Markets, Rights and Power in Australian Social Policy

PUBLIC AND SOCIAL POLICY SERIES

Marian Baird and Gaby Ramia, Series Editors

Markets, Rights and Power in Australian Social Policy

Edited by Gabrielle Meagher and Susan Goodwin

SYDNEY UNIVERSITY PRESS

Sydney University Press
Fisher Library F03
University of Sydney NSW 2006
AUSTRALIA
Email: sup.info@sydney.edu.au
sydney.edu.au/sup

National Library of Australia Cataloguing-in-Publication Data

Title:	Markets, rights and power in Australian social policy / edited by Gabrielle Meagher and Susan Goodwin.
ISBN:	9781920899950 (paperback)
ISBN:	9781920899967 (ebook : epub)
Notes:	Includes bibliographical references and index.
Subjects:	Social service--Australia.
	Social service--Contracting out--Australia.
	Social service--Evaluation.
	Social work administration--Australia.
	Australia--Social policy--21st century.
Other Authors/ Contributors:	Meagher, Gabrielle, editor.
	Goodwin, Susan, 1963- editor.
Dewey Number:	361.994

Cover image: © iStock.com/Qweek. Cover design by Miguel Yamin

Markets, Rights and Power in Australian Social Policy

Edited by Gabrielle Meagher and Susan Goodwin

SYDNEY UNIVERSITY PRESS

First published in 2015 by Sydney University Press
© Individual contributors 2015
© Sydney University Press 2015

Sydney University Press
Fisher Library F03
University of Sydney NSW 2006
AUSTRALIA
Email: sup.info@sydney.edu.au
sydney.edu.au/sup

National Library of Australia Cataloguing-in-Publication Data

Title:	Markets, rights and power in Australian social policy / edited by Gabrielle Meagher and Susan Goodwin.
ISBN:	9781920899950 (paperback)
ISBN:	9781920899967 (ebook : epub)
Notes:	Includes bibliographical references and index.
Subjects:	Social service--Australia.
	Social service--Contracting out--Australia.
	Social service--Evaluation.
	Social work administration--Australia.
	Australia--Social policy--21st century.
Other Authors/ Contributors:	Meagher, Gabrielle, editor.
	Goodwin, Susan, 1963- editor.
Dewey Number:	361.994

Cover image: © iStock.com/Qweek. Cover design by Miguel Yamin

Contents

Acknowledgments

This book has had a long gestation, and our warm thanks go to the contributors and Sydney University Press for their patience.

A small grant from the Faculty of Arts and Social Sciences at The University of Sydney brought the contributors together in 2011, and we would like to thank Dr Gyu-Jin Hwang for his support in the early stages.

We would also like to thank Rhondda Hollis, Assistant Editor of the *Australian Review of Public Affairs*, for her always cheerful and careful assistance with copyediting and proofreading.

Gabrielle would like to thank her colleagues at Stockholm University's Department of Social Work, especially Tommy Lundström and Marta Szebehely, for giving her time to finish the book when they had the right to demand her full attention.

Gabrielle Meagher and Susan Goodwin
April 2014

Foreword

We have all experienced that frustration in meetings called to solve a problem when no one seems willing or able to name its cause. We talk about it as the 'elephant in the room'. In this book, Gabrielle Meagher, Susan Goodwin and their fellow contributors have exposed a genuine elephant in the room of Australian social policy: the marketisation of social services. It is my fervent hope that *Markets, rights and power* proves the catalyst for a revolution in the way we think about the role of social services and their governance in Australia.

It is not as though we have not had a thriving research industry focused on bits of the market animal. Public policy researchers have peered through the lens of 'new public management' searching for traces of hierarchy, market and network. The Grand Pooh Bahs of the Productivity Commission have worn themselves to a frazzle in the quest for ever-new market mechanisms to generate more 'efficiency'. But none of these has been asking the basic questions of social policy about what and how social services can best contribute to the welfare of the nation. This book does just that. It demands that, before we even mention the words management and efficiency, we ask what are the economic and social goals we are trying to achieve? And who is best placed to deliver on these: state, market or civil society?

You would think that there would be ready answers to these questions within the social policy research community. But there are not. This book really breaks a silence. As the reader will see, the triumph of economic rationalism in the 1990s sought to replace the logic of citizenship with the logic of the market in the social services as much as in the economy. I believe that one effect of this was to create an increasingly timorous and defensive social policy discipline which narrowed its focus to issues of compensation and protection, becoming almost exclusively taken up with the role of the tax and transfer system in combating poverty. Social policy shrank to the dimensions of 'welfare' while social services were abandoned to a netherworld overseen by experts in productivity and management.

Nevertheless, I imagine most readers have had an uneasy sense that there was something amiss in the land of social services. People like myself with a footing in the voluntary welfare sector have long bemoaned the distortion of civil society organisations into 'little fingers of the state'. Others, like Stebbing in this book, have pointed out the way so-called privatisation has masked huge transfers of public monies to prop up private health insurance and the retirement savings of the rich.

But, to date, these kinds of studies have been more or less single issue concerns. What is so important and path-breaking about this book is the way it lines up the experience of all the social services to show just how pervasive the impact of marketisation has been on the welfare state and thereby on Australian society. And from a social policy perspective what a sorry story it makes!

As we read in the Introduction, the welfare state was built on the idea that the social services – especially education, health and housing – should deliver equal opportunities for all citizens to participate in society regardless of their class, race or gender. But chapter by chapter we observe the myriad of ways in which this national aspiration to 'civilise capitalism' has been undone by the opposing agenda of marketisation, in which our governments have sought to offload these responsibilities for society on to private markets and to leave it to individuals to get what they can pay for. If you ever doubted that market freedoms for the pike brings death to the minnows then read on to see what the book calls the 'vicious cycle of public sector decline, as underfunded public services become services for the poor, and a two-tiered system emerges'.

Seeing it all together in the synoptic view of this book you might well shake your head and wonder how it all happened. I surmise that the social services simply got caught up in that indiscriminate microeconomic reform frenzy of the 1990s. Deaf to social policy researchers, policymakers listened only to economic rationalists bent on extending market forces into a social service sector which, after all, constitutes a significant proportion of the national economy. Thanks to Gabrielle and Susan, we can now see the social damage that has been done and begin the task of constructing a new reform agenda for the social services.

Indeed, it is a most opportune time to bring on the revolution. For the first time since the 1990s policymakers doubt the market principle as the one size fit for all occasions. Some Australian politicians might be talking of the end of the 'age of entitlement', whatever that might really mean. But no international agency today takes seriously the old economic rationalist assumptions about 'growth first' with the social benefits left to trickle down. Economic growth with social equality is the new game in town. What will this mean for social services?

On this point I offer my final congratulations to our authors. In the recent past too much social policy scholarship in this area has seemed a sheep-like bleating about the evils of markets and 'neoliberalism' with no framing of alternative, progressive possibilities. Our authors are not out to say that the market mechanism is some kind of force for evil but rightly recognise that it is indeed appropriate in the more 'economic' domains of society. Their point is that when it comes to broader, more complex, social goals then the instruments of market competition are simply not the right ones.

Here they point to the alternative logic of 'association' and I believe that their case is compelling. A strong cohesive society will shoulder responsibility for all its members and do so in a way which gains their trust and gives them an effective 'voice' over the decisions that affect their lives. If we are to truly embrace the new global aspirations to end poverty and promote inclusive growth then we must learn from the lessons of this book. Competitive markets in the social services are not suited to these goals. It is time to reconstruct our social services on the very different logic of 'association'.

Paul Smyth
April 2014
Melbourne

Introduction: Capturing marketisation in Australian social policy

Gabrielle Meagher and Susan Goodwin

Australia has never had a large public social service system like those of the Nordic countries, or even of the United Kingdom. Instead, most social services have been delivered by a range of organisations that has included, but not been dominated by, the public sector. However, the mixed economy of Australian welfare services has not been static. In recent decades, both the *organisational mix* and the *modes of coordination* have changed significantly. Successive governments have expanded publicly funded social provision without expanding the public sector, by directly subsidising private provision, by contracting private agencies to deliver services, and by subsidising consumer purchases from approved private providers using tax expenditures and voucher-like instruments. Policies have been rolled out at different rates and with different instruments across the range of areas of Australian social policy. Yet the direction of change overall is clear – market organisations and market logics are playing an increasing role.

One consequence is that the profile of social service providers has changed. Although non-profit organisations continue to have a leading role in provision, for-profit, often corporate, organisations have grown

Meagher, G. & Goodwin, S. 2015, 'Introduction: Capturing marketisation in Australian social policy', in *Markets, rights and power in Australian social policy*, eds G. Meagher & S. Goodwin, Sydney University Press, Sydney.

considerably and have become an influential constituency in the social policy process. For-profit provision now dominates long day care for children and some forms of residential care for older people, and has a growing presence in other fields, including job placement services and community care. Meanwhile, public sector provision has stagnated, declined or disappeared altogether, depending on the field (see Table 1).

In addition to changing 'provider' arrangements, there has been an evolving role for the 'consumer' in social service systems, as the trend towards 'individualisation' or 'personalisation' of social provision has gathered strength. It has been argued that a new 'hybrid' subject of social policy has been created: the 'citizen-consumer', or the 'citizen as consumer of public services who expects to exercise choice in the provision of public services, just as s/he exercises choice in "consumer society" ' (Clarke et al. 2007, p. 1). This dimension of marketisation has altered relationships between citizens and the state, and between citizens and the organisations and professionals that they interact with in social service systems.

The state may not be the dominant actor in social policy *provision* in Australia, but it remains the dominant *funder* of human and social services. Thus, private organisations receive billions in public funds to deliver social services to citizens or to provide for social needs. The result is a service system with complex combinations of individual and collective financing, private and public provision, and public, market and associational rationalities. This raises important questions about how financial flows from the public to the private sector, within the private sector, and to and from citizens, are organised and monitored. Given that the key purposes of social policy are to reduce inequality and poverty (Goodin et al. 1999, pp. 26–27; Korpi & Palme 1998, p. 661), it remains necessary to trace 'who benefits?' from Australian social policy (Bryson 1992; Marston & McDonald 2013), even in the context of this complexity. Beyond questions about the distribution and redistribution of resources, marketisation in Australian social policy also raises questions about the distribution of social advantage and disadvantage (that is, 'who suffers?'), and about the democratic steering of social policy (that is, 'who decides?'). This book aims to capture some of the complexity of marketisation in Australian social policy, and thereby contribute some answers to these questions.

Marketisation: a multifaceted lens

Looking at Australian social policy through the lens of marketisation involves marking out and marking off territory for analysis. A threshold decision is the choice of term – privatisation is an alternative, and has been broadly defined and used in ways which make it more or less synonymous with marketisation.[1] However, despite its encompassing meaning-in-use, the word privatisation suggests a one-way movement from public to private, while marketisation suggests a more comprehensive process that takes in the importation of characteristically private sector ways of doing things into the public sector. In fact, contributors to this volume use both terms, and we have not enforced a single definition.

Marking out our analytical territory is a complex endeavour, for a range of reasons. One is that the concept of marketisation is itself somewhat protean. This is partly because the concept attempts to capture sweeping social transformations, and so is very abstract, and partly because the concept has been framed and mobilised in diverse ways across the social sciences, in which each discipline has its characteristic starting points, objects, methods and questions. Even if there is some agreement that marketisation is about ideologies, politics and policies, how these are related is much more contested. Another challenge is that any attempt at synoptic analysis of this complex process confronts the divergent trajectories of change across time and policy domains: market reforms have been introduced at different times and have unfolded at different rates in different policy domains, so that the nature and pace of change varies between them. This means that general statements about the 'extent' of marketisation overall are difficult, if not impossible, to make. Yet another is that if we focus on market-making policies, we find a range of different instruments and rationales that do not form a cohesive whole. Enhancing consumer choice, for example, does not always result in efficiencies and cost-savings, the other common goals of marketising reform. In other words, in practice, marketisation is not one thing. Nor is marketisation a project solely of right-wing parties and governments – both right and left have undertaken marketising re-

---

1 'Liberalisation' is yet another widely used term, which to us seems even more encompassing, not to say diffuse.

forms, although they tend to use different rationales and instruments consistent with the divergence in their natural constituencies (Gingrich 2011; Zehavi 2012). Related, some forms of marketisation appear to enhance rights, while others seem to reduce them. Actually, rather than some measures being rights-enhancing and others rights-reducing, it is more likely that different measures create different arrays of gains and losses, and of winners and losers in an uneven mosaic. The diversity of effects is also complicated by the subjective corollaries of marketisation; positioning people as customers instead of citizens or clients or patients not only changes their relationships with service organisations and professionals, but also their experiences and assessments of social services.

In short, the diversity of practices, rationales, trajectories, actors and impacts makes it difficult to establish marketisation definitively as a phenomenon which can be tied to a specific set of principles, strategies and effects that apply uniformly across the field of Australian social policy. Nevertheless, we – researchers and citizens alike – apprehend that profound shifts have occurred and are occurring. Thus, complexities notwithstanding, the contributions to the book document the various elements in their current form, and hold them both still and together to reflect on them as though they *are* a phenomenon.

So how *have* we marked our analytical territory? In relation to marketisation, we include any and all of those processes through which policymakers shift ownership, provision, financing, and/or regulation of an asset or activity from the public to the private (for-profit or non-profit) sector (Aulich & O'Flynn 2007). We also include those processes through which rationalities and practices from the private sector are brought into the internal operation of public sector organisations themselves. Often called the 'new public management' (NPM), these processes have sought to introduce 'market discipline' into how public sector organisations run themselves, and into their modes of coordinating their relationships with the external organisations they increasingly fund and regulate to provide services (Diefenbach 2009; Pierre 1995).[2] Marketising measures include output-based funding,

---

2 Note that Aulich and O'Flynn (2007) call these processes 'privatisation'; Diefenbach (2009) uses the term 'New Public Management', and Pierre (1995) uses the term 'marketisation'.

contracting out, competitive tendering, asset sales, voucher systems, public–private partnerships and user pays.[3]

But a list of measures does not quite communicate the character of marketising change, which, as noted above, has altered the profile of organisations that provide social services, and the ways they relate to each other, to the state and to service users. Developments such as the growth of a for-profit private sector and the use of competition to organise social markets are changing the array of *institutional logics* that are organising the field of social policy in Australia. Here we take insights from the sociology of institutions, which theorises society as 'an inter-institutional system of societal sectors in which each sector represents a different set of expectations for social relations and human and organizational behavior' (Thornton & Ocasio 2008, p. 104). Thornton and colleagues (2012, p. 73) identify the following 'institutional orders' or 'sectors': family, community, religion, state, market, profession and corporation. In ideal type, each sector has distinctive sources of legitimacy and authority and a distinctive basis of norms (among other elements). Although all sectors are relevant, to some degree, in the field of social services, community, state and market are most important for this book. According to Thornton and colleagues (2012, p. 73), the institutional logic of the community – what we also call an associational logic in the book – has trust and reciprocity as its sources of legitimacy, commitment to community values as its source of authority and group membership as the basis of its norms. The institutional logic of the state has democratic participation as its source of legitimacy, bureaucratic domination as its source of authority, and citizenship as the basis of its norms. In the market sector, the source of legitimacy is share price, the source of authority is shareholder activism and the source of norms is self-interest. Importantly, given our focus on marketisation, competition as a strategy is also a defining feature of a market logic (Thornton et al. 2012, p. 100).

These ideas offer further means of capturing marketisation: it is a process through which the institutional logic of the market is crowding out the associational logic within (and carried by) non-profit organisa-

---

3 Not all are considered in detail in the book. See Whitfield (2006) for a comprehensive typology and Mudge (2008) for an analysis situating these developments under the umbrella of neoliberalism.

tions and the bureaucratic and democratic logics within (and carried by) the state. According to some organisational theorists and policy analysts, public and private organisations are becoming less distinctive as they 'hybridise' in mixed economies undergoing market reforms (Clarke 2004; Evers 2005; but see also Andersen & Sand 2011). It is true that 'structural overlap' (Thornton & Ocasio 2008, p. 116) between public and private organisations is increasing, as they are forced into association by marketising reform, and that we would expect their new relationships to change the institutional logics guiding both. However, it does not seem true that 'publicness' no longer has meaning, or that private corporations and non-profit organisations have (iso)morphed into copies of one another. Thus, the categories of public, for-profit and non-profit are critical in organising analysis in the book, even as their limitations are explored and discussed.

Since the book is about social policy, we also comment briefly on how we have marked out this terrain, and point out that contributors have addressed more traditional and less traditional policy domains. Most deal with social *services* rather than *income support*, because income support policies for people of working age have been transformed by related rationales but with quite different measures to those that are the primary focus here. The volume includes studies of community aged care, housing, superannuation and health care but also of schooling, banking and immigration skills assessment. Further, the way contributors have engaged marketisation in Australian social policy is necessarily historical, contextual and empirical. In that sense, the book extends earlier work by Australian researchers (Carney & Ramia 2002; Considine 2001; Healy 1998; King & Meagher 2009; Muetzelfeldt & Briskman 2003; Pusey 1991; Rees et al. 1993; Smyth & Cass 1998)[4] and joins several more recent international volumes that have grappled with market-making and the relationship between public and private in all their diverse expressions in the social policy sphere (see, for example, Ascoli & Ranci 2002; Bevir & Trentmann 2007; Béland & Gran 2008;

---

4   These monographs and edited collections are joined by an extensive body of research reports and journal articles much too large to catalogue here – many such contributions are cited in the following chapters of this volume. There is also important research about privatisation and corporatisation of infrastructure and utilities that we do not catalogue here, some of which is cited in Chapter 1.

Dwivedi et al. 2013; Gingrich 2011; Meagher & Szebehely 2013; Morgan & Campbell 2011; Newman & Clarke 2009). Finally, because, as we have argued, marketisation is a complex process, the contributors have examined different dimensions, from the political, organisational and distributional to the historical, cultural and legal.

The first chapter, 'The politics of market encroachment: policymaker rationales and voter responses to privatisation' by Gabrielle Meagher and Shaun Wilson, examines the policies and politics of marketisation in Australia, from the perspectives of policymakers and voters. The chapter begins by pointing out that while asset sales are highly visible as 'privatisation', the marketisation of social services is much less visible, but no less important, for understanding change in Australian institutions. The authors survey market encroachment into Australian society over the last 25 years, with the aim of understanding the pressures on governments and the policy choices they have made in enacting market reforms. One thing research has clearly established is that asset sales have not been popular with the public, and were certainly not demanded by them. The chapter presents recent data to show that the sales of Telstra, Qantas and the Commonwealth Bank are the most unpopular of the major economic reforms of the last three decades, including the introduction of the GST and floating of the dollar. Meanwhile support for either public or non-profit provision of social services remains overwhelming, which suggests a similar pattern of divergence between the preferences of policy and business elites and the preferences of the public when it comes to the involvement of for-profit organisations.

The divergence between elite and public policy preferences on market reform is partially reconciled at the ballot box through votes on broader economic questions of taxation and redistribution. Australia's majoritarian electoral system, which tends to push the middle class to the right,[5] has left the Labor Party with a persistent challenge of rais-

---

5   Here we draw on Torben Iversen's and David Soskice's (2006) explanation of the relationship between electoral institutions (majoritarian versus proportional representation) and the extent of redistribution (lower versus higher, respectively). They hypothesise that in majoritarian electoral systems (such as Australia's) '[m]iddle-class voters will not like a right-wing government, but they have less to fear from it [than from a left wing government], because if it lowers taxes and

ing revenue for social purposes (Wilson 2013). One response to this challenge has been for Labor to resort to market reform – a preferred strategy by the conservative parties – as a means to build up service provision. The result is a rough consensus on this direction, if not on the distance to be travelled, among policymakers of both parties.

As governments have relied on market measures to grow social service provision, they have profoundly changed the way they engage non-profit organisations, and these organisations have themselves been profoundly changed as a consequence. Thus, in a necessary complement to the analysis of for-profit organisations that also threads through the volume, Susan Goodwin and Ruth Phillips chart how marketisation has also driven the growth of *non*-profit organisations (NPOs) in their chapter, 'The marketisation of human services and the expansion of the not-for-profit sector'.

Goodwin and Phillips argue that marketisation has not just led to the expansion of the 'non-profit sector' in social services, but has, in important ways, *produced* it from a disparate collection of large and small charities and churches, and mostly small associations with roots in their local community or in social movements. On the one hand, these organisations have been brought into a unified field by the technologies of marketisation (such as competition, contracting out and performance monitoring), in ways that have shaped a collective identity but have also changed their internal operations. On the other hand, these organisations have been drawn more closely into the state itself, as they take its money and implement its policies. The strange consequence – since the state and civil society (within which non-profits are very often positioned) are the institutions most associated with democracy – is that the public logic of democratic participation has been crowded out.

Finance in social markets

Proponents of market reform often argue that it will save money. To many ears this is alluring, since in recent decades, despite growing national incomes (the Global Financial Crisis [GFC] notwithstanding),

---

spending below the preferred level, it also allows the middle classes to increase private spending' (2006, p. 170).

debate about the affordability of social policies has been intense. As Hujo and McClanahan (2009, pp. 1–2) put it, 'the current approach to financing social policy is dominated by a microperspective on how to allocate a given amount of resources'. These 'efficiency' arguments 'shift the burden of proof regarding the value of social policy to the expenditures side, and at the same time, assume a glass ceiling for state revenues'. The result is a policy frame that positions social policy systems as, following Paul Pierson,[6] 'trapped in conditions of "permanent austerity"'.

Despite the topicality of the 'unaffordability' of social policies, Morel and Palme point out that how social provision is financed 'remains somewhat of a black box of the welfare state', and that the hidden nature of some financing mechanisms has 'added to the confusion about existing policy alternatives' (2013, p. 401). But, as they continue, these issues are of critical importance: the choice of instrument for financing social provision has an impact not only on the redistributive outcomes of social policy, but also on the political legitimacy of social policy systems. Taking up these issues, contributors to the book examine three different types of financing mechanisms in Australian social policy: a now entrenched mechanism of financing of retirement income through occupational and fiscal welfare, a new mechanism of financing the 'social benefit bond', and an old financing mechanism, the 'state-owned enterprise'.

In 'The devil's in the detail: The hidden costs of private retirement incomes policy', Adam Stebbing charts the institutionalisation of compulsory occupational superannuation in Australia. Several key themes of market reform are evident in the story of the expansion of superannuation, including extensive public subsidies for private provision, the consolidation of a large and powerful for-profit sector, the individualisation of risks and benefits, and important partisan differences in instrument design, despite an apparently bipartisan overall direction.

Since the early 1990s, policy has shifted from commitment to collective responsibility for income support in old age in the form of the age pension, to encouraging individuals to 'save' for their retirement, primarily through superannuation. Governments rationalised manda-

---

6 Hujo and McClanahan cite Paul Pierson's formulation from his *The new politics of the welfare state* (2001).

tory superannuation as required by the costs of population ageing and the need to increase national savings. Stebbing unpacks this simplistic understanding of what compulsory occupational superannuation is, how it works and who benefits most from it. First, unlike the age pension, accessed as *social welfare* by older citizens who meet the means test, superannuation in Australia is a form of *occupational welfare*, the benefits of which accrue to individuals on the basis of their employment, paid for by their employer (and perhaps by themselves). A second, and less visible, aspect of superannuation is that it is also arranged as a form of *fiscal welfare:* that is, through generous tax concessions, social provision is made for beneficiaries via the taxation system. When the occupational and fiscal welfare elements of superannuation are taken into account, the inequitable consequences of privatising retirement incomes become very stark. People on low incomes – the majority of whom are women who work part-time, often for decades and often in low-paid jobs – face living on a residual universal payment in their old age. Meanwhile, those with the highest incomes – those in lifetime, full-time, well-paid employment, and so mostly men – receive the highest benefits, not just from their occupational superannuation, but also from regressive tax expenditures, which amounted to $30.2 billion in revenue forgone from the public purse in 2011–12. To put this figure into perspective, it is almost two-thirds as much as total Commonwealth expenditure on support for older people, including both the age pension and aged care services.[7] Stebbing argues that superannuation tax reform is required to address these anomalies.

As Stebbing notes, one of the processes driving reform of retirement incomes around the world is 'financialisation', through which financial calculation and financial institutions increasingly dominate the economy and the social world. Individual superannuation accounts and superannuation choice are just a couple of ways that every person who takes a job in Australia is exposed to financial risks and obliged to engage in their calculation (Bryan 2010). In 'Social benefit bonds: Financial markets inside the state', Dick Bryan and Angela Mitropoulos

---

7   According to the 2012–13 Budget, the Commonwealth spent $48.7 billion on assistance to the aged in the fiscal year 2011–12 (Treasury 2012, table 9.1). Figures (and their source) on tax expenditures on superannuation and other social purposes are reported in Meagher and Wilson, this volume.

explore how financialisation is changing how policymakers think about funding social services, and opening even more opportunities for profit-making from social activities.

Bryan and Mitropoulos introduce a very recent innovation in Australian social policy: a financing mechanism called the social benefit bond (SBB). These instruments bring the logic – and resources – of the (financial) market into social provision, by enabling private sector actors to finance public service provision, on the basis that their 'investments' will result in a private financial return. In what the authors say are 'essentially social experiments', the role of the state in providing for social needs is dramatically re-cast. Under the pervasive account of social welfare as 'unaffordable', the welfare state is represented as unable to find or to raise enough funds to meet social needs – even those as serious or important as prisoner rehabilitation or alternative care for abused and neglected children, the service areas in which SBBs have been developed. In this context, a discourse of 'alternative financing mechanisms' has arisen to support a shift away from the conventional tax-spend funding in social policy. These alternatives have been pounced upon by non-profit (non-state) social service organisations, which were drawn into provision of publicly financed social services partly as a cost-saving measure and are themselves caught in the 'unaffordability' frame.[8] Indeed, it is highly unlikely that SBBs would have emerged if activities such as foster care had remained in the public sector. Through instruments such as SBBs, collective endeavours within a public logic, through which social needs were met from contributions from the community as a whole via taxation, are re-cast as private opportunities for businesses to make money out of (solving) social problems, with a veneer of philanthropy.

For all their novelty, SBBs are not the first or only way that the state and the financial markets have been institutionally entwined. Leanne

---

8　A colourful but anecdotal example illustrates this point. The marketing pitch for a conference called 'Social finance: progressing impact investing in Australia', put together by a for-profit conference organising company in mid-March 2014 was: 'Are you a Not-for-Profit organisation struggling for funding? Unfortunately, for most Not-for-Profits, the answer to that question is a resounding "yes". The simple fact is, there isn't enough money coming from government (or corporate or philanthropic organisations) to tackle the social challenges we face. The good news is there is a way to access more funding. It's called Social Finance'.

Cutcher and Johann Loibl's chapter, ' "Which bank?" Competition and community service obligations in the retail banking sector', draws attention to the role the state has long had as a market player. Their narrative of the privatisation of banking in Australia also tells of the loss of a collective logic in the wake of financialisation, and but also of the possibilities and fragilities of structural overlap in institutional orders.

Australia has a strong tradition of state-owned enterprises, and in banking they have had a range of purposes. In the colonies of 19th-century Australia, state-owned banks were a bulwark against the perceived avarice and incompetence of private banks and early after Federation, the Commonwealth Bank of Australia (CBA) was established with a similar rationale. Cutcher and Loibl show the *social effects* of publicly owned financial institutions, which are distinctive because they are impelled (by virtue of being public) to operate under two institutional logics: the market logic of competition and the community logic of ensuring equitable access to financial services. The privatisation of the CBA – also justified as increasing competition – resulted in a loss of community logic in banking, under which the CBA served the whole community, rather than individual persons or individual companies. The now private Commonwealth Bank is today part of a highly concentrated banking sector, dominated by four large private banks. Swept along by the process of financialisation, consumers face a bewildering array of financial 'products', offered by fewer organisations, from which they are expected to choose with risk-calculating foresight. However, a set of small financial institutions that continue to balance community and market logics persists, in the form of non-profit financial 'mutuals'. Cutcher and Loibl conclude by pointing out that these hybrid organisations are unlikely, alone, to be able to redress the trouble with Australian banking today; the Big Four also need to change their ways of doing business.

The changing mix in the mixed economy

As noted above, both for-profit and NPOs are engaged in providing publicly funded social services in Australia, in a complex mixed economy, and in most service fields, for-profit providers are increasing their share. Table 1 presents available data about the organisational composition of provision in residential aged care, child care, employment services and school education, showing change over time. The clearest trend is the decline of the public sector.

Table 1: Organisations in Australian social services, 1980–2014. For sources and notes, see appendix at the end of the chapter

Residential aged care (operational places, 30 June, %)

	1994	2000	2005	2010	2013	% change 1994–2013
Public	12	10	8	6	6	−6
Non-profit	61	63	61	59	58	−3
For-profit	28	27	31	35	36	+8
n=	131,418	141,237	158,901	179,749	186,278	+54,860

Long day care for children (approved/licensed providers, %)

	1994	2000	2004–05	2008–09	2012–13[†]	% change 1994–2013
Public	16	10	3	3	6	−10
Non-profit	26	24	26	22	31	+5
For-profit	58	67	71	75	63	+5
n=	3,015	4,012	n. a.	n. a.	6,409	+3,394

Employment services (provider organisations, %)

	1995[*]	1998[**]	2003	2009	2014	% change 1994–2013
Public	80	37	3	0	0	≥−80
Non-profit	20	30	47	61	68	~+50
For-profit		33	50	39	33	~+25

Schools (full-time students, %)

	1980	1990	2000	2013	2013	% change 1980–2013
Public	78	72	69	66	65	−13
Private	22	28	31	34	35	+13
n=	2,984,562	3,041,657	3,247,425	3,486,879	3,633,438	+648,876

Another clear trend is not visible in this data: the growth of private corporate entities in service provision. One stark example is the profile of providers in Job Services Australia (JSA), through which publicly funded job placement services are provided to people who are un-employed. The three largest for-profit providers will receive a total of more than $1.5 billion, which amounts to 21 percent of the total value of all JSA contracts, for the current contract period of July 2009 to June 2015.[9] Of the three largest for-profit providers, two are inter-national companies. One of the international companies, MAXNet-Work Pty Ltd, received the largest contract of more than $750 million. MAXNetWork is a subsidiary of Maximus, a company listed on the New York Stock Exchange with market capitalisation of US$3.9 billion in March 2015. As its primary business model, Maximus targets public programs in health and human services in the United States and several other countries, now including Australia. Since 2006, MAXNetWork has been awarded contracts to the total value of $812 million in tenders by the Australian Goverment. The second largest for-profit provider of employment services, with JSA contracts worth $362 million, consists of three subsidiaries of Employment Services Holdings Pty Ltd (ESH). ESH has operations in the United Kingdom as well as Australia. The three subsidiaries operating in Australia have or have had contracts to the value of a further $59 million to provide general personnel, Indige-nous job training and placement and humanitarian settlement services between 2007 and 2015. The three largest non-profits are the Salvation Army, Campbell Page and Mission Australia, and together they have JSA contracts amounting to 17 percent of the total value for the con-tract period. (Brief accounts of the establishment of the Job Network, the predecessor to JSA, and of the rise and fall of ABC Learning, a cor-porate child care provider, are discussed in Chapter 1 of this volume. Chapter 7 discusses the development of corporate health care.)

There are a range of theoretical approaches to the shift of respon-sibility for defining, providing, financing and controlling of social ser-vices from the state to private organisations. First, there are theoretical

---

9   Data about contract values for these and other services is publicly available data on AusTender, the web portal for the Australian government's tender system. The figures quoted here are based on the authors' calculations of contract data taken from AusTender.

arguments for public involvement in social services as a remedy for market failure, and which emphasise the public logic of universality, democracy and citizenship organised through bureaucracies. Second, there are theoretical arguments for private involvement in social services. Those which advocate for-profit involvement emphasise the logic of the market through competition, innovation, efficiency and choice, while those advocating non-profit involvement emphasise a community or associational logic through participation, responsiveness and reciprocity. Third, there are arguments for a revised role of government in the provision of public services, characterised in the catch-phrase of NPM, as 'steering not rowing', such that political decision-making is separated from the management of public services, and public–private 'partnerships' are a substitute for public services. Several contributions to the book explore the extent to which the second and third have informed change in Australian public administration in recent decades, resulting in a changing mix in the mixed economy.

In 'Community aged care providers in a competitive environment: Past, present and future', Bob Davidson examines the structure and evolution of an area of Australian social policy that has, by and large, conventionally been 'outsourced' by government. Indeed, community aged care is a clear example of the dominant 'Australian way' of social service provision: since the 1970s, the state has sponsored private organisations in several major domains, including aged care, but also neighbourhood and family support services, women's services, crisis housing services and legal services (Goodwin 2003). Community aged care, then, is a clear example of the state 'not rowing', and Davidson uses industrial organisation theory and historical analysis to show that state steering has shaped the mix of types of boats and types of rowers (to stretch the metaphor) in making the 'quasi-market' for these services.

In community aged care, the share of for-profit provision is relatively low, unlike residential aged care or child care, in which for-profit providers have considerable shares, and listed corporations are important players within the for-profit sector. Davidson explains why this is so, and how recent policy developments might change the profile of providers in the future. The legacy of a strong, pre-existing non-profit sector and a careful use of selected market instruments have meant that, to date, the operation of the community care quasi-market has worked to select *social* maximisers, rather than *profit* maximisers. Thus, service quality has generally been good – for those who have received services, at any rate; the rate of unmet need is high. However, as 'consumerist' service models gain increasing currency in policy discourse, major changes to the instruments through which the community care quasi-market is organised are under discussion. Davidson argues that although service users would apparently have more choice under consumerist models, a 'freer' market in community care would also endanger the stability, equity, efficiency and service quality delivered by the current arrangements.

Australian governments have been playing an increasing role in social service areas such as community aged care, child care and others, even if they do so by making and coordinating markets for those activities. In housing, however, private markets have always been dominant and have become increasingly so in recent decades, as Lucy Groenhart and Nicole Gurran explain in 'Home security: Marketisation and the changing face of housing assistance in Australia'. Since colonisation, a property development industry has existed and most Australians have provided for their housing through private transactions with commercial providers. However, governments have intervened outside these private arrangements with housing assistance measures aimed at meeting the needs of citizens for whom the private housing market is unaffordable. Groenhart and Gurran document the changing rationales and instruments of government housing assistance, and show how these are connected to the dissemination of NPM in housing policy internationally.

The best known form of housing assistance is direct provision of housing itself, through government construction, ownership and subsidisation of the costs of (public) housing. But this is now a vestigial and residual offering – the number of public housing dwellings has fallen in recent decades, and access to them has been increasingly targeted on the most disadvantaged members of the community. Meanwhile, expenditure on vouchers to assist other low-income households pay rent in the private market has grown considerably, and a range of other measures have sought to bring more private resources and private actors into housing assistance. Increasing choice for residents in what is now called 'social housing' has been one goal of marketising reform in the sector, but without a substantial increase in the quantity of social housing, it is not clear whether this goal can genuinely be realised.

A similar trend is evident in the Australian health care system, although the public sector has historically had a much larger role in health than in housing. In 'Money and markets in Australia's health care system', Fran Collyer, Kirsten Harley and Stephanie Short put health care marketisation in the context of the history of the Australian health care system. They argue that this system has been dramatically transformed in recent decades, such that decisions about health care provision are based increasingly on market rather than medical considerations. This is perhaps the community's greatest concern about marketisation – that concern for the public good will be replaced by self-interest, especially profit maximisation. The authors portray a shift from a sector dominated by public and not-for-profit institutions to a sector in which private corporations now play a considerable role, especially private hospitals and private health insurers. They argue that the emergence of 'corporate health care' in a 'highly protected market system' has been enabled by successive governments. The shift matters for a number of reasons, they contend. Government subsidies for private health care and health insurance markets are a drag on the health care budget. Commercial interests in the system distort health care planning and service delivery – services are placed where they will garner the best return for shareholders, not where they are most needed. The overarching consequence, they argue, is that Australian people are no longer assured access to a universal health care system in which a uniformly high standard of timely health care is available to all.

Questions about if and how marketisation works are at the centre of Anna Boucher's contribution, 'Marketisation of immigrant skills assessment in Australia'. Boucher provides a forensic view of the outsourcing state, through her analysis of marketised immigration skills assessment. This area of social policy is particularly significant in Australia, where immigration policy has become increasingly oriented towards labour market goals. Before 1999, officers of the Department of Immigration assessed the skills of immigration applicants: in other words, public servants made decisions that could be appealed under public law. Since 1999, these assessments have been carried out by a range of independent assessing bodies, some private professional associations, others commercial arms of government agencies. In her focus on a single, relatively bounded area of provision, Boucher is able to develop a framework for assessing the extent to which marketisation can be justified in this arena, but her approach has wider application and her findings wider implications.

The effects of marketisation of skills assessment, Boucher argues, have been mixed. Timeliness and accuracy have increased, but other problems have arisen. Marketisation has involved significant cost-shifting to immigration applicants, who must be able to afford to pay for skills assessment in order to be even considered. Perhaps most importantly, rights to review of assessments have been truncated, because the position of private providers under public law is unclear. The tight focus of this chapter establishes a general question for other subcontracted and commodified areas of social provision: when services are no longer provided as public services, what mechanisms are available to assure service users' administrative rights?

Markets, consumers and 'choice'

Market logic, with its central concepts of competition and choice, is both a powerful 'cognitive lock' (Blyth 2001) and very highly valorised in public policy discourse. Policy goals such as enhancing efficiency or choice seem self-evidently positive and to reject them is not politically feasible, nor perhaps even desirable. Indeed, the concept of choice has functioned as a bridge between elite policy preferences and those of the public.

Choice has clearly become a very powerful concept in policy discourse. In almost all areas of Australian social policy increasing choice for people using services has become an important justification for marketisation. This is partly because the alternative to choice is framed as *someone else deciding* on one's behalf. This is politically and psychologically unattractive, even though social service systems necessarily continue to rely to some extent on elements of prescription and even compulsion, whether exercised through professional expertise, statutory authority or market dynamics. But it is also because choice is a protean concept. While it is a keyword of neoclassical economic theory, which formalises the logic of the market, 'choice' has a place in other policy frames or discourses, each of which motivates, justifies and mobilises it differently. Accordingly, the meaning of choice itself changes, depending on the frame/discourse in which it is used.

Within the market frame, choice as a policy idea has been propagated by an elite epistemic community, drawing on public choice theory, neoclassical economics and NPM. The concept of the individual in this frame is atomistic: an agent with wants who maximises utility through exchanges; and choice is abstract and instrumental. At the individual level, choice is a means to meeting wants; at a system level, aggregated individual choices are a means for reaching an efficient distribution of resources that meet those consumer wants. There is not much concern within this frame for the *contents* of choices. The perspective is *system-wide*: the sum of individual choices drives competition in markets, leading to increased efficiency and quality. The suite of policy prescriptions is familiar: outsourcing, vouchers, personal budgets, introduction of new providers who compete to provide services, including promotion of private sector and specifically for-profit providers. Because this frame has a rather empty concept of choice, it does not necessarily align with policies seeking to give people choices over things that mean something to them. In practice, choice of *provider* has been the typical offering, on the assumption that individuals will find a provider that suits them from the more diverse array that market reforms are assumed to present to them.

But choice has also been a central concept in what we might call a human rights frame in social services policy. This frame has 'bottom up' origins, in the women's and disability rights movements. Its concept of the individual is a person with rights to autonomy and participation in their personal, social and political worlds, and choice is one means through which each person can enact self-determination. The perspective within this frame is *person-centred*: choice is a means of expressing and maintaining identity, dignity and autonomy. Self-determination or control over one's own life is the goal, and choice enables this. Typical policy prescriptions include removing barriers to participation and provision of necessary support in ways that enable choice and control over that support, including through user-led organisations. As a frame that has most purchase within the disability field, personal budgets controlled by the individual requiring assistance are also a typical policy proposal – one shared with the market frame. Because the perspective within this frame is person-centred, making choice *meaningful* for people is an important policy goal – people should have a choice over the dimensions of service design and execution that mean something to them and that enhance their dignity and control over their lives.

What these frames share is that choice is a good in itself, and this gives some insight into the irresistibility of policies rationalised as increasing choice. However, these frames construct who people are (that is, they constitute subjects) and the circumstances and contents of their choices in quite different ways. The policy prescriptions of these two frames overlap only partially. Meanwhile, in general, the market frame has prevailed in the design of social service reform.

The impact of marketisation in education policy, specifically on parents choosing a school for their children, is explored by Helen Proctor and Claire Aitchison in 'Markets in education: "School choice" and family capital'. They point out that school choice has, ironically, itself become compulsory, and that old patterns of inequality are reproduced in new ways through it. Parents' wealth and knowhow have always been important, even decisive, in the educational fortunes of their children, but this dynamic is exacerbated under current arrangements, which are producing and affirming a particular kind of entrepreneurial, hyper-involved parent. In other words, school choice policies produce students, families and teachers as particular types of subjects. In the school choice case studies they explore, the authors find that school choice favours particular kinds of children, families and educational forms and that the exercise of school choice is highly constrained. They also find that the process of school choice is labour intensive and emotionally and intellectually challenging. For many parents, the outcome was tinged with dissatisfaction as they recognised and experienced the limitations of choice in practice.

Marketisation is changing social services, but it is not the only trend reshaping social policy in Australia. In the final chapter, 'Conditional income transfers and choice in social services: Just more conditions and more markets?', Terry Carney contrasts marketisation in residential aged care services with increasing conditionality in income support (social security) payments for people of working age. While most welfare services are being re-arranged in ways that ostensibly expand consumer choice, in income support, precisely the reverse is happening. Certain groups of people have become subject to authoritarian and involuntary 'management' of their social security payments, which removes personal control over half or more of their income, and withdraws benefits if they do not comply with detailed behavioural management requirements. The groups subjected to income management are among the most socially excluded and disadvantaged Australians, notably (but not exclusively) Aboriginal people in the Northern Territory.

Yet despite the apparently wide discrepancy between income management and marketisation, the two policy approaches share a common and deep root in *individualising* the subjects of the welfare state. Carney points out that the design of conditional income support programs assumes that the causes of social disadvantage are individual, and that the people involved have or retain sufficient agency to (choose to) act in response to the measures' incentives. In this way, the structural causes of disadvantage are obscured, just as the market frame obscures the structural inequalities of distribution that arise in choice-based service systems.

Examining these apparently divergent policy approaches side-by-side makes it less possible to see marketisation in Australian social service systems as a genuine attempt to improve citizens' lives through the provision of greater 'choice'. Carney considers several explanations for these developments. The most striking, from our perspective, is that contemporary social policy is an 'exercise in the construction of citizens capable of exercising "regulated freedom"', that is, the welfare state must 'responsibilise' citizens, and only responsibilised citizens are deserving of choice.

Was there no other way?

Australian social services are arranged through a complex mix of organisations, institutional logics, and policy instruments. In some sectors, the mix is more complex than others and the direction of change more difficult to discern. However, to a lesser or greater extent, market instruments and actors have come to play a larger role across all fields of social services. Yet marketisation was not the only possible direction for reform to address perceived problems with the public sector and for developing the social service system. In Australia and elsewhere, policies, strategies and actors working within the community logic of the associational sphere have emerged and contended with the logic of the market to (re)shape social policy.

In the 1970s, the Whitlam Labor government (1972–75) sought to expand new organisational bases for social service provision, framed within a community logic. The policy vehicles for these developments included the Australian Assistance Plan and its associated Regional Councils for Social Development (RCSD) and the Community Health Program. The Australian Assistance Plan (AAP), for example, was part of a radical reconceptualisation of decision-making about the allocation of social welfare resources in line with new social movement objectives of self-determination and the creation of more participatory, inclusive and responsive social policy. A variety of grants were dispersed to volunteer RSCDs who worked with community development workers and social planners funded by the AAP to mobilise 'grass roots' action around welfare and to encourage the formation of local associations to deliver welfare services to the whole community (Byrne & Davis 1998; Oppenheimer 2008).

The AAP, like other Whitlam experiments, was short-lived – one of the first actions of the incoming Fraser government in 1976 was to withdraw support from it. But it had a lasting legacy: historians and social policy analysts have argued that the AAP and related developments underpinned the formation of a 'community sector' of locally organised, often government-funded, community groups in Australia (Broom 1991; Eisenstein 1996; Melville 1993). This 'state-sponsored community sector' (Goodwin 2003, p. 15; see also Goodwin & Phillips, this volume) was less an attempt to develop an alternative between the bureaucratised state and the competitive market (for which see, for example, Botsman & Latham 2001); but rather an alternative to the bureaucratised state and the paternalism of the charity sector.

The AAP did not succeed in generating a participatory revolution in Australian social policy. One reason was, of course, as Melanie Oppenheimer (2008) points out, the Labor defeat in 1975. But Oppenheimer canvasses several other reasons, some related to professional and organisational rivalries, some to the AAP's weakly developed base in the federal bureaucracy and others to institutional and political barriers of Australian federalism (2008, pp. 177–81; see also Graycar 1977). These proximal causes are no doubt important, but so too is the emergence and consolidation of market ideas and practices in social policy. With the rise of NPM and the increasing marketisation of social policy since the 1990s, the 'expectations for social relations and human and organizational behavior' (Thornton & Ocasio 2008, p. 104) that take shape within a community logic have diminished. The 'community sector' has become increasingly incorporated into the marketised state, dominated by large charities now steered as much by market and corporate logics as by associational ones (see Goodwin & Phillips, this volume).

But at least as important as the decline of the community logic in the non-profit sector is the declining effect of a *public* logic in social policy. Shortly after the end of the AAP, Adam Graycar (1977, p. 20) wrote that the only avenue for major change in Australian social policy is through forms of community participation and citizen control. The major impediments here are the difficulty in establishing a participatory culture, the limited scope of the objectives of citizen participation, difficulties in establishing legitimacy for citizen groups, and difficulties in gaining access to sufficient resources to make the participatory process a politically powerful process.

It is difficult to imagine that policies promoting consumer choice will contribute to fostering the participatory culture – the deeper democracy – required. It is not least for this reason that marketisation is a disturbing trend for those concerned about inequality and democracy, and about rights and power in Australian social policy.

Appendix

Sources and notes to Table 1.

- Residential aged care: *Australia's welfare 1995* for 1994; Report on government services for 2000, 2005, Reports on operation of the *Aged Care Act, 1997* for 2010 and 2013.
- Long day care for children: *Australia's welfare 1995*, authors calculations based on table 4. 2 for 1994; *State of child care in Australia* April 2010, published by the Office of Early Childhood Education and Care, Department of Education, Employment and Workplace Relations, for 2004–05 and 2008–09; *Report on government services* for 2012–13, authors' calculation, note that data for South Australia are from 2011–12.

- Employment services (Job Network/ Job Services Australia): Senate Employment, Education and Training Legislation Committee, Hansard, 23 November 1995, for 1995, Riggs (2001, p. 378) for 1998, Eardley (2003, p. 7) for 2003, personal communication, Director, Director Deed Administration, Business Partnerships Branch, Employment Services and Support Group, Department of Employment, March 2014, for 2009 and 2014. * Contracted case management services only, delivered under the ALP's Working Nation program. ** Figures for 1998 and 2003 are the results of the tendering processes that ran for 2–3 years after those dates.
- Schools: Australian Bureau of Statistics, *Schools Australia*, various years. Note, the vast majority of private schools are formally non-profit.

References

Andersen, N. Å. & Sand, I. J. (eds) 2011, *Hybrid forms of governance: Self-suspension of power*, Palgrave Macmillan, Basingstoke.

Ascoli, U. & Ranci, C. (eds) 2002, *Dilemmas of the welfare mix: The new structure of welfare in an era of privatization*, Springer, New York.

Aulich, C. & O'Flynn, J. 2007, 'From public to private: The Australian experience of privatisation', *Asia Pacific Journal of Public Administration*, vol. 29, no. 2, pp. 153–71.

Béland, D. & Gran, B. 2008, *Public and private social policy: Health and pension policies in a new era*, Palgrave Macmillan, Basingstoke.

Bevir, M. & Trentmann, F. (eds) 2007, *Governance, consumers and citizens: Agency and resistance in contemporary politics*, Palgrave Macmillan, New York.

Blyth, M. 2001, 'The transformation of the Swedish model: Economic ideas, distributional conflict, and institutional change', *World Politics*, vol. 54, no. 1, pp. 1–26.

Botsman, P. & Latham, M. 2001, *The enabling state: People before bureaucracy*, Pluto Press, Sydney.

Broom, D. 1991, *Damned if we do: Contradictions in women's healthcare*, Allen & Unwin, St Leonards.

Bryan, D. 2010, 'The duality of labour and the financial crisis', *Economic and Labour Relations Review*, vol. 20, no. 2, pp. 49–59.

Bryson, L. 1992, *Welfare and the state: Who benefits?*, Macmillan, London.

Byrne, J. & Davis, G. 1998, *Participation and the NSW policy process. A discussion paper for the Cabinet Office, New South Wales*, NSW Cabinet Office, Sydney.

Carney, T., & Ramia, G. 2002, *From rights to management: Contract, new public management and employment services*, Kluwer Law International, The Hague.

Clarke, J. 2004, 'Dissolving the public realm? The logics and limits of neo-liberalism', *Journal of Social Policy*, vol. 33, no. 1, pp. 27–48.

Clarke, J., Newman, J., Smith, N., Vidler, E. & Westmarland, L. 2007, *Creating citizen-consumers*, Sage, London.

Considine, M. 2001, *Enterprising states: The public management of welfare-to-work*, Cambridge University Press, Melbourne.

Diefenbach, T. 2009, 'New public management in public sector organizations: The dark sides of managerialistic "enlightenment" ', *Public Administration*, vol. 87, no. 4, pp. 892–909.

Dwivedi, Y. K., Shareef, M. A., Kumar, V. & Kumar, U. 2013, *Public administration reformation: Market demand from public organizations*, Routledge, New York.

Eardley, T. 2003, *Outsourcing employment services: What have we learned from the Job Network?*, paper presented to the Centre for Applied Economic Research Conference on the Economic and Social Impacts of Outsourcing, University of New South Wales, 4–5 December.

Eisenstein, H. 1996, *Inside agitators: Australian femocrats and the state*, Allen & Unwin, St Leonards.

Evers, A. 2005, 'Mixed welfare systems and hybrid organizations: Changes in the governance and provision of social services', *International Journal of Public Administration*, vol. 28, nos. 9–10, pp. 737–48.

Gingrich, J. R. 2011, *Making markets in the welfare state: The politics of varying market reforms*, Cambridge University Press, Cambridge.

Goodin, R., Headey, B., Muffels, R. & Dirven, H-J. 1999, *The real worlds of welfare capitalism*, Cambridge University Press, Cambridge.

Goodwin, S. 2003, 'States, communities, individuals', *Communities and their capacity to address disadvantage*, ACOSS Paper 130, pp. 12–7.

Graycar, A. 1977, 'The politics of social policy in Australia', *Social Policy & Administration*, vol. 11, no. 1, pp. 3–20.

Healy, J. 1998, *Welfare options: Delivering social services*, Allen & Unwin, St Leonards.

Hujo, K. & McClanahan, S. 2009, *Financing social policy: Mobilizing resources for social development*, Palgrave Macmillan, Basingstoke.

Iversen, T. & Soskice, D. 2006, 'Electoral institutions and the politics of coalitions: Why some democracies redistribute more than others', *American Political Science Review*, vol. 100, no. 2, pp. 165–81.

King, D. & Meagher, G. (eds) 2009, *Paid care in Australia: Politics, profits, practices*, Sydney University Press, Sydney.

Korpi, W. & Palme, J. 1998, 'The paradox of redistribution and strategies of equality: Welfare state institutions, inequality and poverty in Western countries', *American Sociological Review*, vol. 63, no. 5, pp. 661–87.

Marston, G. & McDonald, C. 2013, *The Australian welfare state: who benefits now?*, Palgrave Macmillan, Melbourne.

Meagher, G. & Szebehely, M. (eds) 2013, Marketisation in Nordic eldercare: A research report on legislation, oversight, extent and consequences, Stockholm Studies in Social Work 30, Stockholm University.

Melville, R. 1993, Turbulent environments: Women's refuges, collectivities and the state, unpublished PhD thesis, School of Social Work, University of New South Wales.

Mudge, S. L. 2008, 'What is neo-liberalism?', *Socio-Economic Review*, vol. 6, no. 4, pp. 703–31.

Muetzelfeldt, M. & Briskman, L. 2003, *Moving beyond managerialism in human services*, RMIT Publishing, Melbourne.

Morel, N. & Palme, J. 2013, 'Financing the welfare state and the politics of taxation', in *The Routledge handbook of the welfare state*, ed. B. Greve, Routledge, London.

Morgan, K. J. & Campbell, A. L. 2011, *The delegated welfare state: Medicare, markets, and the governance of social policy*, Oxford University Press, New York.

Newman, J. & Clarke, J. 2009, *Publics, politics and power: Remaking the public in public services*, Sage, London.

Oppenheimer, M. 2008, 'Voluntary action, social welfare and the Australian Assistance Plan in the 1970s', *Australian Historical Studies*, vol. 39, no. 2, pp. 167–82.

Pierre, J. 1995, 'The marketization of the state: Citizens, consumers and the emergence of the public market', in *Governance in a changing environment*, eds B. G. Peters & D. J. Savoie, McGill-Queen's Press, Montreal.

Pusey, M. 1991, *Economic rationalism in Canberra: A nation-building state changes its mind*, Cambridge University Press, Melbourne.

Rees, S., Rodley, G. & Stilwell, F. (eds) 1993, *Beyond the market: Alternatives to economic rationalism*, Pluto Press, Sydney.

Riggs, L. 2001, 'Introduction of contestability in the delivery of employment services in Australia', *Labour Market Policies and the Public Employment Service: Proceedings of the Prague Conference*, July 2000, OECD, Paris.

Smyth, P. & Cass, B. 1998, *Contesting the Australian way: States, markets and civil society*, Cambridge University Press, Melbourne.

Thornton, P. & Ocasio, W. 2008, 'Institutional logics', in *The SAGE handbook of organizational institutionalism*, eds R. Greenwood, C. Oliver, R. Suddaby & K. Sahlin, Sage, London.

Thornton, P., Ocasio, W. & Lounsbury, M. 2012, *The institutional logics perspective: A new approach to culture, structure, and process*, Oxford University Press, New York.

Treasury 2012, Budget Paper No. 1, Statement No. 6: Expenses and net capital investment, Department of Treasury, Canberra.

Whitfield, D. 2006, A typology of privatisation and marketisation, ESSU Research Report No. 1, European Services Strategy Unit. http://tiny.cc/e1r1qx

Wilson, S. 2013, 'The limits of low-tax social democracy? Welfare, tax and fiscal dilemmas for Labor in government', *Australian Journal of Political Science*, vol. 48, no. 3, pp. 286–306.

Zehavi, A. 2012, 'Welfare state politics in privatization of delivery: Linking program constituencies to left and right', *Comparative Political Studies*, vol. 45, no. 2, pp. 194–219.

1

The politics of market encroachment: Policymaker rationales and voter responses

Gabrielle Meagher and Shaun Wilson

In recent decades, market ideas and practices have increasingly encroached on activities previously organised by different logics, primarily the bureaucratic logic of the public sector and the associational logics of churches and non-government organisations. One highly visible trend has been privatisation of public assets. Universally accessed public utilities in telecommunications, energy and water have been sold off, along with publicly owned financial institutions and transport carriers. Less visible, but no less important, has been the marketisation of publicly funded social services. The growing use of contracts, competition, and quasi-vouchers to allocate funds and service users to the organisations that provide services are examples of this development. Another has been the disproportionate growth of the share of for-profit providers in Australia's mixed economy of social services.

In Australian social policy, market practices and organisations have played an increasingly significant role in shaping the delivery of services, but in ways that ordinary voters may not identify as connected to 'privatisation', understood as asset sales. Asset sales have also taken place in social services (for example, publicly owned residential care fa-

Meagher G. & Wilson S. 2015, 'The politics of market encroachment: policy maker rationales and voter responses', in *Markets, rights and power in Australian social policy*, eds G. Meagher & S. Goodwin, Sydney University Press, Sydney.

cilities have been sold to private organisations), but other marketising instruments have been more common. For example, child and family welfare services, such as foster care placement, have been contracted out to private providers in several states. User fees have increased households' contributions to the cost of many social services. And, across child care, school education, health care and superannuation, public policies have promoted the growth of private provision.

Marketisation has changed the texture of social services, pushing service users into new roles and relationships with the state (see, for example, Carney and Proctor & Aitchison, this volume). These changes raise important questions about the trajectory of the social service system. This chapter first describes the process of marketisation in Australian policy then explores how the public has responded. It begins with an account of the pressures that led governments of divergent political persuasions to introduce marketising policies and then offers an overview of asset sales and service marketisation in Australia during the last 25 years. Finally it explores how the Australian public has responded not only to visible marketisation via asset sales but also to the less visible processes that are reorganising social services. Do voters recognise the trend to private provision and what do they think about it? Do voters endorse privately run services of all kinds? Are there pressures emerging within this model of service provision? Answering these questions helps identify the future tension points within a more privatised system of social services.

Pressures on the state for privatisation and marketisation

A dynamic view of market encroachment, addressing the *why* as well as the *what*, must engage with the politics of this process: why policymakers decide to sell assets, contract out and offer quasi-vouchers, and how they rationalise these decisions on one hand, and how the public has responded on the other. Table 1.1 sets out some of the internal and external pressures that encourage greater privatisation of assets, and increasingly, marketisation of social services.

In the 1980s, policymakers in both centre-right and centre-left governments around the world began to look to the market for solutions when the institutions of state management of the private economy

Table 1.1: Pressures on the state for privatisation and marketisation

	Internal pressures (politics and bureaucracy)	External pressures (business, consumers, voters, media)
Asset sales	• Pragmatic need to finance budget deficits • Overlapping political and business networks that favour, gain from privatisation • Response to 'overburdened' state – bureaucratic and political interest in shifting blame for utility and service failures • Strong ideological and administrative framework in the benefits of *systemic* market provision among bureaucratic and political elites ('new public management' [NPM], for instance)	• Corporate interest in asset acquisition • Financial markets seeking assets and pressuring for market reforms • Media-publicised consumer and business dissatisfaction with inefficient state-owned utilities • Class interest in de-unionisation and reducing the size of the public sector
Service marketisation	• Resource constraints that favour cheaper, contracted services • Overlapping political and business networks that favour and gain from marketisation • Bureaucratic and political interest in shifting responsibility for (failures in) social provision • NPM framework that favours 'steering' not 'rowing' (cost control, competition) and individualised modes of provision	• Public pressure to finance (expensive) social services • Increasing business interest in the social service 'market' • Media-publicised consumer dissatisfaction with publicly provided social services

and the public sector came under pressure from slow growth, inflation and rising unemployment. The privatisation response was prompted by a number of influences. Some pressure for privatisation was fairly pragmatic: with no great attachment to ownership, privatisation emerged as an administrative option to raise resources to fund budget deficits and to resolve management problems of large state utilities (see Feigenbaum & Henig 1994, p. 187).

But the privatisation agenda had deeper political significance. Governments and market actors often have overlapping ideological and financial interests in increasing the scope of the market at the expense of the public sector. McAllister and Studlar argue that privatisation was driven by elites seeking either greater commercial access to public assets and services or, more ideologically, greater popular participation in a new 'property-owning democracy' (1989, p. 158). The authors make clear that, despite the rhetoric of participatory capitalism, 'privatisation is a policy which did not emerge because of popular demands among voters; rather, privatisation was a product of elites' (1989, p. 174).

Exceeding mere advocacy for privatisation on the basis of apparently 'neutral' economics, business organisations, thinktanks, political parties, and government leaders in many countries launched political programs for public asset sales that would 'realign institutions and decision-making processes so as to privilege the goals of some groups over the competing aspirations of other groups' (Feigenbaum & Henig 1994, p. 191). Feigenbaum and Henig (1994) develop a typology of the political underpinnings of privatisation that helps us understand why and how governments use it. They argue that *pragmatic* privatisations are typically understood by those undertaking them as a technical solution to an immediate problem. Tactical privatisation is directed at achieving party political goals in the short term, including attracting allies and rewarding supporters. *Systematic* privatision, as the name suggests, seeks to transform economic and political institutions and interests more comprehensively. Describing systematic privatisation, Feigenbaum and Henig state that 'the withdrawal of the state results in a substantial and not readily reversible decrease in the power of working classes relative to that of organized elites' and may also involve a 'values' shift that promotes 'a shrinking of the sphere of activities considered to be legitimate areas for public scrutiny and intervention' (1994, p. 200). Furthermore, systemic privatisation may entail 'nontransient restructuring of the institutional arrangements of the society ... so that the array of incentives presented to individuals and groups encourages a greater reliance on private and market-oriented solutions' (1994, p. 201). No doubt, these institutional and value shifts both promoted and were reinforced further by the internal reorganisation of the public sector. The adoption of 'new public management' thinking by public sector managers committed to private sector managerial styles and 'public service provision by private organizations' (Hood 2002, p. 12,554) helped normalise privatising strategies.

The most dramatic examples of systemic privatisation followed the collapse of command economies in the Soviet-dominated world in the late 1980s, which precipitated and normalised subsequent mass privatisation in that region. This huge experiment in rapid transfer of public assets to the private sector had disastrous consequences, from the entrenchment of the financial and political power of oligarchs to the mortality crisis[1] caused by the mass job loss that characterised transition across the former Soviet bloc (Stuckler, King & McKee 2009). The collapse of the Soviet model also further undermined the 'mixed economy' models in Western Europe and the English-speaking democracies. In these countries, public ownership of several industries had long been accepted on the grounds of natural monopoly or public interest. However, this state of affairs came under strong political attack, particularly during Conservative Prime Minister Thatcher's rule in the United Kingdom during the 1980s.

Privatisation programs under the British Conservatives, Australian Labor and the French Socialists, for example, have all involved overlapping pragmatic, tactical and systematic objectives. Feigenbaum and Henig's (1994) analysis focuses on objectives defined *internally* within governments, which attract interest from bureaucrats, budget-minded politicians and reformers. More recently, research has emphasised the role of *external* pressures and interests in sustaining and deepening the privatisation agenda. Financialisation has increased the power of market actors who have an interest in asset sales and service marketisation. The rapid accumulation and internationalisation of private financial assets in recent decades has created a massive pool of private funds seeking investment opportunities, while pressures on public finances – partly created by tax cuts on high-income earners and corporations –

---

1 In an article in *The Lancet*, Stucker and colleagues find that 'Mass privatisation programmes were associated with an increase in short-term adult male mortality rates of 12.8%' and that 'One mediating factor could be male unemployment rates, which were increased substantially by mass privatisation' (2009, p. 399).

have led governments to reconsider the size and structure of their budgets and balance sheets. In this context, as Huffschmid (2008, p. 220) puts it, 'privatisation appears to be a solution to the problems of both the wealthy and the state: it gives the former a new area for investment, while at the same time easing the financial burden on the latter'.

Indeed, new capitalist actors have come to specialise in gaining ownership of government-run assets and access to publicly funded services. Australia's Macquarie Bank, for example, largely built its international market position on the basis of handling Australia's energy, transport and road infrastructure privatisations. One journalist remarked that the bank had become '[a]n unelected elite making big money from handling what the public used to own: it's a target-rich environment, if ever there was' (Haigh 2007, p. 33). Macquarie Bank also has substantial investments in publicly funded aged care services. As Crouch notes, firms engaged in privatisation and marketisation go on to cultivate very specialist capacities for dealing with the privatisation process: 'the core business of these firms is not therefore the substantive activity; providing defence equipment does not have much to do with educating children. ... The core business is the art of winning government contracts' (2013, p. 228). On the other side, public sector organisations and managers have also steadily built up skills and techniques in contract management.

The next two sections provide an indicative overview of how these pressures to sell public assets and marketise social services have played out in Australia since the 1980s. Although not comprehensive, this historical sketch demonstrates the complex politics and process of marketisation, as governments and oppositions seek to realise their ideologies while managing public expectations, the electoral cycle and fiscal and institutional constraints.[2] And although our primary interest is social policy, we begin with asset privatisation because it is useful for

---

2   Our overview is necessarily selective; for more detail, see Aulich and O'Flynn (2007a, 2007b), Colley and Head (2013), Fairbrother and colleagues (2002), Walker and Walker (2008), and 'Privatisation: a review of the Australian experience', a special issue of *Growth*, the journal of the Committee for the Economic Development of Australia, edited by Margaret Mead and Glen Withers (2002). The sources we cite in this section also deal with particular dimensions of the topic in detail.

understanding the parallel process of change in social services, in which market encroachment is less immediately visible.

Asset sales in Australia: what has happened and why

Early rationales for asset privatisation

In Australia, extensive public development of economic infrastructure, for example, utilities, transport, communications and financial services, had its roots in colonial history and was essential to nation building during the first three-quarters of the 20th century (Aulich & O'Flynn 2007a, pp. 371–72). However, this began to change as privatisation came squarely onto the policy agenda in the early 1980s, with the release by the Liberal–Country Party Coalition government (1975–83) of the report of the Committee of Review of Commonwealth Functions (soon known by its critics as the Razor Gang). In his ministerial statement on the report's release in April 1981, Prime Minister Malcolm Fraser outlined the government's objectives under the heading 'Transfer of functions to the private sector'. These were:

> strengthening private economic activity and the influence of individuals over the economy through their choices in the market place. In the view of the Government, activities of a commercial kind are generally best performed in the private sector, where they are open to greater influence from consumers and to the disciplines of competition (Fraser 1981, p. 1,832).

Announced reforms included asset sales, contracting out, and encouragement of private sector involvement in a wide range of activities. In his endorsement of the report, then-Treasurer John Howard argued that Fraser's 'statement and the response of the Opposition have demonstrated what a sharp philosophical difference there is between we on this side of the House and the Opposition about the size and role of government in Australia' (Howard 1981, p. 1,986).

As it happened, the Review of Commonwealth Functions was more aspirational than effectual as a marketisation manifesto, not least because the Fraser government lost power early in 1983. Despite Mr

Howard's remarks on party differences, it was Labor governments led by Bob Hawke (1983–91) and Paul Keating (1991–96) that began divesting public properties and eventually government business enterprises. Nevertheless, the ALP was never united on privatisation, and some researchers argue that its asset sales were 'pragmatic' rather than ideological (Aulich & O'Flynn 2007a; see also Feigenbaum & Henig 1994, p. 194). Still, over 13 years in government, Labor clearly moved away from its pronounced ideological hostility to privatisation.

Researchers have pointed to a range of structural and contingent causes behind this shift in Labor's approach. One was the strong pull of neoliberal ideas on Labor, a social democratic party that found itself in office dealing with economic stagnation in ways that compromised its traditional redistributive goals (Lavelle 2005). Another was the growing influence, or at least receptive disposition, of neoclassically trained 'econocrats' in the federal bureaucracy (Hawker 2006; Pusey 1991). Public service reforms also gave unprecedented influence to policy entrepreneurs within the formal policy process, as the use of ministerial advisors and consultants became institutionalised (Hawker 2006). According to Geoffrey Hawker (2006), former merchant banker David Block, who was appointed to lead an 'Efficiency Scrutiny Unit' in the Department of Prime Minister and Cabinet in September, 1986 was particularly important during the Hawke years.[3] Hawker argues that Block drove the marketisation agenda behind the scenes, following the crisis precipitated by a collapse in the terms of trade in 1986. This agenda included asset sales as well as the comprehensive introduction of commercial principles into the internal operation of the Commonwealth public service (Hawker 2006; Holmes & Wileman 1997).

Overall, then, it seems that economic crisis and the rising influence of small government ideas conspired to generate political and policy opportunities for market encroachment. Practically, this resulted in La-

---

3   A media report at the time collected several quotations from Prime Minister Bob Hawke extolling Mr Block's virtues and efforts, among which were: 'I wanted to get the toughest, leanest, meanest, most efficient bloke in the private sector, and bring him into the Australian public service to undertake a series of efficiency scrutiny surveys' and 'I pay tribute to the magnificent work that he has already done in, bringing to an examination of the practices of the Commonwealth public service, the rigours of the private sector' (Stephens 1987).

bor committing to balance budgets without raising taxes as a share of GDP, as part of the 'Trilogy' announced in the 1985–86 budget (Head 1988). Inevitably, this commitment would create multiple pressures for budget restraint and hence further policy reform, including the use of private providers in social services and the eventual sale of assets. These asset sales would help Labor to reduce budget deficits, fund popular programs, and avoid future capital expenditure on state-owned assets.

Given the lack of internal consensus in favour of this approach, it took a series of political and financial crises to give the ALP leadership the political authority to push major privatisation. In 1987, Prime Minister Hawke had unsuccessfully sought the approval of the ALP National Conference for asset sales (Goldfinch 1999, p. 14). Three years later, the impending collapse of the State Bank of Victoria (SVA), caused by the failure of its merchant banking arm, Tricontinental, opened the way for the partial privatisation of the Commonwealth Bank (CBA). Raising equity through privatisation enabled Treasurer Keating to sell part of the CBA and use the funds to purchase (rescue) the SVA (*The Economist* 1990). After the proverbial privatisation horse had bolted, a special party conference in September 1990 approved the sale of Australian Airlines and 49 percent of Qantas (Goldfinch 1999, pp. 13–14) and these, along with a range of other specialised defence and research organisations were sold over the subsequent years. Together, sales under Labor raised well over $6 billion (Aulich & O'Flynn 2007a); see Table 1.2. Other sales were announced but not carried out; yet others were carried over into the Howard era (Hawker 2006, pp. 250–51).

By the mid-1990s, the Labor government had overseen a transition in which market encroachment into the public sector had become part of normal policy. Most indicative was the Keating Labor government's active pursuit of National Competition Policy (NCP) in the early–mid-1990s. This was an ambitious blueprint for microeconomic reform prepared by a committee of inquiry chaired by management professor Fred Hilmer in 1993 (Commonwealth of Australia 1993). NCP was agreed by the state and Commonwealth governments in 1995. It amounted to a framework for marketisation through microeconomic reform of government business enterprises (many of which were owned by the states) and in the economy more broadly, mandated via changes to the *Trade Practices Act 1974*. The policy's organising principles were

Table 1.2: Indicative summary of asset sales, federal and state governments, 1987–2013. For sources and notes, see appendix at the end of the chapter

Jurisdiction	Party of government[a]	Year	Asset	Proceeds ($m)
Federal	ALP	1988	Defence Service House Corporation Loan Portfolio	1,515
		1993, 1995	Qantas	2,115
		1993	Commonwealth Bank (first tranche)	1,700
		1988–95	Other	1,037
	Coalition	1996	Commonwealth Bank (second tranche)	5,100
		1997	Melbourne, Brisbane and Perth airports	3,337
		1997–2006	Telstra (three tranches)	45,200
		2002	Sydney Airport	4,233
		1996–2004	Other	3,781
NSW	Coalition	1989–95	State bank, investment and insurer, grain handling	1,943
	ALP	1995–98	Tab Ltd, Axiom Funds Management	1,177
		2010	NSW Lotteries	1,011
	Coalition	2012	Kurnell desalination plant (50 yr lease)	2,300
		2013	Port Botany, Port Kembla (99 yr leases)	5,000
		2013	Electricity generators	160
Qld	ALP	1994	Gladstone Power Station	750
	National [b]	1996–2000	TabQ, Bank of Qld, Suncorp-Metway/QIDC, State Gas Pipeline	2,878
	ALP	2010	Queensland Rail	4,600

Jurisdiction	Party of government[a]	Year	Asset	Proceeds ($m)
		2010–11	Other (Abbot Pt Coal terminal, infrastructure and resource assets)	4,500
SA	Labor	1992–93	Sagasco, SA Financing Trust	451
	Liberal [c]	1994–96	State Bank of South Australia	730
		1994–2000	Other infrastructure and resource assets	719
		1999	Esta Power and Power Utilities	3,500
Tas.	Liberal	1993	State insurance office	42
	Labor	2005	Hydro's Roaring Forties wind energy generation (50%)	110
Vic.	Liberal [d]	1992–98	Electricity industry	22,522
			Other (incl. Tabcorp, ports, grain handling, State Insurance Office)	1,227
WA	Labor	1993	State Govt Insurance Office	165
	Liberal	1993–2000	Dampier-Bunbury Natural Gas Pipeline, AlintaGas, Bank West, other	4,129

contestability, which warranted the break-up of monopolies, and *competitive neutrality*, which meant in practice that the public sector could not receive special treatment or protection in economic transactions. Removal of a range of industry-specific protections under NCP angered farmers and small business owners, raising doubt about the viability of rural communities (Boswell 1996).[4] At the same time, NCP judged

---

4   National Party senator Ron Boswell spoke on behalf of these constituencies in this critical assessment of NCP. Later, Pauline Hanson's One Nation Party would be a beneficiary of small business and rural hostility to NCP (van Fossen 1998).

public sector subsidies to assist less well-off consumers and clients to be inefficient and uncompetitive, a move that raised concerns about the policy's impact on poorer Australians (Carver 1996). As we discuss later, this model for marketising public services has had a very significant impact on social service provision through the expansion of contracting out, including increased use of mechanisms such as competitive tendering.

Howard's privatisation program

Under John Howard's Coalition government (1996–2007), market encroachment on the public sector was pursued in all its forms at the federal level (Aulich & O'Flynn 2007a). The new government convened a National Commission of Audit, in the tradition of the Fraser government's Review of Government Functions and in keeping with its election promise. The Commission's terms of reference and underpinning principles were informed by market logic: to identify whether or not the federal government *should* be involved in the activities in which it *was* involved.[5] Its report included the recommendation that 'The Government should shut down or sell public sector assets where there appears to be no public interest reason for continued government ownership' (National Commission of Audit 1996, recommendation 3.4). The definition of public interest was correspondingly narrow.

The Howard government ran with this advice. Between 1996 and 2006, it sold the remainder of the Commonwealth Bank, Telstra, most major and minor airports, the National Rail Corporation, and Australian Defence Industries, among other assets, which, at a total of more than $61 billion, yielded nearly 10 times more than earlier sales under Labor (Aulich & O'Flynn 2007a, appendix 2). The Howard government

---

5   According to Hawke and Wanna (2010, p. 71) the recommendations of the Commission of Audit were more 'managerial than neoliberal, oriented towards doing more with less and improving "value for money" . . . based on a presumption that program managers (spenders) would manage their own budgets better'. The distinction between managerial and neoliberal is valid, albeit rather fine. David Block's proposals, which used private sector models to reform the public sector, were based on the same assumptions (Hawker 2006), and asset sales and other marketising reforms are prominent among the commission's recommendations.

also embarked on a massive program of contracting out of IT and other 'non-core' services from the federal public sector (Aulich & O'Flynn 2007a; Australian Public Service Commission 2003; Pittard 2007).

Coalition policy towards privatisation clearly followed the Liberal Party's stronger embrace of free-market economics, most forcefully expressed in the *Fightback!* program of 1991 (Liberal Party of Australia 1991). Still, mass privatisation needed public legitimation, and the question was central in the election of 1996. In 1988, around the time that the ALP had begun selling off some Commonwealth assets, public support for whole or part privatisation of Telstra was measured at 61 percent (Goot 1999, p. 217). However, by 1996, when the Coalition under John Howard's leadership was seeking election on a platform that included privatising Telstra, support for the sale had fallen to 33 percent (Goot 1999, p. 217). Thus, the Coalition needed to manage the electoral risk of persisting with privatisation, and the related problem of National Party resistance to a reform with the potential to hurt rural communities. As Goot (1999) argued at the time, Howard crafted a complex and electorally successful strategy to neutralise criticism from the left. He promised funds from the Telstra sale to undertake environmental projects, while also making the (now credible) argument that Labor would privatise anyway.

The Liberals also actively promoted privatisation by encouraging small 'mums and dads' shareholders to buy shares in the staged privatisation of Telstra. Designed to appeal to middle-class and aspirational Coalition voters, this strategy repositioned the sale of major public assets as a step towards genuine popular ownership. In his closing address to the Liberal Party's 1998 national convention, John Howard exalted popular share ownership as his 'great goal' for the future:

> just as Robert Menzies made Australia the greatest home-owning democracy in the Western world, so it is my goal that my Government will make Australia the greatest share-owning democracy in the world. Already we have sold one-third of Telstra and we're along the way towards that goal ... we have made a firm policy decision, that if re-elected we will proceed to allow the people of Australia, the men and women of Australia, to buy the remaining two-thirds of Telstra (Howard 1998).

To overcome National Party resistance, the Coalition restricted foreign ownership in Telstra (just as the ALP had restricted foreign ownership of Qantas in 1992) so that its sale would not arouse excessive nationalist concern about foreign takeovers of land and assets – a rallying cry of populist right-wing resistance to free markets that continues today.[6]

Although privatisation was clearly and increasingly unpopular with the electorate, the Howard government persisted with attempts to sell assets well into its final term. It passed legislation to privatise Medibank Private, a huge government-owned health insurer, late in 2006 and began to arrange the sale by share market float (Department of Finance 2007, p. 44). Following public outcry, the sale was then postponed until after the 2007 election (Aulich & O'Flynn 2007b, p. 161), which the government lost, so 'the sale process was promptly terminated' (Department of Finance 2008, p. 49). Public opposition was also decisive in the government's 2006 decision not to proceed with the sale of the Snowy Mountains hydroelectricity scheme, which was at an advanced stage of planning. In June of that year, the sale of this 'Vegemite of national infrastructure' (Andren 2006, p. 22) was withdrawn. The prime minister justified the decision by saying that 'The decision to sell has created a lot of unhappiness in the Australian community right across the political spectrum. I am not such a zealot about privatisation that you sell everything under the sun irrespective of the circumstances' (Howard 2006).[7]

The return of Coalition government in 2013 – and of privatisation

The final asset sales planned by the Howard government did not go ahead, and during the years of ALP federal government under Kevin Rudd (2007–10, 2013) and Julia Gillard (2010–13), privatisation, at least in the form of public asset sales, was off the agenda. The GFC may

---

6 Chan (2013) describes the 'explosive entry' of the issue of foreign ownership, especially of land, into the 2013 federal election campaign.
7 With an election coming, in the same press conference, Mr Howard also admitted to succumbing to the persuasion of his cabinet colleague, member for the bellwether seat of Eden-Monaro, to withdraw the proposal. He also blamed the NSW Labor government, a major shareholder in the Snowy Mountain scheme, for proposing the sale in the first place (Howard 2006).

have had a role here, as Labor returned to a more traditional Keynesian deficit-funded stimulus strategy (Colley & Head 2013, p. 869).

The re-election of a Liberal–National Coalition government in September 2013 immediately revived discussion about reducing the size of the public sector. Further asset sales were not mentioned in the Liberal Party's 'Real Solutions' election policy statement, although the sale of Medibank Private was foreshadowed, along with massive cuts to public sector jobs. After winning, the government returned to the Coalition's longstanding marketising agenda, justified by reference to the (apparent) weak fiscal position of the federal government.

Action was swift. Announced in October 2013, a 'Commission of Audit' reported in February 2014 and advised the government on an aggressive, deep and wide-ranging privatisation and outsourcing program. Recommendation 57 of the report used the Hilmer-era idea of 'contestability' to justify its advocacy of short, medium and long term privatisation of entities including the Snowy Hydro, the Mint, Defence Housing Australia, and the National Broadband Network (National Commission of Audit 2014, pp. 220–24). Proposals for the sale of several of these were announced in the 2014–15 budget.

The Government had already committed itself pre-election to the full privatisation of the largest private health provider, Medibank Private, which was floated in November 2014 and raised the government around $6 billion (Hartge-Hazelman & Baker 2014). This privatisation will likely reshape how price-setting occurs in the private health insurance industry, with ongoing signs the government will allow premiums to continue to rise at a record or near-record pace (Gardner 2015).

Perhaps the most serious threat to public infrastructure emerged with the implementation of the Asset Recycling Initiative, agreed to at a Council of Australian Governments meeting in May 2014 (Dossor 2014). The aim of the program is to provide federal incentives for states to privatise existing assets on the condition that the proceeds fund new public infrastructure (Department of Infrastructure and Regional Development 2014). The success of the proposal is no doubt related to its twin appeal to natural privatisers and those governments desperately looking for infrastructure finance. By early 2015, the South Australian, Victorian and Queensland governments had accelerated privatisation plans to access these funds (two year time limit for access) (Crowe 2014). The federal government's proposals have the potential to unleash a vast program of asset transfer into private control, and to further generate profits for private businesses involved in public-private partnerships financed by the sell-offs.

State governments and asset sales

State governments, which have traditionally owned utilities and which had a major presence in insurance and banking, also began to sell off assets in the 1990s. And, as Table 1.2 shows, over the last two decades, at least one wave of asset sales has occurred in all states, under ALP and Liberal governments. As with the federal sphere, fiscal difficulties have been as much a driver as ideological zeal. Over time, rationales at the state level have also changed, from an emphasis on debt reduction to pleading about the need to raise revenue for infrastructure (Colley & Head 2013). Overall, Liberal governments have privatised more and faced less political resistance than Labor. As such, the return of Liberal governments in Victoria, Queensland and New South Wales (NSW) after 2010 has relaunched the privatisation agenda in those states.

Some of the privatisation experiences of the Australian states are worth chronicling in more detail. In NSW, ALP governments attempted to continue the process of asset sales begun in the 1990s under Premier Nick Greiner's Liberal–National Party government, but mostly failed. Indeed, privatisation initiatives by Labor governments in NSW faced paralysing internal opposition. The proposed sale of electricity generators in NSW under Labor premiers Bob Carr (in 1997 and 2003) and Morris Iemma (in 2007 and 2008) (Colley & Head 2013, p. 871) led to serious internal party revolts, on both occasions led by the union movement, and the sales did not go ahead. A further sell-off attempt in 2010–11, under Labor's Premier Kristina Keneally, was also eventually derailed with the ALP's defeat in 2011. Given the political difficulties Labor had faced, Liberal premier-in-waiting, Barry O'Farrell, made undertakings to unions before the election not to privatise certain entities, including water and ferries (Smith 2011). However, since the election, a significant asset sale program has been underway, involving electricity generators, a desalination plant and the three major ports of NSW (Table 1.2 shows major sales completed between 2011 and 2013). To carry out these large scale asset sales, the government was required to engage in political trade-offs with minor parties (Clune 2012, p. 628).

In the run-up to the 2015 election, Premier Baird (2014–) has foreshadowed the sale of further electricity assets ('poles and wires'), but faces strong public disapproval of the proposal (Nicholls & Hasham 2015). Meanwhile, another program of asset sales has been less visible and so less contested. In late 2012, the NSW government established an agency, Government Property NSW, to manage its portfolio of 200,000 properties, which have a combined value of almost $130 billion. By February 2015, $1 billion worth of these properties had been sold, and many more were slated for future sale (Knowles & McClymont 2015). Like the major asset sales, these divestments have been consistently justified as providing funds for infrastructure development.

Victoria's Liberal government led by Premier Jeff Kennett in 1992–99 embarked on the most ambitious program of privatisation and outsourcing in a highly ideological response to its inherited budget and debt problems (Robinson 1994). More than 50 government businesses were sold, including the electricity generation sector and public transport systems, yielding more revenue than the proceeds of the privatisations of all other states put together at that time (Colley & Head 2013, p. 870). After a long period of ALP government (1999–2010) during which privatisation was not pursued, the Victorian Liberals regained government in 2010 and market reform returned to the centre of policy debate.[8] Although there were no major asset sales under Liberal rule, both premiers Baillieu (2010–13) and Napthine (2013–2014) publicly stated that privatisation was a strategy under consideration, notably to raise revenue for infrastructure projects (Gordon 2012; Napthine & O'Brien 2013).

Queensland came relatively late to large-scale privatisation: starting small under the ALP in 1994, asset sales took off under National Party governments between 1996 and 1998. A hiatus during ALP governments led by Premier Peter Beattie (1998–2007) was followed by a massive second wave of privatisation under Labor Premier Anna Bligh (2007–12), who announced these plans *after* Labor won the 2009 election. These asset sales (which included Queensland Rail) were not

---

8 The incoming government commissioned an Independent Review of State Finances, the report of which they considered too controversial for publication, but which recommended very wide-ranging transfers of public responsibility to the private sector, according to media reports (Uren 2012).

anticipated by voters, who opposed them, and they have consistently factored as a reason for her government's crushing defeat in March 2012 (Quiggin 2012). Not surprisingly – against the recommendations of its own Commission of Audit[9] and in spite of an enormous parliamentary majority – the new Liberal–National Party government of Premier Campbell Newman undertook not to sell any further assets without an explicit mandate. In January 2015, however, Premier Newman took a far-reaching privatisation plan to voters, centred on the sale of electricity assets (Ludlow & Wiggins 2014). His party lost the election, and Mr Newman himself lost his seat, after Labor campaigned primarily on the privatisation issue.

In Western Australia, the first asset sale (of the State Insurance Office in 1993) was undertaken by a Labor government, but this privatisation was overshadowed by the sweeping divestment of infrastructure, energy, banking and other assets under a Liberal government between 1993 and 2001. Following seven years of Labor rule (2001–8), the incoming minority Liberal government did not pursue asset sales immediately. When Western Australia lost its AAA credit rating in September 2013, following significant increases in the state debt, Premier Colin Barnett immediately began to discuss privatisations, despite promises not to do so before the election in March that year (Burrell & Taylor 2013). However, such proposals are clearly politically sensitive, and he has been careful to hedge: 'there will not be asset sales that impact on services to the public ... they will be carefully thought out' (Burrell & Taylor 2013).

In South Australia, privatisation began in a small way under the ALP in 1992, but proceeded apace under Liberal premier Dean Brown, who was elected in a landslide in 1993 and claimed a mandate for large-scale reform, including reducing public debt through asset sales (Martin 2009, p. 141). Colley and Head suggest that when Labor returned to government in 2002, 'the privatization agenda had run its course' (2013, p. 870).

Federal Treasurer Hockey's recent privatisations (noted above) have re-opened the question of asset sales at the state level in the most

---

9   Premier Newman established a Commission of Audit soon after winning the 2012 election. The Commission's report recommended further asset sales and a variety of other marketising reforms (Queensland Commission of Audit 2013).

comprehensive way since the introduction of NCP two decades ago. The premiers of NSW and Queensland responded with caution, citing the need for engaging voters before signing up to the scheme (Coorey 2013). However, with so much privatisation having already occurred, those assets remaining in public hands increasingly seem to political and business elites like an unexploited opportunity.

What can be concluded from this overview of Australia's experience with privatisation? The first conclusion is that governments at federal and state levels, on both sides of politics, privatised. They did so often against political opposition, and typically against public opinion – our focus later in this chapter. Labor in opposition at both state and federal levels tends to oppose privatisations, with state premiers Steve Bracks in Victoria and Wayne Goss in Queensland later expressing regret about the impact of privatisations they instigated on rural rail services in their respective states. Nevertheless, Labor is inclined to promote asset sell-offs when in government, despite voter and union resistance. Coalition governments are persistent and successful privatisers, most using a 'commission of audit' to frame their agenda.

The second conclusion is that, over time, rationales for privatisation change (Colley & Head 2013). At the state level, fiscal difficulties have been a persistent rationale. Ideology has become less explicitly important, but only because the ideas behind privatisation have become normalised in elite discourse. Moreover, in recent years, sell-offs have been increasingly justified to voters as providing funds for much needed infrastructure, both at the federal level and by the states, which are responsible for three-quarters of infrastructure investment (Chan et al. 2009, p. xvi). Once the funds are raised, infrastructure development is increasingly undertaken through 'public–private partnerships', which are a form of market encroachment by other means.

The third conclusion is that, despite difficulties encountered in privatisation, there have been no serious or programmatic proposals to reverse privatisations of any major asset sales at either level of government, or by either major party.

A final conclusion involves assessment of whether privatisation has been a success on its own terms. Two main criteria have justified privatisation: improving efficiency and raising revenue; the latter has dominated in recent years, but the two are connected. Researchers have found that public assets have been underpriced in Australian privatisations (Gong & Skekhar 2001), and that, because most privatisations have *not* been undertaken through open subscription to an Initial Public Offering, the windfall gains have accrued to purchasing companies, not to individuals (Docherty & Easton 2013). In early 2008, Walker and Con Walker estimated that the sale proceeds to date amounted to $56.2 billion, while the market value of assets sold was $151.3 billion, representing, they argued, a transfer of $95.1 billion to the private sector (2008, p. 20). Table 1.3 presents the current market value of a handful of former publicly owned enterprises, to give a hint of the scale of ongoing impact on public balance sheets.

Assessing the fiscal consequences of privatisations in Australia, taking into account the potential for efficiency gains, economists Harris and Lye (2001, p. 319) concluded that generally, governments should not use privatisation with the objective of raising revenue. In particular, selling efficient and profitable government-owned enterprises is most detrimental to the public sector and this reduction in net worth is ultimately borne by the taxpayer. Privatisation is a poor fiscal tool and should not be used as a means of improving economic efficiency.

Furthermore, a program of privatisation targeting inefficient government-owned enterprises might result in a fiscal gain, as was the case with Telstra, Qantas and the Commonwealth Serum Laboratories (CSL). This provides more weight to the case for privatisation of inefficient government-owned enterprises. Too often, governments are intent on selling profitable and competitive enterprises without sufficient justification.

This nuanced view of privatisation, however, is not reflected in political debate in Australia, where asset sales are generally framed as good economic sense. Meanwhile, public–private partnership (PPP) arrangements, which are becoming a preferred model of infrastructure development following privatisation, also raise public interest concerns. Infrastructure PPPs give governments political opportunities, not least because they 'are not recorded on government balance sheets, bypassing expenditure controls and reducing parliamentary and public scrutiny of projects' (Chan et al. 2009, p. 143). PPPs also provide lucrative opportunities to businesses in the finance sector as well as in construction. Critics point out that 'the potential for the interests of the advocating government and the business partners to dominate over the public interest has been palpable' (Hodge & Greve 2010, p. S8).

Table 1.3: Current market capitalisation of major assets

Company name	$ million
Qantas	2,668.54
Commonwealth Bank of Australia	122,490.50
Telstra	64,703.99
Suncorp	16,133.98
Tabcorp	2,715.39
Total	208,712.40

Source: www.bloomberg.com, valuation at 14 February 2014

In the shadows: marketisation in social services

Asset sales appear as highly visible lump sums on the revenue side of the public ledger. And, Australians are aware of changes in service arrangements in new privatised banks, airlines, utilities, and telecommunication carriers. Are techniques involved in the marketisation of social *services* so obvious? The answer is no: measures such as contracting out (outsourcing) or tax expenditures to support market provision are much less visible. One reason is that contracting out appears on the expenditure side of the public ledger, often as part of program outlays and recorded in ways that do not make clear who the government is paying to provide services. Tax expenditures are particularly opaque. Not reported in the budget at all,[10] revenue is 'forgone' in the form of tax concessions to individuals and companies.

Marketisation of social services is different from asset sales in another important way. Most of the assets sold by governments in recent decades provided services for which payments by consumers (whether households or industry) covered the costs of production, and in many cases delivered a surplus to the public purse. Public ownership dealt with the problem of natural monopolies, distributing the surpluses of production to consumers and businesses that would have otherwise

---

10   Tax expenditures are reported separately in Treasury's annual *Tax expenditure statements*.

accrued as monopolistic profits. Many social services are different: consumers (generally households or individuals) typically do *not* pay the full cost of production; indeed, they may pay relatively little. Such services are publicly subsidised for social purposes; in other words, redistribution is an essential feature of their design. They are *social* infrastructure that enables labour market and community participation (for example, of parents of young children and family members of frail older people and people with disabilities), and that provides in-kind specialised support to various vulnerable groups (for example, through support to find work for unemployed people, welfare services for children and families and residential care for older people) and to people in crisis situations (for example, following natural disasters, droughts, homelessness or domestic violence).

These characteristics affect the politics of social service marketisation in different ways. For example, services directed at smaller, disadvantaged groups such as unemployed people, are less likely to attract widespread public attention, especially when the economy is growing, so changes may not be registered, let alone resisted. Meanwhile, services taken up across all social groups, such as child care and aged care, have only quite recently, and partially, emerged as 'public issues' from their prior status as 'personal troubles', to use C. Wright Mills's well-known formulation. Thus, compared to universal services such as health and education that have long been provided collectively, the political salience of child care and aged care to broad publics is still developing.

Regardless, profound shifts have occurred, and in what follows, we point to a few major developments at the federal level[11] to give a sense of the changes that have introduced market practices and actors into social services over the last two decades. We discuss child care, employment services, superannuation, health care, aged care and approaches to the non-government sector. As pointed out in Goodwin and Phillips (this volume), publicly subsidised social services have long been provided by a range of mostly private (non-public) providers in Australia. However, until relatively recently, the 'mixed economy'

---

11   The state governments have primary responsibility for organising delivery of many social services affected by the changes we discuss. Developments at the state level are not chronicled here but deserve a definitive account.

was not primarily coordinated by market instruments and incentives, and the role of for-profit organisations was marginal or non-existent in most policy areas. Other chapters in this volume, especially those by Davidson (on community care), Stebbing (on retirement incomes), Carney (which includes discussion of aged care), Proctor and Aitchison (on schooling), Collyer, Harley and Short (on health care) and Mitropoulos and Bryan (on a new financing method for social services) fill out the account in detail.

Hawke and Keating's welfare model: Labor engages private services

The Hawke and Keating Labor governments made critical reforms to social policy that increased involvement of private sector actors, both non-profit and for-profit. Important for understanding Labor's reforms in these areas is that they were aimed at increasing the scale of service *provision* without increasing the size of the *public sector* – although public *spending* on key service areas did increase significantly. Using the examples of child care, employment services, and retirement income provision, we show how increased service provision was largely achieved by promoting the growth of private sector alternatives to underdeveloped public provision.

Child care had long been provided in a mixed economy, with some, but not all, private providers, enjoying public subsidies. As Brennan (1998; 2007) has documented, only non-profit and local government providers were eligible for federal government funding under the terms of the *Child Care Act 1972*. In limiting eligibility in this way, the then Liberal government accepted the recommendation of early childhood professionals that good quality care 'was best provided in childcare centres under the auspices of non-profit organisations' (Brennan 2007, p. 214) – market ideas were yet to influence this policy domain.

In the 1980s, Labor had changed the model of recurrent funding for these services, in a bid to save money by reducing public spending on what some in the government saw as unjustifiable support to the middle class (Brennan 1998). Before this reform, funding levels had been tied to actual staff costs, and so were formally linked to the costs of providing services. The reforms, which were resisted by unions, childcare workers and women's groups, shifted the funding model to payment per licensed place. The new payment was *not* formally linked to costs of provision, and this payment was supplemented by fee assistance to low-income families. The new approach to funding services delinked the level of public funding from the actual costs of provision, and has been widely used to contain the public cost of social services since the 1980s. User fees typically make up the difference between the subsidy and the cost – a form of privatisation to households.

Other ALP reforms to child care further privatised the system by promoting the expansion of for-profit provision. In 1991, the ALP government increased funding to child care by extending eligibility for public subsidies to parents using for-profit providers. Brennan (1998) has documented how this decision was a compromise, following intense debate within the ALP, pressure from for-profit providers and opposition from women's groups.[12] An important rationale for increasing public funding for child care was Labor's commitment to addressing child poverty; the rationales for the chosen measure – extending subsidies to for-profit providers – included competitive neutrality and the need to draw more capital into the sector (Brennan 2007, p. 215). This round of changes shifted the financing mechanism from one which primarily funded *centres* to provide services to one which primarily funded *parents* to subsidise the costs of child care – effectively a 'voucher system through the back door' (Brennan 1998, p. 188). The impact of these changes was immediate and profound. Between 1990–91 and 1995–96, the number of children using formal child care grew from 153,100 to 570,300, and federal expenditure on child care grew from $245.6 million to $990.6 million (Australian Institute of Health and Welfare 1997, p. 111–12). Over the same period, the number of places in for-profit childcare centres increased from 36,700 to 122,462 (233 percent) while the number of places in community-based, non-profit services increased from 39,567 to 45,601 (15 percent) (Brennan 2007, p. 215).

---

12 The Minister of Finance, Peter Walsh, agreed with the for-profit providers that a voucher system would be the best policy. For market champion Walsh, vouchers would resolve the problems of inequity arising from the disproportionate use of publicly subsidised child care by middle-class families. However, this policy was not adopted (Brennan 1998).

The ALP also sought to widen access and improve benefits without establishing new public institutions in another social policy domain: retirement incomes. In 1992, the government introduced compulsory superannuation, thereby making occupational superannuation available to a much wider range of employees than previously (see Stebbing, this volume, for a detailed analysis). During Whitlam's leadership of the ALP, a national (public) superannuation scheme was added to the party's platform in 1969, based on a collective logic. The ALP under Hawke and Keating did not take this route, and the chosen instrument led to the growth of a massive private funds management industry, underpinned by public subsidies in the form of generous tax concessions. Note, however, that non-profit industry super funds were an important innovation of this time, and were the default funds for workers on industrial awards. With these industry funds, a vestige of an associational logic was retained by the ALP's reforms.

With its employment strategy, *Working nation*, released in 1994, Labor sought to address the high unemployment of that time with a job guarantee for the long-term unemployed and a more flexible model of assistance to job-seekers in finding and training for work. This more individualised assistance was to be achieved through specialised 'case management' services, established as a complement to the mainstream Commonwealth Employment Service. Case management would be offered by a newly constituted public provider, Employment Assistance Australia (EAA), along with services outsourced to non-government organisations, both for-profit and non-profit. Contracts were allocated following a tender procedure run by an independent regulator, with competition between providers (including EAA) on quality, not price. By 1996, 30 percent of case management services were offered by private providers (Considine 2000, pp. 277–78; Considine 2003, p. 66).

In other policy domains, a similar pattern of a blend of social democratic goals on one hand, and fiscal containment and the increasing use of corporate/market mechanisms and private actors on the other, is evident. In 1983, for example, Labor established Medicare, a universal public health insurance system – to fund mostly privately allocated, privately provided medical services. Meanwhile, in aged care, earlier Liberal governments' subsidies to residential care had promoted open-ended, uncoordinated and inequitable development of the nursing home sector. Labor's remedies for these problems combined bureaucratic (regional planning) and market (competitive tendering) logics (Kendig & Duckett 2001; see Davidson, this volume for discussion of developments in community care). As with asset sales and competition policy, many Labor reforms in the social services provided fertile ground for more thoroughgoing marketisation by the Howard government after 1996, and for the consolidation of for-profit provision in many social service fields. Not least was the consolidation of new private interests in social policy, interests that sought to keep funding flowing and to contain regulation that might increase costs.[13]

In an overlapping set of developments, the way governments dealt with non-government service providers also began to change significantly during the 1980s (see also Goodwin & Phillips, this volume, for a more systematic treatment of this issue). As public spending on social services increased and private providers were more systematically included in the welfare state, governments sought tighter control over those providers. To this end, governments at federal, state and local levels began to use a suite of corporate management technologies, including program budgeting, performance measurement and corporate planning to arrange both their internal operations and their relationships with the private organisations they funded to provide social services (Considine 1988; see also Healy 1988; Industry Commission 1996).[14] As these approaches took hold and evolved over the subse

---

13   Brennan (1998; 2007, p. 220) has shown, for example, how for-profit childcare providers first successfully fought for access to public subsidies and then, often successfully, resisted increased quality regulation.

14   The report of an inquiry into competitive tendering and contracting (CTC) by public sector agencies, was commissioned by the ALP government and released in early 1996. Section A. 1 of the report contains an excellent articulation of the principles of public sector management and change abroad at the time. Section A. 2 showed that CTC accounted for a relatively small proportion of public spending at that time. At the federal level, the Defence and Veterans Affairs departments dominated CTC, measured by expenditure (Industry Commission 1996, pp. 60–61), while in New South Wales and Western Australia (the only states for which detailed figures were given), CTC accounted for small but rapidly growing proportions of spending – in NSW, 2.3 percent of expenditure was via CTC in 1992–93, rising to 4.0 percent in the following financial year. In WA the proportion increased from 3.6 percent in 1992–93 to 7.6 percent in 1994–95 (Industry Commission 1996, p. 62).

quent decades, they significantly changed the demands government funders made on their 'suppliers'.

Howard's service marketisation: contracting out and tax expenditures support private service industries

Outsourcing and competitive tendering developed apace during the Howard years. Alongside asset sales, the Howard government outsourced information technology, human resources and knowledge services in the federal bureaucracy. It was also very active in marketising areas of social policy. The Hawke and Keating governments tended to use marketising reform to *expand* service provision by using public subsidies or legislation to increase services. By contrast, Howard's policies tended to encourage the *substitution* of private provision or funding for public. In an analogue to its ambitions for 'mum and dad' share ownership, the Howard government's rationales for social service marketisation included enhancing individual choice. Promoting the growth of the private sector's share of provision was also an explicit policy goal. Here we briefly outline some developments in child care, job placement services, superannuation, health care and aged care, to demonstrate the character of market reform of social services during the Howard years.

The extension of public subsidies to for-profit providers under Labor was a quick-fix solution to the problem of the undersupply of child care, with an uneasy mix of rationales. The Coalition government's approach to child care funding was more unequivocal in its promotion of a market-driven system – albeit one that provided large and growing public subsidies to the families targeted by Howard's politics, which also emphasised traditional gender roles and extended social benefits to those on higher incomes.

In its first budget, the government reduced and restructured child care funding. It removed the operational and capital subsidies to nonprofit, community-based child care services despite promises not to do so before the election, reduced the level of one form of child care subsidy to parents, and imposed a means tests on the other (Brennan 2007, p. 216). However, new funding arrangements brought in as part of the New Tax System in 2000 *increased* the Child Care Benefit (CCB) paid to parents, and increased the eligibility threshold for this benefit. In 2004 – an election year – a further subsidy was introduced, in the form of a tax expenditure: the Child Care Tax Rebate (CCTR), which subsidises parents' out-of-pocket expenditure on child care. While the CCB was means-tested and cut out for families above a certain income threshold, the CCTR was capped but not means-tested. The CCTR considerably reduced the extent of targeting of child care benefits, and injected yet more funds into the system.

The further injection of funds into an unplanned system, which had relatively undemanding quality regulation and no cap on fees, created favourable conditions for the further expansion and corporatisation of for-profit provision. A spectacular example of the business opportunity apparently offered by the new funding regime was the rise of ABC Learning. Listed on the stock exchange with 43 centres in 2001, in 2007 it owned 2,323 centres, of which 1,095 were in Australia, following a building program and the aggressive pursuit of acquisitions (Newberry & Brennan 2013). At its high point, ABC Learning was the world's largest child care company. Along the way, owner Eddie Groves made close relationships, including business deals, with several leading Coalition politicians; indeed, Larry Anthony, the Howard government's minister for Children and Youth Affairs joined the board of the company as a non-executive director within months of losing his seat at the 2004 election (Brennan 2007, p. 218). Critics have pointed out how policies championed as fostering competition and choice in child care instead led to strong market concentration and price inflation (Newberry & Brennan 2013).

Earlier in the 1990s, Labor's *Working nation* expressed a mix of social democratic and marketising impulses, and began the process of contracting out job placement services. The Howard government's reform of labour market programs removed the social democratic elements, notably the job guarantee, and, as Mark Considine puts it, involved 'radical changes ... to strengthen the market elements of this service' (2003, p. 66). Using the now ritual criticisms market reformers use to justify policy change, the government claimed its evidence-based labour market programs were addressing the 'inflexibility, lack of choice and diversity, the absence of competition and unclear objectives and outcomes' of the ALP's *Working nation* (cited in Thomas 2007, p. 10). In 1998, the 'Job Network' was created and all publicly funded job placement services to recipients of income support were put out to competitive tender. The CES and EAA were closed down, and replaced for the time being by a new public entity, Employment National, which competed alongside private providers. Over two rounds of contracting in 1998 and 2000, Employment National's share fell to below 10 percent, and at the third round in 2003, all contracts went to private providers (Thomas 2007).[15]

The Howard government also made a large number of reforms to superannuation policy during its period in office, not all in the same direction.[16] Some early measures sought to decrease inequities in the system arising from the *compulsory* nature of the Superannuation Guarantee, which removed urgently required money from the pockets of people on very low incomes, and from the very longstanding and regressive tax concessions on super contributions, which Labor had not remedied. There were also several measures designed to improve the sustainability of the system, such as increasing the preservation age, and removing disincentives for older people to remain in paid employment. However, the main thrusts of superannuation policy during the Howard years, especially later on, were to enhance the business opportunities of private financial institutions and to increase the benefits received by a core constituency of wealthy voters (see Stebbing, this volume).

The idea of enhancing choice was a key rationale behind the two main reforms that both increased the scope of for-profit private superannuation and reframed superannuation as a financial services 'product' directed at 'customers'. The first was the *Retirement Savings Account Act 1997*, which enabled a wide range of financial institutions to offer alternatives to trustee-controlled superannuation funds, thereby opening up a tax-expenditure-subsidised business opportunity to private banks. These opportunities increased when, after a long gestation, legislation was passed to enable employees to nominate any eligible super-

---

15 The Coalition introduced competition over price as well as quality into the tender processes of 1998 and 2000, but removed price in 2003 because it was evidently counterproductive (Thomas 2007, pp. 2, 19). Over time, detailed control over providers increased, in the attempt to deal with the predictable problems of 'parking' of hard-to-place clients and selection bias towards easier-to-place clients ('creaming') that arise in marketised systems (Thomas 2007, p. 23).
16 For a comprehensive overview, see Warren (2008), from whom much of the following is drawn.

fund, rather than the default fund, in their industrial agreement from 2005 (Warren 2008, p. 18).

As noted above, early changes sought to decrease inequities arising from concessional tax treatment of contributions to superannuation. However, later changes reversed some progressive measures and, over-all, significantly increased the inequity of superannuation arrange-ments.[17] The government argued that the changes would 'dramatically simplify superannuation for retirees and improve incentives to work and save' (Australian Government 2006, p. 9). The government abol-ished the tax surcharge on superannuation contributions by high-in-come earners it had introduced in its first budget, removed *all* taxes on superannuation benefits, and extended arrangements that permitted sharing of entitlements with spouses, which offered significant benefits to high-income breadwinner households. One consequence was the very steep climb in the costs of revenue forgone in tax expenditures during the final years of Howard rule (see Table 1.4).

Increasing choice was also an important justification for Coalition reforms in health policy. In opposition, the Coalition had long opposed universal health insurance: the Fraser government abolished the Whit-lam government's Medibank, and Medicare was an opposition target during the Hawke and Keating governments. In 1995, however, Howard changed his mind – for electoral, not ideological reasons. As he put it to his biographers, Wayne Errington and Peter van Onselen:

> I think that there is a certain bedrock statism in the Australian psy-che. I came to the conclusion that the public would never let us get rid of Medicare and we had to accept the public wanted it and what our responsibility was to try and build on it and develop up the poli-cies and build around Medicare (2007, p. 228).

Accordingly, Medicare was not retrenched after the election of the Howard government. Instead, the Coalition offered support for private

---

17 Measures to encourage low-income earners to contribute to their own superannuation were retained, but were marginal beside the benefits that flowed to high-income earners. It is also important to note that the ALP did not remove regressive concessional treatment of superannuation contributions that had existed for many decades.

alternatives to Medicare, in the form of a 30 percent rebate on private health insurance premiums in 1999. The goals were to revitalise the rate of private health insurance, which had declined significantly since the introduction of Medicare, and, as noted, to enhance choice. To defray public opposition, the Coalition framed the rebate *as a support for Medicare itself*, by diagnosing an 'unsustainable pressure' on the public system, to be relieved *not* by increasing funds to that system, but rather by subsidising private alternatives (Elliott 2006). In 2004, an election year, in the attempt to shore up support of another key Howard constituency – older Australians – the rate of the rebate was increased to 35 percent for people between 65 and 70 years old, and to 40 percent for those aged over 70.

One reason why older people might have needed a sweetener of this kind is that, on the recommendation of the National Commission of Audit in 1996, the Howard government sought to bring a different marketising instrument into aged care policy: user pays. The first Coalition budget brought in user fees for the first time for services under the Home and Community Care program, and new means tests were introduced and fees increased in residential care in 1997. The most controversial change was the introduction of 'accommodation bonds', which bring in service user resources to fund capital deficits in residential care. This measure was strongly resisted by older people and their families, who feared that they would have to sell the family home to gain access to the care they needed (Fine & Chalmers 2000, p. 11).

Also introduced in 1997 was a policy designed to enable those with more resources to pay more to get more within publicly subsidised residential care. Providers would be able to offer 'extra service' facilities or wings, to 'enable residents in aged care services to enjoy a superior level of comfort and choice' (Department of Health and Ageing 2005, cited in Buckmaster 2005, p. 3). While fees, subsidies and standards for *care* remained set by the government, proprietors could set their own charges for *service* dimensions, such as accommodation, food and recreational and personal services. This measure was a deliberate attempt to engender stratification within aged care, and opened a lucrative business opportunity in which corporate providers were particularly interested (Buckmaster 2005, p. 4).

Across most social policy fields, the government took a similar approach. For example, federal funds for private schools were also increased and funding rules relaxed, which the government justified as enhancing educational choice and which lead to significant growth of private education. This, along with changes to the range of policies already discussed, exemplifies some key themes and instruments in Coalition social policy. Promoting private alternatives to public provision, justified as enhancing self-reliance and consumer choice is one; another is the use of tax expenditures as a social policy instrument, not least to extend benefits to higher income households previously ineligible for support within Australia's targeted welfare model. By the end of the Howard era, private provision of social services had increased considerably, as had the share of for-profit companies within the private sector, and stratification in education, health care and aged care had been actively engendered by public policy. Further, despite the focus on cost containment in many policy areas, the extent of public involvement in social policy, as measured by spending, had not shrunk by 2007; indeed, quite the reverse, it had expanded – leading the Howard government's approach to be characterised as 'big government conservatism' (Norton 2006).

One other result of the Howard approach to social policy deserves mention. Conservatives are often thought to favour non-profit or non-government organisations (NGOs) because they express a communitarian spirit of self-help or, more paternalistically, a charitable impulse. The Howard government certainly drew on these themes, with its rhetoric of a 'unique social coalition approach' (cited in Phillips 2007, p. 33), in engaging these organisations in service provision. Yet in reality, the Coalition government's relationship with NGOs was more complex. On one hand, many non-profit organisations gained large income streams from providing publicly funded services, in job placement, homelessness, family relationship counselling and other areas. On the other, in addition to the increasingly detailed control exercised through contracting that began under the ALP, the Coalition government was hostile to the advocacy role taken by some NGOs, which it also sought to neutralise or control. Early in its period in office, the government simply stopped federal funding to several advocacy NGOs in the social welfare and environmental fields (Phillips 2006, p. 60), and contracts with providers often included 'gag clauses' which sought to prevent those receiving federal funds from criticising the government (Franklin & Lunn 2008).[18] Over time the Howard government established a group of favoured – or perhaps captured – organisations, many of them with a religious auspice (Phillips 2007). Meanwhile, the rhetoric of 'coalition' notwithstanding, the non-profit sector was damaged, with its capacity to act with an associational logic undermined by competition with other organisations (both non-profit and for-profit), and by the highly instrumental nature of the contracting process (Wright, Marston & McDonald 2011).

No turning back? Federal Labor and social services 2007–13

Labor's election in 2007 marked a return to the revival of social democratic goals, although these were still pursued with market-inflected strategies, as we shall show. ALP governments under Rudd (2007–10, 2013) and Gillard (2010–13) attempted major expansionary reforms of health care, education, disability support and aged care. One challenge for Labor in power was opposition from entrenched private interests consolidated by Howard-era policies. Another was the federal structure of governance in Australia, which became increasingly difficult to navigate as more states came to have Liberal or Coalition governments over Labor's time in federal government. Yet another was that Labor's ambitious reform agenda was dogged by the perennial problem of Australia's 'low tax social democracy' (Wilson 2013), which left the ALP without the resources required to fully realise its reform goals.

But Labor had also been challenged in realising its social democratic goals by its own ideology, which has pulled it back towards market-oriented policies and away from developing more collective responses to social risks. A 2008 speech by the then Deputy Prime Minister and Minister of Education, Employment and Workplace Relations,[19] and later Prime Minister, Julia Gillard gives a sense of Labor's approach. Ms Gillard spoke about 'the new politics of the progressive centre':

---

18 The Howard government also put forward a Charities Bill in 2003, which sought to redefine the purpose of organisations with tax exemptions to exclude those with political or advocacy purposes. The bill was not passed and was withdrawn (Wright et al. 2011, p. 311).

19 Revealingly, Ms Gillard said she 'would be happy to be described as "the Minister for Productivity" ' following her swearing in to this 'very broad suite of portfolios' (Gillard 2008).

> The next generation of reform challenges are all about how the power of the market interacts with the surrounding framework of institutions and the actions of individuals themselves. That means we are focusing on the fundamentals of *market design* ... How can we develop markets which interact productively with strong public institutions and empower users to participate successfully in them? (Gillard 2008)

Ms Gillard criticised the Howard government's 'version of being pro-market' for having little regard for the overall performance of sectors, including health and education, in which it had simply encouraged the growth of private providers and private consumption. But, she went on:

> Rejecting this approach does not mean that we seek to control and direct market activity from within government. Instead, we need to ensure that, in sector after sector, the design of key institutions, the shared investment in knowledge and skills and the approach taken to regulation increase the distinctive strengths, innovative capacity and adaptability of that field. (Gillard 2008)

Kevin Rudd expressed similar 'Third Way' ideas in his lengthy essay on social democracy in 2009, in which he decried 'neoliberalism, and the market fundamentalism it had produced', but also emphasised 'the creative agency of government' in addressing social inequity and 're-build[ing] confidence in properly regulated markets' (Rudd 2009). A brief overview of Labor policy on child care, schools and health illustrate how the ALP in government enacted this approach, within the political and institutional constraints they faced.

Before the election in 2007 early childhood programs had a prominent place in Labor's campaign, in keeping with the ALP's strong focus on education as a means to social mobility for individuals and prosperity for the nation. In its first budget, Labor increased the non-means-tested tax rebate (CCTR) component of funding from 30 to 50 percent of out-of-pocket expenses, and raised the annual per-child ceiling from $4,354 to $7,500. This approach to increasing child care affordability continued the inflationary and market-oriented approach of the Coalition. Shortly after these changes were brought in, the Rudd government was confronted by the collapse of ABC Learning – the corporate, for-profit provider that had grown to dominate long day care in Australia. The government spent $100 million (in addition to its ongoing child care funding) to prevent the sudden closure of such a large part of the system (Newberry & Brennan 2013, p. 240).[20] Eventually, much of the child care *provision* part of ABC Learning was taken over by a consortium of large, non-profit organisations, underpinned by loans from the government and the NAB – and by capital from self-styled philanthropic private investors, who are now pleased to report that they receive a 12 percent return on their investment in the rebranded 'Goodstart' (Gorman 2013). The property in the centre *buildings* remained in the hands of for-profit property trusts, as it had been under ABC Learning (Newberry & Brennan 2013). Once the transfer of ABC Learning centres to Goodstart had taken place, for-profit providers still retained 64 percent of long day care places (Office of Early Childhood Education and Care 2010, p. 6). Overall, then, Labor did not substantially change the market structure, as predominantly for-profit private providers, complex private business models and demand-side funding were left in place.

However, social democratic goals also shaped the ALP's approach to child care, through policies aimed at increasing quality and accessibility within this 'market'. During its first term, Labor sought to use regulation to increase staff: child ratios and the qualifications of staff – both measures long resisted by for-profit providers – and to extend the reach of national quality regulation to all forms of child care.[21] Other measures included the guarantee of a part-time preschool place to all four-year-olds in Australia and the development of a National

---

20 Newberry and Brennan (2013) give a fascinating account of the 'opco-propco' (operational company–property company) structure that enabled the growth, and led to the demise of ABC Learning. This model of separation of operation and property elements of the 'business' is still in place.

21 The Keating government had introduced an accreditation system for services seeking access to federal subsidies, as a concession to researchers and non-profit providers concerned about the quality of unregulated child care offered by for-profit providers, which had gained access to public subsidies. During its 2007–13 term, Labor established a new national system (and institution) for oversight of quality of all forms of publicly subsidised child care, including preschool, long day care and out-of-school-hours care: the Australian Children's Education and Care Quality Authority.

Early Years Learning Framework.[22] A later intervention in 2013, the 'Early Years Quality Fund', offered $300 million over two years to finance wage increases for staff in long day care centres, in recognition of the low pay and related retention problems in the sector. To access the funds, providers were required to make enterprise bargains with staff and United Voice, the relevant union.

In school education, Labor had to deal with the legacy of the Howard government's funding model, which had given substantial new federal funding to private schools that, in turn, made many private schools and many parents reluctant to see a more egalitarian redistribution. During the 2004 election campaign, school funding policy had been strongly contested. The then Labor leader, Mark Latham, promised federal funding to schools on the basis of need, and created a 'hit list' of 67 elite private schools from which a Labor government would withdraw funding, for redirection to poorer schools (Harrison & Hall 2012). Whether or not this declaration of so-called class warfare and expression of the 'politics of envy' was decisive in the 2004 election outcome (Harrison & Hall 2012; see Browne 2012), Labor was very cautious during the 2007 campaign, promising to preserve the Howard government's arrangements for four years, and to conduct a review of school funding. This review, chaired by David Gonski, was not commissioned until April 2010 – nearly two and a half years after Labor had been elected – and during the election campaign later that year, Labor again promised to extend the existing inequitable arrangements (Harrison & Hall 2012). The committee finally delivered its report to the government in December 2011, and the report, which recommended sweeping changes to redress the significant inequalities it had identified (Gonski 2011), was publicly released in February 2012.

Now constrained by its own promise to bring the budget into surplus, the ALP baulked at implementing 'Gonski'. On releasing the report, the government re-emphasised the importance of education to Australia's economic future. But rather than taking the opportunity provided by an authoritative report – and, likely, the support of the majority of the public (Browne 2012) – to act, it announced a yet further round of consultation, and even proposed to look into whether philan-

---

22   See Australian Institute of Health and Welfare (2009, p. 22) for a complete list of Labor's first term initiatives in this area.

thropic funding might be a possible 'alternative funding stream' (Hall 2012).

The Australian Education Bill was introduced into parliament in late November 2012, for implementation in 2014. In April 2013, the government announced cuts of over $2 billion in university funding, to release resources for schools. At the time of the federal election in September 2013, plans for implementation were underway but incomplete, and a protracted process of haggling with the state and territory governments, several of which were now in Coalition hands, was not completed. In implementing the Gonski reforms, the federal ALP government sought to tie the states to increasing their own funding to schools as a condition of receiving increased funds, among a range of other measures included in a National Plan for School Improvement (Harrington 2013). Thus it appears that Prime Minister Gillard was hampered by political and fiscal problems in achieving her goals of developing 'markets that interact productively with strong public institutions' and of redesigning 'key institutions' in the area of education.

Just as the Coalition's private school funding seemed politically difficult for Labor to reform, so too did the private health insurance rebate. The rebate 'largely directed subsidies to those on higher incomes who are more likely to take out PHI, and to private insurance companies, private hospitals and medical specialists' (Segal 2004, p. 3; see also Collyer et al., this volume), all of which have an interest in its continuation.[23] The benefits to these diverse recipients are handsome indeed: the rebate amounted to $4.67 billion in revenue forgone in 2011–12, the most recent year for which data are available (see Table 1.4). The ALP had opposed the introduction of the rebate: during the debate on its introduction, Jenny Macklin (1998) called it 'the worst example of public policy ever seen in this parliament'. However, once it had been introduced, Labor did not take what it saw as the electoral risk of opposing it, and Kevin Rudd promised to retain during the 2007 election campaign.

---

23 Further, the rebate did not create a corresponding decline in demand for public services, because people with private insurance retain full access to Medicare, and around a quarter continue to present at public hospitals as public patients (Seah, Cheong & Anstey 2013, pp. 1–2).

Table 1.4: Tax expenditures for social purposes, Australia, 2000–12 ($m)

	Superannuation	Private health insurance	Housing	Child care
2000–01	9,920	2,031	13,000	
2001–02	11,140	2,118	13,000	
2002–03	10,100	2,250	–	
2003–04	13,833	2,387	14,000	
2004–05	17,288	2,645	37,000	
2005–06	23,305	2,883	39,500	
2006–07	30,379	3,073	39,500	
2007–08	38,940	3,587	40,500	75
2008–09	33,117	3,643	29,500	1,122
2009–10	25,413	4,262	43,500	1,072
2010–11	27,226	4,000	35,500	1,562
2011–12	30,262	4,671	31,000	1,887
2000–12 (total)	**270,923**	**37,550**	**336,000**	**5,718**

Source: Treasury tax expenditure statements, various years.

The need to find savings in the context of the GFC provided a political opportunity for reform after Labor came to office, and the Fairer Private Health Insurance Incentives Bill, was introduced in 2009. Labor did not directly challenge the private health system with this bill: Minister of Health, Nicola Roxon, avowed in her second reading speech that 'the government supports a mixed model of balanced private and public health services', and justified the changes as increasing the fairness and sustainability of public subsidies to the private sector (Roxon 2009, p. 4435). The Coalition opposed the bill in the Senate, so it failed to pass on two occasions (Biggs 2011, p. 5) and an amended version was enacted in 2011, taking effect on 1 July 2012. Labor's reform removed one incentive for higher income earners to take out private insurance by means testing the rebate, but increased the other, by raising the Medicare surcharge.

Public hospitals were also a politically charged issue at the 2007 election, and Kevin Rudd promised major reform, foreshadowing a 'federal takeover' of hospitals. A lengthy review and consultation process resulted in a National Health Reform Agreement in 2011 (COAG 2011). Through this agreement, Labor aimed to steer state governments by promising significant resource increases in return for cooperation with new national institutions which would set a 'national efficient price' for diagnosis-related activities in hospitals and monitor hospital performance. This agreement continues the corporatisation of the public sector, with its purchaser–provider split, benchmarking and mix of decentralised budgets and centralised regulation – while also conforming to Rudd and Gillard's model of government steering by regulation and market design.

We conclude this brief review of some of Labor's social service re-forms by noting that the ALP in government sought to redefine and develop the relationship between the federal government and the non-profit sector, following Howard government policy that had sought to contain criticism and to control closely organisations under contract to provide services. Early in its first term, Labor announced that it would remove 'gag clauses' from federal government contracts, and promote a more open policy debate with the non-profit sector (Franklin & Lunn 2008). In 2009, it commissioned the Productivity Commission to look into the contribution of the non-profit sector, and a lengthy report was published in 2010. In the following years, a set of new institutions was established, including a National Compact between the federal government and the non-profit sector in 2010, the Office for the Non-Profit Sector in the Department of Prime Minister and Cabinet in 2011, and the Australian Charities and Not-for-Profits Commission in 2012. These institutions were designed to develop and support collaboration between the government and non-government organisations (NGO) (the Compact and Office) and to independently regulate non-profits (the Commission). As researcher John Butcher has put it, whether these efforts succeed in 'putting the genie' of the contracting state 'back in the bottle' remains to be seen, given 'the path-dependent legacies of two decades of microeconomic reform' (2011, p. 50).

The ALP's major social policy reforms confronted entrenched interests, which it mostly failed to challenge head on. The major reforms also had long implementation lead times, with the bulk of federal funding growth held over for several years from the time of the policy announcement.[24] This has left these reforms very vulnerable, following the election of a Coalition government in September 2013.

The Abbott government

As noted above, long lead times on implementation of many of Labor's social policy measures made them vulnerable to retrenchment before they were established. Evidence from the first 18 months of the Abbott Coalition government (2013-) suggests that it will prevent many Labor social policies from being fully implemented. The Coalition has justified many policy retrenchments with claims that Labor left the nation's finances in a poor state. Another rationale the Coalition invokes is the need to remove unnecessary regulation imposed by an interfering ALP government.

Far-reaching and more systematic marketising reform in social services has been foreshadowed by the Abbott government under the rubric of competition policy. In December 2013, the government announced a Competition Policy Review, and the draft report was released in September 2014. The report's preoccupations and modes of reasoning reflect confidence in market mechanisms and private provision, and suspicion of government regulation as burdensome and distorting. According to the review panel, in the area of 'human services',

---

24   The hospital reforms begun by the Rudd government and finalised in 2011 when Julia Gillard was prime minister were to be fully implemented between 2014 and 2019, when an extra $16.4 billion would be spent on public hospitals (Coorey 2011). Only $11 *million* was allocated to DisabilityCare Australia in the budget of 2013–14, the fiscal year during which the scheme was announced after a long gestation that included an inquiry by the Productivity Commission. Only in 2016–17, the last year of the forward estimates period, would significant federal funding of $1.5 billion be allocated (Treasury 2013a, p. 140). The 2013–14 Budget also allocated 'an additional $9.8 billion over six years to implement a new needs-based funding model for schools, as part of the National Plan for School Improvement', less than $1 billion of which was to be paid out before July 2015 (Treasury 2013a, p. 120).

'deepening and extending competition policy ... is a priority reform. Removing barriers to entry can stimulate a diversity of providers, which is a prerequisite for expanding user choice' (Competition Policy Review 2014, p. 26). The report proposed a virtual encyclopaedia of new public management reforms for 'social service markets': separation of funding, regulation and service provision, public-private partnerships, contestable funding and consumer choice (Competition Policy Review 2014, Chapter 10).

In addition to sweeping approaches to market reform such as the Commission of Audit and the Competition Policy Review, the Abbott government has also proposed change in several of the specific fields this chapter has been tracking. In the area of child care, as part of his bid to attract more women voters, Mr Abbott said before the election that one of his first acts in a Coalition government would be to ask the Productivity Commission to explore the costs of subsidising in-home child care by nannies (Peatling 2012). At the time, Labor criticised this proposal to fund the most private of all forms of child care as inequitable and unsustainably expensive, and child care experts expressed concern about how the quality of private, home-based child care could be ensured. Such an inquiry was commissioned in November 2013, with terms of reference honouring Mr Abbott's promise. In turn, the draft report of the inquiry, released in October 2014, recommended that 'approved nannies to become an eligible service for which families can receive ECEC assistance' (Productivity Commission 2014, p. 48).

Meanwhile, on 10 December 2013, the government announced that it would *not* honour the previous ALP government's contracts with childcare providers to increase childcare workers' wages, under the $300 million scheme mentioned above. Two days later, the government announced that it would stop a much larger Labor scheme worth $1.2 billion to increase wages in aged care, introduced as part of the ALP's large-scale reform in that area. The motivation is at least partly political: during the election campaign, the Coalition had characterised this scheme as a means to increase union membership, because like the child care scheme, it also required providers to enter into enterprise bargaining agreements to access the funds (Harrison 2013).

In the area of superannuation, the Coalition is also seeking to reduce the power of unions, through proposed changes to the composition of the boards of trustees of non-profit industry superannuation funds. Currently, the boards of industry superannuation funds include an equal number of representatives of employers and employees, with the latter usually appointed by relevant unions. The Coalition and representatives of for-profit providers position unions as 'special interests' in this role, and changes under consideration would require union nominees to be replaced by 'independent' directors (Tingle & Patten 2013; Treasury 2013b). The Coalition is also seeking to give greater access to for-profit providers to compulsory superannuation contributions made on behalf of workers on awards. Currently, default funds in awards are specified by Fair Work Australia, and in the majority (70 percent) of cases, the default funds are industry superfunds (Productivity Commission 2012, p. 33). The Coalition has opposed this arrangement as an 'anti-competitive closed shop' (Coalition 2013a, p. 8), and for-profit providers have been lobbying for access to this 'market', from which they argue they are currently 'locked out' (Financial Services Council 2012, p. 4). Both the Coalition and for-profit providers propose removing deliberation within Fair Work Australia from the process of designating default funds in awards. Instead, they argue that employers should be able to choose any eligible fund on behalf of employees who do not choose themselves. It is notable that industry superfunds have long demonstrated superior performance, on average, compared to for-profit funds (Productivity Commission 2012, p. 73) and that the Coalition does not frame for-profit providers as a 'special interest' in the superannuation field.

The Coalition has also foreshadowed or attempted other reversals of Labor social policies discussed above. Before the election, the Coalition had promised to reverse the ALP's reforms of the private health insurance rebate 'once fiscal circumstances allow' (Coalition 2013b). At the time of writing, the means test and tax surcharge for private health insurance also remained in place for high-income earners. And although not foreshadowed in its campaign materials, changes to Medicare have also been raised since the Coalition assumed office. In February 2014, the then Health Minister, Peter Dutton, echoing John Howard, called for increasing private contributions to the costs of health care as a strategy for 'modernising and strengthening Medicare', and making it more 'sustainable' (Dutton 2014). This is despite evidence that both total health expenditure and public health expenditure in Australia are comparatively low, which suggests that sustainability problems are not acute. Expenditure data notwithstanding, out-of-pocket contributions by patients – which the government has sought to increase – are already comparatively high (OECD 2013). After legislative setbacks in 2014 and a retreat on an administrative manoeuvre to introduce copayment in 2015, the future of the Coalition's plans is unclear.

The Coalition also promised to *keep* some major ALP initiatives before it was elected. Mr Abbott and then Shadow Education Minister, Christopher Pyne, promised to honour Labor's school funding policy, calling it a 'unity ticket'. Once in government, however, the Coalition changed its mind on this question – more than once. At the end of November 2013, now Minister for Education, Christopher Pyne, announced that school funding agreements that Labor had come to with several states would be honoured in 2014 only, and a new funding system would be implemented in 2015, modelled on the Howard government's approach. A week later, the government had retracted this proposal, following strong criticism, including from Coalition Ministers of Education in Victoria and NSW (Hurst 2013). The revised position retained the expenditure Labor promised, but Mr Pyne proposed to remove important conditions required in Labor's agreements. One that has definitely been removed is the requirement that states also contribute additional funds, to ensure a net increase in education spending. At the time of writing, the fate of the needs-based formula for distribution of funds, which was at the heart of the Gonski report's recommendations for redressing inequality, was at best uncertain.

The Coalition has been active in the area of government–third sector relations, too. Before the election, it promised to abolish the Charities and Not-For-Profits Commission, established by Labor in 2012. In a speech reiterating the promise in January 2014, the then Minister for Social Services Kevin Andrews argued that the commission 'imposes an unnecessary and ponderous compliance burden on the sector'. Instead, he proposed a US-style 'centre of excellence' to replace 'coercive compliance and regulation' with 'collaborative education, training and development' (Andrews 2014). Like many of the Abbott government's social policy measures, legislation abolishing the commission was not passed by the Senate during 2014.

Problems of marketised social services in Australia

The encroachment of market ideas and practices into Australia's social service system has raised a new set of problems for governments and public.

First, governments have often used market practices to save money, leaving services systematically underfunded. Unmet demand – whether for child care, aged care, high quality schooling, timely medical treatment or genuinely individualised labour market support – is one result; a second is on the supply side, expressed in the low pay, high turnover and often inadequate level of training in the social services workforce.

Second, in several policy areas, notably health, education, child care and aged care, public underfunding combines with choice-co-ordinated provision to generate significant inequality. Market-derived rationales of increasing choice, diversity and competition in social services justify public subsidies to a wide range of private providers, both non-profit and for-profit, often without appropriate system planning or scrutiny. Moreover, a patchwork approach to services weakens programmatic responses to complex welfare problems. In this kind of mixed economy of social services, people with more resources may opt out of the public sector and purchase private services, which are resourced by a combination of public subsidies and their own funds. This has clearly happened in school education in Australia, for example. The result can be a vicious cycle of public sector decline, as underfunded public services become services for the poor, and a two-tiered system emerges.

Third, there is substantial international evidence that for-profit organisations, especially corporations, provide social services that are, on average, lower quality than those provided by public or non-profit organisations (Meagher & Cortis 2009; Harrington et al. 2012). In child care and residential aged care, where public provision is vestigial at best in Australia, the risk of poor quality services for the poor is more likely to arise in the for-profit sector, where lean service subsidies, weak consumer efficacy and the profit motive are combined. Meanwhile, those with more resources can pay more to escape both public services and poor quality private ones. Here the conflict between the logic of the market and the nature of social services seems most acute.

Fourth, there is the problem of ensuring that services in marketised social service systems are of good quality. As Braithwaite, Makkai and Braithwaite (2007, p. 219) argue in their book about regulating residential aged care, as for-profit provision has displaced non-profit provision in Australia and elsewhere, 'the density of rules and resources to enforce them has increased'. And as this regulatory apparatus has increased, so have the problems of ritualistic compliance and regulatory capture, as private providers seek to limit the impact of quality controls on their cost structures.

Fifth, the ABC Learning case provides spectacular evidence of the *instability* that can also arise in service systems driven by a mixture of consumer choice, public subsidy and the profit motive. Where the primary interest of corporate entities in marketisation is in gaining access to lucrative government contracts or subsidies and maximising shareholder return, privately provided services can lose the features expected of public services: equal treatment, uncompromised commitment to needs, and stable provision over time.

Sixth, while less spectacular than corporate collapses, reports of fraudulent conduct by private contractors point to another systematic problem in marketised service arrangements. Reports of pervasive fraud by providers of publicly funded employment placement services under the Job Network and its successor, Job Services Australia, have recurred over more than a decade (Besser 2011, 2012; Marris 2001; Morris 2007), and have involved both for-profit and non-profit providers. Problems have also been reported in aged care – an internal departmental audit was reported to have found that one in six claims for a government subsidy for nursing home residents had over-charged ('Nursing home rorts clawback' 2012). Likely to be much less prevalent because of the design of the funding system, problems have also been revealed in the child care sector. A report from the Australian Crime Commission noted that 'There are increasing instances of child care benefit fraud schemes perpetrated by the owners of child care centres by means of lodging fraudulent statements of child care usage to the Family Assistance Office' (cited in Viellaris 2013).

Seventh, as we noted in Table 1.1, in marketised systems, governments under political pressure can shift responsibility for service failures to private providers. This raises pressing questions of democratic accountability for social provision – the public are repositioned as customers and governments as purchasers; meanwhile private providers can simply close their business and move on.

Voters' responses to marketisation: support for a mixed economy of ownership and services with a leading role for government

Our account of asset sales and market encroachment into social services in Australia has focused on the role of political, bureaucratic and corporate elites, and we have mentioned public opinion only in passing. Our focus now turns to how Australian voters have responded. That market encroachment is an elite project does not mean that voters are irrelevant to shaping the course and limits of privatisation in rich democracies.

Voter opinions are only one source of information about public policy institutions and social policy arrangements, but they are an important one. This is because understanding how elite-driven policies are 'institutionalised' involves some consideration of the role of 'political feedback' in policy change. The failures of some attempts at large-scale privatisation – such as Thatcher's efforts with the UK National Health Service – to survive major political and economic tests are important examples of such feedback. In developing countries, utility privatisations (water, gas) have led to powerful conflicts and opposing coalitions that hint at doubts about the future for privatisation, even in rich democracies (see Hall, Lobina & Motte 2005). Recent bank and commercial nationalisations during the Global Financial Crisis are reminders of the endemic risks of a highly privatised economy. By considering what mix of government and private involvement the public prefers we gain a useful picture of what arrangements are widely accepted and where possible tension points between policymakers and the public over privatisation lie.

We begin with public attitudes to ownership of enterprises and institutions and public attitudes to who is best suited to deliver social services. Tables 1.5 and 1.6 present findings from the *Australian Survey of Social Attitudes* in 2003 (Wilson et al. 2004) and 2009 (Evans 2010) about the preferred mix of government/private involvement in major enterprises, institutions and services.

Table 1.5: Preferences for ownership of major enterprises and institutions, 2003, percent

	Public	Mix public and private	Private	Can't choose
Australia Post	67	24	5	3
Prisons	67	19	8	6
Public transport systems in cities	63	28	6	3
The electricity system	60	31	9	6
Telstra	57	31	9	4

Source: *Australian Survey of Social Attitudes* 2003 (n>2,114) Question: Do you think the following enterprises or organisations should be in public ownership, private ownership or a mix of public and private ownership?

As Table 1.5 shows, in 2003, public ownership was preferred by Australians in all five areas surveyed, with support ranging from a low of 57 percent for Telstra to a high of 67 percent for (still government-owned) Australia Post and prisons (in which there is limited private involvement). There was some support (low 30s) for partial private ownership of Telstra and electricity; as discussed earlier, both types of utility had been steadily privatised over the 1990s and 2000s. Still, support for *fully* private ownership remained extremely low in 2003 – less than 10 percent across all five enterprises and institutions.

Table 1.6 gives us a better picture of support for private delivery of social services. Government is the widely preferred provider of education and health services, with nearly nine in 10 voters thinking that governments are best suited to deliver in health services. When we consider social and community services – including care for people with a disability, child care, elder care, and employment and welfare support – a slightly different picture emerges. Governments are considered by small majorities to be best suited to deliver care for older people and people with disabilities. Government leads 'best suited' responses by a plurality of respondents for the other two service categories – services for job-seekers and child care. Community organisations and large charities, which became major institutions under the Howard government's social services and welfare model, are preferred by 44 percent of respondents as the best providers of counselling and welfare support. Business involvement in social services gain greatest recognition in the area of employment services (36 percent) where they have played a major role in service provision since the privatisation of the Commonwealth Employment Service.

All in all, support for non-public involvement in social and community service provision is higher, for several reasons. The first is that many of these services have not traditionally been provided as public services. Rather, as discussed earlier, they have expanded at a time when direct government provision is distinctly out-of-favour among policy-makers. One finding in political and policy science is that stable policy institutions and arrangement will gather natural 'constituencies' (Pierson 1996, p. 147); no doubt the prior evolution of the mixed economy of social service provision has influenced public support. But these areas of provision are also ones that not only invite strong contest between state and market provision, but also conflict between government and family – social norms still sanction care for children, people with disabilities and the elderly within private family settings. None of these observations should discount one other finding that, when views about these five social services are averaged, government still leads as best provider with 45 percent of responses. Only when scores for the community sector and family are combined does the number of respondents preferring non-government delivery arrive at a similar percentage. Given growing business interest and involvement in welfare, it is useful to note that business is clearly the least preferred provider; why this is the case should be the subject of further research.

Support for, and opposition to, privatisation

As we have noted, elite enthusiasm for privatisation has not rubbed off on voters – even when they have had years of experience of privatised services. Existing research (looking at data similar to ours) suggests that opposition to privatisation started to grow in the 1990s and has remained consistent and relatively stable since then (Pusey & Turnbull 2005, pp. 165–6). In this section, we draw on other survey research and

Table 1.6: Preferences for delivery of health, education and social services, 2009, percent

	Governments	Community organisa- tions incl. churches and charities	Businesses	Families and relatives	Can't choose
Health services	87	4	5	1	3
Education	85	7	2	2	4
Care for the disabled	51	24	4	10	6
Care for elderly persons	50	23	4	16	6
Services for job-seekers	47	11	36	1	5
Counselling or welfare support	42	44	5	3	6
Child care	36	20	18	21	6
Average social services (last 5 rows)	**45**	**24**	**13**	**21**	**6**

Source: *Australian Survey of Social Attitudes* 2009 (n>3,243) Question: In general who do you think is best suited to deliver the following services?

opinion poll data to explore attitudes to privatisation in further detail. We show that recent data further confirm Pusey and Turnbull's findings, and suggest that a 'new constituency' of voters who have adapted to and warmed to privatisation is yet to arrive. Figure 1.1 presents responses to the AuSSA 2009 question 'Privatisation of government services has more benefits than costs'.

Results show that less than 20 percent of respondents support the proposition that the benefits of privatisation outweigh the costs. A ma-

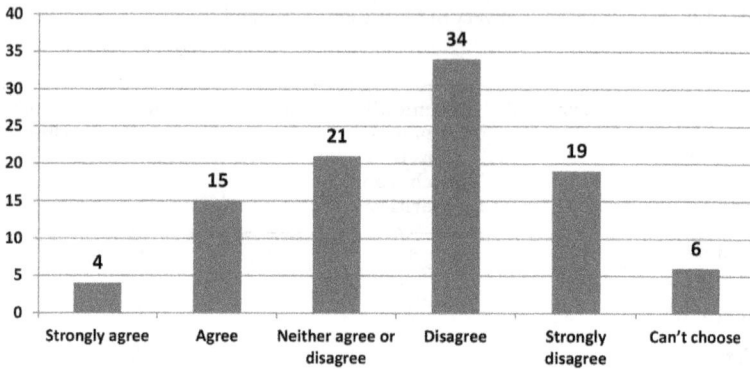

Figure 1.1: Perceptions of the costs and benefits of privatisation, 2009, percent
Source: *Australian Survey of Social Attitudes* 2009 (n=3,097) Question: Privatisation of government services has more benefits than costs.

jority (53 percent) view privatisation as having more costs. Around 27 percent of respondents seemed to have mixed or unclear views, not supporting either proposition or not choosing – a relatively high number which we discuss further below. Still, the balance of opinion among those who express a clear view (by agreeing or disagreeing) is clearly opposed to privatisation.

Widespread scepticism about privatisation as a general policy approach persists. In January 2014, a public opinion poll reached very similar findings to the AuSSA survey. In response to the question 'Generally, do you think that privatisation – that is, having public services owned or run by private companies – is a good or bad idea?', a majority – 59 percent – thought privatisation a bad idea while only 21 percent thought it a good idea (Essential Research 2014). The remainder did not know.

A poll in February 2015 confirmed this general finding, and gives more clues as to why Australians are sceptical about privatisation (Essential Media Communications 2015, p. 13). The poll clearly shows that voters don't believe that private ownership will bring lower prices, more competition or better quality services – the main and long-standing claims of proponents of privatisation. And respondents are clear about who they think *does* gain – 70 percent say that the corporate sector mainly benefits while just 25 percent agree that privatisation helps the economy.

Support for privatisation by social group

Durant and Legge's (2002) study of privatisation views among French voters found that the political and ideological orientations of voters were particularly important. We used data from AuSSA 2009 to see if similar political divides emerge among Australian voters. In addition to the variables included in the French study, we also had a hunch that 'nationalistic' orientations played a role in cleavages over privatisation; that is, that voters wanted big public institutions like utilities to be under *Australian* control, whether public or private. AuSSA 2009 did not include questions measuring nationalist policy stances, so we used the privatisation data in AuSSA 2005 and compared views based on responses to a question seeking views as to whether foreign competition had a bad effect on job security. We considered voters who agreed with this question more likely to be 'economic nationalists'.

Figure 1.2 ranks net support for privatisation for a range of different constituencies available from data included in the *Australian Survey of Social Attitudes 2009*. Net approval was calculated by subtracting total disapproval from total approval so that a negative score represents more disapproval than approval. As is clear from the figure, *none* of the constituencies included had a net *positive* view of privatisation, including a range of groups typically associated with support for free markets (shareowners, Liberal Party identifiers, voters identifying as right of centre). Not surprisingly given the potential for windfall gains, shareowners have the highest net support for privatisation at –20 percent, though still well in negative territory and only narrowly ahead of Liberal Party identifiers (–21 percent). However, much greater opposition was found among 'economic nationalists' (–43 percent), defined as those with negative views of the impact of foreign competition on local jobs, union members (–55 percent) and Australian Greens identifiers (–60 percent). Within the Coalition's base, National Party identifiers had nine percent lower net approval (–30 percent) than Liberal identifiers. Notably, young people, defined as between 18 and 35 years, had slightly less negative views of privatisation than the average voter at –27 percent net approval. Young voters, having grown up in an 'age of pri-

Higher support for privatisation

High income earners (−25%)

Right of centre voters (−22%)

Liberal Party identifiers (−21%)

Shareowners (6 or more shares) (−20%)

Under 35s (−27%)

Somewhere in the middle

National Party identifiers (−30%)

Men (−34%)

Voters with university degrees (−36%)

Women (−36%)

Lower support for privatisation

Economic nationalists (−43%)*

Labor Party identifiers (−44%)

Left of centre voters (−55%)

Union members (−55%)

Green identifiers (−60%)

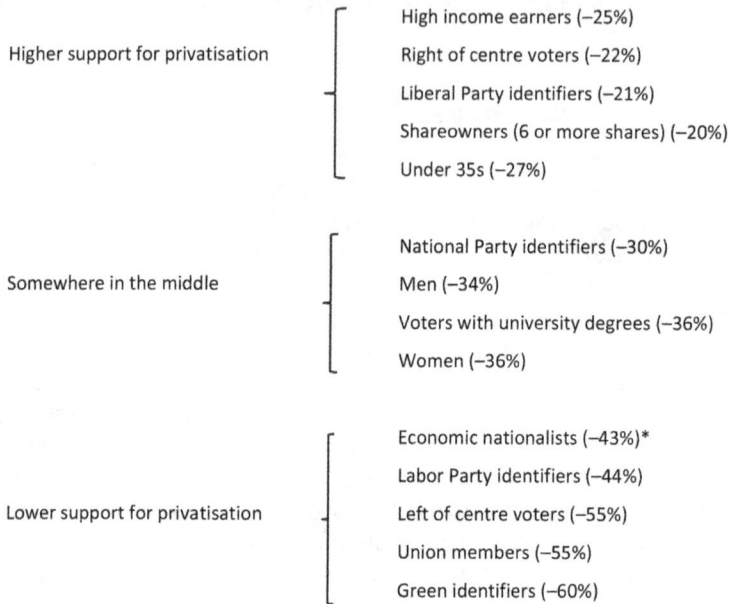

Figure 1.2: Support for privatisation by key constituencies, 2009, net approval, percent. For sources and notes, see appendix at the end of the chapter

vatisation' may have fewer attachments to public ownership – a trend that, if continued, might herald slowly rising toleration, if not acceptance, of privatised services.

Public responses to specific privatisations

To this point our analysis explores voter attitudes to privatisation at a general level, without gauging views on specific proposals. This general survey of opinion leaves unanswered two further questions – does the *general* unpopularity of privatisation among voters translate into opposition for *specific* decisions to privatise major services? And, how does voter support for privatisation of these services compare to other major economic reforms? The commercial Essential Media online panel survey of 1,017 voters from October 2011 helps with answers. Table 1.7

shows voters' assessments of a range of major economic decisions taken by federal governments in the past few decades. Medicare achieves strong support (net approval is 70 percent) and so does compulsory superannuation for workers (72 percent). Although compulsory private super conceals a form of privatisation in diverting worker funds to financial markets, its ultimate popularity stems from its place as a mandated, universal means of financing retirement incomes. Immediately obvious in Table 1.7 is the unpopularity of the sale of three major public enterprises – Telstra, the Commonwealth Bank and Qantas – which have a combined market capitalisation of approximately $190 billion (as at February 2014; see Table 1.3 above) or around half of Australia's net public debt. These privatisations, all with net approval percentages below minus 20 percent, rank well below the public's evaluation of other policy decisions, some of which are hardly free of ongoing unpopularity and controversy (the Goods and Services Tax, for example).

Table 1.8 gives more detail about public opinion on these decisions by respondent voting intentions. Confirming evidence from the *Australian Survey of Social Attitudes* presented above, major privatisations register negative net approval from voters from all four main political parties – Labor, Greens, National and Liberal. Liberal voters are not positive towards privatisation in retrospect. Rather, they are the least negative, albeit only marginally when it comes to the Commonwealth Bank and Qantas. National voters again break with Liberals in holding stronger negative assessments of privatisation. On this measure, Labor voters register stronger anti-privatisation views than Greens (though both groups of voters are strongly hostile). By contrast, responses to AuSSA 2009 on the general question suggested Green identifiers are more hostile; it may be that Labor voters become more critical when prompted about *specific* privatisation proposals. The privatisation of Telstra was the most unpopular of the three, attracting even –20 percent net approval from Liberals.

The same Essential Media poll asks respondents whether they support *reversing* these decisions (see Table 1.9). With the exception of boosting trade protection, the re-nationalisation of Telstra, Qantas and Commonwealth Bank are the only other hypothetical policy reversals that gain net approval from voters (between +5 and +14 percent). However, it should be noted that none of these three propositions reaches majority support. Still, we can conclude there is a sizeable constituency

Table 1.7: View of impact of major government decisions on Australia in 2011, percent

Policy decision	Good	Bad	Net approval
Compulsory super	79	7	+72
Medicare	76	6	+70
Floating the dollar	46	11	+35
Free trade agreements	41	21	+20
Goods and services tax	39	30	+9
Privatise Qantas	23	44	−21
Privatise the Commonwealth Bank	29	49	−21
Privatise Telstra	21	53	−32

Source: Essential Media (2011). Question (Very good–very bad; 5 points): 'Thinking about some of the major decisions the federal government has made over recent years, do you think the following decisions have been good for Australia or bad for Australia?'. Net approval, or the balance of opinion, is calculated simply by subtracting the percentage of those who responded that a decision was bad for Australia from the percentage who responded that the decision was good.

Table 1.8: Attitudes to privatisation of major services by voting intentions in 2011, percent (net approval)

Policy decision	Labor	Green	Liberal	National
Privatise Telstra	−48	−33	−20	−36
Privatise Qantas	−40	−26	−5	−14
Privatise Commonwealth Bank	−36	−15	−1	−20

Source: Essential Media 2011, 24 October. Question: See Table 1.7.

in favour of re-nationalisation, perhaps surprising given that two of these privatisations had been concluded by the mid-1990s. The poll also asked respondents about two other hypothetical changes and the results

Table 1.9: Support for reversing major government decisions in 2011, percent

Policy Reversal	Support	Oppose	Difference
Increasing trade protection	59	20	+39
Buying back Telstra	47	33	+14
Buying back Qantas	44	34	+10
Buying back the Commonwealth Bank	41	36	+5
Abolishing the GST	35	43	−8
Regulating the dollar	32	42	−10
Voluntary super	24	64	−40
Privatising Medicare	10	73	−63

Source: Essential Media (2011), 24 October. Question (Strongly support–strongly oppose; 4 points): 'Would you support or oppose the federal government taking any of the following decisions'.

place responses on re-nationalisation in a wider context. The hypotheticals are privatising Medicare, a major government service, and making superannuation voluntary, which would make it once more a privilege rather than a right. Table 1.9 shows that the privatisation of Medicare would be extremely unpopular (−63 percent) as would be the 'voluntarisation' of super (−40 percent).

The future of privatisation of social services

Recent survey and polling evidence suggests that Australians disfavour privatisation by a large margin. This unpopularity has occasionally altered the pace and content of some privatisations; the examples of ensuring majority Australian ownership of entities like Telstra and Qantas,[25] as well as the active promotion of participation of small shareholders in the sale of Telstra, are examples of the impact of public opin-

---

25   In 2014, Prime Minister Abbott indicated that the government was prepared to review the foreign ownership restrictions with which, he said, Qantas had been 'shackled … by the Labor Party back in the 1990s' (Binnie 2014).

ion. Governments have also been punished for unannounced privatisations, particularly Anna Bligh's Labor government which was sent into opposition with just seven out of 89 seats in the March 2012 Queensland state election. And, electoral threats have occasionally caused privatisations to be postponed or abandoned; the retreat from the privatisation of the Snowy River hydroelectricity operations and Medibank Private during the Howard Coalition government are two examples.

What is clear, however, is that privatisations are difficult to reverse once they have happened. As Feigenbaum and Henig remark, privatisation policies 'may engender new groups as well as behaviour, groups endowed with powers that leave them entrenched and sometimes impossible to remove' (1994, p. 208). Moreover, re-nationalisation is not an active feature of the platforms of the social democratic and labour parties anywhere in the rich democracies, although the Clark Labour government (1999–2008) in New Zealand re-nationalised its accident insurance scheme, Air New Zealand and New Zealand's railway system during its period in office. Major (temporary) nationalisations of an assortment of banks, insurers, and car companies in the United Kingdom and the United States, during Gordon Brown's period as Prime Minister and Barack Obama's period as President respectively, were not commitments to public ownership but rather attempts to stabilise market capitalism in the face of the Global Financial Crisis. Public policies are typically shaped by an underlying policy paradigm (Dillon 1976). The present paradigm provides a 'warrant' for private ownership of major assets; contention over the consequences of private ownership has not been sufficiently influential, or sufficiently grounded in organised, countervailing material interests, to tip policy orientations back towards public ownership.

The same paradigm stabilises the drive for greater marketisation of services: the prevailing view is that governments can do more, and be better, by regulating markets for services currently provided by government (see Le Grand 2007; in Australia, Keating 2004). Australia has been a leading 'marketiser' of services, even promoting international emulation in some areas like case management and market-based employment services. Non-government provision of social services has been institutionalised and extended further. Australia's history of a mixed economy of social services means there is an implicitly higher baseline of public support for (or at least, reduced public opposition to) the development of community and private provision. One of the few studies that touch on this subject gives other reasons for this apparent support. Thompson and Elling (2000) show that, in the case of Michigan voters, privatisation that favours non-profit organisations attracts different constituencies and expectations than privatisation that favours for-profit providers. Moreover, attitudes towards the community sector are more positive than towards for-profit providers. Many on the left as well as the right area are attracted to a 'network society' model of provision where localised, non-bureaucratic forms of care and assistance are envisaged.

Conclusion

Early in the chapter, we outlined the internal and external pressures on governments to sell assets and marketise service provision. In this conclusion, Table 1.10 draws together the threads of the two parts of the chapter, setting out the pressures that might draw governments towards marketising social service provision and those which might make marketisation a less attractive approach.

The creation of a successful 'market' of actors and organised interests in social service provision is at the core of stable marketisation processes. When governments can defray costs, do more with less, 'rule' through contracts, and impose standards on social service providers and workers, the market model can be seen to have stabilising features (squares 1 and 2). But the markets for social services *can and will* change: small, community providers can be out-competed by large, for-profit providers. These processes bring out inequalities in provision that upset localised communities reliant on services, who are in turn capable of organising around their interests and raising the visibility of their needs. Where powerful private providers dominate provision, and substantial inequities in access to and quality of services emerge, governments may have an interest in resuming direct provision or imposing additional regulation (squares three and four), especially if contestation of 'market control' becomes more organised and visible, and attaches itself to paradigmatic activity aimed at redefining the value, role and central place of direct public provision.

Table 1.10: Competing pressures for greater market/government social service provision

	Internal (politics and bureaucracy)	External (business, consumers, voters, media)
Greater market provision	• Reduction of responsibility, especially in difficult service areas • Cost control • Overlapping business and political networks favouring marketisation	• Pre-existing markets for service privatisation / lobbying for resources, contracts • Past successes in market provision • Client pressure for choice and non-profit involvement • Invisibility of the problems of marketisation processes to public scrutiny • Powerful for-profit providers 'capture' government decision-making
Greater government provision	• Service / risk management problems • Budget protection by local bureaucratic agencies • Paradigmatic shifts in favour of public provision	• Visible service and market failure • Inequities (and discrimination) in private delivery • Cost increases from private contracts • Organised, visible resistance to private provision in favour of government provision

Australian governments have enabled broad and deep market encroachment into Australian public institutions. This has been a bipartisan project – up to a point. Labor governments have tended more to pragmatic marketisation, while Liberal and Coalition governments have sought more systematically to spread and consolidate market organisations and practices in Australian society. It is clear that, whether bipartisan or not, marketisation is an elite project, and voter opposition to its various policy expressions is widespread and longstanding. How the tensions identified in Table 1.10 – not least those between public and private sector elites on one hand and the public on the other – play out will shape Australian social policy in the coming decades.

Acknowledgments

We thank Dr Adam Stebbing for research assistance for this chapter, and for providing Table 1.4.

Appendix

Sources and notes to Table 1.2.
Federal – Aulich and O'Flynn (2007a, Appendix 1 and 2); State – Reserve Bank of Australia (1997); Walker and Con Walker (2008); various media reports.
(a) The party recorded is generally the party that decided/legislated the privatisation; in some cases the actual sale occurred following a change of government. The notes below record relevant cases and a divergence from this rule.
(b) Process initiated/commitment made by National Governments 1996–98, but carried through by Labor into the 1999–2000 fiscal year.
(c) *Partial* privatisation proposed by ALP Premier Bannon before Labor lost power in 1992 – allocated to the incoming Liberal government which sold the whole bank, since the size of the part Labor proposed for retention is not known.
(d) Process begun under previous ALP premier, Joan Kirner, with the proposed sale of *one* electricity generator in response to financial difficulties.

Source and notes to Figure 1.2.
Australian Survey of Social Attitudes 2009. Question: (Agree–disagree) Privatisation of government services has more benefits than costs. n=3097.net approval is calculated by subtracting total disapproval from total approval so that a negative score represents more disapproval than approval. High-income earners are defined as earning $2,000 or more per week (n=219). * *Australian Survey of Social Attitudes* 2005 data. Attitude question in the 2005 survey that was used to define 'economic nationalists': 'Many people today talk about Australia becoming more closely linked to the outside world through trade, immigration and politics. Please tell us how much you agree or disagree with each the following statements: Opening up Australia's economy to

foreign competition has a bad effect on job security in this country';
'economic nationalist' respondents coded = Strongly agree + Agree.

References

Andren, P. 2006, House of Representatives, Official Hansard, No. 7, Parliament of
  Australia, 30 May, p. 23.

Andrews, K. 2014, Address to Australian institute of company directors, NFP
  Directors Lunch, 29 January. http://kevinandrews.dss.gov.au/speeches/45

Aulich, C. & O'Flynn, J. 2007a, 'John Howard: The great privatiser?', *Australian
  Journal of Political Science*, vol. 42, no. 2, pp. 365–81.

Aulich, C. & O'Flynn, J. 2007b, 'From public to private: The Australian experience
  of privatisation', *Asia Pacific Journal of Public Administration*, vol. 29, no. 2,
  pp. 153–71.

Australian Government 2006, *Budget overview 2006–07*, 6 May.
  http://www.budget.gov.au/2006-07/overview/download/overview.pdf

Australian Government 2011, *National compact: Working together*, Office of the
  Not-for-Profit Sector, Canberra. http://www.mdsi.org.au/pub/
  National_Compact.pdf

Australian Institute of Health and Welfare 1997, *Australia's welfare: Services and
  assistance*, Australian Institute of Health and Welfare, Canberra.

Australian Institute of Health and Welfare 2009, *Australia's welfare 2009*,
  Australian Institute of Health and Welfare, Canberra.

Australian Public Service Commission 2003, *The Australian experience of public
  sector reform*, APSC, Canberra.

Besser, L. 2011, 'False claims boost chance of survival in jobs game', *Sydney
  Morning Herald*, 19 December.

Besser, L. 2012, 'Employment agency rorts investigated', *Sydney Morning Herald*, 6
  February.

Biggs, A. 2011, Fairer Private Health Insurance Incentives Bill 201, *Bills Digest*, no.
  20, 2011–12, Parliamentary Library, Canberra.

Binnie, K. 2014, 'Qantas Sales Act: Prime Minister Tony Abbott flags lifting
  airline's foreign ownership rules', *ABC News*, 14 February. http://tiny.cc/
  18r1qx

Boswell, R. 1996, 'The implications of National Competition Policy', *Australian
  Journal of Public Administration*, vol. 55, no. 2, pp. 79–82.

Braithwaite, J., Makkai, T. & Braithwaite, V. A. 2007, *Regulating aged care:
  Ritualism and the new pyramid*, Edward Elgar Publishing, Cheltenham.

Brennan, D. 1998, *The politics of Australian child care: Philanthropy, feminism and
  beyond*, Cambridge University Press, Melbourne.

Brennan, D. 2007, 'The ABC of child care politics', *Australian Journal of Social Issues*, vol. 44, no. 2, pp. 213–25.

Browne, P. 2012, 'Latham's list was a hit in the polls', Inside Story, 27 August. http://inside.org.au/lathams-list-was-a-hit-in-the-polls/

Buckmaster, L. 2005, Aged Care Amendment (Extra Service) Bill 2005, *Bills Digest*, no. 183, 2004–05, Parliamentary Library, Canberra.

Burrell, A. & Taylor, P. 2013, 'Assets on the block as WA's AAA lost', *The Australian*, 19 September.

Butcher, J. R. 2011, 'An Australian compact with the third sector: Challenges and prospects', *Third Sector Review*, vol. 17, no. 1, pp. 35–58.

Carver, L. 1996, 'Consumers/citizens and the national competition policy', *Australian Journal of Public Administration*, vol. 55, no. 2, pp. 88–93.

Chan, G. 2013, 'Foreign investment makes explosive entry into election campaign', *The Guardian*, 29 August. http://www.theguardian.com/world/2013/aug/29/foreign-investment-on-election-agenda

Chan, C., Forwood, D., Roper, H. & Sayers, C. 2009, Public infrastructure financing: An international perspective, Productivity Commission Staff Working Paper, March 2009.

Clune, D. 2012, 'Political chronicles: New South Wales January to June 2012', *Australian Journal of Politics and History*, vol. 58, no. 4, pp. 627–32.

COAG (Council of Australian Governments) 2011, *National Health Reform Agreement*, 2 August. http://www.federalfinancialrelations.gov.au/content/Content.aspx?doc=related_agreements.htm

Coalition 2013a, *The Coalition's Policy for Superannuation*, September. http://www.liberal.org.au/our-policies

Coalition 2013b, *Our plan: Real solutions for all Australians – The direction, values and policy priorities of the next Coalition government*. http://pandora.nla.gov.au/tep/22107

Colley, L. K. & Head, B. 2013, 'Changing patterns of privatization: Ideology, economic necessity, or political opportunism', *International Journal of Public Administration*, vol. 36, no. 12, pp. 865–75.

Commonwealth of Australia 1993, *National Competition Policy*, Report by the Independent Committee of Inquiry (the Hilmer Report), Commonwealth Government Printer, Canberra.

Competition Policy Review 2014, *Competition Policy Review Issues Paper*, 14 April. http://tiny.cc/h7r1qx

Considine, M. 1988, 'The costs of increased control: Corporate management and Australian community organisations', *Australian Social Work*, vol. 41, no. 3, pp. 17–25.

Considine, M. 2000, 'Selling the unemployed: The performance of bureaucracies, firms and non-profits in the new Australian "market" for unemployment assistance', *Social Policy & Administration*, vol. 34, no. 3, pp. 274–95.

Considine, M. 2003, 'Governance and competition: The role of non-profit organisations in the delivery of public services', *Australian Journal of Political Science*, vol. 38, no. 1, pp. 63–77.

Coorey, P. 2011, 'Labor clinches national health deal', *Sydney Morning Herald*, 2 August.

Coorey, P. 2013, 'Hockey offers states billions to sell off assets', *Australian Financial Review*, 28 November.

Crouch, C. 2013, 'From markets versus states to corporations versus civil society?', in *Politics in the age of austerity*, eds A. Schafer & W. Streeck, Polity Press, Cambridge, pp. 219–38.

Crowe, D. 2014, 'Joe Hockey public asset sell-off plan tipped to start race between states', *The Australian*, 20 September.

Department of Finance 2007, *Annual report 2006–07*, Commonwealth of Australia, Canberra.

Department of Finance 2008, *Annual report 2007–08*, Commonwealth of Australia, Canberra.

Department of Infrastructure and Regional Development 2014, 'The Asset Recycling Initiative'. http://investment.infrastructure.gov.au/publications/reports/pdf/factsheets2014/Factsheet_The_Asset_Recycling_Initiative.pdf

Dillon, G. M. 1976, 'Policy and dramaturgy: A critique of current conceptions of policy making', *Policy and Politics*, vol. 5, no. 1, pp. 47–62.

Docherty, P. & Easton, S. 2013, 'A note on the pricing of Australian government asset sales', *Australian Journal of Management*, Online early, published 22 October. doi: 10.1177/0312896213503839

Dossor, R. 2014, 'Infrastructure Growth Package—Asset Recycling Fund', *Budget Review 2014-15 Index*, Canberra, Australian Parliamentary Library http://www.aph.gov.au/About_Parliament/Parliamentary_Departments/Parliamentary_Library/pubs/rp/BudgetReview201415/InfrastructureGrowth

Durant, R. F. & Legge, J. S. 2002, 'Politics, public opinion, and privatization in France: Assessing the calculus of consent for market reforms', *Public Administration Review*, vol. 62, no. 3, pp. 307–23.

Dutton, P. 2014, Address to CEDA Conference, 19 February. https://www.health.gov.au/internet/ministers/publishing.nsf/Content/11D2552AD759459CCA257C84007C8C40/$File/PD001a.pdf

Elliott, A. 2006, ' "The best friend Medicare ever had"? Policy narratives and changes in Coalition health policy', *Health Sociology Review*, vol. 15, no. 2, pp. 132–43.

Errington, W. & van Onselen, P. 2007, *John Winston Howard*, Melbourne University Publishing, Melbourne.

Essential Research 2011, Essential Report SPSS data file, 24 October.

Essential Research 2014, 'Opinion of privatisation', Essential Report, 28 January. http://essentialvision.com.au/opinion-of-privatisation-2

Essential Media Communication 2015, 'Privatisation', The Essential Report, 10 February. http://essentialvision.com.au/documents/essential_report_150210.pdf

Evans, A. 2010, The Australian survey of social attitudes, 2009 [Computer file], Australian Data Archive, The Australian National University, Canberra.

Fairbrother, P., Paddon, M. & Teicher, J. (eds) 2002, *Privatisation, globalisation and labour*, The Federation Press, Sydney.

Feigenbaum, H. B. & Henig, J. R. 1994, 'The political underpinnings of privatization: A typology', *World Politics*, vol. 46, no. 2, pp. 185–208.

Financial Services Council 2012, Submission to the Productivity Commission's Inquiry into default superannuation funds in modern awards. http://tiny.cc/54t1qx

Fine, M. & Chalmers, J. 2000, '"User pays" and other approaches to the funding of long-term care for older people in Australia', *Ageing and Society*, vol. 20, no. 1, pp. 5–32.

Franklin, M. & Lunn, S. 2008, 'Critics in "climate of fear": Gillard', *The Australian*, 9 January.

Fraser, M. 1981, Ministerial statement, House of Representatives Hansard, Parliament of Australia, 30 April.

Gardner, J. 2015, 'Health insurance premiums to surge', *Sydney Morning Herald*, 22 January http://www.smh.com.au/business/health-insurance-premiums-to-surge-20150121-12v69s.html

Gillard, J. 2008, Reforming education and skills: Challenges of the twenty first century, Speech to the City of London Corporation, London, United Kingdom, 30 June. http://pandora.nla.gov.au/pan/80087/20090127-1541/www.deewr.gov.au/Ministers/Gillard/Pages/Article_081103_093120.html

Goldfinch, S. 1999, 'Remaking Australia's economic policy: Economic policy decision-makers during the Hawke and Keating Labor governmets', *Australian Journal of Public Administration*, vol. 58, no. 2, pp. 3–20.

Gong, N. & Shekhar, C. 2001, 'Underpricing of privatised IPOs: The Australian experience', *Australian Journal of Management*, vol. 26, no. 2, pp. 91–106.

Gonski, D. (Chair) 2011, *Review of funding for schooling: Final report*, Department of Education, Employment and Workplace Relations, Canberra. http://pandora.nla.gov.au/tep/132421

Goot, M. 1999, 'Public opinion, privatisation and the electoral politics of Telstra', *Australian Journal of Politics and History*, vol. 45, no. 2, pp. 214–38.

Gordon, J. 2012, 'Baillieu flags state asset sales', *The Age*, 23 March.

Gorman, R. 2013, 'The phone call that saved Australia's childcare sector', ABC Radio National, *Saturday Extra*, 19 November. http://tiny.cc/w7t1qx

Haigh, G. 2007, 'Who's afraid of Macquarie Bank? The story of the millionaire's factory', *The Monthly*, July. http://www.themonthly.com.au/issue/2007/july/1240964771/gideon-haigh/who-s-afraid-macquarie-bank

Hall, B. 2012, 'Surplus before schools as Gonski report decries student disadvantage', *Sydney Morning Herald*, 20 February.

Hall, D., Lobina, E. & Motte, R. D. L. 2005, 'Public resistance to privatisation in water and energy', *Development in Practice*, vol. 15, nos. 3–4, pp. 286–301.

Harrington, C., Olney, B., Carrillo, H. & Kang, T. 2012, 'Nurse staffing and deficiencies in the largest for-profit chains and chains owned by private equity companies', *Health Services Research*, vol. 47, no. 1, Part I, pp. 106–28.

Harrington, M. 2013, Australian Education Bill 2012, *Bills Digest*, no. 73, 2012–13, Parliamentary Library, Canberra.

Harris, M. & Lye, J. N. 2001, 'The fiscal consequences of privatisation: Australian evidence on privatisation by public share float', *International Review of Applied Economics*, vol. 15, no, 3, pp. 305–21.

Harrison, D. & Hall, B. 2012, 'Back to schools: The end of Howard's way?', *Sydney Morning Herald*, 13 February.

Harrison, D. 2013, 'Government puts stop to aged care pay rise scheme', *Sydney Morning Herald*, 12 December.

Hartge-Hazelman, B. & Baker, P. 2014, 'Medibank to raise "$5.7 billion"', *Sydney Morning Herald*, 23 November. http://www.smh.com.au/business/medibank-to-raise-57-billion-20141123-11s5zy.html

Hawke, L. & Wanna, J. 2010, 'Australia after budgetary reform: A lapsed pioneer or decorative architect?', in *The reality of budgetary reform in OECD nations: Trajectories and consequences*, eds J. Wanna, L. Jensen & J. de Vries, Edward Elgar, Cheltenham, pp. 65–90.

Hawker, G. 2006, 'Ministerial consultants and privatisation: Australian federal government 1985–88', *Australian Journal of Politics and History*, vol. 52, no. 2, pp. 244–60.

Head, B. 1988, 'The Labor Government and "economic rationalism"', *Australian Quarterly*, vol. 60, no. 4, pp. 466–77.

Healy, J. 1988, 'Packaging the human services', *Australian Journal of Public Administration,* vol. 47, no. 4, pp. 321–31.

Hodge, G. & Greve, C. 2010, 'Public-private partnerships: Governance scheme or language game?', *Australian Journal of Public Administration*, vol. 69, no. S1, pp. S8–S22.

Holmes, J. W. & Wileman, T. A. 1997, *Reform in the Australian Public Service 1983–86*, Office of the Auditor General of Canada. http://www.oag-bvg. gc. ca/internet/English/meth_lp_e_10214.html.

Hood, C. 2002, 'Public management, new', *International encyclopedia of the social and behavioral sciences*, Elsevier, Oxford.

Howard, J. 1981, Ministerial Statement, House of Representatives Hansard, Parliament of Australia, 30 April.

Howard, J. 1998, Transcript of the Prime Minister, the Hon. John Howard MP, address at the close of the Liberal Party national convention, Brisbane, 15 March. http://pmtranscripts.dpmc.gov.au/browse.php?did=10903

Howard, J. 2006, Transcript: Joint Press Conference with the Special Minister of State, the Hon. Gary Nairn MP, Parliament House, Canberra, 2 June. http://pmtranscripts.dpmc.gov.au/preview.php?did=22308

Huffschmid, J. 2008 'Finance as a driver of privatisation', *Transfer: European Review of Labour and Research*, vol. 14, no. 2, pp. 209–36.

Hurst, D. 2013, 'Coalition's second Gonski U-turn: Labor model to be largely retained', *The Guardian*, Australian Edition, 2 December.

Industry Commission 1996, *Competitive tendering and contracting by public sector agencies*, Report No. 48, Australian Government Publishing Service, Melbourne.

Keating, M. 2004, *Who rules? How government retains control of a privatised economy*, The Federation Press, Sydney.

Kendig, H. & Duckett, S. 2001, *Australian directions in aged care: The generation of policies for generations of older people*, Australian Health Policy Institute Commissioned Paper Series 2001/05, AHPI, University of Sydney.

Knowles, L. & McClymont, A. 2015, 'New South Wales government sells $1 billion worth of public assets in the past two years', *ABC News*, 10 February.

Lavelle, A. 2005, 'Social democrats and neo-liberalism: A case study of the Australian Labor Party', *Political Studies*, vol. 53, no. 4, pp. 753–71.

Le Grand, J. 2007, *The other invisible hand: Delivering public services through choice and competition*, Princeton University Press, Princeton.

Liberal Party of Australia 1991, *Fightback! It's your Australia: The way to rebuild and reward Australia*, Presented by John Hewson and Tim Fischer on behalf of the Liberal Party of Australia and the National Party of Australia.

Ludlow, M. & Wiggin, J. 2014, 'Queensland to sell power network', *Australian Financial Review*, 16 September. http://www.afr.com/p/national/queensland_to_sell_power_network_4oj25koqSkruawUQ3Nb32L

Macklin, J. 1998, House of Representatives, Hansard, Parliament of Australia, 10 December, p. 1,964.

Marris, S. 2001, 'Job agency rorts worse than feared', *The Australian*, 25 July.

Martin, R. 2009, *Responsible government in South Australia: Playford to Rann, 1957–2007*, Wakefield Press, Adelaide.

McAllister, I. & Studlar, D. 1989, 'Popular versus elite views of privatization: The case of Britain', *Journal of Public Policy*, vol. 9, no. 2, pp. 157–78.

Mead, M. & Withers, G. 2002, *'Privatisation: a review of the Australian experience'*, Committee for the Economic Development of Australia, Melbourne.

Meagher, G. & Cortis, N. 2009, 'The political economy of for-profit paid care: Theory and evidence', in *Paid care in Australia: Politics, profits, practices*, eds D. King & G. Meagher. Sydney University Press, Sydney, pp. 13–42. http://ses.library.usyd.edu.au/handle/2123/7289

Morris, S. 2007, 'Job Network agencies accused of fraud', *Australian Financial Review*, 18 April.

Napthine, D. & O'Brien, M. 2013, Transcript of media conference by Premier Denis Napthine and Treasurer Michael O'Brien, 14 October. http://tiny. cc/a90zqx

National Commission of Audit 1996, Report to the Commonwealth Government, June. http://www.finance.gov.au/archive/archive-of-publications/ncoa/coaintro.htm

Newberry, S. & Brennan, D. 2013, 'The marketisation of early childhood education and care (ECEC) in Australia: A structured response', *Financial Accountability & Management*, vol. 29, no. 3, pp. 227–45.

Nicholls, S. & Hasham, N. 2015, 'Support falling for Mike Baird's electricity privatisation plan despite $20 billion infrastructure promise', *Sydney Morning Herald*, 9 February.

Norton, A. 2006, 'The rise of big government conservatism', *Policy*, vol. 22, no. 4, pp. 15–22.

'Nursing home rorts clawback' 2012, *The Australian*, 9 May. http://tiny. cc/w0h1qx

OECD 2013, OECD health statistics 2013 – Frequently requested data, Organisation for Economic Co-operation and Development, Paris. http://www.oecd.org/els/health-systems/health-at-a-glance.htm

Office of Early Childhood Education and Care 2010, *State of child care in Australia*, Department of Employment, Education and Training, Canberra.

Peatling, S. 2012, 'Now for Abbott's nanny state', *Sydney Morning Herald*, 25 March.

Phillips, R. 2006, 'The role of nonprofit advocacy organizations in Australian democracy and policy governance', *Voluntas*, vol. 17, no. 1, pp. 27–48.

Phillips, R. 2007, 'Tamed or trained? The co-option and capture of "favoured" NGOs', *Third Sector Review*, vol. 13, no. 2, pp. 27–48.

Pierson, P. 1996, 'The new politics of the welfare state', *World Politics*, vol. 48, no. 2, pp. 143–79.

Pierson, P. 2001, *The new politics of the welfare state*, Oxford University Press, Oxford.

Pittard, M. 2007, 'Outsourcing and new employer entities: Challenges to traditional public sector employment', in *Public sector employment in the twenty-first century*, eds M. Pittard & P. Weeks, ANU E-Press, Canberra, pp. 189–228.

Productivity Commission 2012, *Default superannuation funds in modern awards*, Inquiry report no. 60, Productivity Commission, Canberra.

Productivity Commission 2014, *Childcare and early childhood learning: draft report*, Canberra, Productivity Commission. http://www.pc.gov.au/inquiries/completed/childcare/draft/childcare-draft.pdf

Pusey, M. 1991, *Economic rationalism in Canberra: A nation-building state changes its mind*, Cambridge University Press, Melbourne.

Pusey, M. & Turnbull, N. 2005, 'Have Australians embraced economic reform?', in *Australian Social Attitudes*, eds S. Wilson, G. Meagher, R. Gibson, D. Denemark & M. Western, UNSW Press, Sydney, pp. 161–81.

Queensland Commission of Audit 2013, *Final report*, Queensland Government, Brisbane. http://www.commissionofaudit.qld.gov.au/reports/final-report.php

Quiggin, J. 2012, 'Asset sales, their part in Labor's downfall', *The Drum Opinion*, Australian Broadcasting Corporation. http://www.abc.net.au/unleashed/3913872.html

Reserve Bank of Australia 1997, 'Privatisation in Australia', *Reserve Bank of Australia Bulletin*, December, pp. 7–16.

Robinson, M. 1994, 'The financial management strategy of the Victorian coalition government', *Australian Journal of Public Administration*, vol. 53, no. 2, pp. 232–47.

Roxon, N. 2009, Fairer Private Health Insurance Incentives Bill 2009, Second reading speech, House of Representatives Hansard, Parliament of Australia, 27 May, p. 4435–36.

Rudd, K. 2009, 'The Global Financial Crisis', *The Monthly*, February.

Seah, D. E. S, Cheong, T. Z. & Anstey, M. H. R. 2013, 'The hidden cost of private health insurance in Australia', *Australian Health Review*, vol. 37, no. 1, pp. 1–3.

Segal, L. 2004, 'Why it is time to review the role of private health insurance in Australia', *Australian Health Review*, vol. 27, no. 1, pp. 3–15.

Smith, A. 2011, 'O'Farrell quashes privatisation jibes', *Sydney Morning Herald*, 8 March.

Stephens, T. 1987, 'Efficiency expert who wields a scalpel, not an axe', *Sydney Morning Herald*, 15 July, p. 15.

Stuckler, D., King, L. & McKee, M. 2009, 'Mass privatisation and the post-communist mortality crisis: A cross-national analysis', *The Lancet*, vol. 373, no. 9661, pp. 399–407.

The Economist 1990, 'Private hatred', 1 September, p. 32.

Thomas, M. 2007, *A review of developments in the Job Network,* Research paper no. 15, Parliamentary Library, Department of Parliamentary Services, Canberra.

Thompson, L. & Elling, R. C. 2000, 'Mapping support for privatization in the mass public: The case of Michigan', *Administrative Review,* vol. 60, no. 4, pp. 338–48.

Tingle, L. & Patten, S. 2013, 'Unions, employer groups may lose control of super boards', *Australian Financial Review,* 28 November.

Towell, N., Kenny, M. & Smith, B. 2013, 'Razor taken to CSIRO', *Sydney Morning Herald,* 8 November.

Treasury 2013a, 'Expense measures', *Budget Paper,* No. 2, Department of Treasury, Canberra.

Treasury 2013b, Better regulation and governance, enhanced transparency and improved competition in superannuation, Discussion Paper, Australian Government, Canberra, 28 November.

Uren, D. 2012, 'Secret government plan to end big bureaucracy', *The Australian,* 28 August.

Van Fossen, A. B. 1998, 'One Nation and privatisation: Populist ethnic nationalism, class and international political economy', *Queensland Review,* vol. 5, no. 2, pp. 44–53.

Viellaris, R. 2013, 'Childcare centre cheats rob taxpayers of more than $1 million in fraudulent claims', *The Courier-Mail,* June 22.

Walker, B & Walker, B. 2008, *Privatisation: Sell off or sell out: The Australian experience,* Sydney University Press, Sydney.

Warren, D. 2008, *Australia's retirement income system: Historical development and effects of recent reform,* Melbourne Institute Working Paper No. 23/08, Melbourne Institute: Melbourne.

Wilson, L. 2013, 'Commission of Audit to look for more privatisation opportunities', *The Australian,* 27 October.

Wilson, S. 2013, 'The limits of low-tax social democracy? Welfare, tax and fiscal dilemmas for Labor in government', *Australian Journal of Political Science,* vol. 48, no. 3, pp. 286–306.

Wilson, S., Gibson, R., Meagher, G., Denemark, D. & Western, M. 2004, Australian survey of social attitudes, 2003 [computer file], Australian Data Archive, The Australian National University, Canberra.

Wilson, S., Gibson, R., Meagher, G., Denemark, D. & Western, M. 2006, Australian survey of social attitudes, 2005 [computer file], Australian Data Archive, The Australian National University, Canberra.

Wright, S., Marston, G. & McDonald, C. 2011, 'The role of non-profit organizations in the mixed economy of welfare-to-work in the UK and Australia', *Social Policy & Administration,* vol. 45, no. 3, pp. 299–318.

2

The marketisation of human services and the expansion of the not-for-profit sector

Susan Goodwin and Ruth Phillips

There is extensive evidence that, over the past two decades, non-government organisations have taken on a dramatically significant role in the Australian welfare state, as governments increasingly fund them to deliver human services. Mark Considine argues that this trend in Australia 'can be viewed as the most important and most radical change to state–society relations since the advent of the modern welfare state' (2003, p. 63). This chapter explores this development in an effort to consider how not-for-profit welfare services have come to be positioned in the marketisation agenda that this collection seeks to capture.

The organisations discussed in this chapter are variously referred to elsewhere as non-government organisations (to specify separateness from government); third sector organisations (to specify a distinctiveness from two other sectors, the market and the state); civil society organisations (to specify a basis in associations formed voluntarily, rather than through the family, state or market) and community sector organisations (to specify a concern with local or particularised needs). In this chapter, the relationship of these organisations with government, with the market, with civil society and with 'the community' is brought

Goodwin, S. & Phillips, R. 2015, 'The marketisation of human services and the expansion of the not-for-profit sector', in *Markets, rights and power in Australian social policy*, eds G. Meagher & S. Goodwin, Sydney University Press, Sydney.

into question. As such, the term not-for-profits (NFPs) is utilised. Thus the defining characteristics of the organisations under discussion are 1) that they do not seek to distribute profits and 2) they seek to provide a range of public goods and services (taken, partially, from Casey & Dalton 2006, p. 25). Here then, their distinctiveness hinges on the common feature that they are not, as Davidson puts it, 'in it for the money' (Davidson 2009, p. 65). While 'the NFP sector' encompasses a huge diversity of organisations, including sporting, hobby and cultural groups, this chapter focuses on NFPs that provide human services.

However, there are important differences *within* the category of NFP human services: between organisations constituted as charities, and those constituted as incorporated associations; between those with a religious auspice and those founded in social movement, consumer rights or self-help activities; between the very large and the very small; between the highly bureaucratised and those with quite ad hoc administrative structures; and between those with a single service focus and those that work across a range of human services. Indeed, part of the narrative in this chapter concerns the way 'the NFP sector' has been historically produced as a unified category of services *through* marketisation processes.

In 2010, the Productivity Commission found that not-for-profit organisations were the major providers in most human service areas across Commonwealth, state and territory government agencies and that there were around 20,000 non-profit organisations in the humans services sector that relied on government for their main source of funding. The Productivity Commission also reported that total government funding to non-profit human services had increased from $10.1 billion in 1999–2000 to $25.5 billion in 2006–7 (Productivity Commission 2010, pp. 300–62). By way of contrast, research conducted in 1995 by the Industry Commission identified some 11,000 'community sector social welfare organisations' that were receiving government funding, and most of the organisations identified employed fewer than five staff (Industry Commission 1995). These data establish that the NFP human services sector in Australia is substantial and that government funding to it has increased exponentially over the past two decades.

Historical threads to NFP welfare sector expansion

In Australia, NFPs have historically played a role in maintaining the welfare of citizens, intervening where the market and the family have failed them. Prior to nationhood and throughout the early and mid-20th century, charities and mutual aid societies provided the majority of social services. In the case of charities, these activities were sustained by support from religious organisations, some government grants and subsidies, and donations from the public (Berman et al. 2006). Many of the charities were church-based, fragmented along sectarian lines and, in addition to providing public goods, were 'partly motivated by competition for souls' (Murphy 2006, p. 44.10). Mutual aid societies, such as the friendly societies, developed along self-help lines, and provided insurance and services to group members and their families. Paul Smyth (2008) suggests that NFPs were historically located outside of government and relied on a culture of voluntarism. Indeed, Leslie Chenoweth claims that, in Australia, governments have historically distanced themselves actively from funding and providing services, favouring a culture of 'Australian self-reliance' (2008, p. 54).

Extensive public funding for human services to replace the 'somewhat haphazard coverage of voluntary organisations' (Fawcett et al. 2010, p. 99) did not really emerge until the postwar period when, as Smyth suggests, 'there came a point when Australia needed a welfare state' (2008, p. 215). For example, throughout the 1960s state governments (with the exception of Victoria) began establishing large welfare departments, taking on the work of the voluntary Child Protection Societies (Lamont & Bromfield 2010). However, a similar consolidation of state responsibility for service delivery, based in principles of universality, entitlement and professionalism did not occur in the full range of personal social services, as was the case, for example, in the United Kingdom. Even during the 1970s, when state *funding* of social services escalated significantly, the overall model of a mixed economy of welfare did not alter much. In the Australian welfare state, government *provision* of community services 'developed slowly, in a sketchy, residualised and uneven manner' (Harris & McDonald 2000, p. 54).

Berman and colleagues' (2006) detailed history of funding to two of the major NFP organisations on the contemporary welfare services landscape, the Brotherhood of St Laurence (BSL) and the Salvation

Army, illustrates the Australian mixed economy model in practice from the postwar period on. For example, in the 1950s, under the *Aged Person's Home Act 1954*, these church-based organisations were encouraged by the Commonwealth government (through matching funds for capital expenditure) to build and operate accommodation for the aged. In the 1970s, they were funded by the Commonwealth government to provide labour market programs to deal with growing unemployment, and during the 1970s and the 1980s they received government 'project funding' for poverty alleviation programs (particularly for the elderly and low-income families), community development projects, unemployment services, emergency and crisis accommodation services, alcohol and drug treatment programs, and domestic violence services. Children's services were another major service area where governments funded NFPs (although in this case, not the BSL or the Salvation Army) to provide services, including funding for orphanages and institutions for children with disabilities.

In the 1970s and 1980s an array of new NFP organisations appeared on the social policy landscape. In what Anna Yeatman (1990) called the 'democratic-participative' era in Australian public administration, new social movements politicised a new range of social needs: women's rights, consumer rights, environmental issues, disability rights, gay and lesbian issues, migrant rights and so forth. These movements made claims on the state, both for government services (such as legal aid offices[1] and community health centres) and for funding for community-based organisations to provide services (such as community legal centres, women's health centres, neighbourhood centres and refuges). What is distinctive about the advocacy of these movements is that they were claiming not just a redistribution of resources, but the democratisation of state institutions and practices: service delivery models were pitched as an alternative to professionalised, bureaucratised, and disempowering models of welfare bureaucracy (see, for ex-

---

1 The Legal Aid Commissions in the states and territories were established between the 1970s and 1990s. However, in NSW, the first *Legal Assistance Act* was passed in 1943, and this established the Public Solicitors Office. On its website, NSW Legal Aid state that it was at this point that 'Legal aid was no longer a charity but a social right. It was the first time in the western world that lawyers were employed to give legal aid to low income earners'.

ample, Broom 1991; Weeks 1994). But the new organisations were also established as an alternative to the traditional NFPs, the charities. Social movements were particularly critical of the historical role that charities had played in determining citizens as deserving or undeserving of service, and also of the reliance on religiously motivated volunteers and faith-based analyses of social problems. Martin Painter (1992) argues that government responded to the new social movement organisations with an official discourse of participation. Christine Everingham (2003) suggests that what emerged was a state-sponsored community sector that was quite distinct from the charity sector.

However, in the early 1990s, the state-sponsored community sector lost much of its legitimacy. Public choice discourses contributed a rationale for the de-funding of services provided by women's groups, environment groups and migrant rights groups (Fawcett et al. 2010). Public choice proponents argued that many of the NFP groups actively involved in the delivery of community-based services not only failed to reflect the public good, but also seriously distorted social policy by promoting 'special interests' over the interests of the general community and, in some cases, building 'service empires' for themselves. They had 'captured the state'. In addition, the rise of managerialism and economic rationalism in public administration rendered community-based NFPs vulnerable in the new efficiency paradigm. The development of technocratic approaches to public sector program planning and resource allocation, referred to as the 'new public management' (NPM), demanded that funded services demonstrate measurable outcomes. This entailed a broad shift from grants and project funding to output-based funding. The new financing models involved new data collection requirements, new standards of professionalisation and new organisational structures. For many organisations, accountability mechanisms were undeveloped and some activities (such as advocacy, democratisation and empowerment) were hard to measure, and these new frameworks were introduced 'without the necessary funding investment in agencies to fulfil their obligations' (Inglis & Rogan 1993, p. 7). The dual affronts of public choice discourse and NPM significantly undermined the 'self evident worth' (Harries 1993, p. 193) of community-based organisations. 'Performance management' was the beginning of the application of 'market discipline' to the state-sponsored community sector that, in turn, laid the foundations for the marketisation of NFPs more generally.

NFPs and the marketisation of human services: contractualism and outsourcing

Throughout the 1990s, the public sector reforms focused on ensuring that market principles applied to the public sector involved inducing competition between all types of service providers – public sector, for-profit and not-for-profit – for government funding. Competition, it was argued, would mean that government expenditure on service provision would be based on principles such as cost effectiveness and productivity rather than traditional bureaucratic decision-making processes. However, valorising competition in decision-making processes in this way also implicitly de-legitimised the new social movement goal of more democratised public decision-making. Competition positions service delivery as an *output* of policy that has already been decided. This contrasts significantly with the ideals of community-based human service organisations as social policy-in-action and of a more diffuse and de-volved social democracy.

Competition was to be fostered through the contracting out of services, and non-government organisations were to tender for government contracts. This approach is referred to as the 'purchaser–provider split', in which the role of government is conceptualised as primarily the buyer (steerer), rather than the provider (rower) of public services. According to Dalton and colleagues (1996, p. 100), the purchaser–provider split was 'supposed to allow governments to distance themselves from the day-to-day operation of services ... by contracts or contracting out services'. The centrality of contractual arrangements in these reforms led some public policy analysts to refer to a shift to 'the contract state' or 'New Contractualism' (Dalton et al. 1996; Davis 1997; Sidoti et al. 2009; Yeatman 1995). Commenting on this shift in the 1990s, Glyn Davis (1997, p. 217) argued that in the emerging contract regime:

> [m]uch bureaucratic attention is on monitoring performance of distant contractors, and regulating private markets ... however the price of supervising and enforcement – the transaction costs of contracting – can sometimes overwhelm any financial benefit. Yet the drive towards contracts is on across Australia, a triumph of hope over experience.

A common theme in narratives of the marketisation of human services in Australia is privatisation through 'outsourcing'. The now iconic example of the outsourcing program involved the delivery of services to unemployed people. (In 2001, an OECD report called the Job Network a 'radical transformation of employment service delivery ... without parallel in OECD countries' (2001, p. 262).) Until 1998, publicly funded employment services for job-seekers had been delivered by the Commonwealth Employment Service (CES), a public sector agency. In 1998, the CES was replaced by the Job Network, a network of 300 public, private and not-for-profit providers. Aulich (2011, p. 208) describes the move in terms of privatisation, explaining Minister Amanda Vanstone's rationale for outsourcing in the following way:

> Vanstone argued that a privatised service would cost less, give more choice and personalised services to job-seekers and would be better for employers. Private providers would be paid on the basis of outcomes, to drive down costs and drive up labour market participation.

In the second round of contracts in 2000, the network had reduced to 197 providers, consisting almost exclusively of for-profit and not-for-profit organisations. Reflecting on the development of Job Network, the then Minister for Employment and Workplace Relations, Tony Abbott, explained:

> As the purchaser but not provider of employment services, the Government has created what might best be described as a 'social market' – a competitive market which exists because government has summoned it in to being. In this sense, the Job Network is an 'arm' of government and Job Network members are the government's partners and allies in so far as they are bound to one another in the delivery of services the public has come to expect (2003, p. 200).

Outsourcing of human services by governments has continued apace. By 2014 the employment services sector, which had been renamed Job Services Australia by the Rudd Labor government in 2009, consisted only of NFPs and for-profit-providers. Australian governments outsource homelessness services, personal and family services, drug and alcohol services and services for people with disabilities and for older people. Most recently in the state of New South Wales (NSW) the government has transferred a significant amount of public housing to community housing providers and has committed to transferring the majority of out-home-care (foster care) services to non-government providers by 2022 (Legislative Assembly of NSW 2013). As the data provided in the Introduction show, the majority of providers that governments outsource human services to are NFPs.

The Third Way?

An important hinge in the expansion of the NFP sector's role in human service delivery has been the deployment of Third Way ideas. The Third Way can be traced to communitarian visions of the role of the state, particularly in the work of Anthony Giddens, which were taken up and applied in the United Kingdom by the Blair Labor government and promoted in Australia by Labor Party politicians such as Mark Latham. A central plank of the Third Way is the devolution of social services to local community groups and associations. Giddens, for example, suggested going beyond the welfare state to develop a 'social investment state', or a 'positive welfare society' by altering the balance between the forms of welfare support government provides directly and those that emerge out of the 'third sector', or community-based organisations and associations (Giddens 1998, p. 117). Crucial to the logic of Third Way politics was a construction of the welfare state as disabling – as cumbersome, inefficient and unresponsive to the community (see Botsman & Latham 2001). Interestingly, Third Way ideas have also been attractive to conservative parties elsewhere, and to Coalition governments in Australia. Tony Abbott, for example, claimed that 'the Third Way may have actually come further in Howard's Australia than in Blair's Britain' (2003, p. 204).

NFPs have been able to work with Third Way ideas to justify their position in welfare markets. By way of example, in its submission to the Productivity Commission's study of the contribution of the not-for-profit sector, the peak organisation for Australian non-government community services, ACOSS (2009, pp. 2–3), prefaced their recommendations with a list of '10 key features and benefits of a strong, diverse and effective not-for profit community services and welfare sector'. The list included statements such as:

> The sector is mission driven rather than market driven. This means that surpluses are reinvested back to provide a dividend for community stakeholders, rather than individual shareholders...
>
> The sector can be more responsive to previously unrecognized needs resulting from market or government failure...
>
> An ability to respond holistically and flexibly ... Such responsiveness and flexibility cannot be guaranteed by contracted commercial services and probably not by more bureaucratic and siloed government structures.
>
> Participation and representation of clients in management structures, program development and delivery can be empowering and lead to more effective outcomes...
>
> Meaningful community involvement in, and responsibility for, providing community services is an important tool for weaving community cohesiveness. This can serve as a safeguard against some parts of our society becoming marginalized and alienated.

So, while economic rationalism, managerialism, contractualism and outsourcing disciplined the activities of the NFP sector, it certainly did not kill it off. Indeed, the more intense marketisation of human services that has continued into the 21st century created a new space for NFPs in newly legitimised welfare markets. This special place has been justified by governments and by NFPs alike through reference to historical legacy (that is, that NFPs had a longstanding involvement in humans service provision), social purpose (that is, that NFPs are driven by altruism rather than profit) and market competitiveness (that is, that NFPs could provide cheaper and better services).

Bringing the charities back in

Importantly, the NFP space is inclusive of charities *and* of community sector organisations, who champion their value in similar ways: by contrasting themselves to both government *and* for-profit human service providers. There is some evidence that the larger Christian charities benefitted from their religious identity under the conservative Howard government (1996–2007), as it made significant references to the values and role of such organisations in addressing human need and social problems throughout its term (Phillips 2007). Further, an analysis of state departments of community services spending demonstrates that, apart from the major secular NGOs, such as the Red Cross, the Benevolent Society and Barnardos Australia, the larger faith-based NGOs gained the largest contracts for the delivery of major state services. For example, in NSW in 2010–11, 101 NFP agencies were funded to deliver services in the key human service area of 'family and individual support'. Grants started at $12,000, but the large faith-based agencies typically received total funds of more than $500,000 each, with some receiving grants of more than $2.5 million (Family and Community Services 2011).

Many of the charities have expanded on the basis of status as preferred welfare providers in the market in welfare services, although it is not easy to pinpoint *why* they were so interested in expansion in this direction. For the church-based organisations, Murphy's statement about 'capturing souls' seems anachronistic. Some recent research on NGOs gives some insight into how faith-based organisations frame their motivations (Goodwin & Phillips 2011; Phillips & Goodwin 2013). Participants tied the expansion of their organisations to mission, but referred to a broad 'social justice' mission rather than a specifically religious one. This framing very much overlapped with the agenda described by participants from secular NFPs. Examples of responses about expansion from both types of organisations included: 'It's part of our vision to improve the lives of vulnerable people'; 'Our organisation has a strong commitment to social justice' and 'because of a commitment to social justice that comes out of our links to [a particular] church' (quoted in Goodwin & Phillips 2011, p. 30). Thus the charities and community-based organisations' rationales for delivering government-funded welfare services can be seen to converge: they are responsive, flexible, have the capacity to innovate *and* they are motivated by social justice principles.

Marketisation of human services and NFP policy research

While the increased role of NFPs as human services providers has been analysed in detail in the contemporary literature, one area of expansion that has been less focused upon is the way that some NFPs in the sector have grown their policy research activities. Since the 2000s, Australian NFP human service organisations have been increasingly allocating resources to policy research through the establishment of policy research units and policy research positions. Indeed, most of the large charities referred to above, as well as some smaller community-based organisations, now have specialised units (sometimes referred to as 'social justice' units), in which policy research is a central activity and policy researchers are key personnel. This development can be related to marketisation in a number of ways. First, the professionalisation of organisations that accompanied NPM techniques of disciplining NFPs resulted in the more regular employment of staff with research backgrounds and research degrees: the change in workforce demanded by the new requirements promoted an internal culture of developing a research base that fitted with the external pressure from funders for 'evidence'. Second, when governments began contracting out service provision, they also began dismantling existing government research and policy units that sat alongside the service provision programs, opening a space and need for in-house research. As one policy researcher explained:

> Prior to contracting out, the departments used to do evaluations of their programs. For example, governments had the data to ask questions such as whether training or work experience is more effective in moving people into the workforce. Once services were contracted out, they could no longer ask these questions because they weren't providing the services ... the fact that government is no longer producing evaluation research has created an opening for other players. (quoted in Goodwin & Phillips 2011, p. 27)

A third rationale for the expansion of NFP policy research activities relates directly to the competitive funding environment, which placed pressure on organisations to gain reputational advantage with government funders as well as with donors and other constituencies. This advantage could be gained through research production: conducting policy research was seen to have 'cachet' with funders, and so was important for 'branding' the NFP as a serious player in the field of human services (Goodwin & Phillips 2011, p. 28). Finally, the de-legitimising of alternative forms of democratised decision-making, discussed above, created a need for alternative ways of influencing policy processes. Policy research became an effective form of working for social justice in a context where 'evidence-based change' was privileged over other forms of community and consumer participation and social movement activism (Goodwin & Phillips 2011, p. 31). Because NFPs had taken on such a significant role in the human services market, their proximity to end users meant they came to be regarded by government as having important intelligence for social policy and, as such, were provided opportunities to participate in policy processes via their research-based practices. In addition, because NFPs are seen as 'not being in it for the money', the evidence they produce is largely regarded as objective, or at least more disinterested than for-profit providers. In the context of marketisation, this final point, however, must be regarded as moot. As can be seen, in the competition state, NFPs *are* in it for the money, even if that money is for community stakeholders (which, as organisations grow, includes organisational staff) rather than individual shareholders.

NFPs in the human services market: community, market or state organisations?

The ostensibly powerful arguments about the distinctive nature and role of NFPs in human services are, ironically, also precisely the arguments that lose force as a result of the marketising processes described in this chapter. For example, Kerry Brown and Robyn Keast (2005) suggest that new ways of funding and providing social services may have strengthened government control through the introduction of coercive regulatory arrangements. Through these arrangements, services are governed at a distance and this can have a stifling effect on NFP's putative capacity to innovate and be responsive to localised and individual circumstances. While NFPs continue to claim a base in 'the community', their activities are increasingly constructed by government as services *for* the community, rather than *from* the community.

Similarly, contractualism and competitive tendering encourage business-like practices in NFPs and orient them toward achieving the best financial outcomes, rather than the best social outcomes. The so-called gaming of performance measurement regimes (Pollitt 2007) by both NFPs and for-profits and the professionalisation of government contract tender writing are two examples of shifts in practices that blur the boundaries between these two types of organisations. In its sub-mission to the Productivity Commission inquiry into the not-for-profit sector, the Brotherhood of St Laurence suggested that contracting out 'led to the rise of mega not-for-profit and for-profit service delivery agencies in the non-government welfare sector whose size and ag-gressive business practices have sometimes crowded out and displaced more traditional sector functions' (2009, p. 3). Again, while NFPs con-tinue to claim separateness from the market primarily through their eschewal of a profit motive, in welfare markets they function as private organisations, deploying market strategies.

One of the most highly contested aspects of outsourcing to NFPs has been the use, by governments, of funding contracts to control criti-cism of government policy, particularly the use of so-called gag clauses (Maddison 2009, p. 26). This practice goes to the heart of the dis-tinctiveness of NFPs as independent of government and advocates for social justice. Under the Howard Coalition government, confidential-ity clauses were a feature of many of the contracts drawn up between the government and NFP service providers. These required organisa-tions to seek approval of the funding agency before making public comment and were similar to clauses applied in contracts with for-profits, who were seen as ostensibly similar – as primarily contracted service providers. The Gillard Labor government sought to overturn this approach on the basis it supported a 'strong and independent not-for-profit sector', and the *Not For Profit Sector Freedom to Advocate Act* was enshrined in 2013. Interestingly, however, the Queensland gov-ernment has maintained its position on confidentiality clauses, but for different reasons. Its position is that where NFP organisations receive a majority of their funding from government, they are, 'to all intents and purposes, government agencies. And, given that this is the case, it fol-lows they should be subject to the same conditions that apply to any other government agency' (Thomas & Knowler 2013, p. 8).

The positioning of NFPs as either quasi-private organisations or quasi-government organisations in government-funded human services markets works against the notion that they are civil society organisations, formed voluntarily outside of the domains of the state, market or family, and the NFP sector is grappling with reasserting its identity as the third sector. Wright and colleagues (2011) contend that perhaps the most significant, and most widely accepted, outcome of the contracting out of human services to not-for-profit organisations is the government's appropriation of third sector discourses. They argue this appropriation has led to the 'automatic positioning' of the state in an 'unfavourable and undesirable light as a desirable arena of service provision' (Wright et al. 2011, p. 303). This is perhaps the most radical way in which the marketisation of NGOs has changed state–society relations.

References

Abbott, A. J. 2003, 'The Job Network: A view from the minister', *Australian Journal of Labour Economics*, vol. 6, no. 2, pp. 199–205.

ACOSS (Australian Council of Social Service) 2009, Submission to the Productivity Commission into the contribution of not-for-profits, ACOSS Submission, June 2009, Sydney, http://tiny. cc/hij1qx

Aulich, C. 2011, 'It's not ownership that matters: It's publicness', *Policy Studies*, vol. 32, no. 2, pp. 199–213.

Berman, G., Brooks, R., & Murphy, J. 2006, 'Funding the non-profit welfare sector: Explaining changing funding sources 1960–1999', *Economic Papers: A Journal of Applied Economics and Policy*, vol. 25, no. 1, pp. 83–99.

Botsman, P. & Latham, M. 2001, *The enabling state: People before bureaucracy*, Pluto Press, Sydney.

Broom, D. 1991, *Damned if we do: Contradictions in women's health care*, Allen & Unwin, St Leonards.

Brown, K. & Keast, R. 2005, 'Social services policy and delivery in Australia: Centre–periphery mixes', *Policy & Politics*, vol. 33, no. 3, pp. 505–18.

Casey, J. & Dalton, B. 2006, 'The best of times, the worst of times: Community-sector advocacy in the age of "compacts" ', *Australian Journal of Political Science*, vol. 41, no. 1, pp. 23–38.

Chenoweth, L. 2008, 'Redefining welfare: Australian social policy and practice', *Asian Social Work and Policy Review*, vol. 2, no. 1, pp. 53–60.

Considine, M. 2003, 'Governance and competition: The role of non-profit organisations in the delivery of public services', *Australian Journal of Political Science*, vol. 38, no. 1, pp. 63–77.

Dalton, T., Draper, M., Weeks, W. & Wiseman, J. 1996, *Making social policy in Australia: An introduction*, Allen & Unwin, Sydney.

Davidson, B. 2009, 'For-profit organizations in managed markets for human services', in *Paid care in Australia: Politics, profits, practices*, eds D. King & G. Meagher, Sydney University Press, Sydney, pp. 43–79.

Davis, G. 1997, 'Toward a hollow state? Managerialism and its critics', in *Managerialism: The great debate*, eds M. Considine & M. Painter, Melbourne University Press, Melbourne, pp. 208–223.

Everingham, C. 2003, *Social justice and the politics of community*, Ashgate, Hampshire.

Family and Community Services 2011, 'Funds Granted to Non-Government Organisations, 2010–2011', NSW Department of Family and Community Services Annual Report, NSW Government, Sydney.

Fawcett, B., Goodwin, S., Meagher, G., & Phillips, R. 2010, *Social policy for social change*, Palgrave Macmillan, Melbourne.

Giddens, A. 1998, *The third way: The renewal of social democracy*, Polity Press, Cambridge.

Goodwin, S. & Phillips, R. 2011, Researching the researchers: policy research in non-government organisations in the human services sector, Social Policy Research Network Research Report 2011, University of Sydney.

Harries, M. 1993, 'Quality and accountability in community services', in *Beyond swings and roundabouts: Shaping the future of community services in Australia*, eds J. Inglis & L. Rogan, Pluto Press, Sydney.

Harris, J. & McDonald, C. 2000, 'Post-Fordism, the welfare state and the personal social services: A comparison of Australia and Britain', *British Journal of Social Work*, vol. 30, no. 1, pp. 51–70.

Industry Commission 1995, Charitable Organisations in Australia, Report 45, AGPS, Melbourne.

Inglis, J. & Rogan, L. (eds) 1993, 'Introduction', in *Beyond swings and roundabouts: Shaping the future of community services in Australia*, eds J. Inglis & L. Rogan, Pluto Press, Sydney.

Legislative Assembly of NSW 2013, *Outsourcing community service delivery*, *Report 2/55*, NSW Parliament Legislative Assembly Committee on Community Services, Sydney.

Maddison, S. 2009, 'Lessons to be learned: Reviving advocacy organisations after the neo-con men', *Cosmopolitan Civil Societies: An Interdisciplinary Journal*, vol. 1, no. 2, pp. 18–29.

Murphy, J. 2006, 'The other welfare state: Non-government agencies and the mixed economy of welfare in Australia', *History Australia*, vol. 3, no. 2, pp. 44.1–44.15.

OECD (Organisation for Economic Co-operation and Development) 2001, *Innovations in labour market policies: The Australian way*, OECD, Paris.

Painter, M. 1992, 'Participation and power', in *Citizen participation in government*, ed. M. Munro-Clarke, Hale & Iremonger, Sydney, pp. 21–36.

Phillips, R. & Goodwin, S. 2013, 'Third sector social policy research in Australia: New actors, new politics', *VOLUNTAS: International Journal of Voluntary and Nonprofit Organizations*, 1–20, online February 2013, doi: 10.1007/s11266-013-9351-z.

Phillips, R. 2007, 'Tamed or trained? The co-option and capture of "favoured" NGOs', *Third Sector Review*, vol. 13, no. 2, pp. 27–48.

Pollitt, C. 2007, 'The new public management: An overview of its current status', *Administration and Public Management Review*, vol. 8, pp. 110–15.

Productivity Commission 2010, *Contribution of the Not-for-Profit Sector, Research Report*, Canberra.

Thomas, M. & Knowler, K. 2013, Not-for-profit sector Freedom to Advocate bill, *Bills Digest*, no. 116, Parliamentary Library, Department of Parliamentary Services, Canberra.

Sidoti, E., Banks, R., Darcy, M., O'Shea, P., Leonard, R., Atie, R., Di Nicola, M. & Stevenson, S. 2009, '*A question of balance: Principles, contracts and the government-not for profit relationship*', UWS The Whitlam Institute, Sydney.

Smyth, P. 2008, 'The role of the community sector in Australian welfare: A Brotherhood of St Laurence perspective', in *Strategic issues for the not-for-profit sector*, ed. J. Barraket, UNSW Press, Sydney, pp. 212–35.

Lamont, A. & Bromfield, L. 2010, *History of child protection services*, National Child Protection Clearinghouse Resource Sheet, Australian Institute of Family Studies, Melbourne http://www.aifs.gov.au/nch/pubs/sheets/rs22/rs22.pdf

The Brotherhood of St Laurence, 2009, *Submission to the Productivity Commission into the contribution of the not-for-profit sector*, Brotherhood of St Laurence, Melbourne, http://www.bsl.org.au/pdfs/BSL_subm_Productivity_Comm_inquiry_NfP_sector_Jul09.pdf

Weeks, W. 1994, *Women working together: Lessons from feminist women's services*, Longman Cheshire, Melbourne.

Wright, S., Marston, G. & McDonald, C. 2011, 'The role of non-profit organizations in the mixed economy of welfare-to-work in the UK and Australia', *Social Policy & Administration*, vol. 45, no. 3, pp. 299–318.

Yeatman, A. 1990, *Bureaucrats, technocrats, femocrats: Essays on the contemporary Australian state*, Allen & Unwin, Sydney.

Yeatman, A. 1995, 'Interpreting contemporary contractualism', in *Governing Australia: Studies in contemporary rationalities of government*, eds M. Dean & B. Hindess, Cambridge University Press, Cambridge, pp. 124–39.

3

The devil's in the detail: The hidden costs of private retirement incomes policy

Adam Stebbing

Australian governments have shifted the focus of public policy onto the private sector in recent decades. Retirement incomes policy offers an important case study of this shift as a major target of efforts to privatise social provision. Rather than involving cutbacks to public provision, the privatisation of retirement incomes has extended occupational welfare offered as a condition of employment and fiscal welfare delivered via the tax system (Titmuss 1958, p. 42). In fact, the introduction of compulsory occupational superannuation represents the largest transfer of social provision to the private sector in recent memory. This scheme has established private super as a secondary source of retirement savings for most Australians and channelled record investments into private super funds.

The unprecedented growth of private super has stimulated debate about the economic and distributive impacts of private retirement incomes policy. This policy shift continues to be justified as a means to promote the key economic objectives of containing public expenditure, particularly over the long term as the population ages, and advancing national savings. That said, the capacity of current policy settings

Stebbing, A. 2015, 'The devil's in the detail: The hidden costs of private retirement incomes policy', in *Markets, rights and power in Australian social policy*, eds G. Meagher & S. Goodwin, Sydney University Press, Sydney.

to meet these goals, although often assumed, has been challenged by recent evidence. At the same time, the distributive effects of private retirement incomes policy have become of mounting concern, with attention focusing on the tax treatment of super and how private super has shifted the risk profile of retirement incomes. This 'risk shift' is particularly concerning because of the financialisation of private super, which has involved super funds reorganising their operations to maximise short-term profit and minimise fund exposure to long-term risk (Cutler & Waine 2001, p. 100). The financialisation of private super reflects a broader institutional reorganisation of the superannuation market, brought about by the demutualisation of several large not-for-profit operators and the growing market share held by for-profit providers including banks and other financial entities.

This chapter explores both the *fiscal impact* and *distributive effects* of private retirement incomes policy to better understand the strengths and limitations of recent developments. The fiscal impact of private retirement incomes policy is gauged by surveying the available evidence on its capacity to meet key policy goals. The distributive effect of private retirement incomes policy is examined by analysing current policy settings and the impact of private super on the risk profile of retirement incomes. After reviewing the evidence, I conclude by canvassing the prospects for reform in this critical policy domain.

Retirement incomes in Australia: A two-tiered system

The Australian retirement incomes system is a mixed economy that can be understood as a two-tiered system of social risk management (see Stebbing & Spies-Butcher 2010). The first and primary tier collectively pools protection from the social risk of income insecurity in old age. This tier consists of the publicly financed age pension (and related benefits) that excludes the wealthy through means tests. Providing a modest income stream, the age pension's full fortnightly rate was $776.70 for singles and $585.50 (each) for couples in January 2015 (Department of Human Services 2015). The pension forms the bedrock of the retirement incomes system, covering 76 percent of the population aged 65 years and over (AIHW 2013, p. 238).

In contrast, the second-tier individualises protection from income insecurity in retirement, through private investments managed in individual accounts. This tier mainly consists of private superannuation and voluntary savings, both of which are financed by contributions from individuals (or made on their behalf). Lacking the redistributive mechanism typical of European social insurance schemes, private super benefits are predominantly calculated in relation to individual contributions and investment returns. Because the government does not appear to finance the second tier (despite the generous concessions discussed below), retirees who draw retirement incomes from private sources are widely perceived to be self-funded (and are referred to as 'self-funded retirees'). Private super has become an important secondary source of retirement income and is now held by around 90 percent of income earners (Nielson & Harris 2009, p. 9).

The Commonwealth government supports both tiers of the retirement incomes system. The first tier consists of income transfers directly financed by the Commonwealth, such as the age pension, rent assistance and benefits provided to Concession Card holders (AIHW 2011, p. 11). Accounting for most expenditure on the first tier, the age pension cost $42.3 billion in 2014–15 (Australian Government 2014). The second-tier is supported via indirect means; this support includes regulations and tax expenditures, which provide tax payers with selective tax breaks. The major regulatory scheme is the Superannuation Guarantee Scheme, which mandates that employers pay nine percent of their employees' wages into private super. As contributions were increased from three to nine percent between 1992 and 2002 and will only increase to 12 percent in 2025, this scheme is not set to mature until at least 2050 (assuming a working life from 18 to 67 years of age). This scheme channels tens of billions of dollars into private super each year, without mandating financial contributions from the government. The super tax concessions discount the tax levied on super at all three stages of the super income stream – when employers make super contributions on their employees' behalf, when individuals earn interest on their super investments and when individuals withdraw benefits. These tax expenditures account for most public spending on the second tier, costing $32.1 billion of revenue forgone in 2013–14 (Treasury 2014). And, salary-sacrificing arrangements exist for employees who forgo income in return for their employers making additional contributions to super funds (which have the benefit of being subsidised by the tax expenditures).

The shift to private retirement incomes: A brief policy history

The two-tiered structure of retirement incomes policy has a long history, with the Commonwealth establishing the foundations of both tiers in the early 20th century. The age pension was the first social program established after Federation and the super tax concessions formed part of the first federal income tax. Despite these early origins, private retirement incomes policy played a minor role for most of the 20th century. The current emphasis of retirement incomes policy on private superannuation is a novel development. This section outlines the major developments in retirement incomes policy and explains how this shift coincided with the financialisation of private super.

The age pension

At Federation, age pensions received in-principle support from all major political parties and were one of only two social provisions explicitly identified in the Constitution. Political support for a national age pension was buoyed by the pre-existence of colonial and state schemes in NSW and Victoria, as well as concerns about aged poverty following the economic downturn in the 1890s (Dixon 1977, p. 22). Despite featuring on their agendas, early federal parliaments failed to introduce a national age pension because of fiscal constraints that stemmed from unresolved issues with the states about the distribution of taxing responsibilities (Kewley 1973, p. 67). After the Deakin minority government developed a means of skirting these fiscal constraints in 1908, Labor made support for increasing taxes conditional on the establishment of an age pension (Kewley 1973, p. 72). The government proved receptive to this request as it relied on Labor's greater numbers to retain office (Sawer 1956, p. 71). Legislation for the age pension was swiftly introduced to parliament in 1908 and passed into law with support from the major parties.

The age pension marked a watershed in retirement incomes policy, providing a modest income stream for eligible members of the population aged 65 years and over. Like earlier state schemes, the pension was financed out of consolidated revenue and means tests established eligibility. The age pension's design reflected a compromise between Deakin's Protectionists and Labor. Labor supported a universal age pension and opposed social insurance (Kewley 1973, p. 83). The Protectionists (and Free Traders) opposed universalism because of its cost (Kewley 1973, p. 83). They also rejected social insurance because of perceptions that it would expand direct taxation and was unsuitable to Australia's English heritage at the time (Kewley 1973, p. 82). Labor agreed to support the means-tested age pension backed by the Protectionists, but indicated the intention to establish a universalist age pension when the Commonwealth's financial position improved (Kewley 1973, p. 82). At its introduction, the age pension covered a small minority of the population since average life expectancy was less than 60 years (AIHW 2009, p. 83). Despite early reforms that reduced the eligibility age for women from 65 to 60 years and exempted the family home from the means test, the age pension was only received by around one-third of the eligible age group by the 1930s (Kewley 1973, p. 22).[1]

Over the following 50 years, the age pension became established as the primary retirement incomes policy. On the one hand, the age pension's role was firmed up by the failure of alternative policy proposals to take hold. After reversing their opposition to social insurance in 1913 (following the establishment of such a scheme in the United Kingdom in 1912), the non-Labor parties introduced several proposals to parliament before the Second World War but were unable to garner the support necessary to implement them (Dixon 1977, p. 43). Labor continued to support a universal pension and remained opposed to social insurance over this period. On the other, the age pension became entrenched as coverage gradually rose with rising life expectancy and the liberalisation of the entitlement criteria. Liberal and Labor gov-

---

1 The family home was exempted from the means test of the age pension in 1912 (Nielson & Harris 2009). This critical decision, which was extended later by a similar exemption in the Capital Gains Tax, has become an entrenched feature of the Australian tax and transfer system. These exemptions for owner-occupier housing has created perverse incentives to over-invest in housing, as well as to use super benefits on housing improvements and mortgage payments (for more on housing policy see Groenhart & Gurran, this volume).

ernments both liberalised the age pension between the 1950s and mid-1970s. This trend culminated in the Whitlam's Labor government abolition of the means test for those aged more than 70 years in 1975 and the move by the Fraser Liberal government to remove assets from the means test in 1979 (Bateman & Piggott 2003, p. 31).

However, the age pension has increasingly been targeted since the late 1970s. Reversing the direction of its earlier policy, the Fraser government froze the non-means-tested component of the age pension for recipients aged more than 70 years to reduce government spending (Daniels 2011, p. 35). The Hawke Labor government re-established both income and assets tests for all recipients in the mid-1980s as part of its efforts to redirect spending to new programs like Medicare (Daniels 2011, p. 35). The Hawke government also announced that it would increase the age pension by indexing it to 25 percent of male full-time average earnings (rather than index it to the Consumer Price Index) (Whiteford 2004, p. 85). Although this goal was mostly achieved from 1990, this reflected a fall in male average earnings and the reform was not legislated at this time (Whiteford 2004, p. 85). The Howard Liberal–National Coalition government largely retained the policy settings that it inherited, but enacted legislation to index the age pension at 25 percent of male full-time average earnings in 1997 and liberalised the means test as compensation for the Goods and Services Tax in 2000 (Daniels 2011, p. 36). And, the Rudd Labor government increased the rate of the pension to 27.7 percent of male average earnings (an increase of $60 per fortnight for singles), while tightening the means test and lifting the eligibility to those aged 67 years by 2019 (APL 2009, p. 171). Subsequently, the Abbott Coalition government (2013–) proposed raising the eligibility age of the pension to 70 years by 2035 and reducing the payment by indexing it to inflation rather than average male wages (Australian Government 2014). A century after it was introduced, the age pension remains the primary source of retirement income for most retirees despite the recent shifts to targeting and private provision.

The rise of compulsory private superannuation and the super tax concessions

While compulsory superannuation has recent origins, the Fisher Labor government established the super tax concessions when it introduced the income tax to fund Australia's role in the First World War in 1915 (Harris 2002, p. 180). Applying to the three stages of the super income stream, these tax concessions provided tax discounts that increased with the amount of income earned and super held. But, at the time they were introduced these tax concessions also had a low budgetary cost because income tax was levied on a minority of high-income earners and fewer than five percent of workers held super (Olsberg 1997, p. 58).

As minor provisions of a new income tax system, it is unsurprising that the inequality of the super tax concessions escaped controversy when introduced. Moreover, these tax concessions reflected the practice of not taxing mutual aid organisations, as not-for-profit life insurance funds administered most super schemes at the time (Rafter 1986, p. 232). It also streamlined the Commonwealth income tax with similar provisions for super in the states' schemes (Harris 2002 p. 177). However, even if they had had a larger cost, these tax concessions are still likely to have had a low profile because tax expenditures were not reported in either the Budget or other reports of public finance. In fact, reflecting their low profile, the super tax concessions were not subject to systematic review until the Asprey Tax Review of 1975 – around 60 years after their introduction.

The secondary role of superannuation grew steadily over the mid-20th century and this coincided with a shift in the composition of the super industry. Super came to cover 32 percent of the workforce by 1974, with coverage concentrated amongst men on higher incomes in managerial, professional and public sector roles (ABS 1976). The rising coverage of public sector employees was the result of governments establishing their own super schemes for their employees from the 1920s (Bateman & Piggott 2003, p. 31). The coverage of public sector super funds gradually expanded, with 44 percent of those with super covered by public sector schemes by 1974 (NSCI 1976, p. 11). Life insurance offices continued to play the major role in the private sector, with estimates suggesting that they held more than 60 percent of private super accounts in 1974 (NSCI 1976, p. 11). The remaining private sector employees were largely covered by small private funds overseen by trustees (NSCI 1976, p. 9).

In the mid-1970s, concerns about the pension's adequacy received wide attention, including in academic reports and union campaigns for national superannuation (a super scheme that covered the workforce and was administered by the state) (Olsberg 1997, p. 76). Both major parties responded to these concerns with proposals to extend state support. Notably, in 1969, Whitlam responded by placing national super on Labor's policy platform (this move was also a tactic to court the middle-class vote). Although not eventuating in reform, this put national super on the agenda and reversed decades of Labor opposition to social insurance.

Meanwhile, union campaigns extended private super to some workers from the mid-1970s. When confronted with a political climate hostile to wage growth, unions pursued private super in award negotiations to improve the lot of workers in lieu of wage increases (Olsberg 1997, pp. 75–76). Viewing award super – that is, super included in industrial awards – as deferred wages, unions perceived these payments as having the benefits of supplementing the age pension and extending the super tax concessions to workers (Combet 2004, p. 17). Unions, such as the Pulp and Paperworkers Federation (PPF) and the Federated Storemen and Packers Union (FSPU), also sought to increase worker control of super investments (and thereby reduce that of employers) by introducing their own super funds (Olsberg 1997, p. 78).

The union campaign experienced some success, with award super a key factor in expanding super coverage to 44 percent of the workforce by 1982 (Olsberg 1997, p. 78; ABS 1982, p. 8). This increase in coverage was not accompanied by a radical overhaul of the super industry. Public sector schemes slightly increased their share of super accounts to 48 percent, while private sector schemes held 52 percent of accounts (Rafter 1986, p. 241). The most significant change to the super industry during this period involved the drop in the share of super accounts administered by life insurance offices, which fell to around 42 percent of private super accounts in 1983, as other financial organisations increased their involvement in super (Rafter 1986, p. 241). But, the share of super accounts remained concentrated within the life insurance industry itself; Klumpes (1992, p. 124) estimates that the then non-profit Australian Mutual Provident (AMP) and National Mutual accounted for about 69 percent of the life insurance industry's superannuation business in the late 1980s.

Award super reached new heights through its inclusion in the Accord Mark II negotiated by the Hawke Labor government and the Australian Council of Trade Unions (ACTU) in 1986 (Olsberg 1997, p.

76, 81). The Accord Mark II gave unions both the capacity to negotiate award super of up to three percent of wages and a role in administering the not-for-profit industry super funds, which were the default funds into which award super was to be paid (for awards that covered multiple employers) (Kingston, Piggott & Bateman 1992, p. 141). Industry super funds, an Australian innovation, have industry-wide coverage and are mostly financed by compulsory employer contributions (Olsberg 1997, p. 81). Managed by a board comprising an equal number of appointees selected by employers and unions, these not-for-profit funds select investment strategies aimed at maximising members' benefits. In addition to increasing super coverage to 51 percent by 1988 (ABS 1988), this campaign gave Labor and the union movement a stake in the success of private super.

In this piecemeal way, private super came to replace a national, public superannuation scheme as Labor's second arm of retirement incomes policy in the late 1980s. A series of official reports dismissed national super as being no longer viable because of its start-up costs (see Foster 1988, p. 190; SSCHA 1988, p. xliv). At the same time, compulsory private super was presented as a solution to the long-term pressures of population ageing on the federal budget – which had emerged as a major social issue – because it would not increase public expenditure. Both these views were reinforced by neoliberal ideas, which added to perceptions that a public scheme would place undue costs on the Budget and that financial markets allocate resources more efficiently than the state (Quiggin 2011, p. 34). The popularity of these ideas made national super increasingly unpalatable politically because such a scheme would increase the government's stake in the financial sector (Quiggin 2011, p. 34; Sharp 2009, p. 202).

Formally adopting private super in 1989, Labor argued that it would improve the adequacy of retirement incomes and help to increase national savings (Howe 1989, p. 4). After unsuccessfully attempting to increase award super through later Accords, Labor directly extended private super to the workforce by legislating the Superannuation Guarantee Scheme in 1991 (Mann 1993). This scheme requires employers to contribute super contributions on their employees' behalf; the rate of compulsory employer contributions gradually increased from three to nine percent of wages between 1992 and 2002 (Kerin 1991). In 1994, the Keating government announced that it would defer previously promised tax cuts as a further increase to the Super Guarantee after 2002. But, the Howard government chose to not implement this increase in 1997 (Nielson & Harris 2009). In 2012, the Rudd and Gillard governments announced that the Super Guarantee would be gradually increased to 12 percent of wages between 2013 and 2019 (Australian Government 2012, p. 9).[2] However, in 2014, the Abbott Coalition government delayed the increase in the Super Guarantee, so that it would not reach 12 per cent until 2025 (Martin & Hutchens 2014). The Super Guarantee represents one of the most significant shifts of provision to the private sector; between 1990 and 2012, this scheme contributed to coverage expanding from 64 to 90 percent of the workforce and to super investments ballooning from $123 billion to $1.4 trillion (Nielson & Harris 2009; APRA 2013).

The extension of private super to the workforce also extended the super tax concessions from $5.6 billion of revenue forgone in 1984 to $32.1 billion in 2013–14 (Treasury 2014, p. 12). Despite their growing significance, the super tax concessions were subject to minor reforms between 1915 and the election of the Hawke government. In 1983, the first reform package reduced the budgetary cost of the super tax concessions by limiting access to superannuation benefits to those aged 55 years or over and increasing the taxes levied on lump-sum super benefits.[3] The government set the tax rates at 15 percent for the first $50,000 of lump-sum super benefits and at 30 percent for any benefits above this amount (Keating 1983). This reduced the inequality of the super tax concessions by increasing the tax paid on larger super benefits. In 1984, a second reform removed the 30/20 rule that, since 1961, had required super funds to invest 30 percent of their portfolios in government bonds to receive tax discounts (Wallis 1997, p. 572). As a response to recommendations of the Campbell Committee and Martin Report, this reform was one of a suite of measures that deregulated the

---

2   Initial increases to the Superannuation Guarantee were legislated by the Gillard government before Labor lost office in September 2013. In Opposition, the Liberal party committed to raising the Super Guarantee to 12 percent of wages, but indicated that it would delay implementation.

3   Until 1983, lump-sum super benefits were taxed at the highly concessional rate of five percent and there was no minimum age at which super benefits could be drawn.

financial sector (Sharp 2009, p. 201).[4] These reforms aimed to minimise state interference in the financial sector because investors operating in competitive markets were perceived to make more efficient decisions that would maximise return (Sharp 2009, p. 201). In 1988, the third set of reforms brought forward revenue by establishing 15 percent tax concessions on employer super contributions, super fund earnings and benefits (Daniels 2011, p. 36). The government argued that this reform was revenue neutral because tax increases at earlier stages of the super income stream (on contributions and investments) would be offset by reducing the tax on super benefits.

Initially, the Howard government reduced the inequality of the super tax concessions and expanded the options workers had available to them in regards to choice of fund. In 1996, the government reduced inequality by introducing the Superannuation Surcharge, which required those earning more than $75,000 per year to pay an additional 15 percent tax on super contributions (Treasury 2001, p. 87). The government also supported low-income groups by establishing an 18 percent rebate for private super invested on behalf of low-income spouses and the Superannuation Co-contribution Scheme, which matched voluntary private super contributions made by low-income earners dollar-for-dollar up to $1,000 per year (Warren 2008, p. 18). And, in 2002, the Howard government was able to introduce legislation for Super Choice (first announced in 1997), which gave workers the ability to choose between five funds nominated by their employers rather than the fund nominated in their industrial agreement (Warren 2008, p. 18). Super Choice made super more like a consumer product, giving individuals greater scope to select a fund and assume responsibility for their investments. This reform aimed to marketise super by increasing both competition between funds for customers and the lucrative opportunities available to private providers.

However, toward the end of its term, the government changed its focus by introducing reforms that increased the benefits received by a core constituency of wealthy voters. Arguing that it was reducing complexity, the government decreased the Super Surcharge to 7.5 percent

---

4   The Hawke government set up the Martin Committee in 1983 to assess the Campbell Report. The Campbell Committee, which was tabled in 1981, recommended sweeping financial de-regulation (Sharp 2009, p. 201).

in 2004 and then abolished it in 2005 (Warren 2008, p. 19). Then, in 2006, the government announced the Simplified Super package, which made super benefits exempt from tax and halved the taper rate for the age pension (Warren 2008, pp. 21–23). These reforms simplified the taxation of super but increased inequality by reducing the tax paid by those who had large super investments, which assisted a core Coalition constituency of older and wealthy voters – including those nearing retirement (Fraser 2006, p. 7).

Both the Rudd and Gillard Labor governments reformed these concessions. In 2010, the Rudd government announced that those on annual incomes of less than $37,000 would receive a 15 percent tax rebate on their super contributions from July 2012. Previously, this group of lower income earners had received no tax discount, as the 15 percent concessional tax rate was equal to their marginal tax rate. In 2012, the Gillard government halved the tax discount on super contributions received by the top 1.2 percent of income earners who receive incomes of more than $300,000 to 15 percent from July 2012 (Australian Government 2012, p. 35). These reforms have not radically reduced the incidence or scale of those concessions. Overall, the rapid expansion of the super tax concessions in the last few decades is clearly the result of the policy shift to private retirement incomes that has extended compulsory private super to the workforce.[5]

The 'financialisation' of private superannuation

The two decades following the establishment of compulsory super have coincided with structural change to the private super industry. Similar to the United States and the United Kingdom, the Australian superannuation industry has been transformed by financialisation. Financialisation refers to the increasing role of financial actors, motives, markets and institutions in organising the economy (Epstein, cited in Martin, Rafferty & Bryan 2008, p. 122). Cutler and Waine (2001, pp. 99–100)

---

5   Revenue forgone in super tax concessions accounts for less now than before the Global Financial Crisis. As recently as 2008, the super tax concessions were estimated at $38.9 billion of revenue forgone (Treasury 2013, p. 4). However they fell to $24.1 billion in 2009–10 reflecting the lower returns that super funds have received on their investments (Treasury 2013, p. 4).

usefully distinguish between three features of financialisation: first, it involves the elevation of financial criteria to assess fund performance (and the marginalisation of other criteria); second, super funds are operated to maximise 'shareholder value', rather than value for stakeholders such as account holders; and, third, regulatory frameworks are deregulated to advance the pursuit of profit (Cutler & Waine 2001, p. 100). These features of financialisation are evident in the deregulation of the financial sector, as well as changes to both the composition of the Australian super industry and structure of benefits offered to fund members over recent decades.

The regulatory framework that private super funds operate in was altered by broad-sweeping deregulation to financial markets in the 1980s and 1990s. These reforms aimed to increase the efficiency (and thus profit) of financial markets by opening up the financial sector to competition, reducing the barriers to market entry, and discouraging market segmentation (Keneley 2001, p. 163). The abolition of the 30/20 rule was of particular significance for the super industry because it gave funds the freedom to pursue more profitable ventures than bonds. On a broad level, these reforms resulted in a regulatory framework that gave private super funds, not-for-profit and for-profit alike, greater scope to pursue profits.

Financial deregulation has encouraged life insurance funds to transform their structure and role in the private super industry (Keneley 2001, p. 164). An important development has been that several large life insurance funds – including major players in the private super industry such as National Mutual in 1995 and AMP in 1997 – have responded to deregulation by demutualising their operations (Keneley 2001, p. 164). Demutualisation has financialised the super industry by converting not-for-profit funds into for-profit entities. This replaced an associational logic of risk-sharing among members, dating back to the 19th century in some cases, with a market logic of profit maximisation. It also transformed fund members of NFPs into consumers and shareholders. With key providers now operating on a for-profit basis, the distinction between not-for-profit life insurance funds and other forms of for-profit private super can no longer be sustained. A further significant development was that not-for-profit life insurance funds were under pressure to act as if they were for-profit because they had to compete with banks for capital to expand their business and they experienced increased competition from industry super funds (Keneley 2001, p. 162). Another major development has been deregulation of (some) restrictions on mergers and acquisitions that has enabled the formation of conglomerates that specialise in multiple financial services (Keneley 2001, p. 163). These financial conglomerates have blurred the distinction between the life insurance industry and other parts of the finance sector (Keneley 2001, p. 164). These three processes have significantly contracted the traditional role of life insurance funds as not-for-profit providers and expanded their involvement in for-profit provision.

The restructuring of the life insurance sector reflects a wider shift in the composition of the private super industry. The Australian Prudential Regulatory Authority (APRA) classifies super funds into five categories: public sector funds; the non-profit industry funds; retail funds privately operated on a commercial basis; corporate funds run by employers for their own employees; and, small (or self-managed) funds with fewer than five members (2013, p. 10). Table 3.1 displays how the overall share of super accounts and assets held by each type of fund changed between 1996 and 2011. The table shows that industry super funds increased their share of super accounts from 33 to 37 percent, while their share of super assets has increased from eight to 19 percent. As the proportion of assets held by these funds is much lower than their share of super accounts, it suggests that those with lower super balances benefit most from the industry funds. It also reveals that the accounts managed by retail super funds have markedly grown from 39 to 48 percent, whereas their assets increased from 24 to 28 percent of the total. And, the table shows that small funds have marginally increased their share of accounts from one to three percent, but had the greatest growth in assets from 12 percent to 32 percent of those held by the super industry. This suggests that small funds are predominately held by the very wealthy. In contrast, corporate and public sector funds decreased their share of both super accounts and assets; public sector funds now account for about 11 percent of super accounts and 14 percent of assets. Although somewhat offset by the growth of not-for-profit industry funds, these figures indicate that for-profit funds (that maximise shareholder value), and self-managed funds favoured by the well-off, have increased their market share since the establishment of the Super Guarantee.

Table 3.1: Proportion of super accounts and super assets held by the main types of funds, 1996 and 2011

| | Super accounts | | | | Super assets | | | |
| | 1996 | | 2011 | | 1996 | | 2011 | |
	'000s	%	'000s	%	$b	%	$b	%
Corporate	1,300	8	593	3	45.6	19	56.6	5
Industry	5,200	33	11,449	37	20.2	8	226.2	19
Public sector	3,000	19	3,373	11	48.1	20	172.9	14
Retail	6,100	39	15,063	48	59.6	24	339.5	28
Small	200	1	846	3	28.2	12	392.9	32
Total*	15,800	100	31,324	100	202.0	100	1,299.0	100

Source: APRA (2007, 2012) * Percentages may not sum to 100 due to rounding

While the Super Guarantee does not require compulsory super contributions to be invested in accounts with particular benefit structures, it has nevertheless coincided with a dramatic shift in the structure of the super accounts offered by private super funds from defined benefit schemes to accumulation accounts. Defined benefit schemes provide private pensions that are calculated according to both a member's final salary and the duration of their contributions (APRA 2007, p. 5). In contrast, accumulation accounts manage super in individual savings accounts, providing benefits in relation to the contributions made and interest earned (or loss) from investment (APRA 2007, p. 5). Whereas 82 percent of super accounts had a defined benefit structure in 1982, less than 14 percent of super accounts had this structure by 2000 (Treasury 2001, p. 85). In 2000, accumulation accounts comprised 86 percent of super accounts.

The shift toward accumulation accounts has continued in the last decade. Table 3.2 provides data on the benefit structures of super accounts held by Australians in 2010. In addition to the two types of schemes already discussed, the table includes data on hybrid accounts that combine features of accumulation accounts and defined benefit schemes. The table displays the number of super accounts held with

Table 3.2: Benefit structures of superannuation accounts in Australia, 2010

Benefit structure	Accounts		Assets	
	'000s	%	$ billion	%
Accumulation account	19,589	60	750.4	63
Defined benefit	645	2	57.9	5
Hybrid account	12,624	38	379.8	32
Total	32,857	100	1,188.1	100

Source: APRA (2011, p. 21)

each benefit structure (like Table 3.1), but does not reveal the portion of Australians with each type of account (as multiple accounts may be held by an individual). Nonetheless, accumulation accounts have spread further, with the table showing that about two percent of super accounts have only a defined benefit structure. Of these defined benefit schemes, 98 percent of accounts are held in public sector funds and have since been replaced with accumulation accounts (APRA 2011, p. 37). Because of this, the number of accounts in the defined benefit category is expected to drop further. Table 3.2 also shows that accumulation accounts hold 63 percent of super assets and hybrid accounts hold a further 32 percent. Taken together, this data confirm that accumulation accounts have become the main form of private super since the advent of award super and the Super Guarantee.

The shift to accumulation accounts reflects broader international trends in other private pension markets, especially those in other English-speaking countries (see Langley 2004; Cutler & Waine 2001). This shift is associated with the financialisation of the private super industry because the risk profile of accumulation accounts is more conducive to maximising shareholder return than defined benefit schemes (Cutler & Waine 2001, p. 108). In defined benefit schemes, the investment risk is borne by the fund and the employer-sponsor, who guarantee account holders a set benefit level at retirement (Davis & Hughes 1992, p. 167). Accumulation accounts, in contrast, leave the account holder responsible for the investment risk, with employers guaranteeing only a set level of contributions and the funds not specifying the level of benefit (if any) that will be received at retirement (Davis & Hughes 1992, p. 168). The shift of investment risk to account holders with accumulation accounts has been appealing to private super funds that aim to maximise shareholder value because they limit the funds' exposure to shortfalls and provide greater certainty of their liabilities by passing losses onto account holders (Cutler & Waine 2001, p. 108).

Financialisation has also coincided with the growth of accumulation accounts through its impact on industry super funds. The growing role of industry super funds has accelerated the uptake of accumulation accounts, with only three of 100 such funds offering defined benefit schemes in 1992 (Kingston, Piggott & Bateman 1992, p. 141). Kingston and associates (1992, p. 141) contend that industry funds seem to have offered accumulation accounts because of issues in securing sponsors that would be legally responsible to guarantee defined benefits (if funds went into deficit) when multiple employers are involved. APRA (2007, p. 5) further argue that this reflected a broader shift in employer preferences for accumulation accounts since they found the high cost of defined benefit schemes and their potential to increase their liabilities unappealing. The provision of accumulation accounts by industry funds reflects financialisation to the extent that employers sought to limit their liability (and maximise profits) and that the state chose not to regulate sponsoring arrangements. In turn, Davis and Hughes (1992, p. 168) claim that the prevalence of accumulation accounts has led industry funds to manage their investments to maximise short-term profit (like retail funds) since their members follow annual performances more closely than those with defined benefits. The overall implication here is that the industry funds are managed in similar ways and offer similar benefits to 'financialised' private super funds despite their not-for-profit status. In fact, Bryan, Ham and Rafferty (2008, p. 44) found that not-for-profit funds – including the industry super funds – outperformed private retail funds between 2004 and 2008. As will be seen in the ensuing discussion, both the financialisation of the private super industry and the rise of accumulation funds have implications for the efficiency and equity of private retirement incomes policy.

Value for money? Interactions between private super and retirement incomes policy

What to make of this recent shift to private provision? Has privatisation and financialisation made retirement incomes policy more efficient? A useful starting point for assessing the shift to private super is to examine how efficiently it has met the official rationales that governments have offered for recent reforms. As the policy history above shows, the Super Guarantee has been linked to three major policy goals: boosting retirement incomes; advancing national savings; and reducing the fiscal pressure of population ageing on future governments. On a more general level, Labor and the ACTU came to prefer private super over a public scheme because, as in other cases of privatisation, of perceptions that the private sector would more efficiently allocate funds and that expanding the public sector would cost too much. Support for a private scheme from Treasury, the Cass Social Security Review and the financial sector reinforced these perceptions (Sharp 2009; Mann 1993). At first glance, the superannuation guarantee appears to have met these goals with flying colours. Private super offers almost all workers a secondary source of retirement income and seems to have contributed $1.4 trillion to national savings and reduced future fiscal pressures – all without seeming to expand public spending. However, a closer look at the interactions between private super and other second-tier policies casts doubt on the efficiency of current retirement income policy.

Boosting retirement incomes?

The superannuation guarantee's contribution to increasing retirement incomes might seem to be its most self-evident achievement. The scheme has expanded super coverage and investments to new heights. But, it is one thing for private super to have increased retirement incomes and quite another for it to have done so efficiently. For the Super Guarantee to boost retirement incomes efficiently, retirees would, at the very least, have to use their super investments as income. Both the structure of super benefits and available evidence on how super is spent by retirees suggest that this link is more tenuous than generally assumed.

Superannuation is available to those aged 55 years or older who retire and to those who continue to work past the age of 65 years. Nevertheless, the structure of super benefits is a key factor in whether funds are used as retirement income. Defined benefit schemes, as well as the defined benefit component of hybrid schemes, are most likely to be used as retirement income because they are receivable only as a private pension that provides a regular income to beneficiaries once they reach a certain age. Benefits from accumulation accounts or components can be used as retirement income or potentially put to other uses as they are mostly received as lump-sum payments. As Disney points out, super benefits from accumulation accounts can 'be expended at the onset of retirement, or passed on to relatives for tax avoidance purposes, rather than used as retirement income' (2007, p. 3). The potential for super benefits to be put to other uses is exacerbated by the tax exemption of super benefits received after age 60 years – five years before retirees are eligible for the age pension, provided they meet its eligibility criteria. Because of the prevalence of accumulation accounts and the relatively low level of super held by most current retirees, there is no guarantee that private super is drawn on as retirement income (even though people receive it at retirement age).

In fact, the available evidence suggests that lump-sum private super tends to be used to pay off household debt rather than used as retirement income. Kelly and associates (2004) compare household debt and the super held at retirement with the amounts of each held in the years leading up to it. They note that in households with at least one person aged 50–69 years in the workforce, the average super balance was $170,000 and mean household debt was $85,500 in 2002 (Kelly, Farbotko & Harding 2004, p. 8). For households where people aged 50–69 years had retired, the average super balance was $93,000 and household debt was $22,700 in 2002 (Kelly et al. 2004, p. 8). Because of these different levels of debt and higher home ownership among retired people, Kelly and colleagues (2004) argue that super appears to be used to pay off debt accrued when in the labour force. This is consistent with more recent data that show 69 percent of individual retirees who received lump-sum super between 2003 and 2007 did not use their benefits primarily for retirement income (ABS 2011, p. 92). These 'other' uses of private super undermine the compulsory nature of super to the extent that individuals use their benefits to bring forward consumption and accrue debt before retirement.

Retirees' use of lump-sum super to pay off mortgages or reduce debt from housing upgrades is unsurprising, considering the incentives for investing in owner-occupier housing. The favourable tax treatment of owner-occupier provides incentives to individuals from all age groups to invest in housing over other investments. Owner-occupier housing is exempt from capital gains tax and imputed rent is not taxed (Smith 2004, p. 194; Yates 2010, p. 32). Retirees have a further incentive to invest in their primary residence, since owner-occupier housing has long been excluded from the assets test of the age pension (as noted above). Taken together, these policies offer retirees incentives to invest their super in owner-occupier housing (potentially to over–invest) and to claim the age pension as their retirement income (also see Spies-Butcher & Stebbing 2011).

Although spending lump-sum super on housing or servicing debt may increase household wealth, it does not, in itself, boost retirement income. It could be argued that this does not prevent private super spent from contributing to retirement income through reverse equity mortgages, which allow retirees to access income or lump-sum from housing assets that they own. However, this industry is in its infancy in Australia, with only 1.4 percent of individuals aged more than 60 years holding a reverse mortgage in 2007 (Henry 2008, p. 28). The evidence thus casts doubt on the significance of the direct, or indirect, contribution made by lump-sum super benefits from accumulation accounts to retirement income.

Reducing the pressures of population ageing?

The capacity of private retirement incomes policy to offset the public costs of the age pension over the long term as the population ages also seems straightforward. The Super Guarantee and other second-tier policies relating to private super are widely assumed to reduce budgetary costs by directing funds into private super that will then be used as retirement income instead of the age pension. As the assumption that private super provides retirement income has already been shown to be suspect, the focus here is on the projected impact of the super tax concessions on the efficiency of private retirement incomes policy as the population ages.

Like other affluent societies, Australia's population is projected to age in coming decades because of declining fertility and rising life expectancy. Fertility rates have fallen from 3.5 to two births per woman between 1961 and 2008 (Treasury 2010, p. 7). Average life expectancy has also risen by (at least) 24 years for men and women since 1901, reaching 79.2 years for men and 83.7 years for women in 2006–7 (Treasury 2010, p. 6). Table 3.3 displays projections from the third *Intergenerational report* on the impact that these trends are expected to have on the age structure of Australia's population. These official projections show that the proportion of the population aged over 65 years is expected to grow from 13.5 to 22.7 percent between 2010 and 2050 – projected growth of almost 70 percent. Population ageing will increase outlays on the age pension, but care has to be taken to avoid overstating by how much for two reasons. First, these projections are likely to over-estimate the scale of the problem because they are based on conservative assumptions and are sensitive to small changes due to their long-term nature (Dowrick & McDonald 2002, pp. 9–10).[6] Evidence of this is that the third *Intergenerational report* has scaled down the projected costs of population ageing found in the first two reports (released in 2001 and 2007). Second, Australia has a 'favourable demographic profile' compared to many similar countries (OECD 2009, p. 150). Both these considerations suggest that the budgetary impact of population ageing will be modest in Australia.

However, in the event that population ageing were to considerably add to fiscal pressures, the evidence suggests that the current policy settings for private super are not particularly efficient. This is because private super has limited capacity to act as a substitute for the age pension and thereby reduce public spending. The *Intergenerational report*

---

6 Dowrick and McDonald (2002, p. 10) argue that the projections in the *Intergenerational report* are pessimistic because they underestimate the potential for: the participation rate to increase; low unemployment to stimulate the economy; and, healthier lifestyle choices to counterbalance the cost of health and aged care. Moreover, they argue that the report does not give due attention to the projected growth of real after tax incomes because of its focus on the state of public finances (Dowrick & McDonald 2002, pp. 10–11).

Table 3.3: Age structure of the Australian population, 1970–2050

	1970 (% of population)	2010 (% of population)	2050 (Projected % of population)
0–14 years	28.8	19.1	17.2
15–64 years	62.8	67.4	60.2
65–84 years	7.8	11.7	17.6
85+ years	0.5	1.8	5.1

Source: Treasury intergenerational report (2010, p. 10)

projects that the pension's cost will rise from 2.7 to 3.9 percent of GDP in 2049–50 (Treasury 2010, p. 47). But the Treasury estimates that private super will only reduce public spending on the age pension by six percent in 2050 when the Super Guarantee matures (Harmer 2009). Extrapolating from this, private super is subsidised by $30 billion of super tax concessions, which amounts to 2.1 percent of GDP, and is projected to reduce spending on the age pension by less than 0.2 percent of GDP in 2050.[7] As super is projected to save less than 10 percent of what the super tax concessions currently cost as a proportion of GDP, it is difficult to avoid the conclusion that private super provides an expensive and inefficient means to combat any fiscal pressures associated with population ageing.

The high cost and inefficiency of the super tax concessions often escapes attention because their tax expenditure design has afforded them a low profile. These concessions are still excluded from official reports such as the Budget and *Intergenerational reports*. The omission from the latter is particularly concerning, since these reports represent official projections of population ageing and the super tax concessions are one of the more expensive social policies associated with this demographic trend, currently costing just less than the age pension itself. This omis-

---

7   This figure is calculated as six percent of 3.9 percent of GDP. The latter figure is what the age pension is projected to cost in 2050. Moreover, in 2010, the super tax concessions were lower than they previously had been because super funds made few returns in volatile global markets. This suggests that the potential saving is likely to be even less when global financial conditions improve.

sion considerably reduces the usefulness of the *Intergenerational reports* and makes private super seem to appear more efficient and cost-effective than it is. Despite these data limitations, it is clear that the high cost of the super tax concessions is a major source of inefficiency that thwarts the long-term sustainability of current policies for private super.

Increasing national savings?

At first glance, the trillion dollars invested in private super appears to have made progress on the economic goal of boosting national savings. Both Labor and Coalition governments have promoted national savings because of concerns that dwindling local savings would leave the economy reliant on global financial markets for investment funds and exposed to shocks (such as the Global Financial Crisis of 2008). This, in turn, would lead to lower economic growth and employment (FitzGerald 1993, p. 5). As private super is preserved until retirement, governments have argued private retirement incomes policy promotes national savings by channelling funds into more productive capital investments than housing (Edey & Gower 2000, pp. 277, 288).

The link between super and national savings has, however, proven difficult to establish in practice, because it is difficult to calculate the extent to which compulsory super contributions replace other forms of household savings that would have been made in their absence (FitzGerald et al. 2007, p. 6). Projections calculated by researchers complicate this further, with estimates of compulsory super's contribution to new household saving ranging from 37 to 75 percent (Edey & Gower 2000, p. 297). A further reason for this difficulty is that record household debt has offset increases to national saving from private super (FitzGerald et al. 2007, p. iii). On the one hand, households have limited savings capacity because they are, on average, servicing high mortgage and credit card debt. On the other hand, the potential of private super to increase national savings is undermined by retirees' use of lump-sum super benefits to service household debts.

But, more fundamentally, Coates (2004) contends that national saving is an abstract concept with increasingly limited practical use. National saving has become difficult to separate from foreign savings because of the global integration of finance and capital markets (Coates

2004, p. 83). This means that a national savings pool cannot be presumed and its definition and size are arbitrary to some extent (Coates 2004, p. 90). For example, it is difficult to calculate how much owner-occupied housing contributes to national savings because its roles as a vehicle of household savings and source of household debt are not easily separated (Coates 2004, p. 91). At the same time, housing values are inflated by tax and pension asset test exemptions. Just as importantly, Coates (2004, p. 93) argues that economic globalisation challenges the concept of national saving by implicating household assets and mortgages, as well as private super funds and their portfolios, in international processes. Since the national element of these savings cannot always be easily separated, Coates claims that private super provides 'savings for investment ... not national savings for domestic investment' (2004, p. 97). This is borne out by recent evidence, which suggests that only 39 percent of super assets actually are held in Australia, with 29 percent of these assets held in Australian shares and 10 percent in Australian fixed interest accounts (APRA 2011, p. 40).

In sum, the economic benefits of private super are more often asserted than defended by evidence. The analysis presented here casts doubt on the efficiency of private retirement incomes policy as a means of boosting retirement income, offsetting future fiscal pressures from population ageing and increasing national savings. It also reveals that the super tax concessions undermine the efficiency of private super because of their immense budgetary cost.

The hidden inequalities of private super: Shining light on regressive super tax concessions

As retirement incomes policy is a major area of social provision, the distributive effects of the shift to private super are not incidental. The capacity of social provision to address inequalities is important because material differences impact on the distribution of individual opportunities and societal wellbeing (Wilkinson & Pickett 2009). In contrast to the redistributive impact of the first tier of retirement incomes policy, recent reform to private retirement incomes policy has reinforced inequality by individualising risk and expanding the cost of the inequitable super tax concessions.

Reinforcing inequality by individualising risk

The Super Guarantee has reinforced labour market inequalities between high- and low-income earners, especially as it has coincided with the financialisation of the private super industry. The spread of accumulation accounts, which has been promoted through financialisation, has served to individualise the social risk of income insecurity in retirement (Cutler & Waine 2001). This risk shift is particularly obvious when accumulation accounts are contrasted with their alternatives. Accumulation accounts involve neither the redistributive mechanisms of state-administered social insurance schemes, nor the commitments from employers and financial markets to guarantee a certain benefit in retirement typical of defined benefit schemes. The spread of accumulation accounts has thus shifted risk onto individuals and away from the state, employers and financial institutions (see Cutler & Waine 2001; Langley 2004). Accordingly, the benefits retirees can draw from their super in accumulation accounts are vulnerable to downturns in unpredictable global financial markets – such as the Global Financial Crisis and its unfolding aftermath – but the financial institutions that manage private super funds and the state are largely insulated from liability.

Although retirees with defined benefit schemes tend to receive more benefits and experience less risk than other retirees, the inequalities between those who hold accumulation accounts are the focus here because the latter are the predominant form of private super and most defined benefit schemes have been closed to new members. Accumulation schemes provide individuals with benefits in relation to the rate and length of individual contributions, as well as the earnings from their investments. The advent of compulsory superannuation at a time when accumulation accounts became the norm has provided high-income earners with a cumulative advantage since their contributions are larger and they have the potential to earn more interest than low-income earners. The upshot of this is that second-tier retirement incomes policy mainly benefits those employed full time, while offering little to low-income earners, casual and part-time workers, or those who have extended absences from paid employment (such as the long-term unemployed and full-time carers). Indeed, low-income earners are likely to be adversely affected by the requirement that they defer nine percent of their income via super that could be put to other uses. This has particular implications for gender inequality because gender pay gaps persist; women perform most casual and part-time work; and, they still undertake the bulk of care work (see Sharp & Austen 2006; also see Spies-Butcher & Stebbing 2011, p. 53).

The next two tables confirm that private super reinforces these inequalities. Again, these tables show the percentage of super accounts (again, individuals may hold multiple accounts). Table 3.4 compares super benefits with the gender, gross weekly income and labour force status of those who held them in 2007. The table shows that women tend to hold less private super than men, lower income earners tend to hold less than higher income earners, and unemployed people hold less than those in paid employment. Table 3.5 compares the median and mean of the super benefits held by the gender, gross weekly income and labour force status of account holders. The mean shows how much super each account would hold if super assets were evenly spread, while the median is the mid-point for each grouping if super assets were ranked by how much super they hold. For example, half of the accounts held by women have $18,489 or less, but these accounts would each hold $52,272 if super was spread evenly. Table 3.5 also reveals that median super benefits for each gender, income and labour force grouping is proportionately much lower than the respective mean (or average) – thus the top half of the super accounts in each category hold much more than the bottom half. Although not conclusive, this provides further evidence suggesting that super assets are concentrated among employed men with the highest incomes.

Hidden and inequitable: the super tax concessions

The super tax concessions are, however, the major source of inequality in second-tier retirement incomes. Although the evidence supports this conclusion, the hidden nature of these concessions makes it difficult to ascertain their distributive effects. These policies remain hidden because of limits to existing sources of information about them and their low profile. The *Tax Expenditures Statement*, which remains the most reliable source on the super tax concessions, provides only aggregate estimates. Long-term projections, such as the aforementioned *Intergenerational reports*, do not estimate the revenue forgone from super tax concessions. And, existing research tends to be hypothetical, often us-

Table 3.4: Super benefits by gender, gross income, and labour force status in 2007, percent

	Current account balance/withdrawal benefit					
	$1–$9,999	$10,000–$24,999	$25,000–$49,999	$50,000–$99,999	$100,000+	Total
Gender						
Male	46	44	53	58	66	52
Female	54	56	47	42	34	48
Gross income**						
$1–$299	23	12	8	6	8	13
$300–$599	28	19	13	8	7	17
$600–$999	27	36	34	26	16	27
$1,000–$1,499	6	16	23	29	25	17
$1,500–$1,999	2	3	6	11	15	6
$2,000+	1	2	4	10	18	6
Labour force***						
Employed	79	89	90	92	87	86
Unemployed	5	2	2	1*	1	3
Total	100	100	100	100	100	100

* High standard error of estimate. ** Gross weekly individual income; column totals do not add to 100 as data for nil, negative and unknown income have been excluded. *** Those not in labour force excluded from analysis as it is difficult to calculate this data due to the inclusion of retirees. Source: ABS (2011, p. 81)

ing estimates based on the policy design of the super tax concessions rather than actual data (for example, see Denniss 2007 and Ingles 2009). Moreover, it is difficult to estimate the distributive effects of these policies because the Super Guarantee will not mature for at least three decades. Before this time, it is difficult to estimate the extent to which salary-sacrificing provisions have been used, how these tax concessions impact on final super balances and financial market returns over the

Table 3.5: Comparison of mean and median superannuation balances, 2007

	Median ($)	Mean ($)	Median as a proportion of Mean (%)
Sex			
Male	31,252	87,589	36
Female	18,489	52,272	35
Gross income*			
$1–$299	6,719	41,498	16
$300–$599	8,787	33,246	26
$600–$999	20,000	44,672	45
$1,000–$1,499	47,591	89,884	53
$1,500–$1,999	70,851	135,375	52
$2,000+	108,558	220,774	49
Labour force			
Employed	25,084	69,193	36
Unemployed	3,500	30,556	11
Total	23,698	70,670	33

* Gross weekly individual income; data for nil, negative and unknown income excluded. Source: ABS (2011, pp. 82–83)

longer term. Nevertheless, given that the concessions reduce tax revenue by around $30 billion, it is surprising that *so little* is known about their distributive implications.

The super tax concessions may appear to treat taxpayers equally, but the flat tax rates they levy on super deliver inequitable benefits because of how they interact with the progressive income tax scales. As Table 3.6 shows, these tax concessions provide inequitable benefits at each stage of the super income stream. The tax discount received on super contributions depends on the amount of income earned. Super contributions made by those who earn incomes less than $37,000 per year are subject to a 15 percent tax rebate. The 15 percent concessional tax rate that applies to contributions made by those who earn above

$37,000 but less than $300,000 delivers a tax discount between 15 and 30 percent. And, the 30 percent tax concession for contributions made by those who earn over $300,000 provides a tax discount of 15 percent. Annual limits currently apply to the amount of super contributions that can be taxed at these concessional rates; for those under 50 years, the annual limit is $25,000, while it is $50,000 for those aged 50 years and above (ATO 2012). The flat rate 15 percent concessional tax rates on super earnings offers no benefit to income earners with incomes below $37,000, but delivers a 30 percent tax discount on investment returns for those earning $180,000 or more each year (up to annual limits). The tax exemption of super benefits is more inequitable, providing the biggest tax discounts to those receiving the largest super benefits (see Table 3.6).

Clearly, these tax concessions grant the largest reductions to those who have income and/or super assets that are sufficient for them to pay the highest marginal tax rates. Moreover, higher income earners are more likely to be able to take advantage of the salary-sacrificing provisions and benefit further from these concessions. Compared to both the equitable age pension and the Super Guarantee that merely re-inforces labour market inequalities, the super tax concessions actively extend them. Extrapolating from the above, the evidence suggests that employed men with the highest incomes benefit most from these concessions.

In claiming that second-tier retirement incomes policy is inequitable, I am not arguing that the Australian retirement incomes system is more inequitable overall than those in other countries. This is not only beyond the scope of this chapter, but is unclear because the Super Guarantee has not matured. Rather, my intention is to display how the privatisation of retirement incomes policy has entrenched, and even extended, inequality. It is clear that the super tax concessions are difficult to justify in light of their $30 billion cost and inequity. It also follows from the earlier policy history that the tax concessions that currently subsidise the operations of for-profit super funds were intended to support the not-for-profit sector and that their current scale was inconceivable at their introduction.

Table 3.6: Tax benefits provided by the super tax concessions in 2012–13, percent

Income range ($)	Margi-nal tax rate (%)	Tax paid on super contri-butions (%)	Tax dis-count on super contri-butions (%)	Tax dis-count from 15 percent flat rate tax on fund earnings (%)	Tax dis-count from ex-emption on super benefits (%)
0–18,000	Nil	0	0	0	0
18,001–37,000	15	0	15	0	15
37,001–80,000	30	15	15	15	30
80,001–180,000	37	15	18	17	38
180,000–300,000	45	15	30	30	45
300,001+	45	30	15	30	45

The challenge for reform: A case of politics before policy?

The analysis presented in this chapter calls into question the benefits of privatisation of retirement incomes. Evidence suggests that the recent shift onto second-tier retirement incomes policy, which culminated in the Super Guarantee, has increased inequality – and gender inequality in particular – without efficiently meetings its policy goals. This is not to argue that the Super Guarantee should be abolished, or that private super is not an important source of secondary household savings. Rather, it is to highlight the need for further reform. Importantly, the ability of private super to increase retirement income, reduce public spending and boost national savings are much more tenuous than often assumed. This, in turn, makes it more difficult to justify the large and inequitable subsidies that the super tax concessions provide to private super funds and the well-off. The clear implications of these findings are that reform to the super tax concessions and Super Guarantee could simultaneously improve efficiency and reduce inequality. So, what prospects are there for reform?

Reform to the super tax concessions is a top priority because they are costly policies that deliver most benefit to those who need it least.

However, the major political parties do not currently prioritise reform to these tax concessions. Admittedly, this is less of an issue for the Coalition parties, which extended the benefits these concessions granted to key well-off constituencies at the end of their last term in office. The Rudd and Gillard governments introduced limited reforms that have reduced the inequality of the concessions. Remarkably, even their minor reforms have had an impact because of the immense scale of these concessions; the Gillard government's decision to halve the tax discount on super contributions received by those earning more than $300,000 per year was projected to raise revenue by around $1 billion over the 2012–13 Budget's forward estimates (Australian Government 2012, p. 41). Labor may have been expected to propose more ambitious reform, considering that during their period in office, the super tax concessions were the focus of a series of reports that highlighted their inefficiency and inequality (for example, see Davidson 2012; Denniss 2007; Henry 2009; Ingles 2009; Spies-Butcher & Stebbing 2009). Most notably, the Henry Tax Review – which Labor framed as a blueprint for future tax reform – proposed that the tax concession for super contributions be converted into a flat rate tax offset for up to $25,000 of annual contributions (Henry 2009, p. 100). Nevertheless, there is little to suggest that Labor supports more systematic reform beyond that delivered by the Rudd–Gillard government.

Labor's lack of appetite for reform seems to stem from the fact that the super tax concessions are established policies that have a low profile and receive support from well-resourced interests. As tax expenditures, the inequity of these concessions is concealed and they tend to be viewed as tax cuts for 'self-funded retirees' (Henman & Marston 2008, p. 192). The low profile of the super tax concessions has not been redressed by the annual publication of the *Tax Expenditures Statement* since 1986 as it provides limited information and does not report distributive effects (see Burton 2005). At the same time, these tax concessions enjoy quasi-legitimacy due to their long history. As Pierson (1993) argues, policies that operate over the long term tend to become resistant to reform as they come to inform the expectations of beneficiaries. Reform that reduced the inequity of the super tax concessions could be expected to be unpopular among financial entities that may expect to receive fewer deposits and those voters that would, or expect to, pay more tax. It is thus unsurprising that key representatives of private super funds and the finance industry – including the Association of Super Funds of Australia (ASFA), the Self-Managed Superannuation Professionals Association and the Financial Services Council – have recently reaffirmed their support for these concessions (Hepworth 2012; Korporaal 2012). Focusing on benefits received by self-funded retirees rather than the finance industry, these associations framed the concessions as vital to reducing dependence on the age pension and advocated their extension (Korporaal 2012). Against this backdrop, the prospect of reform to the super tax concessions appears very limited indeed.

Another priority for reform that would increase income security in retirement is to amend the Super Guarantee to reduce both gender inequality and the extent of the investment risks borne by individuals. However, the major political parties have not proposed policies to address these inequalities that are reinforced by the current private super arrangements. The Rudd and Gillard governments focused their superannuation policy on increasing the Super Guarantee contribution rate to 12 percent of employees' wages, which has been a long-term Labor goal that was first flagged by the Keating government. The Coalition parties have largely supported this reform; although the Coalition did not vote to increase the Super Guarantee, Prime Minister Tony Abbott promised to retain the reform when Opposition leader (Franklin & Hepworth 2012). In office, the Abbott government has delayed the increase to the Super Guarantee to beyond its first term, but claims to still support the policy (Martin & Hutchens 2014). Ironically, considering it was used to justify the increase by the Rudd government, the Henry Review explicitly advised against raising the contributions level of the Super Guarantee because it was likely to disadvantage low-income earners (Henry 2009, p. 109). In fact, Labor's move to raise the Super Guarantee is likely to exacerbate gender inequality, as well as the inequalities between low-and high-income earners discussed previously. At the same time, this reform has also increased the investment risks borne by the majority of Australians who hold super in accumulation accounts and does not prevent super from being used for purposes other than retirement income. This implies that recent reform to the Super Guarantee has not just failed to address shortcomings of current policy, but has actually reinforced them.

So, will future reform address the major issues with private retirement incomes policy? On balance, it does not seem likely, but time will ultimately tell. What is clear, however, is that the current scale and inequality of the super tax concessions is a largely unnoticed by-product of the privatisation of retirement incomes policy. It is also clear that it is premature, as the government proposes, to increase the Super Guarantee to 12 percent of wages when the inequalities of private super have not been addressed. From a policy perspective, reform to these concessions could do so much to enhance the efficiency of retirement incomes policy, while simultaneously reducing budgetary pressures and improving equity.

References

ABS (Australian Bureau of Statistics) 1976, *Superannuation Australia*, ABS, Canberra.

ABS 1982, *Superannuation Australia*, ABS, Canberra.

ABS 1988, *Superannuation Australia*, ABS, Canberra.

ABS 2011, *Employment arrangements, retirement, and superannuation Australia*, ABS, Canberra.

Australian Government 2012, *Budget overview 2012–13*, Australian Government, Canberra.

Australian Government 2014, *Budget overview 2014–15: Social Services*, Australian Government, Canberra. http://www.budget.gov.au/2014-15/content/glossy/welfare/download/Social_Services.pdf

AIHW (Australian Institute of Health and Welfare) 2009, *Australia's welfare 2009*, Australian Institute of Health and Welfare, Canberra.

AIHW 2011, *Australia's welfare 2011*, Australian Institute of Health and Welfare, Canberra.

AIHW 2013, *Australia's welfare 2013*, Australian Institute of Health and Welfare, Canberra.

APL (Australian Parliamentary Library) 2009, *Budget review 2009–10*, Department of Parliamentary Services, Canberra.

APRA (Australian Prudential and Regulatory Authority) 2007, 'A recent history of superannuation in Australia', *APRA Insight*, vol. 2, pp. 3–10.

APRA 2011, *Annual superannuation bulletin June 2010*, Australian Prudential and Regulatory Authority, Canberra.

APRA 2013, *APRA Insight*, Issue 1, Australian Prudential and Regulatory Authority, Canberra.

ATO (Australian Taxation Office) 2012, 'Salary sacrifice limits'. http://tiny.cc/siu1qx

Bateman, H. & Piggott, J. 2003, 'The Australian approach to retirement', in *Taste of pie: Searching for better pension provisions in developed countries*, eds N. Takayama, H. Daigaku, & K. Kenyujo, Maruzen Co Ltd, Tokyo, pp. 3–36.

Bryan, D., Ham, R. & Rafferty, M. 2008, *Fund performance in the Australian superannuation industry*, Workplace Research Centre, Sydney.

Burton, M. 2005, 'The Australian tax expenditures statement', *Journal of Australian Taxation*, vol. 8, no. 1, pp. 1–68.

Coates, N. 2004, 'Still "Saving the nation" twelve years on?', *Journal of Australian Political Economy*, vol. 53, pp. 81–99.

Combet, G. 2004, 'Superannuation: Past, present and future: An interview with Greg Combet, Secretary of the ACTU', *Journal of Australian Political Economy*, vol. 53, pp. 17–26.

Cutler, T. & Waine, B. 2001, 'Social insecurity and the retreat from social democracy: Occupational welfare in the long boom and financialization', *Review of International Political Economy*, vol. 8, no. 1, pp. 96–118.

Daniels, D. 2011, *Social security payments for the aged, people with disabilities and carers, 1909 to 2011*, Department of Parliamentary Services, Canberra.

Davidson, P. 2012, *Building super on a fair foundation: Reform of the taxation of superannuation contributions*, ACOSS Paper No. 185, Australian Council of Social Services, Sydney.

Davis, K. & Hughes, T. 1992, 'Long-term goals and short-term horizons: Conflicts in superannuation policy', in *Superannuation and the Australian financial system*, eds K. Davis & I. Harper, Allen & Unwin, Sydney, pp. 157–66.

Denniss, R. 2007, 'Crisis of cash or crisis of confidence: The costs of ageing in Australia', *Journal of Australian Political Economy*, vol. 59, no. 1, pp. 30–49.

Department of Human Services 2015, 'Payment rates for age pension'. http://www.humanservices.gov.au/customer/enablers/centrelink/age-pension/payment-rates-for-age-pension

Disney, J. 2007, *Superannuation and lifelong saving*, University of New South Wales Faculty of Law Research Series Paper 28, University of New South Wales, Sydney.

Dixon, J. 1977, *Australia's policy toward the aged: 1890–1972*, Canberra College of Advanced Education, Canberra.

Dowrick, S. & McDonald, P. 2002, *Comments on the intergenerational report*, Australian National University, Canberra.

Edey, M. & Gower, L. 2000, 'National savings: Trends and policy', *The Australian economy in the 1990s*, Reserve Bank of Australia, Sydney, pp. 277–311.

FitzGerald, V. 1993, *National saving: A report to the government*, Australian Government, Canberra.

FitzGerald, V., Shamlian, T., Doss, T., Read, A., Goldsmith, J., Locke, P. & Scanlan, B. 2007, *Australia's national saving revisited: Where do we stand now?*, The Allen Consulting Group, Canberra.

Foster, C. 1988, *Towards a national retirement incomes policy: An overview*, Social Security Review Issues Paper No. 6, Department of Social Security, Canberra.

Franklin, M. & Hepworth A., 2012, 'Abbott lashes extra super costs for employers', *The Australian*, 24 March.

Fraser, A. 2006, 'No one budgeted for crazy senators', *The Canberra Times*, 20 May, p. 7.

Harmer, J. 2009, *Pension review report*, Department of Families, Housing, Community Services and Indigenous Affairs, Canberra.

Harris, P. A. 2002, *Metamorphosis of the Australian income tax: 1866 to 1922*, Australian Tax Research Foundation, Sydney.

Henman, P. & Marston, G. 2008, 'The social division of welfare surveillance', *Journal of Social Policy*, vol. 37, no. 2, pp. 187–205.

Henry, K. 2008, *Australia's future tax system: Retirement income*, Consultation Paper, Department of Treasury, Canberra.

Henry, K. 2009, *Australia's future tax system: Final report to the Treasurer*, Department of Treasury, Canberra.

Hepworth, A. 2012, 'Cut superannuation tax breaks, says ACTU', *The Australian*, 12 January.

Howe, B. 1989, *Better incomes: Retirement incomes policy into the next century*, Australian Government, Canberra.

Ingles, D. 2009, 'The great superannuation tax concession rort', Research Paper No. 61, The Australia Institute, Canberra.

Keating, P. 1983, 'Economy', Ministerial Statement May 1983: Statement delivered on 19 May 1983 by the Hon. Paul Keating, M. P., Treasurer of the Commonwealth of Australia, Australian Government, Canberra.

Kelly, S., Farbotko, C. & Harding, A. 2004, 'The lump-sum: Here today, gone tomorrow', *AMP. NATSEM Income and Wealth Report Issue 7*, National Centre for Social and Economic Modelling, Canberra.

Keneley, M. 2001, 'The evolution of the Australian life insurance industry', *Accounting, Business & Financial History*, vol. 11, no. 2, pp. 145–70.

Kerin, J. 1991, *Budget speech 1991–92*, 20 August, Australian Government, Canberra.

Kewley, T. H. 1973, *Social security in Australia 1900–72*, Sydney University Press, Sydney.

Kingston, G., Piggott, J. & Bateman H., 1992, 'Customised investment strategies for accumulations superannuation' in *Superannuation and the Australian financial system*, eds K. Davis & I. Harper, Allen & Unwin, Sydney, pp. 139–56.

Klumpes, P. 1992, 'Financial deregulation and the superannuation boom: A crisis in Australian financial services regulation?' in *Superannuation and the Australian financial system*, eds K. Davis, & I. Harper, Allen & Unwin, Sydney, pp. 122–38.

Korporaal, G. 2012, 'Targeting super tax breaks would be a "disaster" ', *The Australian*, January 4.

Langley, P. 2004, 'In the eye of the "perfect storm": The final salary pensions crisis and financialisation of Anglo-American capitalism', *New Political Economy*, vol. 9, no. 4, pp. 539–58.

Mann, K. 1993, 'Supermen, women and pensioners: The politics of superannuation reform', *International Journal of Sociology and Social Policy*, vol. 13, no. 7, pp. 29–62.

Martin, P. & G. Hutchens (2014) 'Low-income earners hit hardest by Abbott super changes', *Sydney Morning Herald*, 3 September. http://www.smh.com.au/federal-politics/political-news/lowincome-earnershit-hardest-by-abbott-super-changes-20140903-10by18.html

Martin, R., Rafferty, M. & Bryan, D. 2008, 'Financialization, risk and labour', *Competition & Change*, vol. 12, no. 2, pp. 120–32.

NSCI (National Superannuation Committee of Inquiry) 1976, *Occupational superannuation in Australia: Final report of the Superannuation Committee of Inquiry, part two*, Australian Government, Canberra.

Nielson, L. & Harris, B. 2009, *Chronology of superannuation and retirement income in Australia*, Department of Parliamentary Services, Canberra.

Olsberg, D. 1997, *Ageing and money: Australia's retirement revolution*, Allen & Unwin, Sydney.

OECD (Organisation for Economic Co-operation and Development), 2009, *Pensions at a glance: Retirement incomes systems in OECD countries*, Organisation for Economic Co-operation and Development, Paris.

OECD 2011, *Pensions at a glance: Retirement-income systems in OECD countries*, Organisation for Economic Co-operation and Development, Paris.

Pierson, P. 1993, 'When effect becomes cause: Policy feedback and policy change', *World Politics*, vol. 4, no. 3, pp. 595–628.

Quiggin, J. 2011, 'To sell or not', *Finance & Development*, vol. 48, no. 4, pp. 34–7.

Rafter, B. 1986, 'Superannuation in Australia: The place of life offices', in *Finance of old age*, ed. R. Mendelsohn, Centre for Research on Federal Financial Relations, Canberra, pp. 231–49.

Sawer, G. 1956, *Australian federal politics and law, 1901–1929*, Melbourne University Press, Melbourne.

SSCHA (Senate Select Committee on Housing Affordability in Australia) 1988, *A good house is hard to find: Housing affordability in Australia*, Australian Government, Canberra.

Sharp, R. 2009, 'The Super revolution', in *The Hawke legacy*, eds G. Bloustein, B.comber & A. Mackinnon, Wakefield Press, Kent Town, pp. 198–211.

Sharp, R. & Austen, R. 2006, 'The 2006 federal budget: A gender analysis of the super taxation concessions', *Australian Journal of Labour Economics*, vol. 10, pp. 61–77.

Smith, J. 2004, *Taxing popularity: The story of taxation in Australia*, 2nd edn, Australian Tax Research Foundation, Sydney.

Spies-Butcher, B. & Stebbing, A. 2009, Reforming Australia's hidden welfare state: Social tax expenditures as welfare for the rich, Occasional Paper No. 6, Centre for Policy Development, Sydney.

Spies-Butcher, B. & Stebbing, A. 2011, 'Population ageing and tax reform in a dual welfare state', *Economic and Labour Relations Review*, vol. 22, no. 3, pp. 45–64.

Stebbing, A. & Spies-Butcher, B. 2010, 'Universal welfare by other means? Social tax expenditures and the Australian dual welfare state', *Journal of Social Policy*, vol. 39, no. 4, pp. 585–606.

Titmuss, R. 1958, *Essays on the welfare state*, Unwin University Books, London.

Treasury 2001, 'Toward higher retirement incomes for Australians: A history of the Australian retirement incomes system since Federation', *Economic Roundup*, Centenary Edition, pp. 65–92.

Treasury 2010, *The intergenerational report 2010*, Department of Treasury, Canberra.

Treasury 2012, *Tax expenditure statement 2012*, Department of Treasury, Canberra.

Treasury 2014, *Tax expenditure statement 2014*, Department of Treasury, Canberra.

Wallis, S. 1997, *Financial system inquiry: Final report*, Australian Government, Canberra.

Warren, D. 2008, Australia's retirement income system: Historical development and effects of recent reforms, Melbourne Institute Working Paper No. 23/08, Melbourne Institute, Melbourne.

Whiteford, P. 2004, 'Reforming pensions: The Australian experience' in *Rethinking the welfare state: The political economy of pension reform*, eds M. Rein & W. Schmahl, Edward Elgar, Cheltenham, pp. 83–101.

Wilkinson, R. & Pickett, K. 2009, *The spirit level: Why more equal societies almost always do better*, Allen Lane, London.

Yates, J. 2010, Housing and tax: The triumph of politics over economics, paper prepared for the conference on Australia's future tax system: A post-Henry review, Sydney, 21–23 June.

4

Social benefit bonds: Financial markets inside the state

Angela Mitropoulos and Dick Bryan

Social benefit bonds (SBBs), also referred to as social impact bonds (SIBs), are a very recent innovation in the fields of social policy and finance.[1] They are profoundly challenging the conventional division between states and markets, and public and private sectors, since they involve the private funding of programs that are embedded within the provision of state services. So, unlike privatisation and subcontracting, where the state cedes high levels of control to non-state providers, SBBs bring financial calculation and the pursuit of financial yield inside the state. To date, they have applied exclusively to welfare programs (specifically recidivism in the prison sector and juvenile offence in the context of foster care). For politicians preoccupied with fiscal austerity, SBBs are depicted as an instrument that creatively breaks the impasse of restricted public policy funding and passes the risk of policy initiatives outside the state. For welfare service providers strapped for cash,

Mitropoulos, A. & Bryan, D. 2015, 'Social benefit bonds: Financial markets inside the state', in *Markets, rights and power in Australian social policy*, eds G. Meagher & S. Goodwin, Sydney University Press, Sydney.

1   The first such bond was issued in September 2011, in relation to Peterborough Prison in the United Kingdom (Social Finance 2011).

SBBs anticipate a significant expansion of resources, albeit with added dimensions of performance accountability and metrics. For private financial investors, these bonds are presented as alternative investment devices that promise yield and the ability to diversify risk in their portfolios.

While many currently operate as only pilot schemes, SBBs represent a significant transformation in the conception, funding and operation of an increasing number of social policy domains. They warrant close consideration, both in terms of their merits as a form of funding of state initiatives and their applications beyond their present focus. In this chapter, we will develop:

1. A brief account of the background of the policy environment in which SBBs have emerged.
2. An overview of the recent development of SBBs in Australia.
3. An analysis of the SBBs as financial instruments: What is the *bond* in social benefit bonds?
4. An analysis of SBBs as social policy instruments: What is the *social* in social benefits bonds?
5. A conclusion about the wider social and policy significance of the arrival of SBBs.

The policy context of the emergence of SBBs

While SBBs express a financial logic – which we will explain shortly – it would be misleading to present them merely as a new financial invention without social and historical context. Building on the concepts of social entrepreneurship, social investment and social enterprise, SBBs articulate an agenda of blending philanthropy and profitable investment. Social Finance UK has been at the forefront of initiating this on a global scale. Their depiction of their role is revealing:

> Many charities and social enterprises face serious financial challenges that stop them from carrying out their work effectively. We believe that, if social problems are to be tackled successfully, organisations seeking to solve them need sustainable revenues and investment to innovate and grow ...

Social Finance brings together individuals with substantial expertise in finance, strategy consultancy and the social sector to drive innovative, sustainable and scalable investment propositions. We combine a deep understanding of social issues with expertise in financial modelling, business case development and investment structuring (see Social Finance 2011).

The implementation of such an initiative would not have been possible had there not been a culture advocating empowering 'communities' rather than 'bureaucrats', and 'investment' rather than 'public expenditure'. At their base, SBBs involve a particularly novel approach to, and understanding of, state capacities.

SBBs came into existence in the United Kingdom in 2011 and soon after they were being developed in Massachusetts and in New York, but the United Kingdom most clearly reveals their social foundations. SBBs were given focus by the Blair Labour government (1997–2007) through the Social Investment Taskforce, established by Gordon Brown as Chancellor in 2000. By 2010 the taskforce was clearly an advocate for the introduction of SBBs (Social Investment Taskforce 2010), but their realisation awaited the broader social politics of the subsequent Conservative–Liberal government (2010–). SBBs became a significant component of that government's 'Big Society' program. According to the Prime Minister David Cameron, the stated aim of Big Society is to take power away from politicians and empower local people and communities. This vision of social policy promises to replace the massive receipt of state help with a new culture of voluntarism, philanthropy and social action (Cameron 2010). In this context, Big Society Finance is central, offering to 'tap into the huge pool of capital for social purposes, and thereby transforming the prospects of the socially disadvantaged' (Cohen 2012). Situated within this vision, SBBs make use of financial techniques to break down social policy into components that can be invested in and traded and, more specifically, they depict the act of financing as an instance of community involvement. The same process can be described as an agenda of reducing dependence on the state in the name of individual responsibility, or more specifically as the transfer of certain kinds of risks from the state to investors, individuals and households.

In Australia, this same focus on social transformation is critical. While it has not been characterised as part of a Big Society agenda, it has nevertheless evolved in connection to it. The federal government explains SBBs in its social investment and philanthropy hub[2] in this way:

> The financial viability of the [charitable] sector depends on the ability of organisations to generate new sources of income. For example, many charitable organisations are now providers of community services funded by state and federal government. These services include child care, aged care and community transport services for people with special needs, just to name a few.
>
> Social investment (also called impacting investing) seeks to address the limitations on the funding of social organisations by improving the flow of capital. Social investment involves actively sourcing and placing capital in investment products that generate social, environment or cultural good while delivering some financial return to the investor. This capital may be in a range of forms including quasi-equity, debt, working capital, lines of credit, and loan guarantees (Australian Government n.d.a).

This is the context in which the federal government is evaluating SBBs, although it notes that they are largely state and territory initiatives, and there is the caveat that 'there is limited research on the long-term effectiveness of [SBB]s' and they involve 'long trailing costs for government' (Australian Government n.d.b).

---

2   This hub remains ongoing despite the change in government. Indeed, it is reasonable to anticipate that it will develop increasing prevalence if the Liberal–National Party government follows even broadly the direction of the UK Conservative Party. The Federal government website states: 'The purpose of the social investment and philanthropy hub is to create a forum to share information and promote initiatives that can facilitate greater private capital flows into areas that had previously been the domain of government' (Australian Government, n.d.a).

The emergence of SBBs in Australia

Presently in Australia, SBBs exist only as pilot programs. In September 2011, NSW Treasurer Mike Baird announced that the Liberal government would establish a trial of the bonds. The government identified the reduction of prisoner re-incarceration rates and a decrease in government-subsidised foster care as the two areas in which it will conduct pilot schemes of the bond. In March 2013, contracts were signed for Australia's first SBB. The 2013–14 NSW budget announced:

> $7 million in private capital has been raised by the Newpin Social Benefit Bond to expand UnitingCare Burnside's Newpin [New Parent and Infant Network] program, which supports children in foster care to be safely restored to their families and prevents children at risk from entering care in the first place.
>
> $1 million will be provided in 2013–14 for the implementation of the Newpin Social Benefit Bond ($8.5 million over four years) (NSW Government 2013).

As summarised by the NSW Department of Family and Community Services (2013):

> The $7 million bond will initially fund four centres and pay for the expansion of UnitingCare Burnside's Newpin program which aims to break the destructive cycle of family relationships that lead to abuse and neglect.
>
> By providing intensive support to improve parenting styles, behaviour and practices, the program helps parents to build positive parent-child relationships. Newpin safely restores children in care to their families and prevents entry into care.
>
> When Newpin achieves agreed social outcomes, such as safely restoring children in care to their families or preventing entry into care, this generates significant social and economic benefits. These benefits mean the government needs to spend less on acute services and is able to spend taxpayers' money helping families in other ways. The savings delivered by successful outcomes are used to pay back the investors' upfront funding as well as provide a return to investors.

The $7 million bond is issued through a special purpose trust managed by Social Ventures Australia (SVA) with a maturity profile of seven years and three months. According to Treasurer Baird (Baird & Goward 2013), 'if the social program is effective and reaches pre-set targets, the investor is repaid their principal plus an agreed return, which is based on performance and capped at 15 percent [per annum].' SVA expects the bond to yield between 10 percent and 12 percent per annum: about double the rate of return on corporate bonds (Rose 2013).

Interest payments on the bond are to be funded by periodic performance payments to Burnside. Performance here is measured by comparing the percentage of Newpin participants deemed fit by the courts to be reunited with their children against parents outside the program whose children are in foster care. Of course, if the performance does not measure up, there is no interest payment. For the overall bond, performance is measured by whether the program achieves a 55 percent restoration rate. It is not a difficult target to meet. It is certainly above the 25 percent restoration rate among parents of fostered children without access to the program, but in 2012 the Newpin program achieved a 74 percent restoration rate (Rose 2013).

This performance measure suggests that this trial SBB is a relatively low risk investment, for the required success rate is already being surpassed. It is, no doubt, driven by the NSW government's desire to ensure the success of the bond for investors, as a foundation for further bond issues in the state. Indeed, further bond issues have already been announced. In May 2012, NSW Treasurer Baird (2012) announced the selection of:

> Social Finance and Mission Australia to jointly develop the pilot in recidivism, which aims to assist 500 repeat offenders released from Junee and Parklea prisons. The proposed bond is approximately $7 million over a term of five to six years.

As in Britain, where they are located within Big Society Finance, and in the United States where the then New York City Mayor Michael Bloomberg's direct links to finance were critical,[3] the development of

---

3   In August 2012, New York City Mayor Michael Bloomberg announced his Bloomberg Foundation, combined with Goldman Sachs, would offer an initial

SBBs in Australia has required political influence to promote an alternative vision of the public sector and to construct avenues for private finance to enter the state. In Australia, Peter Shergold has been pivotal to the unfolding of the bonds, situated at the intersection of finance and public policy, and particularly welfare policy. He has previously held senior public service positions, including Secretary of the Department of the Prime Minister and Cabinet in the Howard government and Head of the Aboriginal and Torres Strait Islander Commission. Shergold is at present a director of AMP Limited, chairman of the NSW Public Service Commission and head of the Centre for Social Impact's joint collaboration between four university business schools. He also has notable experience in welfare, having been central to the welfare reforms precipitated by the Northern Territory Emergency Response (otherwise referred to as the Intervention) introduced by the Howard government (Shergold 2013). Drawing on each of these domains, he was commissioned by the NSW government to oversee the development of SBBs in NSW (Shergold 2012).

Critically, Shergold was active in the 2012 visit to Australia by Phillip Blond, the leading intellectual in the UK Conservative government's Big Society program. As James Whelan (2012) points out, Blond 'was introduced as a "friend of Australia" by the Prime Minister (then Opposition leader) Tony Abbott to address a forum convened by the Liberal Party's thinktank, the Menzies Research Institute. During his visit, Blond briefed senior Liberals and local government officials' (2012, p. 6). Whelan goes on to note that '[e]lements of Cameron's agenda have been endorsed by the Centre for Civil Society, the Centre for Social Impact, the Sydney Institute and by the Institute of Public Af-

---

US$10 million in SBBs to fund a pilot program to reduce the recidivism rate among young offenders jailed at the Rikers Island correctional facility. Also critical in the United States is the Harvard Social Impact Bond Technical Assistance Lab (SIB Lab). Established by Harvard John F. Kennedy School of Government professor Jeffrey Liebman and funded by the Rockefeller Foundation, the lab serves as a hands-on thinktank for helping governments foster innovation and improve the results of their social-service spending. The Rockefeller grant supports current students and recent graduates of the school's Master in Public Policy program who provide pro bono assistance in government offices on all aspects of a SIB start-up phase (Pettus 2013).

fairs whose director, John Roskam, urged Tony Abbott to adopt the "Big Society" program' (2012, p. 6).

What is the bond in social benefit bonds?

Bonds are familiar as ways of issuing debt for state and corporate treasuries. Corporations and states issue bonds (corporate and treasury bonds) in which they receive money now and, in return, pay interest at specified times and repay the principal at maturity. Conventionally, the funds raised by a bond issue go into consolidated revenue, and from there are used for funding all sorts of state expenditures.

Social benefit bonds are different from these conventional bonds. Indeed, the use of the term 'bond' may be something of a misnomer, designed to give an image of solidity when the process involved is closer to a version of venture capital in the domain of social policy. Their bond-like characteristic is simply that they operate for a fixed period in the sense that there is a final payout: the dividends are not in perpetuity as is the case, for example, with corporate shares.

Through SBBs, investors fund a program/intervention undertaken within or under the auspices of the state and the rate of return on the bond is contingent on the extent to which the program/intervention achieves its stated aims. The premise here is that there are new projects (though perhaps better understood as new initiatives within existing projects) that are anticipated to have positive outcomes, but for which state funding cannot be found. In this context, a state may leave the project unfunded, and forgo the potential benefits, or it could invite private funding.

The distinctive funding of social benefit bonds means that the private investor takes on the risks of the proposed program/intervention, although the investor does not actually undertake or manage the program/intervention. The investor is purely taking a risk position, much like a bet. If the program/intervention proves unsuccessful, the state has made no expenditure, and the losses are borne by the private investor. If the intervention is deemed successful, the investor will make a profit which must be paid for by the state. The source of the profit is that the state will be willing to provide funding out of the future dollars it will now not have to expend as a result of the successful intervention.

So, for example, a social benefit bond issued in relation to recidivism will, if the intervention is successful, be paid out of the funds that are now saved by the state having fewer future prisoners to house.[4] In this formulation, the state in principle faces no down-side risk (hence they have sometimes been called 'pay for success bonds').

In practice, regarding the specification of the exact terms of each SBB issuance, the sharing of risks is a matter of negotiation, and returns on the bond may well to some degree be underwritten by the state. For instance, in the NSW Newpin Social Benefit Bond, if the initiative fails in the first four years, investors will recover 75 percent of what they put in. The recovery rate drops to 50 percent in the last three years (Rose 2013). Therefore the essential proposition is not that the state faces no risk, but that the sharing of risk between the state and the investor is a critical and conscious factor in the design of each bond issue.

So what is in SBBs for the investor? In the promotional material, SBBs are sold in the name of financial institution *noblesse oblige* but nevertheless with an anticipated positive rate of return. Indeed, it is notable that the terms 'philanthropy' and 'investment returns' are never far apart. Beneath the social benefit vision there are precise financial calculations and SBBs, like all conventional financial investments, are subject to a careful risk/return calculation. We therefore need to understand SBBs in the context of financial assets generally.

In the orbit of financial derivatives, the model of SBBs is a variety of an options contract. As a derivative, SBBs involve the investor acquiring an exposure to the performance of an investment, but involve no ownership of, or say in, the organisation that implements the investment.[5] It is an option in the sense that the investor has purchased a contingent

---

4 In the case of the Peterborough Prison bond, the first SBB issued, the recidivism rates are measured for the prisoners who have received the services (the experimental group) and others with a similar profile who have not (the control group). The government will only pay the investors if the drop is 10 percent or more for the experimental group than for the control group (Hayat 2012).
5 See Bryan and Rafferty (2011) for an outline of the technical meaning and social role of derivatives. Contracts that trade movements in a measure (be it a measure expressed as a price or an index) are said to derive their value from the value of the underlying asset. While that direction of causation is now contested (in many cases derivative prices drive the price of the underlying asset), it gives rise to the term derivative.

claim: they will receive a payout should certain events occur (targets are reached). If those targets are not reached, the bond is valueless on expiry. The fact that particular SBBs may be underwritten by the state then manifests as an undermining of the stated virtue of the SBB model.

In this sense, a SBB is no different in structure from an oil or interest rate option. Alongside this, the appeal for investors is the expectation that SBBs diversify risk. The risk on an SBB is anticipated to diverge from those on corporate equities and bonds and on commodity prices and to respond to quite different determinants. It might be recalled that at the time of the financial crisis of 2007 and 2008, investors believed they had diversified portfolios. However, when the mortgage-backed securities and, subsequently, credit default swap markets started to crash, all sorts of asset markets followed them down as traders headed to cash (or gold) for fear of default by their counterparties. Yet SBBs hold no such (or little[6]) counterparty risks; their counterparty is the state: SBBs are state-guaranteed, as are conventional government bonds. Unlike standard government bonds, SBBs offer possibilities of high rates of return for successful investment: in short, they are higher risk (and hence involve a high expected return) but carry no default risk. That is a valuable set of attributes in any hedge fund portfolio.[7]

The skill in specifying an SBB is, therefore, in conceiving of modes of effective measurement of performance of an intervention, attaching a precise risk measurement to the range of possible outcomes of the intervention, and attaching a credible price to the combined measures and risks. In the same terms, the potential for future diversification of SBBs is premised on the capacity to define new 'packages' of measurable risks that attach to specific interventions and to measure outcomes that might be attributed legally and exclusively to the intervention. This

---

6   State defaults in the European Union open up the possibility that contracts with the state do carry some default risk.

7   Jonathon Greenblatt, Special Assistant to the US President and Director of the Office of Social Innovation and Civic Participation at the Domestic Policy Council has argued that such low-risk instruments [as SBBs] could emerge as an essential element in the balanced portfolios of sophisticated financial managers. Remarking on the introduction of SBBs in Massachusetts, Greenblatt went on to announce that it 'is among the first shots of a modern revolution, a transformative process that could alter the public conversation about how government interacts with the private sector and public citizenry' (Greenblatt 2011).

requirement, we will see shortly, inherently limits the applicability of SBBs to other domains of policy.

What is the social benefit in social benefit bonds?

There is a popular view, articulated in the federal government's social investment and philanthropy hub (cited earlier) that SBBs are a 'win–win' development. It is suggested that funds will flow to worthy areas that would otherwise be underfunded and, moreover, that laterally conceived projects that might otherwise be dismissed because they are risky will be precisely those that appeal to hedge fund investors. The potential benefits seem clear. However, we should note that, as formal financial contracts, SBBs embed a range of assumptions about how social policy is developing and should develop. We will note a number of implicit assumptions in SBBs: assumptions that need to be accepted if not explicitly embraced if SBBs are to become more widely used.

First, as the historical context of their emergence (discussed earlier) implies, SBBs have been conceived in an era of fiscal austerity, in which the state will leave worthy programs unfunded because, for whatever reason, it is reluctant to fund social policy by taxes or to borrow via standard treasury bonds, even if programs are expected to be long-run cost savers. Therefore the embrace of SBBs implies recognition that hitherto standard ways of funding social policy initiatives are fundamentally contested.

Second, it follows that SBBs are challenging historical dichotomies between state and market, and public and private. Unlike activities such as subcontracting and public–private partnerships, SBBs involve recognition that programs remain 'inside' the state in the sense that the domains of prisoner education and foster care are state responsibilities even if specific interventions funded by a SBB may be subcontracted. Yet, although the identification of state rather than market oversight remains critical, policy initiatives must be framed so as to comply with the requirements of commercial financial calculation.

Third, and following on from the previous point: SBBs require the calculation of quantifiable measures of performance, and dollar values attached to those figures, so that the rate of return on an intervention can be estimated in advance. Only on this basis can an investor make their risk-to-return calculations and choose whether to invest. Further, as with all experiments, and in order to calculate the internal rate of return for investors, SBBs presuppose the existence of controlled experiments, with a control group which must be denied access to the intervention, and not simply to determine whether an intervention works (gives positive outcomes), but whether it works sufficiently to generate a commercial rate of return on the investment.[8] Precise measurability of outcomes and differential access to controlled experiments then become the drivers of policy.

Fourth, as financial contracts, SBBs are future-oriented; concerned less with what is happening in the present than with probabilities about what might happen tomorrow. The pertinent question that the bonds pose is not the present but the future – not, that is to say, rates of imprisonment but the probability that prisoners will re-offend; and not with whether children should be removed from unsafe households but with the future probability that they will need removal. Indeed, it is inherent in the design of SBBs that they cannot engage the present but only the future time of intergenerational risk. So while a particular SBB-funded intervention X might be successful in the sense that it generates a positive rate of return for bond holders (and in the process peoples' lives have benefitted), SBBs cannot be used to fund the ongoing implementation of program X. Once the bond has been issued and the performance is known, the risks and the returns are known: the future becomes the present. Program X would no longer be funded by an SBB, for there are no risks to trade. Whether program X continues to be funded in a 'future present' must be determined by the willingness of governments to fund via conventional means such as taxes and standard treasury bonds or by contracting out the service.

Fifth, in the light of these 'specifications', we can appreciate why, until now at least, SBBs have been focused in the domain of crime and retraining (prisons and foster care and recidivism), and not the pursuit of other social goals. For the investor, SBBs permit bets on probabilities. Probabilities require norms, with risks (and hence returns) conceived as distributions around norms. Hence probabilities of returns to normalcy ('rectification of bads') become the natural domain

---

8 The Deed of Implementation Agreement for the Newpin Social Benefit Bond describes the control group as providing the counterfactual rate of restoration.

of SBBs rather than the pursuit of 'goods'. If we think of the possibility of SBBs in relation to, say community art, one can imagine that there would be social benefit from such an investment, but there will be no objective metric to measure the benefit, and no quantifiable future state savings from which the yield on the bond would be paid. In schools, for example, one can imagine a SBB for remedial interventions, in the names of future behaviour problem alleviation and future unemployment. But a SBB to fund advanced student progression has no potential, for there are no future government costs avoided by such current expenditures. So while SBBs are expressions of financial imagination, their innate agenda remains conservative, that is, they frame social diversity as aberrations from statistical norms.

Sixth, these norms are themselves currently presented as the unfolding agenda of social conservatism around gender, race and families that was generated, not surprisingly, by the British Conservative Party that played a critical role in bringing SBBs to life. In highlighting prisons and foster care, SBBs underscore a longstanding preoccupation of social policy with gender as it pertains to men and women perceived in narrow and often normative terms, and the breakdown of traditional familial roles and households. Particular understandings of the causes of 'family breakdown'[9] and breakdowns in 'law and order' set the target areas for SBBs, and the inability of agencies of the state to ameliorate these breakdowns, in turn, then creates the space for investment in the guise of a philanthropy providing social antidotes. In any event, these antidotes cannot address the reasons for breakdowns in families or in law and order; they can only remediate failure because of the way futurity is embedded in the structure of the bonds. Indeed, it is impossible to understand the recent history and future-oriented time of the SBBs without underscoring the ways in which issues of racism, poverty and gender inequality have been reframed as questions of household volatility and risk (Mitropoulos 2012).

---

9 There is here the presumption that 'fragile families' have been the cause of increasing rates of imprisonment and recidivism since the 1970s (Wildeman & Western 2010), as distinct from changes to social policy and criminal law which have enacted vast differences in the treatment of offenders and sentencing rates of comparable crimes (see Wacquant 2009).

Conclusion

While SBBs are currently small in scale and value, they represent a new and important frontier of social policy, premised on integrating global finance and key public policy initiators in what are essentially social experiments. Characterised by Social Finance UK as 'blended (social and financial) return on investment' in which the 'social and financial imperatives are aligned', SBBs enshrine a positive culture of competition and innovation in social and community services, one enabled by the application of market discipline that rewards effective service providers; and therefore crucial to catalysing a new social economy (Bolton & Savell 2010, pp. 7, 10, 19).

This perspective changes the terms of much contemporary social policy debate. While concerns for the growth of neoliberalism focus on the need to defend collective endeavours under the auspices of the state, here we see collective endeavours re-conceived as private opportunities for hedge funds and venture capital. What makes the introduction of SBBs significant in this context is that they open up the domain of the private (and the calculus of profitability) within the state. In a small but significant way, SBBs thereby shift many of the conventional debates about the state and social policy. According to Jane Jensen (2009, p. 450, emphasis in the original):

> In contrast to neoliberalism that focused on restoring market forces 'displaced' by social spending, in the social investment perspective the state may have a legitimate role if it acts to increase the probability of *future* profits and positive outcomes. This objective-setting in future terms is exemplified by the overriding concentration ... on *breaking* the intergenerational cycle of poverty and disadvantage rather than on *ending* poverty.

The advocates of SBBs, and those in the welfare sector who embrace their introduction as manna from heaven, might reflect that while new projects may come online, and some positive outcomes may be achieved, the framework of venture capital and the stamp of profitability will be setting agendas. In the process, the state itself becomes the enforcer of – not a site of alternatives, let alone resistance to – those commercial agendas.

References

Australian Government n.d.a, Social investment and philanthropy hub. http://si.notforprofit.gov.au

Baird, M. 2012, 'NSW Government announces joint development phase for social benefit bonds', Joint media release, 20 March. http://tiny.cc/1rr1qx

Baird, M. & Goward P. 2013, 'NSW government signs Australia's first social benefit bond', Media release, 27 March. http://tiny.cc/8sr1qx

Bolton, E. & Savell, L. 2010, *Towards a new social economy: Blended value creation through social impact bonds*, Social Finance Report, Social Finance UK. http://www.socialfinance.org.uk/towards-a-new-social-economy/

Bryan, D. & Rafferty, M. 2011, 'Deriving capital's (and Labour's) future', *The Socialist Register*, vol. 47, pp. 196–223.

Cameron, D. 2010, Transcript of a speech by the prime minister on the Big Society, 19 July. http://www.number10.gov.uk/news/big-society-speech/

Cohen 2012, 'Big Society capital marks a paradigm shift', *Stanford Social Innovation Review*, Summer. http://tiny.cc/jwr1qx

Greenblatt, J. 2011, 'Social impact bonds bring social innovation to the Bay State', *The Huffington Post*, 5 September. http://www.huffingtonpost.com/jonathan-greenblatt/shot-heard-round-the-worl_b_858961.html

Hayat, U. 2012, 'Social impact bonds: Turning the recidivism rate into an internal rate of return', *Enterprising Investor*, CFA Institute, 20 June. http://tiny.cc/onu1qx

Jensen, J. 2009, 'Lost in translation: The social investment perspective and gender equality', *Social Politics: International Studies in Gender, State and Society*, vol. 16, no. 4, pp. 446–83.

Mitropoulos, A. 2012, *Contract and contagion: From biopolitics to oikonomia*, New York, Minor Compositions/Autonomedia. http://www.minorcompositions.info/wp-content/uploads/2012/10/contractandcontagion-web.pdf

NSW Department of Family and Community Services 2013, Newpin social benefit bond. http://tiny.cc/zpu1qx

NSW Government 2013, 'Investing to improve services and lives', Budget 2013–14, 18 June. http://tiny.cc/0qu1qx

Pettus, A. 2013, 'Pay for progress: Social impact bonds', *Harvard Magazine*, July–August.

Rose, S. 2013, 'UnitingCare Burnside takes first NSW social benefit bond to market', *Australian Financial Review*, 27 March. http://tiny.cc/tru1qx

Shergold, P. 2012, Social impact bonds: New winds of change in Canada, Centre for Social Impact Blog, 16 March https://secure.csi.edu.au/site/Home/

Blog.aspx?defaultblog=https://blog.csi.edu.au/2012/03/
social-impact-bonds-new-winds-of-change-in-canada/

Shergold, P. 2013, 'Foreword' to *In black and white: Australians all at the crossroads*, eds R. Craven, A. Dillon & N. Parbury, Sydney, Connorcourt Publishing.

Social Finance n.d., About us. http://www.socialfinance.org.uk/about/vision

Social Finance 2011. http://www.socialfinance.org.uk

Social Investment Taskforce Final Report 2010, 'Social investment: Ten years on', April. http://www.socialinvestmenttaskforce.org/downloads/
SITF_10_year_review.pdf

Wacquant, L. J. D. 2009, *Punishing the poor: The neoliberal government of social insecurity*, Durham NC, Duke University Press.

Whelan, J. 2012, 'The influence of "Big Society": Abbott borrows from UK conservatives', *The Conversation*, 20 June. http://theconversation.com/
the-influence-of-big-society-abbott-borrows-from-uk-conservatives-7652

Wildeman, C. & Western B. 2010. 'Incarceration in fragile families', *Future of Children*, vol. 20, no. 2, pp. 157–77. http://futureofchildren.org/
futureofchildren/publications/docs/20_02_08.pdf

5

'Which bank?' Competition and community service obligations in the retail banking sector

Leanne Cutcher and Johann Loibl

In all the discussion about the impact of privatisation and marketisation on public service delivery, one area that is often overlooked is banking services. Yet banking is an interesting case because it offers an example of the state deliberately stimulating competition through a government-owned business enterprise (GBE). Acknowledging this potential role of the state and GBEs is important because, as Murray Goot argues, 'for a generation, much of the free market Right as well as the interventionist Left seem to have forgotten the history of state intervention not as a way of stifling competition but as a way of encouraging it' (2010, p. 83). Accordingly, in the first section of the chapter we provide an overview of how the Fisher Labor government (1910–13) aimed to increase competition in banking by establishing the Commonwealth Bank of Australia (CBA). This federal government bank was set up to compete with both the privately owned *and* state government-owned banks. We also highlight how, during the establishment phase of the bank, a discourse of 'community service' ran alongside a 'competition' discourse (Goot 2010, p. 78) and explore how prior to privatisation, the Commonwealth Bank was tasked with twin goals of increasing com-

---

petition in the sector while meeting community service obligations. In other words, throughout this period, the Commonwealth Bank was operating under two institutional logics: a market logic and a community logic. Under a market logic, the sources of legitimacy and authority are the share price and shareholder activity and the norm is one of self-interest (Thornton, Ocasio & Lounsbury 2012, p. 69). Under a community logic, legitimacy and authority are derived from belief in trust and reciprocity and a commitment to community, and values and norms are based on group membership (Thornton et al. 2012, p. 70). This chapter shows how, over time, the community logic came to be overshadowed by the market logic in the CBA.

In the Australian context, state intervention in banking has always been cast as a way to 'increase competition'; however, just what this means has invariably reflected political, historical and economic reasoning (cf. Rosamond 2002). By the 1980s and 1990s, in line with broader neoliberal discourse, it was thought that competition was best achieved by exposing domestic markets to outside pressure and introducing overseas private sector banks into the sector. One consequence of this was the privatisation of a raft of government-owned banks, including the Commonwealth Bank. We show how opening up the banking market and privatising government-owned banks, in particular the Commonwealth Bank, has produced mixed outcomes for retail bank consumers and has allowed the large for-profit banks to argue that market and community logics are not compatible.

Most recently, the pervasiveness of this discourse about the incompatibility of market and community logics has seen the former federal Labor government (2007–13) turn to the smaller, not-for-profit financial mutuals to deliver on community service obligations for the sector, rather than stipulating that the large for-profit banks incorporate such provisions into their practice. Mutual financial organisations derive their legitimacy and authority from an associational logic, much like the community logic Thornton and colleagues (2012) identify, in that their authority and legitimacy come from belief in sharing and reciprocity, embedded in a norm of the equality of all group members.

The promotion of mutuals as hybrid banks, run on both market and associational logics, mirrors international trends in public sector reform with governments increasingly turning to the not-for-profit sector to provide services and increase consumer choice (Kelly 2007).

What is different about moves by the former federal Labor government to champion financial mutuals is that they were seeking to increase competition at arm's length, with no direct involvement of the government in the workings of those institutions. Rather they appear to be using the notion of financial mutuals and mutuality as a discursive foil to the dominance of the sector by the big four banks.

Competition, community service obligations and a Commonwealth-owned bank

Love (1984, p. 42) reports that in 19th-century Australia there was a 'deeply ingrained suspicion of the probity of bankers, and a conviction that private banking, by its very nature, was not serving the interests of the community as a whole'. These sentiments were reinforced by the bank crash of 1893, which created the general belief that 'the existing banks were avaricious and incompetent' (Gollan 1968, p. 18). On one hand, there was a general view that the private banks had saved themselves at the expense of their customers by destroying their deposits (Butlin 1961), while, on the other, the various state government-owned banks were seen to have acted with propriety and, as a result, their customers were less affected by the crash (Singh 1991). Against this backdrop the Labor movement began to campaign for a federal government-owned bank that could wrest control of the financial system from private bankers. A national, government-owned bank was seen as a 'weapon with which Labor could attack the entrenched positions of capital' (Gollan 1968, p. 93) and where the public's deposits would be safe from 'the perils of dividend-hungry shareholders and speculating, reckless directors' (Love 1984, p. 44).

When the Australian colonies became a Federation in 1901, the newly formed Australian Labor Party began the process of developing national policies on a range of issues on which the Commonwealth Constitution gave the federal parliament power to act (Love 1984, p. 48). Section 51 (xiii) specified 'Banking, other than State banking; also State banking extending beyond the limits of the State concerned, the incorporation of banks, and the issue of paper money'. The Labor Party accepted this opportunity with alacrity because it offered a chance to shape the country's monetary system along lines similar to those advocated for state government-owned banks but on a national scale (Love 1984, p. 48). Accordingly, the focus of debate shifted in the Labor Party from the state to the federal arena with support for government banking so strong that when a proposal to establish a Commonwealth Bank came before the 1902 Federal Labor Conference it was approved with very little discussion (Love, 1984).

In 1911 a 'People's Bank' was born, one which would, in the words of the Prime Minister, Andrew Fisher, 'be a bank belonging to the people, and directly managed by the people's own agents' (Fisher 1911, cited in Singh 1991, p. 120). Fisher went on to explain: 'this is a business concern pure and simple; it is not a matter of idealism'. Here Fisher is alluding to the fact that, from the outset, a key reason for establishing the Commonwealth Bank was to engender competition in banking. Quiggin (1995, p. 31) argues that Australia was unique in the extent to which GBEs operated alongside private firms, in industries such as banking, airlines, insurance and telecommunications. In banking, as Goot (2010, p. 82) has observed, the idea of the state as a competitor was pushed one step further with the idea that it would not only compete against private sector banks but other state government-owned banks. In the first years of its existence the Commonwealth Bank did not compete aggressively with the other banks, but its presence did have an impact on the state-owned banks. This was in large part because when the Commonwealth Bank began full operations in 1913 it took up exclusive right to use post offices as branches, closing off this option to the state government-owned banks that had been using the post offices as deposit agencies (McCarthy 2002).

The Second World War provided the Commonwealth Bank with the opportunity to increase its competitive position vis-à-vis the private banks. During the War, the Commonwealth Bank was given the authority of a central bank, and thereby equipped with the power to set interest rates (Merrett 2006, p. 57). The role of the CBA was further strengthened with passing of the *Commonwealth Bank Act* (1945) which set a clear directive for the CBA to compete with the other banks (Merrett 1998) and to expand its general banking business (Singh 1991, p. 11). The 1945 Act constituted the bank as a central bank and reflected the postwar Labor policy approach, which used public bodies to stabilise the market system. Not surprisingly, the private banks were opposed to the fact that the Commonwealth would be a competing commercial bank at the same time that it operated as a central bank. Over time, these two functions were progressively separated within the bank, and their formal separation was legislated in the *Banking Act* (1959), which established two distinct bodies: the Reserve Bank of Australia and the Commonwealth Banking Corporation (Evatt Research Centre 1988, p. 117).

From its establishment, it was believed that, by competing directly with the private trading banks, the CBA would discourage the other banks from taking unfair advantage of their customers by providing competitive home loans, return strong dividends to the government, and ensure good wages and conditions for employees in the sector. It was the case that, until the early 1980s, home loan rates of the CBA were significantly below those of most of its competitors, which led to it becoming the largest lender for housing in Australia (Howard 1991, p. 18). It also lent large sums to local and semi-government bodies for essential services, including roads, electricity and sewerage (Evatt Research Centre 1988, p. 22). Competing in the same segment of the market as the private banks but with the benefit of economies of scale and the backing of the federal government enabled the CBA to generate significant profits and pay reasonable dividends to the government. For example, in 1987, in addition to paying taxes of $1.316 million, the Commonwealth Bank transferred $61.4 million to government revenue (Evatt Research Centre 1988, p. 138). Competition in the financial services labour market also led to improved wages and working conditions across the sector. With the CBA offering more attractive salaries, the private banks had to follow suit in order to attract highly skilled workers.

The CBA also generated business banking and increased its competitive position by means of its Development Bank arm, founded in 1959. The Commonwealth Development Bank lent to small and rural businesses which had potential but, because of a lack of security and/or personal contacts, were either ignored by the private banks or could not get access to reasonable funding (Jones 2002). The Commonwealth Bank also played a crucial role in the development of the Australian manufacturing industry by underwriting the original loans for both BHP and General Motors Holden (Evatt Research Centre 1988, p. 22).

At the same time that the *Commonwealth Bank Act* (1945) set out a clear aim for the CBA to compete with other banks, it also legislated for the bank to act in the national interest. As set out in Clause 8 of the Act:

> It shall be the duty of the Commonwealth Bank, within the limits of its powers, to pursue a money and banking policy directed to the greatest advantage of the people of Australia, and to exercise its power under this Act and the Banking Act, 1945 in such a manner as, in the opinion of the Bank, will best contribute to: a) stability of the currency of Australia, b) the maintenance of full employment and c) the economic prosperity and welfare of the people of Australia (cited in Evatt Research Centre 1988, p. 22).

This clause made manifest the community service obligations of the CBA, which had been loosely framed with its establishment in 1911. As Martin (1996, p. 111) explains:

> A community service obligation arises when a government specifically requires a public enterprise to carry out activities relating to outputs or inputs which it would not elect to do on a commercial basis, and which the government does not require other businesses in the public or private sector to undertake, or which it would only do commercially at higher prices.

The CBA's community service obligations involved lending to charities and non-profit making bodies, and to local government as well as semi-government authorities, occasionally at concessional rates, as well as ensuring service delivery to people with disabilities, low-income earners, people from non-English-speaking background and Aboriginal people (Howard 1991, p. 18). Having a hybrid bank, which operated under both market and community logics, in the sector had consequences not only for the other banks in terms of competition, but also for customers in terms of equitable access to financial services.

We can see how both a market logic and a community logic (Thornton et al. 2012) influenced banking practice when we examine the CBA's prior commitment to the provision of an extensive branch network. The Evatt Research Centre points out that if a bank branch was to be found somewhere in the outback in the 1980s, it was most likely to be a branch of the CBA (1988, p. 136). Prior to privatisation, the CBA had the biggest branch network in the industry, serving approximately 27 percent of the banking industry's retail customers (ACA 1990). The cost of providing such an extensive bank branch network was implied by David Anderson, Secretary of the CBA:

> It would be difficult I think for a privately owned bank to perhaps justify the total spread of branches. If we get to the stage of being totally driven by (the) bottom line, then people are going to have less of a service than they might be enjoying at the moment (cited in Howard 1991, p. 18).

As a result of strict regulatory controls, Australian banks could not differentiate the products they offered, therefore, market advantage was achieved by offering customer service through an extensive branch network, which allowed the CBA to attract more and more customers (Taylor & Hirst 1983, p. 267). Under its charter as a government-owned bank, the CBA's obligation to cross-subsidise the less profitable branches in the rural areas left its competitors little choice but to follow suit and extend their branch networks.

In line with the community logic that informed much of the CBA's practice, this extensive branch network not only helped to ensure access to banking services for Australians living in rural and remote communities, it also helped to ameliorate the consequences of financial illiteracy. Financial literacy is the ability to make informed judgements and to make effective decisions regarding the use and management of money (Noctor, Stoney & Stradling 1992). In the 1980s, levels of financial literacy in Australia were low. One survey of 1500 Australian adults revealed that 27 percent could not fill out deposit slips correctly, 39 percent failed in writing out cheques and 45 percent were unable to keep records of their financial transactions (Wickert 1989, p. 53). However, at that time the limited number of bank products and an extensive bank branch network meant that the level of financial literacy needed to participate in the financial industry was also low. Most of the financial transactions happened face-to-face, over the counter in branches, and bank customer service officers were regarded as trusted advisors who ensured that customers were not disadvantaged (Singh 1989).

The existence of a large, public bank that operated under both market and community logics impacted the sector as a whole. Prior to its privatisation, the Commonwealth Bank shaped the nature of the Australian banking industry by providing greater security and competitive home loans to consumers, returning strong dividends to the Commonwealth, ensuring fair employment conditions for workers in the sector, lending to small and rural businesses and offering an extensive branch network. The bank was a product of government legislation that 'reflected a deeply entrenched view of the past that there is a valuable contribution to be made to the economy by the public sector' (Evatt Research Centre 1988, p. 114). As Goot (2010) has argued, it is possible then for a public sector provider to both drive competition in the sector, not just in terms of price but also to drive higher levels of service delivery. The privatisation of the bank and deregulation of the industry resulted in significant shifts in the banks' relationships with their customers. The consequences of these shifts are outlined in the following section.

Competition, community service obligations and privatisation

In the previous section we outlined the role played by the CBA in ensuring competition in the banking sector, access to affordable banking products and engagement in a range of community service obligations. In this section of the chapter we show how privatisation of the Commonwealth Bank in 1991 has led to mixed outcomes in terms of competition in the retail banking sector. In addition, while rates of financial literacy have remained similar to those prior to privatisation, the number and complexity of financial service products on offer to consumers mean that higher levels of financial literacy are needed if consumers are to make prudent and informed financial decisions.

Prior to its election in March 1983, Labor had condemned the proposals for financial deregulation put forward by the Campbell Committee (1981), which the Fraser Coalition government had commissioned to inquire into the financial system in 1979. After the election, Labor's position on financial deregulation was rapidly reversed and, by 1986, policies of deregulation more radical than those the Campbell Committee proposed had been adopted (Quiggin 2001). All this change was framed within a discourse of increasing competition in financial services. As Schaefer and colleagues (2011) have noted, the idea of competition has, under neoliberal regimes, been a significant driver of efforts to deregulate and privatise. The Australian dollar exchange rate was floated in December 1983 and exchange controls were lifted (Hand 2001, p. 14). In 1984, foreign-owned banks were allowed to operate in all areas of the industry, and as a result 16 licences were issued for foreign banks, although not all were taken up. According to Kitay (2003, p. 136), it was particularly notable that those foreign banks which attempted to establish a retail presence made little impression on the market at that time, and most restricted their activities primarily to merchant banking activities. Around the same time a number of domestic non-banking financial institutions such as building societies were granted banking licences. While extensive financial deregulation was introduced in Australia between 1981 and 1985, at that time privatisation of the Commonwealth Bank and the state government-owned banks was not seriously advocated (Quiggin 1995, p. 31). So while many argue that deregulation and privatisation invariably go hand-in-hand, the case of banking shows that deregulation can occur without privatisation of GBEs. This is important because, as Quiggin (1995, p. 32) argues, it challenges the notion that privatisation is necessary to promote reform of a sector and the association between reform through regulation and privatisation is 'primarily one of political compatibility rather than of logical implication'.

The privatisation of a number of government-owned banks, including the federal government-owned Commonwealth Bank began in the 1990s. The *Commonwealth Banks Restructuring Act* of 1990 converted the Commonwealth Bank from a statutory authority to a public company with conventional share capital and part-government ownership. On 17 April 1991, the organisation became a public company with a share capital governed by the Corporations Law but subject to certain overriding provisions of the *Commonwealth Banks Act 1959*. The Commonwealth Bank was fully privatised in three stages between 1991 and July 1996. Quiggin (2001) notes that, at each stage in the privatisation of the Commonwealth Bank, the government made solemn assurances that this sale would be the last. However, these apparently binding commitments to continue major public ownership were made and subsequently broken. The need to rescue the State Bank of Victoria was eventually used to force through the full privatisation of the Commonwealth Bank (Quiggin 2001).

While all this change was underpinned by a mantra of 'increased competition' and better choice for banking consumers, the outcomes of opening up the market to foreign competition and privatisation of government-owned banks have been mixed. This is in part because at the same time that bank licences were granted to building societies and government-owned banks were privatised, there was a series of retail bank mergers which resulted in the domination of the industry by the big four banks: the Commonwealth, ANZ, NAB and Westpac. As a result, Australia now has one of the most concentrated retail banking markets in the world, with only 12 domestic banks, nine foreign subsidiaries and 35 foreign branch banks (not all of which offer retail banking services) (APRA 2010).

Further consolidation of the industry is not possible because of the 'four pillars policy'. In 1990 the then Labor Treasurer, Paul Keating, introduced the 'six pillars policy' which precluded mergers between the four major banks and the two largest insurers (AMP and National Mutual) (Wu 2008). In 1997 the Wallis Inquiry into banking argued for the removal of 'six pillars policy' and in response the then Coalition Treasurer, Peter Costello, removed the ban on mergers between insurance companies but maintained a ban on mergers between the four banks. By April 1997, the 'six pillars policy' had become a 'four pillars policy', which removed the previous prohibition of foreign takeovers of Australian banks but still prevented mergers among the four biggest banks (Wu 2008).

While all these changes were intended to increase choice for consumers, this did not occur across all product segments. In the home mortgage area, consumer choice increased dramatically, with the Australian Banking Association (ABA) reporting that 'prior to deregulation in 1995 customers had the choice of only 26 different home mortgage products' and just four years later the market was offering nearly 2,500 varieties of mortgages' (Local Government Banking and Financial Services Taskforce 1999, p. 11). Conversely, in the areas of retail transaction accounts and small business banking competition remained very weak (Connolly & Hajaj 2001, p. 7). In these product segments there is very little price or product differentiation across the banks, particularly the big four banks. Kitay and Rimmer (1997, p. 105) found that bank managers did not consider competing on price or product innovation to be a viable strategy.

Innovations in service delivery afforded by technological innovation offered the banks a significant way to increase profits through the closure of branches and staff redundancies. The shift away from 'bricks and mortar' service to service via a machine or in cyberspace has lead to the widespread closure of bank branches across Australia. Between 1980 and 2011, the number of bank branches fell from 11,760 to 5,588 (APRA 2011). In 1998, Anthony Aveling, the then Chief Executive Officer (CEO) of the ABA, outlined the process involved in decisions about branch closures to a House of Representatives Inquiry into regional banking services (1999), in the following terms:

> An individual bank will review the trends in an area. They will look at what has been happening to their business over a long period of time and they will make projections. If the conclusion that an individual bank comes to is that the bank branch is no longer profitable, or will not be profitable in the near future, then work is done on what are the alternative services that may be provided in that particular location (Standing Committee on Financial Institutions and Public Administration 1998).

While the ABA claimed that only unprofitable banks were closed, the House of Representatives Inquiry (1999, p. 21) found that it was not only the unprofitable branches that had been closed, concluding that: 'it is neither fair nor constructive to perpetuate this impression which in some ways could be seen to put the responsibility for a bank closing on the township rather than on the banks'. The inquiry was correct to argue that communities themselves should not bear responsibility for branch closures, yet, it is the case that closures were spatially uneven, focusing on remote settlements and deprived urban areas (Connolly & Hajaj 2001) and that this had negative consequences for those living there because they lost access to fair and safe financial products from mainstream suppliers (Beal & Ralston 1997). At the same time, financial service consumers faced an increasing array of financial service products with less access to face-to-face delivery channels through which these products could be explained. The need for financially literate consumers has also been exacerbated by the rise of 'self-service' options and the extended marketing of financial service products. Shifting attitudes towards money from an old-economy focus on wages, cash and short-term investments towards a new-economy focus on wealth and assets, savings and investments for the longer term has also increased the need for more financially literate consumers (Finlayson 2009, p. 411).

It is perhaps not surprising, then, that in the lead-up to the 2001 federal election, banking polled as the third most important issue in voters' minds. The Financial Services Union (FSU), the Australian Consumers Association (ACA), the Financial Service Centre, the Australian Pensioners and Superannuants' Federation (APSF) and the Consumer Credit Legal Centre were actively campaigning for the government to adopt a social charter for the banking industry. The social charter included minimum service standards for customers, guaranteed access to banking facilities for all Australians and an ongoing monitoring of fees and charges (Workers Online 2000). In response to this discontent and campaigning, the ABA commissioned a review of its Banking Code of Practice. The review recommended sweeping changes to the Code and took both banking industry and consumer groups by surprise in the scope of the issues raised by the independent consultant, Mr Richard Viney (Nixon 2001).

Three of the four major retail banks (notably not the CBA) responded by introducing a degree of self-regulation. This self-regulation has led to some benefits for low-income customers. In July 2001 Westpac launched its Customer Service Charter which, according to the then Westpac Group Executive, Ann Sherry, 'provides the community with information on the way in which Westpac plans to deliver a better outcome for its customers' (Bland 2001). The latest version of this document was produced in August 2011 and is entitled 'Principles for doing business'. The ANZ launched its Customer Charter in September of 2001 and it is still prominent on their website. The two-page document sets out clear benchmarks for the provision of service to customers, including commitments on access to services, personal information and an improved complaint resolution process. The NAB held a consultation forum chaired by social justice campaigner Reverend Tim Costello, in May 2001 and this led to the introduction of a basic (fee free) bank account for low-income customers (Bland 2001).

Privatisation of the government-owned banks has failed to deliver on its promise of increasing competition, with Australia continuing to have a highly concentrated banking market. In some segments, financial services consumers have very little choice; in other areas, product choice has expanded greatly, increasing the need for higher levels of financial literacy. Widespread branch closures have left many communities without local financial services. Change has been fast-paced in this sector and has not benefited all financial consumers. As the impact of the loss of government-owned state banks became evident, a range of government inquiries were called into the retail banking sector. The most wide-ranging of these, the Wallis Inquiry, concluded that it is not the role of the banks to meet community service obligations because cross-subsidisation of banking services would counteract efficiency in a competitive market (Wallis 1997, p. 196). The ABA argued to the Wallis Inquiry that it was the duty of the government or smaller deposit-taking institutions to ensure equitable access to financial services in Australia (Griffith 2000, p. 4). This final section of the chapter shows how this argument has impacted on those smaller deposit-taking institutions, with some of those organisations embracing calls to be the 'fifth pillar' in banking.

Competition, community service obligations and mutuals

As a result of the Global Financial Crisis (GFC), the Australian retail banking market has undergone a structural shift. As Johnston (2009) reports, the big four banks – Westpac, ANZ, NAB and CBA – have used their position to acquire weaker rivals and take over banking business from smaller banks, non-bank lenders and mortgage brokers. In 2009, the big four banks were writing more than 90 percent of the nation's new mortgages, compared with approximately 60 percent before the GFC (Johnston 2009, p. 7). In response to further consolidation of the market following the acquisition of BankWest by the Commonwealth Bank in 2009, the architect of much of Australia's banking reform and the driver of privatisation of the Commonwealth Bank, Paul Keating, reiterated the need for the federal government to retain the 'four pillars policy' to ensure adequate competition in the sector.

In response to the increasing consolidation of the sector, in 2010 Wayne Swan, Treasurer in the Gillard Labor government, announced a number of reforms aimed at increasing competition in the sector. The central plank of these reforms was the creation of a fifth banking pillar, which he envisaged as the combined power of the mutual sector. Financial mutuals are not-for-profit organisations that are owned by and for their members. Mutualism can be described as a sort of radical communitarianism or collectivism, in which individuals are tied to others through a variety of economic and social links (Parker, Fournier & Reedy 2007, p. 186). A mutual organisation, then, is owned by the people that do business with it. All members of the mutual have equal voting rights, with one vote per member, and any profits are reinvested back into the mutual for the benefit of members. As noted above, mutuals operate under an associational logic, which as Cato (2013) argues is based on notions of reciprocity and mutualism that long predate the market-based economy that is so often presented as the (ahistorical) norm.

In Australia, credit unions are the most common form of financial mutual. The early Australian credit union movement drew on both Raiffeisen philosophy, which influenced the movement in Europe, and Catholic teaching, which underpinned the development of credit unions in Canada and the United States. In the 1850s in Europe, Friedrich Wilhelm Raiffeisen, a German burgomaster, adapted the Schulze-Delitzch concept of self-help people's banks to establish an independent farmer-based credit association (Lewis 1996, p. xxi). The idea of mutual self-help is central to the Raiffeisen notion of 'limitless liability', achievable through a bond of association, whereby a person's trusted standing in the community and the knowledge co-operators had of each other acted as security in seeking loans from a community pool of funds' (Lewis 1996, p. xxi). Across the Atlantic, in Canada, Alphonse Desjardins, a parliamentary reporter inspired by the Papal Encyclical *Rerum novarum* (1891), developed his own philosophy for credit unions. This philosophy shared many of the principles of the European movement, including the notion of limitless liability, open membership, education in cooperation and economic and financial responsibility. Perhaps in keeping with a particular pragmatic Australian identity, the motivation of the early credit union pioneers in Australia has been characterised as simply a way to make personal credit available to ordinary working people (Cutcher & Kerr 2006). During this time, the personal credit market was dominated by loan sharks and hire-purchase finance companies, which often charged interest rates in excess of 80 percent (Cutcher & Kerr 2006). In a bid to regulate this burgeoning market, the NSW government enacted the *NSW Small Loans Facilities Act* in 1941. Credit unions were formed around bonds of association that related to working for the same employer, involvement in a social group or residing in a particular geographical area.

A small number of mutual building societies continue to operate in Australia today. Originally, the benefits of property ownership and the difficulty in obtaining housing finance from banks or private mortgagees saw the concept of building societies transplanted from the United Kingdom and take seed in Australia. Malcolm Hill (1959, p. 10) reports that, 'while there is little information on the early history of building societies in Australia, it seems that the first societies were formed in the 1840s'. However, it was in the 1880s when Australian building societies experienced their first expansion (Hill 1959, p. 4). The second period of growth for building societies came during the period of prosperity that followed the Second World War during the 1950s and 1960s (Lyons 1988, p. 388).

In Australia, up until the 1980s, mutuals were subject to their own legislative requirements and were afforded tax incentives. Not being subject to the same strict reporting requirements as the large mainstream banks and the benefits from the reduced taxes helped sustain a wide range of credit unions and mutual building societies who serviced discrete memberships (Cutcher & Mason 2013). However, a range of structural changes, most notably, demutualisation of many consumer and producer co-operatives, privatisation of the public sector, and deregulation of the financial services sector, made it increasingly difficult for smaller credit unions to survive. The result was a raft of amalgamations which saw credit union numbers fall from 549 in 1983 (Lewis 2001, p. 4) to fewer than 90 today. In 2014, the Customer Owned Banking Association, the peak industry body for financial mutuals, represented 77 credit unions, seven building societies, 11 mutual banks and 13 friendly societies.

Treasurer Swan's reforms sought to improve the mutual sector's ability to compete with the major banks. He instructed the Australian Prudential Regulatory Authority (APRA) to fast-track approval of more than 20 mutuals using the term 'bank' if they apply (at the time of writing, 11 credit unions had moved to calling themselves mutual banks). Further, mutuals were to be able to display a new, official 'government protected deposits' symbol that confirms customer savings are protected in the same way as bank deposits, and Treasury was instructed to help mutuals raise cheaper funding (Gluyas 2010). Not surprisingly, mutuals welcomed the Treasurer's endorsement. However, many commentators are doubtful that the mutual sector has the capacity to be considered a viable fifth competitor in the sector. Most of these concerns relate to insufficient capital, lack of scale and the capacity of a highly diverse grouping of relatively small institutions to act in concert and in united opposition to four major banking corporations (Johyn 2010; Oldfield 2012).

Nevertheless, the persistence of financial mutuals remind us that it is possible to combine market and associational logics in hybrid banking organisations that strike a balance between making profits and meeting community service obligations. One example is Traditional Credit Union (TCU), Australia's only Aboriginal-owned deposit-taking institution, which has been involved in service delivery to Indigenous people living in remote communities across the Northern Territory. With a head office in Darwin, it provides banking services in local languages delivered by Indigenous staff in 11 remote Aboriginal communities. TCU reinvests any surpluses they generate back into the credit union and, in particular, to the education and training of their Indigenous staff. Their approach to employing Indigenous people, delivering financial literacy programs and crafting locally responsive banking services has seen them win a number of national awards.

As noted above, following the GFC, the Australian retail banking market has become even more consolidated. At the same time that there are fewer suppliers of banking products, the range and complexity of those products has increased and this has created challenges for the significant number of financial consumers with low financial literacy. In March 2011, the Gillard Labor government launched the National Financial Literacy Strategy, which aimed to provide a set of 'initiatives to improve the financial literacy of all Australians and enhance their financial wellbeing' and transfered responsibility for delivering on the strategy to the Australian Securities and Investments Commission (ASIC 2011, p. 1). The strategy acknowledges that consumers now have greater responsibility for their financial wellbeing but have been essentially left alone to gain the capability to make the right decisions on financial matters. ASIC's key development in this area has been the construction of a new website, Money Smart, which aims 'to engage people and help consumers and investors make financial decisions that improve their lives, by providing information, tools, guidance and motivation' (ASIC 2011, p. 7). The Appendix to ASIC's strategy report sets out the financial literacy priorities and lists goals they wish to achieve against a somewhat vague timeline (short-term, medium, ongoing) in partnership with schools, the Vocational Education and Training sector, government departments and agencies and unions. Nowhere is there mention of working in partnership with financial service institutions or peak industry bodies such as the ABA. Bringing banks and their representatives back in as part of the solution is important because, as Erturk and colleagues (2007, p. 571) argue, financial literacy programs need to be accompanied by a 're-think of the design of complex financial products that reflect the kinds of risk-return preferences and innate inertia of many financial consumers'. Rather than looking towards not-for-profit charities and non-government agencies to meet the challenge of educating Australians in financial literacy, the government should have the banks as a central plank of their strategy, making them responsible not only for the delivery of educational programs, but also for the provision of consumer-friendly and affordable products and services.

By championing mutuals with their associational logic as a fifth pillar, there is a danger that they alone will be left with responsibility for meeting the community service obligations of the industry as a whole. There is no doubt that mutuals have played, and should continue to play, a key role in the financial sector. The associational logic which shapes their culture, practice and structure means that they are, in many cases, best placed to meet the needs of bank consumers who might otherwise find themselves excluded from access to necessary financial services. However, even when combined, the mutual sector cannot match the reach of the four major banks. The majority of Australians continue to bank with one of the four majors. Therefore, to ensure equitable access to affordable and appropriate financial services and products, governments need to regulate the sector so that all banking organisations operate as hybrids, combining both market and community logics, so that they derive their legitimacy from both their profit-making activities and their community service initiatives and responsibilities.

Conclusion

One hundred years ago, the then Labor government established a bank which would, in the words of Clyde Cameron, a member of the Whitlam Labor government, 'provide genuine competition to private companies which would otherwise co-operate with each other to defraud the public' (cited in Goot 2010, p. 80). The Labor government was keen to increase competition in the banking industry, this time by encouraging consumers to shift their banking business to the mutual sector. It is unclear what the conservative government's position will be. However, if they accept that the government's role in the sector is to ensure the ready availability of fair and reasonably priced financial services, then they should look for ways to ensure that banking organisations operate under both market and community logics. Creating these hybrid organisations will require the government to regulate for community service obligations in the same way that they were legislated for the Commonwealth Bank when it was established. Mutuals, rather than being a fifth pillar for the sector, could work as models of the kind of hybrid organisations needed to ensure the financial inclusion of all Australians.

This chapter has demonstrated that over time, the structure and operation of financial services in Australia have been the outcome of the interplay of a market logic, a community logic and an associational logic. This chapter has sought to show that financial service consumers are best served when a community logic operates alongside a market logic in the same organisations. Both the case of the government-owned Commonwealth Bank and the case of financial mutuals shows that it is possible for these two logics to co-exist and that bringing them together is a way to ensure equitable access to financial knowledge products and services.

References

ACA (Australian Consumers Association) 1990, Privatising without losing the People's Bank, September.

APRA (Australian Prudential Regulatory Authority) 2010, Monthly banking statistics, September (issued 29 October).

APRA 2011, Statistics: ADI points of presence, June (issued 24 August).

ASIC (Australian Securities and Investments Commission) 2011, *National financial literacy strategy*, March, pp. 1–61.

Beal, D. & Ralston, D. 1997, *Economic and social impacts of the closure of the only bank branch in rural communities*, Centre for Australian Financial Institutions, Toowoomba.

Bland, L. 2001, 'Time to be accountable', *Sydney Morning Herald*, 26 September.

Butlin, S. 1961, 'Australia and New Zealand bank', in *Laissez-faire banking*, ed. K. Dowd, Routledge, London.

Campbell, K. 1981, *Final report of the Committee of Inquiry into the Australian financial system*, AGPS, Canberra.

Cato, M. 2013, 'The bioregional economy: Reclaiming our local land', in *The Routledge companion to alternative organization*, eds M. Parker, G. Cheney, V. Fournier & C. Land, Routledge, Abingdon, pp. 220–35.

Connolly, C. & Hajaj, K. 2001, *Financial services and social exclusion*, Financial Services Consumer Policy Centre, University of New South Wales, Sydney, March, pp. 1–66.

Cutcher L. & Kerr M. 2006, 'The shifting meaning of mutuality and co-operativeness in the credit union movement from 1959 to 1989', *Labour History*, vol. 91, pp. 31–46.

Cutcher, L. & Mason, P. 2013, 'Credit unions', in *The Routledge companion to alternative organization*, eds M. Parker, G. Cheney, V. Fournier & C. Land, Routledge, Abingdon, pp. 251–266.

Erturk, I., Froud, J., Johal, S., Leaver, A. & Williams, K. 2007, 'The democratization of finance? Promises, outcomes and conditions', *Review of International Political Economy*, vol. 14, no. 4, pp. 553–75.

Evatt Research Centre 1988, *The capital funding of public enterprise in Australia*, H. V. Evatt Research Centre, Evatt Foundation, Sydney.

Finlayson, A. 2009, 'Financialisation, financial literacy and asset-based welfare', *The British Journal of Politics and International Relations*, vol. 11, pp. 400–21.

Gluyas, R. 2010, 'No concrete steps to hold up a fifth pillar', *The Australian*, 13 December.

Gollan, R. 1968, *The Commonwealth Bank of Australia: Origins and early history*, ANU Press, Canberra.

Goot, M. 2010, 'Labor, government business enterprises and competition policy', *Labor History*, vol. 98, pp. 77–95.

Griffith, G. 2000, *Banks and community obligations*, NSW Parliamentary Library Research Service, Briefing Paper No. 1/2000.

Hand, G. 2001, *Naked among cannibals*, Allen & Unwin, Sydney.

Hill, M. R. 1959, *Housing finance in Australia*, Melbourne University Press, Carlton.

House of Representatives Standing Committee on Economics, Finance and Public
Administration 1999, *Regional banking services: Money too far away,*
Parliament of the Commonwealth of Australia, March, pp. 1–123.

Howard, M. 1991, *Response to deregulation: The recent and future role of the
Commonwealth Bank,* Public Sector Research Centre, Kensington, NSW.

Johnston, E. 2009, 'Banks given too much power, says Keating', *Sydney Morning
Herald,* 23 September, p. 7.

Johyn, D. 2010, 'Small players lack muscle to challenge the big four', *Sydney
Morning Herald,* 20 December, p. 5.

Jones, E. 2002, 'Rural finance in Australia: A troubled history', *Rural Society,* vol.
12, no. 2, pp. 160–80.

Kelly, J. 2007, 'Reforming public services in the UK: Bringing in the third sector',
Public Administration, vol. 85, no. 4, pp. 1003–22.

Kitay, J. 2003, 'Continuity and change: Employment relations practices in
Australian retail banking', *Bulletin of Comparative Labor Relations,* vol. 45, pp.
1–16.

Kitay J. & Rimmer M. 1997, 'Australian retail banking: Negotiating employment
relations change', in *Changing employment relations in Australia,* eds J. Kitay
& R. Lansbury, Oxford University Press, Melbourne, pp. 102–30.

Lewis, G. 1996, *People before profit: The credit union movement in Australia,*
Wakefield Press, Kent Town.

Lewis, G. (2001), Laughing all the way to the credit union: The CreditCare
experience in 'no bank' towns, Accord Seminar Paper, University of
Technology Sydney.

Local Government Banking and Financial Services Taskforce 1999, *The roles and
responsibilities of NSW local government in providing banking and other
financial services to the community,* April, pp. 1–39.

Love, P. 1984, *Labor and the money power: Australian Labor populism 1890–1950,*
Melbourne University Press, Carlton.

Lyons, M. 1988, 'Ted Tytherleigh', in *Australian financiers,* eds R. T. Appleyard & C.
B. Schedvin, Macmillan, Melbourne.

McCarthy, G. 2002, *Things fall apart: A history of the State Bank of South Australia,*
Australian Scholarly Publishing, Kew.

Martin, J. 1996, 'Corporatisation and community service obligations: Are they
incompatible?', *Australian Journal of Public Administration,* vol. 55, no. 3, pp.
111–17.

Merrett, D. 1998, 'The development of central banking in Australia'.
http://www.abc.net.au/money/currency/features/feat7.htm

Merrett, D., 2006, 'Some lessons from the history of Australian banking', *Economic
Papers,* vol. 25, no. S1, pp. 52–60.

Nixon, S. 2001, 'Banks' own man gives them lessons in fair play', *Sydney Morning Herald*, 7 March, p. 1.

Noctor, M., Stoney, S. & Stradling, R. 1992, Financial literacy: A discussion of concepts and competences of financial literacy and opportunities for its introduction into young people's learning, Report prepared for the National Westminster Bank, National Foundation for Education Research, London.

Oldfield, S. 2012, 'Tough out there for niche players', *The Australian*, 11 February.

Parker, M., Fournier, V. & Reedy, P. 2007, *The dictionary of alternatives: Utopianism and organization*, Zed Books, London and New York.

Quiggin, J. 1995, 'Does privatization pay?', *The Australian Economic Review*, 2nd Quarter, pp. 23–42.

Quiggin, J. 2001, The People's Bank: The privatization of the Commonwealth Bank and the case for a new publicly owned bank, Research Paper, School of Economics, Faculty of Economics and Commerce, Australian National University, pp. 1–5.

Rosamond, B. 2002, 'Imagining the European economy: "Competitiveness" and the social construction of "Europe" as an economic space', *New Political Economy*, vol. 7, no. 2, pp. 157–77.

Schaefer, Z., Conrad, C., Chene, G., May, S. & Ganesh, S. 2011, 'Economy justice and communication ethics: Considering multiple points of intersection' in *Handbook of communication ethics*, eds G. Cheney, S. K. May & D. Munshi, Routledge, New York, pp. 436–56.

Singh, S. 1989, 'Australian banking: Customer revolt begins to tell', *Asian Finance*, vol. 15, no. 9, pp. 31–3.

Singh, S. 1991, *The bankers: Australia's leading bankers talk about banking today*, Allen & Unwin, North Sydney.

Standing Committee on Financial Institutions and Public Administration 1998, Inquiry into regional banking services, Transcript of evidence, 18 February, Parliament of Australia, Canberra.

Taylor, M. J. & Hirst, J. 1983, 'Australian banking: The current round of rationalisation and restructuring', *Australian Geographical Studies*, vol. 21, no. 2, pp. 266–71.

Thornton, P. H., Ocasio, W. & Lounsbury, M. 2012, *The institutional logics perspective: A new approach to culture, structure and process*, Oxford University Press, Oxford.

Wallis, R. 1997, *Financial system inquiry final report*, AGPS, Canberra.

Wickert, R. 1989, *No single measure: A survey of Australian adult literacy*, Institute of Technical and Adult Teacher Education, Sydney.

Workers Online 2000, 'Union and community groups call for bank social charter', issue 73, November. http://workers.labor.net.au/73/news3_bank.html

Markets, Rights and Power in Australian Social Policy

Wu, S. 2008, 'Bank mergers and acquisitions: An evaluation of the four pillars policy in Australia', *Australian Economic Papers*, vol. 47, no. 2, pp. 141–55.

6

Community aged care providers in a competitive environment: Past, present and future

Bob Davidson

In Australia, as in many other nations, the ageing of the population, coupled with other social and demographic changes, has underpinned significant growth in aged care in recent years, a development that is projected to continue during the first half of the 21st century.[1] At the same time, there has been an increasing recognition by government and aged care service providers that most older people wish to remain within their own home and remain independent as much and for as

---

Davidson, B. 2015, 'Community aged care providers in a competitive environment: Past, present and future', in *Markets, rights and power in Australian social policy*, eds G. Meagher & S. Goodwin, Sydney University Press, Sydney.

---

1 In 1970, 8.3 percent of the Australian population was 65 years and older, while 0.5 percent was 85 years and older. By 2010, this had risen to 13.5 percent and 1.8 percent respectively; by 2030 it is projected to be 19.3 percent and 2.7 percent, and by 2050 to be 22.7 percent and 5.1 percent (Treasury 2010, p. 10). The growth in aged care, however, arises from a range of factors other than simply more people needing care, including greater participation of women in the workforce with its effects on the number of informal (unpaid) carers, and the greater wealth and political activity of older people relative to past generations. In Australia, the growth of the aged care industry may accelerate after the announcement in April 2012 that the number of funded aged care places will be significantly increased over the next decade (Australian Government 2012).

long as possible (ageing-in-place), rather than go into residential care (such as a nursing home).[2] This has led in recent years to significant 'de-institutionalisation' of older people needing care (AIHW 2001, pp. 96–139). In this context, community aged care, which provides care services to people in their own home and community[3] has experienced particularly high growth and is destined to become a major human services growth industry in future years (Productivity Commission 2008, 2011).

Alongside these developments, the growing political dominance of neoliberalism (Davidson 2012; Stilwell 2005; Nevile 1998) has led to provision of most human services becoming increasingly marketised over the last two decades. This is reflected in the use of a wide range of market mechanisms to distribute government funding and determine who will provide funded services; a greater emphasis on the right of service users (as 'consumers') to choose their services and providers; an increasing obligation on users to make a financial contribution to the cost of services; a greater focus on efficiency in the production of services; and the delivery of many government-funded services by non-government (or 'third party') providers, both non-profit organisations (NPOs) and privately owned 'for-profit' organisations (FPOs). Another aspect of neoliberalism during this period has been the increased pressure on governments to limit public expenditure, a factor with added salience in aged care given the need to ensure that services will be financially sustainable as the population ages in the coming decades. These themes, reflected in contributions to this volume, are all relevant to community aged care in Australia.

As the marketisation of human services has continued apace, a major issue in many sectors has been its impact on the supply side of services, both at the level of individual providers and at a systemic level. One important aspect of this has been a focus on the *types* of organisations that have emerged as providers, and whether different types of

---

2   The term 'ageing-in-place' is also used where someone remains in the same retirement village or nursing home as they age and their care needs increase.
3   In Australia, these services have been known as community care, but other names are used elsewhere, such as domiciliary care or home care. In the United Kingdom 'community care' is used to refer to both domiciliary care and residential care.

providers differ in their capacity to achieve the core objectives of the services, namely that the services are high quality and responsive to user needs (effectiveness), accessible to all people who need them (equity), and make the best use of available resources (efficiency). Within this context there is concern that trends such as the increasing presence of FPOs, the effect of 'new public management' on government agencies (MacDermott 2008), the 'corporatisation' of many NPOs, the ever-growing presence of large providers, and the pressures on all providers to compete to remain viable, will lead to an excessive focus by providers on efficiency, growth and profits, rather than on the individual needs of each service user and ensuring the best services and outcome for all users.

This chapter examines how these processes have played out in terms of who provides paid community aged care services in Australia, and is thus a case study of how the structure of one human services sector has evolved under marketisation. After giving a brief overview of the current structure (the present) (based on Davidson, 2011), it examines *why* that structure has emerged (the past) and how it may change (the future). This account points to some distinctive features of this industry that illustrate important aspects of the impact of marketisation more generally in relation to how and why certain kinds of organisations may become prominent in the provision of human services and the potential implications of this for service users.

These questions are examined from the perspective of service providers, drawing on an economic framework that is based on industrial organisation theory,[4] but which also takes account of the special features of human services and the major political and social forces that have shaped the industry in the past and are likely to shape it in the future. Much of the discussion here is framed in terms of understanding how the 'markets' for community aged care function, but it is important to note that there are more fundamental questions about the validity of using markets in the organisation and delivery of aged care, given,

---

4 Industrial organisation is 'the broad field within microeconomics that focuses on business behaviour and its implications both for market structures and processes, and for public policies toward them' (Schmalensee & Willig 1989, p. xi), or 'the study of the structure of firms and markets and their interactions' (Carlton & Perloff 2005, p. 782).

for example, the dangers in the 'commodification of care' (Himmelweit 2008; Ungerson & Yeandle 2007) whereby personal and relationship values are replaced by 'care' as a tradeable product.

The chapter draws in part on my own current research into the community aged care industry in New South Wales (NSW) as a case study of the impact of contestability on human services providers.[5] In particular it draws on my analysis of funding data for one of the major funding programs (the Commonwealth government's community care packages[6]) and on 43 interviews with senior representatives of funding agencies, industry bodies, and providers between October 2009 and March 2011. These interviews included 30 with CEOs, owners or senior managers of 22 providers in NSW, including eight of the nine major providers that together receive over 40 percent of the funds for community aged care in the state. While much of the data used here is from NSW, and there are some differences between states in the structure and functioning of the industry, this state in many respects reflects the situation in other states. Moreover, given that it is the most populous Australian state and has around one-third of national community aged care funding and clients (SCRGSP 2011), it is a major part of the overall national picture.

Community aged care in Australia is currently in a state of flux following major changes to funding programs announced since 2011. The research reported here was largely conducted before 2011, but the industry structures and processes described remain fundamentally in place. As the chapter shows, however, much of that is likely to change in the next few years.

The community aged care industry (the present)

Community aged care is now a substantial industry in Australia, the value of which was around $4 billion in 2010, including at least $3.2 billion from government funding (SCRGSP 2011). The industry is very

---

5   Ethics approval for the research was obtained from the University of New South Wales.
6   The funding data is in Excel format by individual provider for each of service outlet in Australia for each year from 2002–3 to 2010–11 (DoHA 2003, 2010a).

diverse, in terms of the sources of demand, the range of service types, and the types of services providers.

The demand for community aged care – who needs care and who pays?

The majority of care provided to older people living at home is unpaid care ('informal care') from relatives and friends (ABS 2010). However, paid care may be needed to supplement informal care or where there is no informal carer,[7] and at least one-third of the 2.1 million people in Australia who are aged 70 years or older receive paid care (SCRGSP 2011, pp. 13, 28). There is a wide diversity among older people in both their need for paid community care (for example in terms of the level of need and personal agency arising from frailty or disability, the types of services they require, the need for other services, availability of informal care, and cultural and language background) and their financial capacity to pay for or contribute to the cost of services.

From an economic perspective, the 'demand' for any service is a function of 'need' backed by 'purchasing power' (or money to pay for the service). With community aged care, as with human services more broadly, many people needing care are not able to pay for it and much of the purchasing power must come from government.[8] Over time, in re-

---

7 Note that the term 'carers' is used for those who give informal care, while 'care-workers' refers to paid staff.

8 Within the context of purchaser–provider models, which underpin the marketisation of human services, the level of government funding determines the *demand* for services. In this context, there may be 'unmet need' either because of 'unmet demand' (arising from input or organisational constraints on supply, such as a shortage of staff, even though there are funds available to pay for services) and/or because of inadequate funds to meet all the needs of older people (demand constraints). In recent debates on aged care, limits on government funding are commonly described as 'controls on supply', but this overlooks the nature – and intent – of a purchaser–provider model, a distinction that is important in analysing the role of government in a managed market. In fact, industry-wide, there currently appears to be no major supply constraints in community aged care, given that the main 'input' is staff time and the current workforce is under-utilised (Martin & King 2008; Productivity Commission 2011; Mears 2012) with 'workers wanting … more hours far outnumber[ing] those wishing to work fewer hours' (Howe et al. 2012, p. 87). There are, of course, long-term and some localised concerns about the availability of sufficient care-workers.

sponse to the diversity of need, Commonwealth and state governments in Australia have introduced an extensive array of government-funded community aged care programs. In addition, a range of other non-government sources of funding have emerged. This has led, from the perspective of service providers, to the development of a number of market segments. Table 6.1 shows these segments, which fall into two main 'arenas' of competition.

The *first arena* consists of an array of government-funded programs where a government agency plays at least some part in choosing the possible provider(s) for a designated group of users. The core of the industry is based on two of these programs, the Home and Community Care program (HACC, $1.9 billion in 2009–10), and the Commonwealth government's community care 'packages' ($0.8 billion) (SCRGSP 2011, p. 13, 16) which together provide over 80 percent of government funding and over two-thirds of the total revenue of all providers in the industry. HACC, which was established in 1985 and caters for a lower level of need, funds a multiplicity of block grants for different types of services in each local area, with providers essentially determining the eligibility of users on the basis of common guidelines. The community care packages, which were introduced in 1992 and cater for people with a higher level of need equivalent to those in residential care, operate via a two-part process whereby an independent Aged Care Assessment Team (ACAT) determines the eligibility of an older person and the level of assistance he/she can receive; and (by a totally separate process), a limited number of providers in each region are allocated a maximum number of users at each level that they can assist.[9]

The *second arena* includes an array of situations in which service users (or an agent on their behalf) select their own provider using their own funds or funds that have been previously allocated to them from another (government or non-government) source. This includes a subcontracting segment whereby some funded providers sub-contract care-workers from other providers. It also includes an unsubsidised

---

9 The term 'community care packages' collectively describes the Community Aged Care Packages (CACP), Extended Aged Care in the Home (EACH) and EACH Dementia (EACH D). CACPs are for people whose needs are assessed as equivalent to low-level residential care, while EACH and EACH D are for people with needs equivalent to high-level residential care.

(fee-for-service) segment where people buy services without any government subsidy, either because they are not eligible for a government program; or because they are eligible but on a waiting list, or wanting more hours, or wanting to avoid government.

It is important to note that community aged care is unusual amongst human services in the range of sources of revenue for providers for the core service, both in terms of the number of separate government programs and the existence of services that operate with no government funding.[10] As discussed later, this diversity of revenue sources underpins a number of the distinctive features of this industry. Market mechanisms are used to allocate the available funds for each of the government programs, and thus all operate as *managed markets* (quasi-markets).[11] In this context, three forms of managed market are relevant, namely (i) where government chooses a monopoly provider for each type of service or group of users in a given area, generally via competitive tendering and contracting (CTC); (ii) a quasi-voucher licensing (QVL) system, where users themselves can choose from any licensed provider, with the cost largely subsidised by government, and which is more akin to a conventional market;[12] and (iii) a hybrid of the CTC and QVL systems, with licensed providers having to go through a CTC process that limits the number of providers from which users can choose and where the funding agency (at least to some extent) determines the market share of providers. Historically, CTC systems were

---

10   For example, with government funding, in Australia there is only one source for residential aged care, child care is funded via two linked levels of contributions to parents, and the core funding for schooling comes from one state and one federal agency. Virtually all these services have some level of government funding or subsidy.

11   Davidson (2012) sets out a framework of possible market regimes in which human services are delivered, encompassing both conventional markets where users pay for their own services, and managed markets, where government is the major source of purchasing power for services. A discussion of the differences between the various types of managed markets can be found in Davidson (2008, 2009, 2011).

12   QVL systems encompass what are commonly called 'consumer choice' or 'demand-side-funding' models, and include 'cash-for-care' (Ungerson & Yeandle 2007) and 'individual budgets' (Wilberforce et al. 2011). In QVL systems, the government subsidy may be paid by cash vouchers, tax deductions or reimbursement of the provider (Davidson 2008).

Table 6.1: Sources of demand for community aged care in Australia: arenas of competition and market segments. For sources and notes, see appendix at the end of the chapter

Arena and market segment	Examples of program / buyer
Arena A – Government-funded CTC and hybrid programs	
1 HACC – funding and administration by Commonwealth – prior to 2012, funding was jointly by states and the Commonwealth, with administration by states (ADHC in NSW)	HACC – (Home and Community Care program)
2 Community care packages – funding and administration by Commonwealth	CACP (Community Aged Care Package) EACH (Extended Care at Home) EACH Dementia (EACH D)
3 Other Commonwealth community care programs	NCRP (National Carers Respite Program) Commonwealth Respite Centres Assistance with Care and Housing for the Aged
4 Dept Veterans Affairs (DVA) – programs for war veterans	Veterans' Home Care Veterans' Home Nursing
5 Mixed Delivery Programs – funded by Commonwealth and state – in NSW, delivered by NSW Health	Multi-Purpose Services (integrated residential and community care services in rural areas (Commonwealth) Transition Packages (Commonwealth) and Compacks (NSW) – short-term care for people leaving acute health care

Arena and market segment	Examples of program / buyer
Arena B - Individual Selection of Providers [a]	
6 Quasi-voucher licensing (QVL) models[b]	Attendant care (currently mainly disability)
– government funding/ user choice of provider	Productivity Commission (2011) proposal
7 Sub-contracting from government-funded services (also known as 'brokering')	Providers that have been funded under programs in Segments 1–5
8 Guardianship and insurance (compensable) arrangements [c]	NSW Office of Protective Commissioner (OPC)
	NSW Long Term Care Support Agency (LCSTA)
	Other insurance and compensation payments
9 Funded by non-government bodies (NPOs and FPOs)	NPOs (additional to government funding)
	FPOs (e.g. for employees with aged parents) [d]
	Paid through NPOs (e.g. Claims Convention) [e]
10 Unsubsidised individuals	People approved for Segments 1–5, but either on a waiting list or wanting more ('top-up') hours
	People not approved for Segment 1–5

most likely to be used in the early years of marketisation, but with the greater emphasis in recent years on the need for users to have choice and some power over their services, QVL and hybrid systems are increasingly being used (Davidson 2012).

In the Australian aged care system there are virtually none of the QVL ('choice') models, although such a system was recommended by the Productivity Commission (2011). HACC uses CTC or hybrid systems to determine who receives the block grants, although 'direct allocation' by the department without any formal competitive process is often used in NSW to minimise the transaction costs of tendering where there is no obvious competitor for an existing provider; the community care packages use a hybrid system, and most other programs use a CTC or hybrid system, to appoint a single provider or panel of approved providers in each region. With all of the government programs, a user's eligibility is based on his/her level of frailty or disability, and there is no financial means test for basic eligibility, although an income test is applied to determine the level of financial contribution by the user. However, funding is significantly less than demand, with more people approved for assistance than there are places, leading to waiting lists ('queues') for places in most programs in most areas. For example, the Productivity Commission (2011 Appendix E, p. 20) estimated that the unmet need for packages in 2011 was 49 percent of current places.

In principle, with the Commonwealth community care packages and some of the other programs, users can choose from the providers in their region that have been allocated places, but with long waiting lists, users must often take whatever they can get and thus the potential for users to exercise choice is severely limited. In practice, a government agency determines the total market share of each provider of packages based primarily on an annual tendering round for places or funds. Moreover, for both HACC and the packages, only growth funding is contestable. Subject to a provider meeting its contractual and regulatory requirements, the places and dollars it has been allocated in earlier years are never re-tendered, so that allocations received by a provider in past years are effectively locked in as recurrent funding indefinitely (Davidson 2012).

A major focus in the following sections is on the packages segment for a number of reasons. First, it is the main object of the ambitions, if not activity, of many community aged care providers. This is largely because, while the total funds from HACC are much larger, the packages have much higher per user funding, with payments in 2009–10 ranging from $15,000 to $49,000 annually compared to the mean cost of just over $2000 for each HACC recipient (Productivity Commission 2011, Appendix E, p. 3). The packages also support people with higher needs and are thus of most interest to providers for whom social objectives are paramount. Second, it is a good case study of how an industry has developed under marketisation. The current hybrid system of allocating places has operated since the inception of packages in 1992, and despite the strong limits on contestability for funding, the segment is considered by most providers to be very competitive. Third, the packages have been administered by the Commonwealth funding agency (the Department of Social Services) that is now taking over HACC programs for older people, and which will be increasingly responsible for community aged care in the future.[13] Fourth, it allows a comparison with another related type of service (residential aged care) for which funding is also allocated by DSS using the same basic system, and for which similar data is available.

The supply of community aged care – who are the providers?

On the supply side there is a wide range of providers and types of providers that differ, in organisational terms, in the form of ownership (whether government, NPO, or FPO), scale (size), the scope of services they provide, the geographical spread of their operations and the time for which they have operated. There are several major groupings of providers:

- *Government:* There are three main types of government providers, namely (i) state government specialist home care agencies, although only in NSW is such an agency still significant;[14] (ii) local government, which has a larger role in some states (such as Victoria) and in non-metropolitan areas; and (iii) state health departments, which are becoming increasingly involved as healthcare transition programs are expanded.
- *Non-profits (NPOs):* As a group, the *religious and charitable NPOs* receive the most government funds, both nationally and in NSW. These are mostly longstanding bodies with wide geographic cov-

---

13 The department has been called the Department of Social Services (DSS) since September 2013, following the election of the Abbott Coalition Government. Before that, it was called the Department of Health and Ageing (2001–03).
14 The NSW government's Home Care Services (HCS) is the largest single provider in NSW with an annual budget of over $200 million based solely on community care (both aged and disability). HCS works primarily in HACC where it is a dominant presence. It received 30 percent of the $552 million of HACC funds in NSW in 2009–10, including 81 percent of the $179 million for HACC personal care and domestic assistance services (NSW DHS 2010).

erage that provide a range of services, both in aged care and in other fields. A number are now large enterprises, run along corporate lines, but their size and scope also enable them to develop more sophisticated models of care (Davidson 2011). The largest number of providers, however, are the *community-based NPOs*, which are mostly small and medium-size organisations limited to one area, controlled and managed by local groups. These bodies, many of which originated in the 1970s and 1980s, service either the broader community, or a sub-group within the population, (such as Aboriginal and ethnic groups, and, more recently, GLBT [gay, lesbian, bisexual and transsexual] groups). In general, they have a distinct ethos, support base, and modus operandi from the larger religious and charitable bodies (Lyons 2001).

• The *for-profit organisations (FPOs)* in the sector are almost entirely small to medium-size organisations that are specialists in community aged care. Virtually no publicly listed multi-service FPOs are present[15] – unlike residential aged care, health care, and child care where they have become increasingly involved in recent years – although some large companies have entered and left the sector in the last decade. For example, Ramsay Health Care took over a small FPO in 2004, reselling it in 2006 to a religious NPO.

Each of the market segments shown in Table 6.1 has a distinctive profile in terms of these various types of providers, although most providers operate in more than one segment and it is common for users to access services from more than one segment, both at any one time and over time as their needs change. The providers in the five segments in the first arena (as shown in Table 6.1) are mainly NPOs, although NSW Home Care Service (HCS) is the major provider of HACC services in NSW. In both these major programs, especially HACC, there is a multiplicity of local community-based NPOs that only operate in one geographic area. The providers in the five segments of the second arena are mainly FPOs, although some NPOs operate in these segments. The two arenas are bridged by the extensive use of subcontracting by

---

15   As of June 2011, there were only two publicly listed FPOs providing packages in Australia (both in Queensland), receiving a total of only $1.2 million (0.1 percent of the $872 million allocated for packages nationally).

government-funded providers, with the effect that staff employed by FPOs provide services for at least 20 percent of all users.

Table 6.2 shows the proportion of place provided by government, NPO, and FPO providers in each state and Australia overall for the Commonwealth community care packages in 2009–10.

Tables 6.3 and 6.4 show the allocation of funds for the packages in NSW in 2003 and 2010[16] in terms of ownership and how this changed in recent years in this segment, which providers consider the most attractive and competitive, and which has a profile of providers that is most likely to be the pattern for the industry in the intermediate term.[17] The major features to note are the substantial market share and continuing growth of large religious and charitable NPOs, the larger number of small local community-based NPOs, the limited role of government providers, and the low share of government funds that is allocated directly to FPOs.

In a number of respects, the profile of providers in the industry differs from that in community aged care in other nations and in a number of other human services in Australia that have been marketised. In particular, for a service directed at the broader population (as distinct from services whose target group is based on socioeconomic disadvantage, such as homelessness), FPOs have a low market share of funded programs with virtually no large corporate FPOs. Why, does the industry differ in this respect from community (domiciliary) care in other nations (Brennan et al. 2012) when the service everywhere has a similar basic production function? Why does it differ from residential aged care in Australia (Table 6.4), when the same government agency, processes and people are used to determine funding allocations as for the community care packages? And why does it differ from child care in Australia (Brennan et al. 2012), given that both sectors were substantially reliant on community-based NPO providers two decades ago?

---

16 As at 30 June each year (DoHA 2003, 2010a).
17 An analysis of the major implications of these tables can be found in Davidson (2011).

Table 6.2: Community aged care package places by state and ownership of provider, Australia, 2009–10, percent. For sources and notes, see appendix at the end of the chapter

State/territory	Non-profit organisations				For-profit organisations	Government			TOTAL	
	Religious	Charitable	Community	Total		State	Local	Total	%	Places
NSW	35.2	32.5	20.9	88.6	5.3	2.3	3.8	6.1	100	16,724
Vic	39.8	22.0	13.6	75.4	3.1	12.4	9.2	21.6	100	12,517
Qld.	46.1	24.5	19.2	89.8	6.2	1.4	2.5	3.9	100	9,381
WA	31.3	43.4	4.5	79.2	13.5	1.8	5.6	7.4	100	5,112
SA	26.8	48.1	11.9	86.8	3.4	7.3	2.5	9.8	100	4,158
Tas.	37.1	22.6	26.1	85.7	6.9	5.3	2.0	7.3	100	1,339
ACT	20.6	62.1	11.6	94.4	5.6	0.0	0.0	0.0	100	800
NT	30.7	9.4	18.5	58.6	15.3	0.0	26.1	26.1	100	773
Total	37.0	30.7	16.3	84.0	5.8	5.0	5.2	10.2	100	50,804

Table 6.3: Funding for community care packages (CACP, EACH, EACH D) and residential aged care, NSW, 2003, by ownership of provider. For sources and notes, see appendix at the end of the chapter

Type of provider	Community care packages					Residential care				
	No	%	$M	%	Mean per provider ($M)	No	%	$M	%	Mean per provider ($M)
NPO Charitable	10	7.9	17.1	16.9	1.71	37	9.9	151.7	9.8	4.10
Religious	28	22.0	47.2	46.6	1.69	61	16.2	512.0	33.6	8.40
Community – general	38	29.9	15.4	15.1	0.40	120	31.9	200.3	13.1	1.67
Community – group	29	22.8	10.4	10.2	0.36	11	2.9	32.7	2.1	2.97
Sub-total NPO	105	82.6	90.1	88.8	0.86	229	60.9	897.3	58.8	3.92
FPO Publicly listed										
Private Incorporated	5	3.9	2.7	2.7	0.54	121	32.2	568.9	37.3	4.70
Private non-incorporated						5	1.3	11.2	0.7	2.24
Sub-total FPO	5	3.9	2.7	2.7	0.54	126	33.5	580.1	38.0	4.60
GOV Local Government	15	11.8	5.2	5.1	0.35	20	5.3	15.1	1.0	0.76
State government	2	1.6	3.5	3.4	1.74	1	0.3	33.0	2.2	32.98
Sub-total government	17	13.4	8.7	8.5	0.51	21	5.6	48.1	3.2	2.79
TOTAL	127	100	101.4	100	0.80	376	100	1525.6	100	4.06

Table 6.4: Funding for community care packages (CACP, EACH, EACH D) and residential aged care, NSW, 2010, by ownership of provider. For sources and notes, see appendix at the end of the chapter

Type of provider		Community care packages					Residential care				
		No	%	$M	%	Mean per provider ($M)	No	%	$M	%	Mean per provider ($M)
NPO	Charitable	17	12.0	44.9	16.3	2.64	38	11.7	298.3	12.4	7.85
	Religious	33	23.2	147.3	53.3	4.47	46	14.2	870.6	36.1	18.93
	Community – general	33	23.2	33.3	12.1	1.01	92	28.4	285.1	11.8	3.10
	Community – group	25	17.6	17.9	6.5	0.72	12	3.7	32.0	1.3	2.67
	Sub-total NPO	108	76.1	243.4	88.1	2.25	184	58.0	1,486.0	61.6	7.80
FPO	Publicly listed						2	0.6	57.4	2.4	28.68
	Private incorporated	17	12.0	19.9	7.2	1.17	114	35.2	811.6	33.6	7.12
	Private non-incorporated						2	0.6	5.0	0.2	2.49
	Sub-total FPO	17	12.0	19.9	7.2	1.17	118	36.4	873.9	36.2	7.41
GOV	Local government	15	10.6	9.1	3.3	0.61	17	5.2	20.1	0.8	1.18
	State government	2	1.4	3.8	1.4	1.89	1	0.3	32.4	1.3	32.36
	Sub-total government	17	12.0	12.9	4.7	0.76	18	5.6	52.5	2.2	2.92
	TOTAL	142	100	276.2	100	1.95	324	100	2,412.4	100	7.45

The origins of the current profile of providers (the past)

The establishment of HACC in 1985[18] was a major watershed in the development of the community aged care industry. HACC consolidated and extended a number of state and national funding programs, and brought more systematic planning and coordination of services, replacing a process of uncoordinated grant submissions by a planned allocation of funding across each region (House of Representatives 1982, 1994, pp. 7–9). At that time, the mix of providers was not dissimilar to today, except that the religious and charitable NPOs had only relatively small-scale community care operations. However, HACC operated essentially through a joint planning model between government and providers, with FPOs initially excluded from applying for funds for HACC services, and it was not until the introduction of the packages in 1992, which used competitive tendering, that a more marketised approach was used in the sector. This section seeks to explain how the industry has moved from there to the current profile of service providers.

Economic theory from the field of industrial organisation, modified to take account of the reality where a human service is the 'product', can help explain how and why the current profile has emerged. Two broad groupings of factors are relevant in determining the incentives for, and barriers to, entry of providers in any human services industry. First, there are factors intrinsic to the type of service, stemming from the nature of demand (the characteristics and needs of users) and the production function (the resources and processes needed to produce and distribute the product). Second, there are 'location' factors, notably the geographical, historical, social, demographic, institutional, and political factors, along with key individuals, that may have an influence from the national to local level and shape the industry, markets, and service system in each place.[19] The policies and actions of national and state governments in relation to regulation and funding systems for the

---

18   A bipartisan House of Representatives (1982) report had recommended a more ordered approach to government support for home care. The Hawke Labor government, elected in March 1983, established HACC drawing substantially on the recommendations of that report.

industry are especially important. In turn, the operation of the industry, markets, and providers that have derived from these two sets of factors, constantly feeds back to influence future developments.

Path dependency and government funding

The history of a sector, especially where path dependency is strong,[20] constrains and shapes its development; and where a sector is substantially dependent on government funding, the form and extent of the funding is obviously a critical determinant of the structure of the sector.

These two factors combine powerfully to form a critical parameter for the profile of providers in the community aged care industry in Australia. It was earlier noted that with both HACC and the packages, generally only growth funding is contestable – and this has been the case since both programs were established. Thus the large bulk of funding each year derives from the accumulation of decisions made in previous years going back over for two decades or more.[21] For example, in the allocations for the three main types of packages (CACP, EACH and EACH D) in NSW in 2009–10, 87 percent of funding derived from decisions made in earlier years. This is a substantial barrier to entry for new providers, but it also facilitates stability in the service system.

---

19 For example, a service system may be shaped at a national level by political and cultural traditions (Esping-Anderson 1990), and at a local level by the distance of a community from a major city. With globalisation, the distinctive impact of international forces on each 'location' is also important.

20 'Path-dependency' (Liebowitz & Margolis 1990, 1995; Bessant et al. 2006, p. 46, 82; Travers 2005, p. 89) refers to the power of established institutions and past policies to shape and limit future policies and events. This goes beyond merely that 'history matters' and refers to past decisions and events that determine and limit future options.

21 Some other government programs in the first arena have a provision for regular re-tendering every few years, but this often does not occur and existing funding and contracts are 'rolled over'; or where there has been re-re-tendering, it has led to little change in who are the providers. For example, the National Carers Respite Program (NCRP) uses a hybrid system with competitive tendering to be held every three years in each region. In practice, the funding for NCRP has generally been rolled over with no re-tendering, and the one time there was re-tendering (2005) is remembered by providers as being very disruptive and costly, with very little change resulting.

In this context, it is inevitable that many existing providers in the funded programs will be longstanding and that the entry of new ones will be limited. This leaves three questions to consider regarding the current profile of funded providers, namely (i) what factors in the early years of marketisation set the foundation for the current profile; (ii) what has determined new entry and growth of providers in the funded programs since then; and (iii) how is the growth of FPOs explained, given the small share of government funding that they receive?

Earlier history

The stability of funding systems

The limits on changes in providers over time noted above are part of a broader stability and continuity in the funding and administration of government community aged care programs over the last quarter century, especially when compared to the major changes imposed in that period on some other human services in Australia, such as child care and employment assistance. Since the establishment of HACC in 1985, there has been a gradual evolution in the services and programs that are available and the way in which they have been run, but currently HACC remains a cornerstone of the industry as the largest government program in terms of funding and client numbers, and in broad terms it operates as it has since 1985.

Nevertheless, there has been an increasing, but gradual, marketisation of the sector since 1985. Competitive tendering was introduced with the packages in 1992 and then extended to HACC in the wake of the Hilmer Report (1993) on competition policy; FPOs were able to tender for packages, at least on a pilot basis, from the early years and for HACC from 1998;[22] funding agencies have continued to refine and extend tendering processes; and there has been some movement towards various 'consumer-directed care' options.[23] These changes, however, have been introduced as a continuity with the past, and most programs

---

22   The actual date varied between states. The Amending Agreement between the Commonwealth and New South Wales, which introduced this change, was signed on 1 July 1998.

now work in a similar way in regard to critical aspects in the operation of 'the market'. Thus, in general, a government agency chooses the providers; competitive tendering (and sometimes direct allocation) is used rather thanQVL systems; and funds are paid to providers and administered by them effectively as block grants, with cross-subsidisation across clients a normal practice accepted by the funding agencies.

The 'original' providers

Given this stability and the lack of contestability for previously allocated funding, the early days of HACC and the packages are particularly important in explaining the current profile of providers in the industry. The current position of the major providers is based on their early start in the industry, the continuing accretion of places in the annual funding round each year, and the consolidation of smaller providers within the large NPOs.

Three points are particularly important from the period in which HACC and the packages were established. First, HACC was established before the marketisation of the industry,[24] and many of today's providers, including virtually all the major ones, were operating even before HACC began. Further, Australia has a long tradition of NPO and voluntary provision of human services at a higher level than most other nations (Davidson 2008; Lyons 2001), a tradition reinforced by various government initiatives during the 1970s to support the development of community-based NPOs. Thus when governments sought to move out of direct provision, to 'steer rather than row' (Osborne & Gaebler 1993), it was much more likely that NPOs would play a key role. In Sweden and the United Kingdom, marketisation began in a context where community aged care services had been wholly provided by lo-

---

23 'Consumer-directed care' is aimed at giving service users greater control over the services they receive. In part this stems from long-standing human rights objectives of social movements (Yeatman 1990), but it also has been driven from another direction by the notion of consumer sovereignty that is central to neo-classical economics.
24 While neo-liberalism began to impact from the mid-1970s, it did not substantially affect human services in a number of nations including Australia (MacDermott 2008) and the United Kingdom (Le Grand & Bartlett 1993) until the late 1980s.

cal government, and thus FPOs have subsequently taken a much bigger share of government funding (Brennan et al. 2012; Meagher & Szebehely 2013).

Second, FPOs were formally excluded from providing HACC-funded services until 1998, (although some, such as Kincare, established NPO arms that enabled them to move into HACC earlier than that (Kincare 2007)). While they were able to apply for packages from the early years (1992), FPOs had less opportunity to demonstrate their capability in a field in which trust and reputation are critical.

The history of FPO access to this sector is indicative of some important broader processes in human services that remain relevant to the present day. On the one hand, as outlined by Hansmann (1980, 1987) in his theory of 'contract failure', where there are strong asymmetries of information, buyers are more likely to rely on trust, and they are more likely to trust NPOs because of their 'non-distribution constraint' (such that financial surpluses are not distributed to individual shareholders).[25] In human services there are major asymmetries of information arising from the limits on the personal agency and financial capacity of many users, and on the measurability and observability of the actual services (Blank 2000; Davidson 2012). Thus there is scope for opportunist providers that are profit maximisers rather than social maximisers to reduce the quality and equity of services in order to lower costs, and concern about this possibility in large part explains the continuing concern about FPOs working in human services.

On the other hand, the history of FPO access illustrates the changed environment and expectations created by neoliberalism and marketisation. In 1985, the exclusion of FPOs appears to have been considered largely unexceptional as 'it was the culture then' (interview with government official) following the strong growth of, and government support for, NPOs, especially community-based ones, in the 1970s; problems with FPO nursing homes that had led to government measures to encourage NPOs in aged care (Lyons 1995); and the fact that publicly funded community care providers at the time of the establishment of HACC were government or NPOs. Then, after over a decade of neoliberal dominance, the decision in 1998 to allow FPOs

---

25 See Davidson (2009) for a discussion of the limits to contract failure theory.

into HACC was similarly considered unexceptional within government. More specifically, there had been the Hilmer Report (1993) on
competition policy; a number of years during which FPOs had access
to the packages with few apparent problems; and the increasing acceptance of FPOs to deliver government programs in a range of fields. The
election of the conservative Howard government may have given some
impetus to admitting FPOs, but it was a bipartisan decision supported
by state Labor governments.[26]

Third, until the 21st century, community care was very much the
'poor cousin' of residential care. For some of the larger NPOs and FPOs,
residential care was their only interest, and they did not look to compete seriously for the new stream of funding from packages until later.
Those who initially saw the opportunities gained a first-mover advantage (Lieberman & Montgomery 1988), although even some of those
were initially persuaded primarily by the argument that it would assist
future residential business. The stability and form of the funding system
has undercut any second or late mover advantage.

The result of the above processes is that the NPOs have had time to
grow and consolidate without competition from aggressively marketing FPOs. In particular, the religious and charitable NPOs that operate
across a wide geographic area have had space to develop as large and
efficient operators now able to successfully compete in a more robust
competitive environment if required, while smaller community-based
NPOs have at least been able to retain their earlier funding, and, to
varying extents, have experienced some growth. This contrasts with
child care in Australia where there were few large NPOs when a QVL
system was introduced in the early 1990s (via both tax deductions and
benefits paid directly to parents) and FPOs subsequently took a majority of the market (Brennan et al. 2012).

---

26 Interviewees for this study who had been government officials who were part
of the process at the time recalled that allowing FPOs in was not considered a
major issue amid other more significant changes to mechanisms in HACC for
planning, decision-making, and accountability.

Entry and growth of providers in the funded programs

While funding from previous years is not contestable, new or 'growth' funding is continually made available, usually within annual funding rounds for packages and HACC. Over time, there has been substantial potential for new entrants and for existing ones to grow, with the real value of funding more than doubling in the last decade (Davidson 2011).

Who has received this growth funding? And what factors explain the types of organisations that have received the funding? While the allocations are the result of decisions made about tenders each year, these largely flow from the broad framework and principles that underpin the design and management of the regulatory and funding systems for the programs. This section briefly examines the change in the allocation of total funding for packages in NSW between 2003 and 2010, and whether there were factors in play that may have favoured certain types of organisations.

Outcomes of the tendering process

The packages segment is considered by providers to be 'very competitive', with the total number of new places in some regions each year being less than 10 percent of the total number being sought by providers in their tenders. There are no formal barriers to *entry* for any provider in terms of ownership or size, although each one must be of sufficient size such that it has the capability to meet the requirements to become an approved provider. There has been both new entry and exit of providers between 2003 and 2010. In 2010, 13 organisations from the 2003 list no longer provide services or have been absorbed into another body, while there were 28 new ones. The main increases have been in the number of FPOs. However the market share of the 114 providers in 2003 who remained in 2010 remained constant at 93 percent.

The major interest, however, relates to the *growth* of existing organisations, and the change in the market share of different types of providers. The funding data reveals a number of features. First, while the largest percentage increase went to FPOs, this was from a very small base. The number of FPO providers has trebled in the period. After eleven years of the packages, there were 6 FPOs with 2.7 per cent of total funds (2003); seven years later, there were 18 with 7.1 per cent of funds. Second, the providers receiving the largest absolute increase in funds (and a percentage increase above the overall rate of growth) were the religious and charitable NPOs. Third, the general community NPOs have also grown substantially, but less than the overall rate of growth. The lowest growth was for group-based community NPOs, a fact reflected in their common concern expressed in interviews that in recent years, they have had difficulty in winning places but are then asked by the larger providers to assist in working with their group. Fourth (not shown in the tables), some individual community-based NPOs have had major increases, reflecting their growth-oriented strategies and innovative approaches. In summary, the major growth has been directed to the large NPOs, FPOs have made substantial gains, and some community-based NPOs have flourished, but the share of funding going to the smaller community-based NPOs has declined.

The reasons

A number of factors explain the above. First is the importance of *incumbency*. In any industry, incumbency is a critical advantage for a supplier and an important factor in explaining the structure of the industry. An incumbent firm, especially one with longevity, has an established infrastructure and networks for the production and distribution of its products, a reputation and trust through demonstrated performance over time, access to better information than new entrants (Demsetz 1982) and brand loyalty. Its position will be further buttressed if buyers are risk-averse. Incumbency has some powerful additional benefits in community aged care, given the importance of trust.[27] Governments, generally being risk-averse, will tend to stay with proven performers even if there may be some reservations. For individual users, changing care providers is a major emotional and logistical disruption, and they cannot be sure that a new one will be better than their current one; this is not the same as changing toothpaste for a week's trial. Finally, the value of incumbency is further reinforced in the Aus-

---

27 However, trust and reputation may also be transferable from work in related fields, where a long-standing NPO wishes to move into a sector, as is currently occurring in community aged care.

tralian community aged care industry given the long-term stability of the funding systems.

A second issue is whether there is *government support for certain types of providers*. In some jurisdictions, government or the funding agency has an objective (possibly explicit, but often unspoken) to encourage the entry and growth of certain types of providers in terms of ownership or size. In Australia, FPOs were excluded from HACC before 1998, and in Sweden in recent years, there has been a strong and deliberate push to increase the presence of FPOs in aged care (Meagher & Szebehely 2013). However, for HACC since 1998 and for all of the other current community aged care programs in Australia from their beginning, there appears to have been no explicit policy to promote certain types of providers, other than the aim of some agencies 'to keep a mix of large and small'. Nevertheless, it was clear from statements in a number of interviews that some providers consider there are various unspoken agendas in funding decisions and that, at least informally, decisions unduly favour NPOs and large providers; ironically, others felt that decisions are often aimed at 'giving everyone something'.

Third, *a high level of regulation* generally favours larger and more established providers, given the administrative and resource requirements it entails, while the limitations on profits that regulation implies also reduces the incentives for some FPOs to enter. Arising from concerns about both protecting vulnerable people and ensuring the best use of government funds, the aged care industry has been subject to increasing regulation, especially over the last 15 years from the *Aged Care Act* (1997) on, while different requirements for each program impose extra costs. In contrast, there is no industry-specific regulation on providers in the unsubsidised segment of the industry (part of the second arena in Table 6.1), nor in 2010 were there any specific requirements set by funding agencies regarding bodies that are subcontracted other than that the funded provider must ensure they meet the requirements of their contract (Davidson 2011).

Fourth, the *processes* by which funding is determined will affect the type of providers.[28] Because of the resources it requires, tendering favours larger and more established providers, and this is exacerbated

---

28 Clearly there are strong arguments that regulation and the information required in tenders are a necessary cost in ensuring quality in a marketised system.

where separate tenders are required for each program in each region. The larger providers have the resources to support market research, professional tender writers, and promotional activities to build a positive image – and thus trust – amongst the funding agencies. The process of direct allocations commonly used in HACC in NSW partly avoids these transaction costs and facilitates the growth of smaller community-based providers, but it further reinforces the position of established providers.

Fifth, the *criteria* by which tenders are decided affect the types of providers chosen. There is much documentation setting out the formal criteria, but my interviews with a range of stakeholders sought to identify what they believed to be the crucial factors in practice.[29] A generally positive picture emerged with the major focus in the packages on the (i) quality of care, as reflected in the capability of staff, well-established models of care, and systems to monitor quality; (ii) the scope of services to ensure a better integrated experience for users; (iii) local appropriateness, in terms of a knowledge of local needs and services, established networks, and senior staff with local experience; (iv) the financial and logistic viability of the organisation; and (v) the capacity to begin the service quickly. While the scale of a provider's operation may not be a criterion per se, many of the factors are substantially dependent on scale, thus favouring larger providers. There is no direct price competition, with a fixed amount for each type of package set by the department. Further, departmental staff explicitly rejected the idea of some indirect price competition whereby a tenderer could gain an advantage simply by offering more places than what it was funded for, and were insistent that any proposal had to be justified in terms of its effect on the quality of care. (Providers could, of course, cut costs and reduce quality once they have received allocations in order to increase their fi-

---

However, the aim here is not to debate that issue, but simply point out the implications for the type of providers that emerge in the industry.
29 Providers can attend feedback sessions as to why they were unsuccessful in tendering for packages. While providers had widely differing views on how useful these sessions were, they are an insight into what was significant in funding decisions. One common comment from providers was that high priority criteria varied from year to year.

nancial 'surplus' (or profit), but there are no obvious incentives to do this to win funding).

In these ways, the system would appear to work towards selecting social maximisers rather than profit maximisers, although there also appeared to be limited focus on equity and discouraging cream-skimming[30] or on protecting the conditions for the low paid care-workers. While most providers generally accepted that the outcome of the process was a set of providers that gave quality care, they commonly complained about the process that success mainly depended on how well the tender was written ('an essay-writing competition') and very little on actual first-hand knowledge of the quality of a provider's current care, and that it was rarely clear why the successful providers were chosen over other good ones.

Taken together, the above factors suggest that established providers, providers with size and scope, and NPOs are most likely to succeed with tenders. However, through the emphasis on localisation and demonstrated capability, the system also gives significant opportunities to existing smaller local bodies, many of which have been able to keep winning growth dollars; indeed, 74 percent of package providers in NSW in 2010 operated in only one region. It also enables small and medium-size FPOs that are not profit maximisers, who have been in the sector for a number of years and developed a good reputation, to win funding. On the other hand, the lack of price competition, high profits and the opportunity to quickly get scale, reduces the incentive for some FPOs to enter the sector, especially the larger corporates.

For-profit organisations in the industry

There are three significant features about the involvement of FPOs in the community aged care industry in Australia – their low share of direct funding from government programs; their prevalence in those markets segments in the second arena of competition where providers are chosen by or for individual users; and the fact that they are all small

---

30   Whereby providers avoid more difficult and resource-intensive users or favour more affluent users who can pay a higher co-payment or buy extra services.

and medium-sized enterprises, with no large corporate FPO presence at this stage.

The low share of direct funding for FPOs from government programs is substantially explained above. The combined effect of the strength of NPOs, concerns about FPOs giving priority to profits rather than good services (as embodied in contract failure theory), low profitability, and formal exclusion of FPOs from HACC for over a decade were particularly powerful in the early years of marketisation in the sector, and the first three of these factors remain important today. Moreover, NPOs have shown limited interest in the segments in the second arena, given that the segments in the first arena have the large majority of revenue and cater for people with the highest need which is consonant with the overall mission of most NPOs. Some NPOs provide unsubsidised services, but this is usually limited to clients who are on a waiting list or who want more hours and/or different services above their government-funded entitlements. Some have gone a step further and sought to develop a business that can subsidise their other services, but some of these say that they 'burnt their fingers', finding that they faced tighter margins which forced a mode of operation that did not allow them to assist clients as fully as they wanted. On the other hand, FPOs, with little direct access to government funds, have been able to use these segments to give themselves a good platform of business, especially through subcontracting.

The fact that currently most FPOs in the industry in NSW are small and medium enterprises is explained by a number of factors. The owners of many of these providers are ex-nurses or other people with a human service background who want to work independently of large bureaucratic organisations (whether government or NPO), and thus are examples of the 'dwarves of capitalism', motivated primarily by a desire for independence and good service rather than profit (Davidson 2009, p. 57; Marceau 1990). Some of these FPOs go back decades, others are very recent, and new ones are always being established. Many of today's FPOs have emerged from this sort of beginning, including some now very substantial ones that were begun by nurses on a part-time basis with one or two clients. (Of course, a number of the FPOs are profit maximisers and/or operated by people with no human service background, while no industry-specific regulation of providers for unsubsidised services leaves the way open for more opportunist providers to enter or emerge.)

The fact that people with limited capital have been able to start their own business in this industry in a way that would not be possible in many other human services is a result of the *production function* of community aged care. At the most basic level, the provider of care for an older person living at home needs no physical equipment, financial outlay, or specialised skills to begin. There can be few industries with so few barriers to initial entry. Allied with this is the fact that the basic service involves short periods of assistance (one to two hours) where care-workers do things that most people do for themselves, and thus staff with limited skills and training can be engaged at the margin as additional hours are needed. These features of the production function also facilitate the use of subcontracting and the development of franchises. Clearly, if a provider wishes to grow and ensure consistent high quality service for large numbers of users, it needs more substantial infrastructure, better training and conditions for staff, and economies of scale and scope, but the ease of entry at a basic level of operation has been a powerful reason for the past and continuing establishment of small FPOs in the industry.

However, even a large-scale provider of community care does not need property or the substantial initial capital that is necessary, for example, with a nursing home or childcare centre (Access Economics 2009; Brennan & Newberry 2010). This critical feature of the production function also helps explain the limited interest of large corporate FPOs, whose interest in other human service sectors is based substantially on the role of property, both as a source of profits and as a security against operational and other risks, rather than the actual provision of care.[31] As well, there are other limits on the incentives for larger FPOs to seek to enter this industry, given that the nature of the target group

---

31 Thus, for example, a nursing home can be seen as an investment in rental property where there is a guaranteed high level of occupancy, rents are underpinned by secure government funding and where there is an asset that can be sold if the return is no longer considered satisfactory or the risk becomes too high. On the other hand, property also involves costs, and currently the regulations and cost structure in residential care makes that sector less attractive for providers (Access Economics 2009), and make 'community care more profitable' (Stewart Brown Business Solutions 2009).

means there are limited profits to be made relative to other industries, while under the current funding system (with previous allocations not contestable) they cannot get scale. Notwithstanding that, the profitability of community care is sufficient to attract smaller FPOs and retain large NPOs, with packages estimated in 2009–10 to return at least seven percent (profit as a proportion of total costs), and potentially 20 percent for some providers (Stewart Brown Business Solutions 2009, 2010).

Possible changes

In addition to the substantial growth arising from the ageing of the population and the increasing emphasis on ageing-in-place, the community aged care industry faces major change over the next decade arising from two sets of government decisions. One is the transfer of full responsibility for HACC services for older people (65 and over) to the Commonwealth. The other is the decisions arising from the report by the Productivity Commission (2011) of its inquiry, *Caring for older Australians*. This section considers some possible impacts of these two sets of decisions, which are likely to have profound effects on the structure and operation of providers in the industry.

Transfer of HACC for older people to the Commonwealth

In 2010, Council of Australian Governments (COAG) decided that the Commonwealth would have full funding and administrative responsibility for HACC for older people and the states would have similar responsibility for HACC for people under 65 with a disability.[32] This was to be phased in, with the Commonwealth taking policy responsibility from July 2011 and funding responsibility from July 2012, with an agreement that there would be no significant change to the program before 2015. The key principle behind this change is that services should

---

32 The Council of Australian Governments is the meeting of heads of the Commonwealth, six states and two territory governments in Australia. Since 1985, the Commonwealth and states have jointly funded HACC and the states have administered the programs.

be client-centred and making one level of government responsible for each of aged care and disability programs will facilitate integration of the planning and delivery of services for each group.

One set of effects on providers will flow simply from the fact that aged care will be the responsibility of only one level of government. This will lead to changes aimed at achieving greater consistency between the states and closer linkages between the different forms of aged care, while any further change will be much easier to achieve without the need for negotiation and agreement with the states. Further, it has already led to a different approach to allocating HACC funds than the states currently use. State agencies have relied strongly on the input of regional and local staff in deciding the allocation of funds, but the Commonwealth currently does not have a presence in this field outside the capital cities and historically has been far more dependent on formal tender processes (which, as noted earlier, tend to favour larger providers).

Some major changes to HACC, both in the short term and ones to apply after 2015, have now been announced (Australian Government 2012). The personal care services are to become a basic level of packages and administered along those lines. The other elements of HACC will be amalgamated with a number of other aged care programs to form a new Home Support Program. These changes, along with the more general effects noted above, are likely to substantially impact on the role that small NPOs play in the operation of HACC.

One significant change in NSW that in part has been driven by the transfer of HACC to the Commonwealth has been the decision by the Liberal government, elected in 2011, to privatise NSW Home Care Service (HCS) during 2015. HCS is currently the largest provider of HACC services in NSW, with total revenue of $200 million from all sources.

Government response to the Productivity Commission Report

The Productivity Commission Report (2011) and the initial government response (Australian Government 2012) were very wide-ranging and it is not possible here to trace through all the possible implications for the profile of providers in the community aged care industry.[33] Two key issues are considered below.

The Productivity Commission (2011) recommended that sufficient funding be made available to ensure that there is a place for all older people eligible for assistance. The then government decided to phase this in over the next decade by gradually increasing the number of aged care places from 113 per 1,000 people aged 70 and over to 125 places by 2021–22. Alongside this, the major theme of the government response was the importance of supporting people to remain at home as long as possible and thus a higher proportion of these places will go to community rather than residential care. Given the current parameters (in terms of population, levels of need and eligibility requirements) these changes will go a long way to meeting, by 2022, the Productivity Commission's recommendation for sufficient places for all eligible people. They will also lead to significant growth for providers, including those in the subcontracting segment. It will also mean that, with fewer waiting lists, users will have greater choice, and thus may lead to providers having to do more to attract and retain clients.

The then government decided to defer a change that has the potential to have a major impact on providers. The Productivity Commission (2011) proposed to replace the current hybrid system of funding packages with a QVL system, whereby all approved providers could freely compete for clients on an ongoing basis. Both the former and current governments have indicated support for this approach in the long-term, but will conduct further analysis. There are no plans to implement such a scheme in the short-term.

Such a system would give service users more apparent options, but (as set out in Davidson 2012), it has a number of major dangers, both in terms of ensuring the quality and efficiency of individual providers, and ensuring stability, equity, efficiency, and quality at a systemic level. Such problems have beset child care over the last decade, largely as a result of this form of funding (Brennan & Newberry 2010; Press & Woodrow 2009).

In terms of the profile of providers, it would be likely to lead to more FPOs and a greater market share for FPOs, which would be able to compete directly for clients eligible for government assistance. It may also increase the presence of large corporate FPOs, since they will be

---

33 The federal Labor government lost office in September 2013. The incoming Coalition government has largely endorsed earlier decisions.

able to obtain larger scale more quickly and can use their marketing experience to achieve this. It may also lead to either an excessive number of providers, or conversely, if regulation is reduced, to greater concentration of ownership.[34] At the same time, however, it may also allow the growth and survival of small specialist providers able to meet a niche, either for groups or to provide a specialist service which can be purchased by larger providers for their clients.

Nevertheless, the large NPOs are likely to remain dominant. They have had the time to develop as strong corporate enterprises and should be able to compete strongly in the marketplace that emerges. This has been the case in Job Network, where the NPOs that had scale in similar programs at the time of the introduction of Job Network have continued to grow. It contrasts with child care, where there were few large NPOs when a QVL system was introduced and FPOs quickly took a major share of the market, although those NPOs that did exist (such as Kindergarten Union) have continued to flourish.

Conclusion

Community aged care in Australia is a diverse and complex industry, and provides a useful study in how the structure of one human services sector has evolved under marketisation, and the impact of marketisation on the profile of providers. In community aged care in other nations and in other human service sectors in Australia, there are numerous examples of how marketisation has led to the extensive growth of FPOs, the reduction of the role of NPOs and the end of the substantial involvement of government providers. That this has not happened here in this case is a result of a number of factors, notably the situation two decades ago at the time that marketisation took hold; the subsequent relative stability of the funding system; limited incentives for the entry of larger FPOs in terms of potential profits; the fact that only growth funding has been contestable in the two major programs;

---

34 Previously, the Productivity Commission (2002, p. 11.5) has noted that the introduction of such a system for funding employment assistance for disadvantaged people under the then Job Network program would be likely to lead to some 'consolidation in the industry'.

and the maintenance of close government control over the entry and growth of providers via a tendering system where a major focus has been on ensuring the quality of care.

Much of this may change, however, in the light of government decisions both taken and still to come, especially if these lead to the introduction of a QVL funding system for the major programs where the users choose their providers and *all* funding is continuously contestable. In this context, the large NPOs are likely to retain their prominent position, but there is likely to be an increase in the number of FPOs, a greater concentration of market share, the appearance of large FPOs, and a reduced market share and uncertain future for small community-based NPOs.

The experience of community aged care in Australia has some broader implications for human services. First, where there is long-term stability of funding, history becomes more significant and the first-mover advantage is especially significant. Second, the limits on the entry and growth of FPOs in the early years of marketisation of this service enabled NPOs to develop a strong presence and the capacity to be successful in a robust competitive environment. Third, it shows that tight government control of entry and contestability aimed at ensuring quality services can co-exist with a system that maintains incentives to improve quality and efficiency alongside strong competition between providers. Fourth, it also shows the benefits of a process that closely controls the entry of new providers so as to minimise the potential problems arising from marketisation.

Change is going to happen in this industry in Australia. It is to be hoped that this does not go too far down the marketisation track in ways that remove some of the strong incentives and requirements for quality in the current system. Whatever the change is, however, it will be interesting as an experiment on the impact of government policy and funding systems on different types of human service providers and on the structure of human service industries – and the effects of this on the quality of services and outcomes for users.

Appendix

Sources and notes to Table 6.1.

(a) This includes services *funded* by government either indirectly (Sub-contracting) or by QVL systems; and services *organised* by government (Guardianship and Insurance Arrangements).

(b) The consumer-directed packages pilots started in 2011 are not included here, but under the Commonwealth community care packages, because the department selects providers to manage the packages, albeit under more direction by users.

(c) In these cases, government agencies assist people to obtain care that is often paid for from their own funds. OPC supports both younger people with a disability and older people. LCSTA is for people who have received compensation payments for a road accident injury, and is mainly used by people under 65 years old.

(d) This can include payments by companies to employees who have aged parents. I have not identified any such schemes in Australia, but they do operate in Europe (Snell, Fernandez & Bennetts 2007). (e) This funding is compensation to survivors of the Nazi Holocaust paid by various European governments, coordinated by the USA-based Claims Conference, and distributed through Jewish Care in Australia. In 2012, Australia received $3.8 million ($1.5 million in NSW), most of which was for community aged care.

Sources to Table 6.2.

Derived from DoHA (2010b p. 29 Tables 9–11). Note that the relatively high proportion and number of places held by state government providers in Victoria and South Australia are primarily state health department agencies.

Sources to Table 6.3.

Derived from DoHA (2003). Note: The data cover only CACP, EACH, EACH D packages. Some more recent minor specialised packages for which there is a single provider. (For example, NSW Health has 100 percent of Transitional Health packages are not included).

Sources to Table 6.4.
Derived from DoHA (2010a). Note: The data cover only CACP, EACH, EACH D packages. Some more recent minor specialised packages for which there is a single provider are not included (For example, NSW Health has 100 percent of Transitional Health packages).

References

Access Economics 2009, Economic evaluation of capital financing of high care, Access Economics, March.

ABS (Australian Bureau of Statistics) 2010, *Disability, ageing and carers, Australia: Summary of findings of 2009 survey*, Cat. no. 4430. 0, ABS, Canberra.

AIHW (Australian Institute of Health and Welfare) 2001, *Australia's Welfare 2001*, Canberra, Australian Institute of Health and Welfare.

Australian Government 2012, *Living longer, living better: Aged care reform package*, April. http://www.health.gov.au/internet/main/publishing. nsf/Content/ageing-aged-care-review-measures-factsheet-7.htm

Bessant, J., Watts, R., Dalton, T. & Smyth, P. 2006, *Talking policy: How social policy is made*, Allen & Unwin, Crows Nest, NSW.

Blank, R. 2000, 'When can public policy makers rely on private markets? The effective provision of social services', *The Economic Journal*, vol. 110, no. 462, pp. 34–49.

Brennan, D., Cass, B., Himmelweit, S. & Szebehely, M. 2012, 'The marketisation of care: Rationales and consequences in Nordic and liberal care regimes', *Journal of European Social Policy*, vol. 22, no. 4, pp. 377–91.

Brennan, D. & Newberry, S. 2010, Indirect policy tools: Demand-side funding and lessons to be learned: early childhood education and care, paper presented to the Asia-Pacific Interdisciplinary Research in Accounting (APIRA) Conference, Sydney, July.

Carlton, D. W. & Perloff, J. M. 2005, *Modern industrial organisation*, Pearson-Addison-Wesley, Boston.

Davidson, B. 2008, Non-profit organisations in the human services marketplace: The impact of quasi voucher-licensing systems, paper presented to the 37th Annual Conference of the Association for Research on Nonprofit Organisations and Voluntary Action (ARNOVA), Philadelphia, 20 November.

Davidson, B. 2009, 'For-profit organisations in managed markets for human services', in *Paid care in Australia: Profits, purpose and practices*, eds G. Meagher & D. King, Sydney University Press, Sydney, pp. 43–79.

Davidson, B. 2011, The community aged care industry, paper presented to the 10th Annual Conference of the Society for Heterodox Economists, Sydney, December.

Davidson, B. 2012, 'Contestability in human services markets', *Journal of Australian Political Economy*, vol. 68, pp. 213–39.

Demsetz, H. 1982, 'Barriers to entry', *The American Economic Review*, vol. 72, no. 1, pp. 47–57.

DoHA (Department of Health and Ageing) 2003, Data on approved service providers and aged care places as at 30 June, Excel spreadsheets, provided to author by DoHA.

DoHA (Department of Health and Ageing) 2010a, Data on approved service providers and aged care places as at 30 June, Excel spreadsheets. http://www.health.gov.au/internet/main/publishing. nsf/Content/ageing-rescare-servlist-download.htm

DoHA (Department of Health and Ageing) 2010b, *Report on the Operation of the Aged Care Act 1997 – 1 July 2009 to 30 June 2010*, Department of Health and Ageing, Canberra.

Esping-Andersen, G. 1990, *The three worlds of welfare capitalism*, Polity Press, Cambridge.

Hansmann, H. B. 1980, 'The role of nonprofit enterprise', *The Yale Law Journal*, vol. 89, no. 5, pp. 835–901.

Hansmann, H. B. 1987, 'Economic theories of nonprofit organisations', in *The nonprofit handbook*, ed. W. W. Powell, Yale University Press, New Haven, pp. 27–42.

Hilmer, F. G. 1993, *National competition policy*, Report by the Independent Committee of Inquiry, Australia Government Publishing Service, August.

Himmelweit, S. 2008, Rethinking care, gender inequality and policies, paper presented to the United Nations Expert Group Meeting on 'Equal sharing of responsibilities between women and men, including care-giving in the context of HIV/AIDS', Geneva, 6–9 October. http://www.un.org/womenwatch/daw/egm/equalsharing/EGM-ESOR-2008-EP-7%20Susan%20Himmelweit.pdf

House of Representatives Standing Committee on Public Expenditure 1982, *In a home or at home*, Report, Australia Government Publishing Service, Canberra, October.

House of Representatives Standing Committee on Community Affairs 1994, *Home, but not alone: A report on the Home and Community Care program*, Australia Government Publishing Service, Canberra, July.

Howe, A., King, D., Ellis, J., Wells, Y., Wei, Z. & Teshuva, K. 2012, 'Stabilising the aged care workforce: An analysis of worker retention and intention', *Australian Health Review*, vol. 36, no. 1, pp. 83–91.

Kincare 2007, Kincare website, http://www.kincare.com.au

Le Grand, J. & Bartlett, W. (eds) 1993, *Quasi markets and social policy*, Macmillan, London.

Lieberman, M. B. & Montgomery, D. B. 1988, 'First-mover advantages', *Strategic Management Journal*, vol. 9, no. S1, pp. 41–58.

Liebowitz, S. J. & Margolis, S. E. 1990, 'The fable of the keys', *Journal of Law and Economics*, vol. 33, no. 1, pp. 1–25.

Liebowitz, S. J. & Margolis, S. E. 1995, 'Path dependence, lock-in, and history', *Journal of Law, Economics & Organization*, vol. 11, no. 1, pp. 205–26.

Lyons, M. 1995, 'The development of quasi-vouchers in Australia's community services', *Policy and Politics*, vol. 23, no. 2, pp. 127–139.

Lyons, M. 2001, *Third sector: The contribution of nonprofit and cooperative enterprise in Australia*, Allen & Unwin, Sydney.

MacDermott, K. 2008, *Whatever happened to frank and fearless? The impact of new public management on the Australian public service*, ANU E Press, Canberra. http://epress. anu.edu.au/frank_fearless_citation.html

Marceau, J. 1990, 'The dwarves of capitalism: the structure of production and the economic culture of the small manufacturing firm', in *Capitalism in contracting cultures*, eds G. Redding & S. Clegg, de Gruyter, Berlin, pp. 198–212.

Martin, B. & King, D. 2008, *Who cares for older Australians? A picture of the residential and community based aged care workforce, 2007*, National Institute of Labour Studies, Flinders University, Adelaide, October.

Meagher, G. & Szebehely, M. 2013, 'Long-term care in Sweden: Trends, actors, and consequences', in *Reforms in long term care policies in Europe: Investigating institutional change and social impacts*, eds C. Ranci & E. Pavolini, Springer, New York.

Mears, J. 2012, The world of care work: Care workers and care managers working in community aged care, PhD Research Thesis, The University of Sydney.

Nevile, J. 1998, 'Economic rationalism: Social philosophy masquerading as economic science', in *Contesting the Australian way*, eds P. Smyth & B. Cass, Cambridge University Press, Melbourne, pp. 169–79.

NSW DHS (NSW Department of Human Services) 2010, *Annual Report, 2009–10*.

Osborne, D. & Gaebler, T. 1993, *How the entrepreneurial spirit is transforming the public sector*, Plume, New York.

Press, F. & Woodrow, C. 2009, 'The giant in the playground: The reach and implications of the corporatisation of child care provision', in *Paid care in Australia: Profits, purpose and practices*, eds G. Meagher & D. King, Sydney University Press, Sydney, pp. 231–52.

Productivity Commission 2002, *Independent review of the job network: Inquiry report, Report No. 21*, Productivity Commission, Canberra.

Productivity Commission 2008, *Trends in aged care services: Some implications*, Productivity Commission, Canberra, September.

Productivity Commission 2011, *Caring for older Australians, Inquiry Report*, Productivity Commission, Canberra, August.

Schmalensee, R. & Willig, R. 1989, *Handbook of industrial organisation*, Elsevier, Amsterdam.

Snell, T., Fernandez, J. & Bennetts, R. 2007, Tax exemptions on care vouchers for working carers: An economic analysis, Personal Social Services Research Unit (PSSRU), London School of Economics.

SCRGSP (Steering Committee for the Review of Government Service Provision) 2011, *Report on government services 2011*, prepared by the Productivity Commission, Canberra. http://www.pc.gov.au/research/recurring/report-on-government-services/2011/2011/rogs-2011-volume2.pdf

Stewart Brown Business Solutions 2009, Aged care financial performance survey for year ended 30 June 2009. http://www.sbbsolutions.com.au

Stewart Brown Business Solutions 2010, Aged care financial performance survey for the 9 months ended 31 March 2010. http://www.sbbsolutions.com.au

Stilwell, F. 2005, *Political economy: The contest of economic ideas*, Oxford University Press, South Melbourne.

Travers, P. 2005, 'Rights and responsibilities: Welfare and citizenship', in *Social science and public policy in Australia*, eds P. Saunders & J. Walter, UNSW Press, Sydney, pp. 85–102.

Treasury 2010, *The 2010 Intergenerational report: Australia to 2050 – future challenges*, Australian Government Treasury, Canberra, January.

Ungerson, C. & Yeandle, S. 2007, *Cash for care in developed welfare states*, Palgrave Macmillan, Basingstoke.

Wilberforce, M., Glendinning, C., Challis, D., Fernandez, J., Jacobs, S., Jones, K., Knapp, M., Manthorpe, J., Moran, N., Netten, A. & Stevens, M. 2011, 'Implementing consumer choice in long-term care: The impact of individual budgets on social care providers in England', *Social Policy & Administration*, vol. 45, no. 5, pp. 593–612.

Yeatman, A. 1990, 'The right of redress', *Australian Journal on Ageing*, vol. 9, no. 3, pp. 27–31.

7

Home security: Marketisation and the changing face of housing assistance in Australia

Lucy Groenhart and Nicole Gurran

Australia's housing system has always been primarily private, with the property development industry delivering the majority of new housing since the early days of colonisation. Since Federation in 1901, strong Commonwealth government support for home ownership reflected and reinforced the great Australian dream of owning a home (Paris 1993). Representing material as well as emotional security, home ownership has been an important aspiration for the majority of Australian households, with short-term private rental accommodation regarded as a secondary and transitional option at the beginning of the housing career (Badcock & Beer 2000). The rate of home ownership, outright or with a mortgage, has only declined slightly over the past 50 years, from 71 percent in 1966 to 67 percent in 2011 (ABS 2010, 2011). A small public rental housing system, funded since 1945 through Commonwealth grants to the states under the Commonwealth State Housing Agreement (CSHA) was originally intended to complement and offset the vagaries of the private land and housing market, but in practice, remained largely divorced from wider government initiatives for home ownership and urban policy (Gleeson & Low 2000).

Groenhart, L. & Gurran, N. 2015, 'Home security: Marketisation and the changing face of housing assistance in Australia', in *Markets, rights and power in Australian social policy*, eds G. Meagher & S. Goodwin, Sydney University Press, Sydney.

Despite a significant program of construction in the postwar decades, much of the public rental housing developed by the State Housing Authorities was sold to tenants during the 1980s and by the early 1990s public rental housing had become a small sector of the over-all housing system, highly targeted towards low-income households (Jones, Phillips & Milligan 2007). This tightening of access to public housing coincided with an ongoing contraction of new public housing supply. A National Affordable Housing Agreement (NAHA) replaced the CSHA in 2009, promising a wider policy framework for public housing, remote Indigenous housing, and homelessness initiatives. The new 'affordable housing' lexicon signalled a conceptual bridge between private market forms of housing delivery and the evolution of a new housing sector, encompassing public, community, non-profit, and for-profit housing providers.

This chapter provides a taxonomy of these new initiatives, concep-tualising them within the larger evolution of Australia's housing assis-tance policy under the influence of 'new public management' (NPM) in the 1980s and 1990s. It discusses the privatisation of rental housing support through the introduction of semi-market measures such as fi-nancial rent assistance and the economic rationalisation of public hous-ing services; the diversification of the social housing sector through the introduction of new housing providers and forms of housing provision; the introduction of new financial incentives to leverage private sector investment in affordable housing development and to encourage new partnerships for mixed-tenure housing development; and the mobili-sation of the land use planning system to secure additional resources and development opportunities for social housing and/or subsidised home purchase. The chapter situates the Australian case in relation to international developments in housing policy, highlighting key influ-ences; particularly the diversification of social housing provision, estate renewal and redevelopment, private rental assistance, incentives for in-vestment in social housing, and the planning system. In conclusion, the chapter highlights some of the tensions that have arisen in the increas-ing adoption of market mechanisms and reliance on private funding in the delivery of housing assistance, and the future security of Australia's hybrid affordable housing sector underpinned by public assets and sub-sidy, but sustained by private investment.

Housing, governments and markets

In the private housing market – rental or owner-occupied – the ability to obtain a home depends on the ability to pay. A household's demand for housing, defined by Harriott and Matthews (1998, p. 3) as 'the desire for housing backed by the ability to pay for it' will be met by the private market. This chapter looks at government intervention when the market fails to meet the housing demands of all households. In Australia, this intervention includes direct provision of housing by the state, private rental assistance, and home ownership subsidies. While 'affordable housing' can be a tenure-neutral term to describe housing that is priced to be accessible to low to moderate income households, for the purpose of this chapter it is defined more specifically for the Australian context as housing that is initiated and owned by non-government not-for-profit providers; financed through a mix of public subsidies, planning benefits, private equity or debt finance; priced at below market rents and restricted to moderate or low-income client groups (Lawson & Milligan 2007, p. 75; Wiesel et al. 2012, p. 13). In Australia, 'public housing' refers to housing which is owned and managed by State Housing Authorities (SHAs), whereas 'social housing' is a more expansive term which encompasses public housing and housing owned or managed by other entities, such as community housing or church groups, on a not-for-profit basis.

National trends in housing assistance

Australian housing assistance policy reflects several international trends in analogous jurisdictions where private home ownership remains the dominant tenure form, such as the United States, the United Kingdom and New Zealand. Within an overall policy framework favouring private home ownership, as well as a smaller private rental market, direct support through publicly developed and managed housing has been a feature of national housing policy since the early the 20th century, but gained particular momentum in the postwar years (von Hoffman 2009). In the latter years of the last century, Australia, like many other nations, began to diversify approaches to direct housing assistance from government to non-government, community-based or non-profit housing providers; renew and redevelop ageing public housing estates; and introduce mixed-tenure models intended to reduce spatial concentrations of social disadvantage. Other international trends influencing Australian housing policy included increasing the use of demand-based subsidies to assist low and moderate income earners meet housing payments (rather than investing in increased affordable or public housing supply); financial incentives for investment in social housing; and planning system mechanisms to preserve existing low-cost homes or secure new affordable housing opportunities during processes of urban development.

Internationally, the era of government housing provision that began in the 1950s was in decline in the United States, the United Kingdom, and New Zealand from the 1960s. In the United States, the federal government was increasingly reliant on the private market, and in 1973 Richard Nixon ordered a freeze on public housing construction (Husock 1997, p. 73), while in the United Kingdom, the 1960s saw the promotion of private, non-profit housing associations as an alternative to council housing (Mullins & Murie 2006, p. 37). In New Zealand, investment levels in public housing diminished and by the 1980s, state-owned housing accounted for only five percent of dwellings (Murphy 2003, p. 119). Following this withdrawal of supply-side subsidies through the direct provision of public housing, there was increased focus on demand-side subsidies and private market led solutions. In many jurisdictions, this meant giving tenants 'vouchers' to purchase rental accommodation in the private market (Harriott & Matthews 1998; Murphy 2003; Jacob 2004).

These housing assistance trends demonstrate broader shifts in the relationship between governments and markets. Since the mid-1980s there has been a transformation in the role of the government in many countries. The traditional, hierarchical, bureaucratic form of public administration, which predominated for most of the 20th century, moved towards a more flexible, market-based form of public management, collectively known as 'new public management' 'managerialism' or 'reinventing government' (Hughes 1998; Norman & Stace 1998). Although NPM is generally associated with the 1980s and 1990s, its origins can be traced back to the economic boom following the Second World War. This began with a rapid expansion of quasi-governmental bodies at the edges of government in the 1960s. It progressed in the 1970s with a 'privatisation boom, in response to 'claimed pathologies of the traditional bureaucratic mode of public administration' (Cheung 1996, p. 38).

Economists in the 1970s devised models of bureaucracy that argued the public sector budget was inflated under pluralist party political systems (Niskanen 1973). Under these models, bureaucracies inherently oversupply outputs by establishing a budget that delivers up to twice the socially optimal level of services (Dunleavy 1986, p. 16). Traditional models of bureaucracy were thought to be 'consumed by incentives to maximise their own power at the expense of public goals' (Kettl 2000, p. 31). This 'public choice school' of economic thought is most closely associated with James Buchanan (Bannock, Baxter & Davis 2003, p. 315). Buchanan (1978) viewed government as a leviathan which aimed to maximise its revenue, exploit its monopoly power and expand its influence. The power of government to tax, borrow and print money should therefore be limited (Bannock et al. 2003, p. 315). From these intellectual sources came the impetus to corporatise, privatise (where possible) and open up the public sector to competition.

The public choice school formed the basis of what Donald Kettl has called a 'global reform movement in public management' (2000, p. 1). He argues that this movement has embodied six core characteristics: an overall focus on productivity, or how governments can produce more services with less tax money; marketisation, or how governments can use market style incentives to rid bureaucracy of its 'pathologies'; service orientation, or how governments can 'better connect' with their citizens; decentralisation of programs to lower levels of government; a focus on improving policy development and delivery by separating policy and provision agencies; and accountability, with a shift in focus from process and structure to outputs and outcomes. Many other authors have also summarised the major tenets of NPM, for example Rod Rhodes (1991), who characterised NPM as embodying a focus on management, not policy; a focus on performance appraisal and efficiency; the disaggregation of public bureaucracies into agencies that deal with each other on a user pays basis; the use of quasi-markets and contracting out to foster competition; cost cutting; and a management style which emphasises output targets, limited term contracts, and monetary performance incentives.

International housing policy and NPM

In international housing policy, NPM was applied chiefly through the marketisation of housing assistance. Approaches to marketisation include extensive privatisation by selling public assets, and relying on the private sector for service delivery. In the United States, HOPE VI was the major federal level housing assistance marketisation intervention. Between 1992 and 2002, 63,100 public housing units were demolished, with housing vouchers provided to enable some of the original residents to rent in the private market (Popkin et al. 2004, p. 2). In the United Kingdom, marketisation was seen in housing stock transfer to arms-length housing associations, and the introduction of market processes into a shrinking public housing portfolio, whereby public landlords were increasingly reliant on private finance (Bramley, Munro & Pawson 2004, p. 3). In New Zealand, the application of NPM to housing assistance occurred from 1990, with key reforms including the creation of a profit-oriented Housing New Zealand Corporation to manage state-owned housing, the privatisation of the state's residential mortgage portfolio, market rents for state houses, and the introduction of housing vouchers to assist low-income households with housing costs in the private rental sector (Murphy 2003, p. 119).

Foundations of Australian housing assistance

Australian Commonwealth and state governments provide assistance for home ownership. The current suite of assistance mechanisms include government outlays, such as the First Home Owner Grant; taxation expenditures, including the non-taxation of imputed rent from owner occupation, rates and land tax concessions, and capital gain and stamp duty exemptions; and government regulations and standards in housing and financial markets (SCRGSP 2006–13).

Housing as a basic human need

In addition to support for home purchase, governments in Australia intervene in the housing market by funding social housing and private rental assistance. The basis of this intervention is the philosophical position that access to housing is a basic human need:

Table 7.1 Australian government housing assistance

Policy	Year intro-duced	Nature of assis-tance	Expenditure in most recent year ($M)
Commonwealth First Home Owner Grant (FHOG) subsidies*	2000	Indirect	$706 (2011/12)
Negative gearing tax concessions**	1930s	Indirect	$7,901 (2010/11)
Private rental assistance (CRA)	1958	Indirect	$3,354 (2011/12)
Subsidised non-government provision through community housing***	1980s	Indirect	$509 (2010/11)
Social housing provision (capital and recurrent expenditure)	1945	Direct	$6,053 (2011/12)

*2011/12 figures are for $7,000 FHOG only, state FHOG boosts and concessions are excluded. ** Australian Taxation Statistics for 2010/11 financial year. ***Community housing expenditure for 2010/11. Sources: (SCRGSP 2006–13; ATO 2012).

Housing is a basic human need. Governments in Australia assist home ownership, and in turn accept that people who are not in home ownership should be ensured some of its benefits – through public housing and rental assistance (Australian Industry Commission 1993, p. xv).

The key elements of government housing assistance are set out in Table 7.1, along with their year of introduction and the level of expenditure in the most recently available financial year. These figures exclude capital gain exemptions on the primary dwelling. The table demonstrates that annual indirect housing subsidies (including private rental assistance) totalled over $12 billion, more than double the $6 billion spent on social housing.

The Commonwealth government in Australia was directly involved in housing policy from the beginning of the 20th century, albeit through subsidies for private homeownership only. The *War Service Homes Act* (1912), provided for loans to returned servicemen and gave power to the War Service Homes Commission to build homes for sale to these servicemen, while the *Commonwealth Housing Act* (1927 and

1928) provided housing finance loans to facilitate home ownership for low to moderate income households (Pettigrew 2005, p. 25). At state level, the first SHAs began to take shape between 1935 and 1941, with the exceptions of Queensland and Western Australia, which focused on the construction of subsidised dwellings for homeowners during this period (Hayward 1996, p. 15). Three conceptions of public housing were predominant up to 1945: as a reward for deserving families who could not afford home ownership; as a tool for the alleviation of poverty; and as a temporary necessity to overcome a housing 'shortage' caused by depression and war (Jones 1972 cited in Pettigrew 2005, p. 30).

The Commonwealth established a Housing Commission in 1943 to examine Australia's housing problems, and recommend solutions to address them. The report set out a national target of 80,000 new public housing dwellings per year. The Commonwealth government would assume the major financial responsibility on account of its superior revenue raising capacity, and the state governments would have direct responsibility for constructing and managing the public housing sector (Berry 1988, p. 98). This represented a shift towards government support for public housing as a legitimate tenure. The Commonwealth periodically negotiated agreements about housing with the states, under the CSHA. The first CSHA in 1954 encouraged Queensland (1945) and Western Australia (1946) to establish Housing Commissions, while Tasmania expanded its housing sales program to include the provision of rental units. Under this first CSHA, the number of public dwelling completions rose from 4,028 in 1945–46 to 14,317 in 1954–55. A total of 96,292 public dwellings were completed through the first CSHA (Hayward 1996, p. 16).

Public housing in the postwar years

In the immediate postwar decades, Australian public housing was aimed at those who had the potential to be economically and socially independent. Eligibility criteria excluded the unemployed, the elderly, sole parents and those with disabilities (see Hayward 1996). The stock constructed from the 1940s to the 1970s reflected this, being largely three-bedroom detached houses (with some high rise in Melbourne and Sydney) (Burke & Hayward 2006). In the 1970s, the Housing Commissions were replaced by Housing Departments. In Victoria and NSW the construction of high rise towers, which was a prominent feature of public housing provision in the 1960s, was wound down by the 1970s. The emphasis began to shift away from the construction of whole suburbs and high rise towers toward infill housing, often in inner and middle suburbs (Hayward 1996).

The CSHA was renegotiated numerous times between 1943 and 2009. The Whitlam government increased the funding of public housing in 1972, but also imposed a stricter means test for public housing tenants in the 1973 CSHA. In 1978, the Fraser government reduced considerably the amount of funding for public housing, and proposed a phased introduction of market rents during the life of the CSHA. Funding for public housing was increased by the newly elected Hawke government between 1983 and 1984. This high level of funding was maintained under the 1984 CSHA. From 1986 to 1987 the Commonwealth reduced the level of funding, but at the same time agreed to replace all loans to SHAs with grants (Hayward 1996).

Despite the fluctuating funding levels, a consistent theme from the 1956 CSHA onwards was the use of public housing as another way to promote owner occupation, through sales programs to tenants. By the end of the 1960s it is estimated that Victoria had sold 43 percent of its public housing (Burke et al. 1985, cited in Hayward 1996, p. 19), while Tasmania had sold 67 percent (Martin 1988 cited in Hayward 1996, p. 19). Therefore, the public housing project in Australia over the period of the CSHAs can be seen within the wider context of state and Commonwealth government support for private owner occupation.

The marketisation of Australian housing assistance

Along with a longstanding focus on the private market and owner occupation from the beginnings of government housing assistance, Australian housing policy was also influenced by NPM ideas. By the 1980s, there was a growing awareness throughout the public housing sector that housing assistance in Australia was in need of reform. Funding declined, with the Commonwealth government redirecting housing assistance payments toward private rental subsidies. The consequences for public housing included record waiting lists, a mismatch between available stock and the needs of households, and a maintenance backlog (Burke & Hayward 2006).

NPM in Australian housing

NPM was applied across the Australian public sector. Until the 1980s, Australia had a traditional public service culture modelled on the British system of public administration. From the mid-1980s, the Commonwealth government embarked on a major series of reforms. Public sector agencies were to be more market-oriented, and if state agencies could not be fully privatised then business practices would be applied to their management (Pusey 1991). It was in the context of these changes to the public sector as a whole that NPM came to be applied to housing policy. The public administration methodology employed in the housing sector (and other government agencies) entailed clear specification of objectives, and funding for the delivery of a set of outputs, which in turn delivered outcomes that helped achieve the original objectives (Burke & Hayward 2006). This system of measurable objectives and outputs fostered a culture of policy and program evaluation.

Terry Burke and David Hayward (2006, p. 8) contend that by the mid-1990s, the Australian public housing system was characterised by a cascading set of performance indicators, 'all intimately linked to the new managerialism', another term for NPM. At the national level, indicators included how well public housing met its objectives, and how public housing agencies were performing compared with other sectors, for example, the private rental sector. These were repeated at the state level, in terms of how well a SHA was meeting its objectives and its performance compared to the private sector. Within individual SHA business units, indicators focused on how well a specific function or business was performing, for example, housing finance, stock production or rental housing management. This cascaded all the way down to an individual SHA employee level, with work performance measured against prescribed targets. The emphasis on performance indicators at all levels of the public housing system demonstrates the shift to measuring outputs and outcomes emphasised by Kettl (2000) and Rhodes (1991).

Within housing policy, NPM principles were also seen in the Mant Report on public housing in NSW (Mant 1992) and the Industry Commission report on public housing nationally (Industry Commission 1993). For example, following the recommendations of the Mant Report, some housing policy and regulatory functions were separated from the NSW Department of Housing and located in another agency (although these were subsequently returned to the Department of Housing) (ShelterNSW February 2006, p. 36). This separation of policy and service delivery functions is one of the six core characteristics of NPM identified by Kettl (2000).

Residualisation of public housing

The tangible consequences of this shift to NPM principles included funding and stock stagnation for public housing, moves towards private market provision with housing vouchers, and looking to the market to assist with housing estate renewal. Between 1984–85 and 1994–95, per capita levels of spending on CSHA housing assistance for public housing decreased by one-quarter, while during the same period expenditure on Commonwealth Rent Assistance (housing vouchers) more than tripled (AIHW 1997, p. 155–57, cited in DOH November 2000, p. 34). From 1996 to 2012 the total social housing stock declined from around 400,000 dwellings to 330,000, now amounting to less than four percent of total housing stock (SCRGSP 2006–13). Figure 7.1 compares real government expenditure on public housing through the last two CSHAs (to the end of 2008) and Commonwealth Rent Assistance (CRA), demonstrating declining funding for direct housing assistance in favour of market-based housing vouchers.

This decline in the proportion of public housing units 'occurred at a time when there was a disproportional growth in the number of low-income households' (Yates 2002, p. 38). Targeting of public housing through rationing allocations was a response to this situation, and by 2010 around 90 percent of tenants were on social security benefits, compared to less than 50 percent in 1981 (Income and Housing Survey 1981/2 and 2009/10). Singles and sole parents, many having experienced domestic violence, drug and alcohol addiction, or mental illness, became the major groups being allocated public housing. This growing proportion of low-income and high-needs households in public housing has been termed the 'residualisation' of the sector, whereby it became housing 'of last resort' rather than a mainstream tenure choice (Atkinson & Jacobs 2008, p. 4).

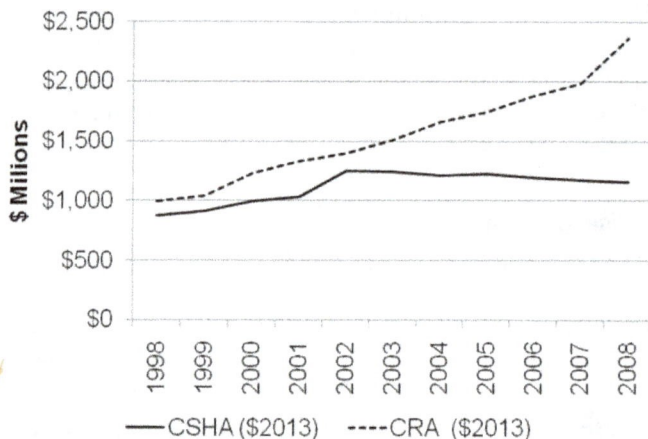

Figure 7.1 Real expenditure on public housing and private rental vouchers, 1998–2008 (AUD2013). Source: SCRGSP (2006–13); ABS (2013)

This residualisation of public housing, combined with the physical design legacies of the 1960s and 1970s, meant that housing estates became highly stigmatised (Arthurson 2004). Consequently, by the 1980s SHAs across Australia began to undertake renewal projects on public housing estates to reduce concentrations of social deprivation (Randolph & Judd 2000). These renewal activities have also provided opportunities to leverage new private market funding in the redevelopment of social housing and, potentially, new forms of housing assistance targeting more moderate income earners now needing modest levels of government subsidy to meet their housing payments (see Parry & Strommen 2001; Hughes 2004; Randolph & Judd 2006). Much of this renewal activity has focused on social mix, by diversifying tenure on public housing estates to introduce private renters and owners (Groenhart 2013a).

A new era of housing assistance?

In 2007, the election of the first of several Labor governments (2007–2013) marked a renewed Commonwealth government interest in housing. The introduction of a new National Affordable Housing Agreement – which replaced the CSHA in 2009 – was a tangible expression of the government's housing policy platform. The NAHA is structured around a single objective, that: 'all Australians have access to affordable, safe and sustainable housing that contributes to social and economic participation' (COAG 2008). The NAHA is much broader in scope than the 60 years of CSHAs it replaced, covering measures at all levels of government that impact on housing affordability. It includes Commonwealth, state and territory and local governments, and embraces a wide range of policy areas, incorporating homelessness, social housing, efficient private housing markets and Indigenous housing.

In addition to the NAHA, the Rudd government also introduced the Nation Building and Jobs Plan, a stimulus package responding to the global economic downturn of 2008 and 2009. This included a National Partnership Agreement on Social Housing, with funding to upgrade 2,500 existing social housing dwellings by 2010 and construct 20,000 new social housing dwellings by 2012. In the wider sphere of housing affordability, the federal ALP government introduced the National Rental Affordability Scheme (NRAS) in July 2008 to stimulate the supply of new affordable private market rental dwellings, through the subsidisation of new dwellings which are rented at below market rates.

Together, these initiatives marked a changing emphasis in Australian housing assistance; with renewed Commonwealth government engagement in housing markets in general, and in affordable and public housing in particular. The question is whether these changes represent a shift away from the marketisation of housing assistance, or are the next stage in the evolution of the NPM project.

Diversity and choice for social housing 'customers'

The diversification of the social housing sector through the introduction of new housing providers was underway from the 1990s. This was achieved when SHAs transferred the management, and in some cases the ownership, of public housing stock to community-based providers.

These transfers continued into the 2000s and accelerated under the NAHA. During the mid-1990s the lexicon supporting stock transfer was very much embedded in concepts of greater housing 'choice' for 'clients or customers' – public housing tenants – for whom diversity of housing delivery from non-profit housing providers acting in competition with each other was to result in better overall housing services. This is a stark example of the use of quasi-markets and the use of contracting out to increase competition. In some ways the promises of this policy were realised, with significant improvements in tenancy management and satisfaction outcomes recorded in areas of NSW where early transfers (of tenancies and management, rather than actual property title) took place (for example, see Department of Families and Community Services 2002). Interventions through intensive tenancy management by Argyle Community Housing on the troubled Claymore public housing estate in NSW in the late 1990s highlighted the potential for community-based organisations to undertake specific engagement programs and to more closely monitor service and maintenance standards for their smaller property portfolios (Randolph & Judd 2000).

Nonetheless, in comparison to international jurisdictions, Australia's community housing sector remained relatively small in scale with supply and growth limitations meaning that ideas of housing choice for low-income households and those with special needs were never really achieved in most jurisdictions. While the community housing sector had just under 46,000 dwellings by 2010 (a 170 percent increase in supply in from 2000), there were still 37,000 applicants on the community housing waiting list (AIHW 2011). Furthermore, public housing dwellings decreased by 6.6 percent over this same period. Because of declining funding for public housing and the transfer of public housing units to community housing providers, there has been no net increase in social housing supply (see Groenhart 2013b).

Leveraging private sector investment

The introduction of new financial incentives to leverage private sector investment in affordable housing development and to encourage new partnerships for mixed housing development and redevelopment have also been central to rhetoric around diversification and provision of 'choice' in the social housing sector.

In 2008 the Rudd government initiated a scheme to provide financial incentives for private sector investment in affordable housing development. The NRAS was intended to support the construction of 50,000 dwellings, with up to 35,000 new homes anticipated by 2014–15. However, the program proved more popular than anticipated and by 2012, support for 40,000 new dwellings had already been allocated. However, these allocations were time limited and expired if the housing was not completed within a specified timeframe. Investors were required to offer the housing to eligible low and moderate income households at 20 percent below market rents, with tax incentives offered in return over a 10-year period. Although such incentive programs may improve overall supply of affordable homes, long-term outcomes are uncertain, particularly as schemes end and investors seek to sell or reposition these homes (Gilmour & Milligan 2008). It has also been argued that the NRAS could have better supported not-for-profit developers, for instance, by dedicating some incentives specifically for non-profit providers, and by connecting the scheme more explicitly with other public funding and policy levers, such as access to developable land (Milligan, Gurran, Lawson, Phibbs & Phillips et al. 2009). At any rate, the NRAS did not survive the change of government in 2013. It was defunded in the Abbott Coalition government's first budget of May 2014 (DSS 2014).

Social housing for nation building

Economic stimulus has also come in the form of government support for the private housing construction sector. In the wake of the GFC, Australia's social and affordable housing supply was boosted by the Rudd government's Nation Building – Economic Stimulus Plan which included funding of $5.238 billion for more than 19,000 new social housing units (2008–09 to 2011–12) (Australian Government 2010). To ensure rapid delivery to achieve the objective of economic stimulus through the construction sector, special purpose legislation to fast-track projects and bypass local planning laws was introduced. By June 2011 over 15,000 new social housing projects had been completed, with an additional 5,000 underway (Commonwealth Coordinator-General 2011, p. 5).

The Housing Affordability Fund

The Rudd government's Housing Affordability Fund (HAF) was another program designed to lift the supply of new homes. Around $450 million was allocated to be spent over five years from 2008, for projects intended to lower the costs of building new homes and result in additional new supply (Australian Government 2008). A total of 75 projects were funded, 23 of which emphasise planning system reform (largely in relation to electronic development assessment) and the remaining a combination of studies and preparatory work intended to reduce developer holding costs, by lowering costs of providing basic infrastructure like water, sewerage, transport or open space. While this subsidy for both the social housing sector and wider housing markets may appear to be a new level of government intervention, Clapham and colleagues argue that such subsidies indicate 'that government eagerness to widen and extend the market can overrule the ultimate "ideal" of non-intervention in the market itself' (1990, pp. 27–28). Subsidies such as the Nation Building stimulus and HAF can be understood as essential to retain a functioning market – in terms of construction employment of private housing supply – in conditions where it may not otherwise be able to operate.

Planning for affordable housing – can the private housing market deliver?

The land use planning system regulates processes of urban development and change by allocating land for particular purposes, stipulating controls on the scale, form and density of development, and coordinating the provision of wider infrastructure and services. In mixed market economies, government intervention in private development through planning is tolerated because it promotes certainty for investors and property owners. From a social welfare perspective, planning regulation minimises negative 'spillover' impacts arising from private development and promotes wider social fairness in processes of urban and regional change. In many jurisdictions throughout the world, these wider societal objectives have extended to the provision of affordable housing for low and moderate income groups (Calavita & Mallach 2010; Whitehead 2007).

While most of the other key international housing system trends under the wider influence of NPM and in particular 'marketisation' (such as stock transfer, estate redevelopment and social mix) have been embraced in some form by Australia's SHAs, there has been much greater ambivalence about using the planning system to secure affordable homes (Beer, Kearins & Pieters 2007). This is in marked contrast to nations such as the United Kingdom, where affordable housing has long been a material planning consideration and where the majority of social housing is now delivered on sites secured through the planning process; and the United States, where most major metropolitan areas and many hundreds of regional cities and towns have introduced legal mechanisms to secure opportunities for affordable housing development or to directly generate new affordable housing supply (Calavita & Mallach 2010; Gurran et al. 2008).

The housing industry

Australia's influential private housing industry may in part explain the reluctance to enable local authorities to mandate affordable housing in new developments. An important sector within Australia's overarching housing system, private housing developers largely kept pace with demand by delivering a steady supply of new homes up until the turn of the millennium (Austin, Gurran & Whitehead 2010). However, this housing was largely delivered in new suburban 'Greenfield' developments which formed the dominant pattern of Australia's urban growth until at least the early 1990s and in many cities so continues. Since the early 1990s there has been a shifting emphasis in urban policy towards containing new growth within existing areas through urban renewal and redevelopment strategies but this has proved a challenging adjustment for the housing industry (NHSC 2010).

The sector has been vocal in criticising the planning system, particularly in relation to land release/urban containment policies, regulatory burden and delay, as well as costs associated with infrastructure provision (Productivity Commission 2011; RDC 2007). These lobbying efforts have been extremely effective over the past decade, influencing the evolution of an ongoing program of planning system reform characterised by an emphasis on 'red tape' reduction; lower fees and charges for infrastructure; and faster planning approvals (for example, Department of Sustainability and Environment 2006; Government of Western Australia 2009; also see Ruming, Gurran & Randolph 2011). However, the reform agenda has rarely included explicit interventions for affordable housing inclusion in new developments. Instead it has emphasised wider deregulation and efficiency which, by implication, will result in a more responsive housing market delivering overall housing affordability (COAG Reform Council 2010).

Nevertheless, several jurisdictions have also experimented with the use of planning mechanisms for affordable housing. Until 2005, these experiments were for the most part a series of bespoke pilot projects driven by dedicated local councils in Victoria and NSW (Gurran 2003). The earliest examples arose in the late 1980s with the establishment of the Port Phillip Housing Company within the former City of St Kilda Council in Victoria. Using a combination of early Commonwealth funding to establish local community housing providers (known as the Community Housing Initiatives Program), as well as concessions and bonuses secured through the planning process, the Port Phillip Housing Association had steadily grown to a portfolio of over 600 dwellings by 2011. However, other attempts to use the planning system for affordable housing in Victoria have been less successful.

In NSW, the nation's first 'inclusionary zoning' scheme (where developments within designated areas must deliver a proportion of development value for affordable housing) was established in 1994 in the urban renewal precinct of Pyrmont and Ultimo. Over time, the special purpose City West Housing Company, established through Commonwealth and state funding to demonstrate a delivery model for affordable housing in renewal contexts, has yielded over 500 housing units through a combination of initial government funding and an ongoing revenue stream through developer contributions and rental income (Milligan et al. 2009). A series of other niche schemes emerged in NSW over the past decade, although overall these have failed to achieve significant momentum or scale.

In contrast to this strictly voluntary approach, the South Australian government has gradually introduced mandatory affordable housing requirements for all new residential areas. The requirement follows the articulation in 2005 of a state affordable housing target to ensure that

15 percent of all new housing is affordable to low and moderate income earners. Over time the implementation mechanisms to support this target have been introduced through successive amendments to state and local planning laws. While initially applied only on government land, the model has steadily gained traction in conjunction with the other Commonwealth subsidies for affordable housing development, such as the National Rental Affordability Scheme and the Housing Affordability Fund. By 2011, over 600 affordable dwellings had been delivered under the model across metropolitan Adelaide, through a combination of affordable rental and home purchase schemes (Davison et al. 2012).

Back to the market?

Housing assistance is, according to Clapham and colleagues, the form of social welfare that lends itself most readily to market provision, given the reliance on the private sector for house building, even for public sector housing, and the nature of housing as a commodity (1990, p. 27). The initiatives described here under 'a new era of housing assistance' marked a temporary reinvigoration of housing assistance policy in Australia. However, this increase in policy 'activity' by government did not signal a retreat from the market towards direct government provision. Rather, these initiatives signified the evolution and maturation of NPM in housing policy. The shift away from public housing to a choice-based social housing sector was imbued with public choice school values, while funding initiatives that facilitate private investment in rental housing were designed to support the continued function of the market in an economic downturn and housing supply crisis, rather than substitute private sector activity. Planning system interventions are intended to improve market conditions by reducing regulatory 'red tape', relying on this as the primary mechanism through which the planning system could contribute to housing affordability by increasing the supply of private sector housing. Other interventions – such as voluntary and mandatory affordable housing requirements – have had limited application and have delivered only a small number of new dwellings. Moreover, Labor's measures of 2007–13 were shortlived; some by design, others by retrenchment by the Coalition government after its election in 2013. The National Housing Supply Council, which the Rudd government had established in 2008 to provide national projections of housing supply and demand, was abolished in November 2013 (Treasury 2013), and, as noted above, the National Rental Affordability Scheme was shelved in May 2014. Meanwhile, as the government has disengaged from housing policy at the federal level, private market pressures have continued unabated. House prices rose on average 10 percent in the capital cities in the year to March 2014 (ABS 2014). The private rental market is also tight, with vacancy rates between 2 and 3 percent in all capital cities except Canberra, and rents increasing in the year to June 2013 (SCRGSP 2014: Table GA.10 and GA.11). The withdrawal of government engagement is therefore leaving housing provision up to a private market that is not delivering for lower income households.

The origins of marketisation are not found solely in the NPM project from the 1980s. Rather, they represent the entrenched tradition of Australian government intervention in housing markets for the purpose of supporting the private housing construction sector and the goal of owner occupation. In contrast to the postwar government commitment towards universal access to appropriate and affordable housing, the role of social housing within contemporary Australian housing assistance policy has shifted. Rather than a reward for deserving families unable to afford home ownership, or even a tool to alleviate poverty, social housing is now a tenure of last resort. Households excluded from home ownership miss out on the significant levels of government subsidy it attracts, including first home owner grants and capital gains tax exemptions, along with negative gearing for landlords. While the policy mechanisms have been dramatically transformed since Federation in 1901, subsidisation and government support for the smooth operation of the private market to deliver housing and support home ownership has remained a constant. As such, housing assistance in Australia has always been marketised.

References

ABS (Australian Bureau of Statistics) 1981/2 and 2009/10, *Income and housing survey*, ABS, Canberra.

ABS 2010, *Year book Australia, 2009–10*, Cat. no. 1301. 0, ABS, Canberra.

7 Home security

ABS 2011, *Basic community profiles*, ABS, Canberra.

ABS 2013, *Consumer price index, Australia,* Cat. no. 6401. 0, ABS, Canberra.

ABS 2014, *Residential Property Price Indexes: Eight Capital Cities, March 2014*, Cat No. 6416.0, Canberra, Australian Bureau of Statistics.

AIHW (Australian Institute of Health and Welfare) 2011, *Community housing 2009–10*, Australian Institute of Health and Welfare, Canberra.

Arthurson, K. 2004, 'From stigma to demolition: Australian debates about housing and social exclusion', *Journal of Housing and the Built Environment*, vol. 19, no. 3, pp. 255–70.

Atkinson, R. & Jacobs, K. 2008, Public housing in Australia: Stigma, home and opportunity, Housing and Community Research Unit Discussion Paper 1, School of Sociology, University of Tasmania, Hobart.

ATO (Australian Taxation Office) 2012, *Australian taxation statistics 2009–10*, Australian Taxation Office, Canberra.

Austin, P. M., Gurran, N. & Whitehead, C. 2010, Planning and affordable housing: Diverse approaches from a common starting point? The experience of Australia, New Zealand and the UK, paper presented to the Cambridge Centre for Housing and Planning Research Conference, 15–16 September, Cambridge.

Australian Government 2008, *Housing Affordability Fund: Consultation paper*, Australian Government, Canberra.

Australian Government 2010, Nation building economic stimulus and jobs plan – Social housing. http://www.economicstimulusplan.gov.au/housing/pages/default.aspx

Badcock, B. & Beer, A. 2000, *Home truths: Property ownership and housing wealth in Australia*, Melbourne University Press, Melbourne.

Bannock, G., Baxter, R. & Davis, E. 2003, *Dictionary of economics*, Penguin Books, London.

Beer, A., Kearins, B. & Pieters, H. 2007, 'Housing affordability and planning in Australia: The challenge of policy under neo-liberalism', *Housing Studies*, vol. 22, no. 1, pp. 11–24.

Berry, M. 1988, 'To buy or rent? The demise of a dual tenure housing policy in Australia, 1945–60', in *New houses for old*, ed. R. Howe, Victorian Ministry for Housing, Melbourne.

Bramley, G., Munro, M. & Pawson, H. 2004, *Key issues in housing: Policies and markets in 21st-century Britain*, Palgrave Macmillan, Basingstoke, Hampshire, UK.

Buchanan, J. 1978, *The economics of politics*, Institute for Economic Affairs, London.

Burke, T. & Hayward, D. 2006, Performance indicators and social housing in Australia, Institute for Social Research, Swinburne University of Technology, Melbourne.

Calavita, N. & Mallach, A. (eds) 2010, *Inclusionary housing in international perspective: Affordable housing, social inclusion, and land value recapture*, Lincoln Institute, Washington.

Cheung, A. 1996, 'Public sector reform and the re-legitimation of public bureaucratic power', *International Journal of Public Sector Management*, vol. 9, no. 5–6, pp. 37–50.

Clapham, D., Kemp, P. & Smith, S. 1990, *Housing and social policy*, Macmillan, Basingstoke.

COAG (Council of Australian Governments) 2008, *National affordable housing agreement: Factsheet*, Council of Australian Governments, Canberra.

COAG (Council of Australian Governments) Reform Council 2010, *National partnership agreement to deliver a seamless national economy: Part 1 – 27 deregulation priorities*, Council of Australian Governments, Canberra.

Commonwealth Coordinator-General 2011, *The nation building – economic stimulus plan: Two year progress report*, Commonwealth of Australia, Canberra.

Davison, G., Gurran, N., Nouwelant, R., Pinnegar, S., Randolph, B. & Bramley, G. 2012, Affordable housing, urban renewal and planning: Emerging practice in New South Wales, South Australia and Queensland, AHURI Final Report Series, AHURI, Melbourne.

Department of Families and Community Services 2002, *National social housing survey with community housing report*, Commonwealth Government, Canberra.

Department of Sustainability and Environment 2006, *Cutting red tape in planning*, Victorian Government, Melbourne.

DOH (NSW Department of Housing) 2000, *NSW social housing: The drivers for being more than simply a landlord*, Occasional Discussion Paper Series, NSW Department of Housing, Sydney.

DSS (Department of Social Services) 2014, *National Rental Affordability Scheme: Questions and answers – outcome of applications for incentives through NRAS Round 5* http://www.dss.gov.au/our-responsibilities/housing-support/programsservices/national-rental-affordability-scheme/national-rental-affordability-schemenras-questions-and-answers-outcome-of-applications-for-incentives-through-nrasround-5

Dunleavy, P. 1986, 'Explaining the privatization boom: Public choice versus radical approaches', *Public Administration*, vol. 64, no. 1, pp. 13–34.

Gleeson, B. & Low, N. 2000, *Australian urban planning: New challenges, new agendas*, Allen & Unwin, Melbourne.

Gilmour, T. & Milligan, V. 2008, Stimulating institutional investment in affordable housing in Australia: Insights from the US, paper presented at the 3rd Australasian Housing Researchers' Conference, Melbourne, 18–20 June, Melbourne.

Government of Western Australia 2009, *Reducing the burden – report of the red tape reduction group*, Government of Western Australia, Perth.

Groenhart, L. 2013a, 'Evaluating tenure mix interventions: A case study from Sydney, Australia', *Housing Studies*, vol. 28, no. 1, pp. 95–115.

Groenhart, L. 2013b, 'Reflecting on a decade of Australian social housing policy: Change and continuity in supply and geography, 2001–2011', *Geographical Research*, vol. 51, no. 4, pp 387–97.

Gurran, N. 2003, 'Housing locally: Positioning Australian local government housing for a new century', *Urban Policy and Research*, vol. 21, no. 4, pp. 393–412.

Gurran, N., Milligan, V., Baker, D., Bugg, L. & Christensen, S. 2008, New directions in planning for affordable housing: Australian and international evidence and implications, AHURI Final Report Series, Melbourne.

Harriott, S. & Matthews, L. 1998, *Social housing: An introduction*, Addison Wesley Longman Limited, Harlow.

Hayward, D. 1996, 'The reluctant landlords? A history of public housing in Australia', *Urban Policy and Research*, vol. 14, no. 1, pp. 5–35.

Hughes, M. 2004, *Community economic development and public housing estates*, Shelter New South Wales, Sydney.

Hughes, O. 1998, *Public management and administration: An introduction*, The Macmillan Press, Basingstoke, UK.

Husock, H. 1997, 'Public housing as a "poorhouse"', *Public Interest*, vol. 129, pp. 72–85.

Industry Commission 1993, *Public housing volume 2: Appendices*, Australian Government Publishing Service, Canberra.

Jacob, B. 2004, 'Public housing, housing vouchers, and student achievement: Evidence from public housing demolitions in Chicago', *The American Economic Review*, vol. 94, no. 1, pp. 233–58.

Jones, A., Phillips, R. & Milligan, V. 2007, Integration and social housing in Australia: Challenges and options, Australian Housing and Urban Research Institute (AHURI) Positioning Paper Series, Queensland.

Kettl, D. F. 2000, *The global public management revolution*, Brookings Institution Press, Washington DC.

Lawson, J. & Milligan, V. 2007, International trends in housing and policy responses, Australian Housing and Urban Research Institute, Sydney Research Centre, Sydney.

Mant, J. 1992, *Inquiry into the Department of Housing, Report of the Commission*, Sydney.

Milligan, V., Gurran, N., Lawson, J., Phibbs, P. & Phillips, R. 2009, Innovation in affordable housing in Australia: Bringing policy and practice for not-for profit housing organisations together, AHURI Final Report Series 134, AHURI, Melbourne.

Mullins, D. & Murie, A. 2006, *Housing policy in the UK*, Palgrave Macmillan, Basingstoke.

Murphy, L. 2003, 'To the market and back: Housing policy and state housing in New Zealand', *GeoJournal*, vol. 59, no. 2, pp. 119–26.

NHSC (National Housing Supply Council) 2010, *Second state of supply report*, Department of Families, Community Services and Indigenous Affairs, Canberra.

Niskanen, W. 1973, *Bureaucracy and representative government*, Aldine-Atherton, New York.

Norman, R. & Stace, D. 1998, *The rich agenda of public sector change*, Australian Graduate School of Management, University of New South Wales, Sydney.

Paris, C. 1993, *Housing Australia*, Macmillan Education, Melbourne.

Parry, S. & Strommen, L. 2001, 'New Living' report: An assessment on tenants and the community in the urban renewal of Lockridge and Langford, research project for Grad Dip in Housing Management and Policy, Swinburne University of Technology, Melbourne.

Pettigrew, D. 2005, *Homes for the people*, Department of Housing, Sydney.

Popkin, S. J., Katz, B., Cunningham, M., Brown, K., Gustafson, J. & Turner, M. 2004, A decade of hope VI: Research findings and policy challenges, The Urban Institute and The Brookings Institution, Washington DC.

Productivity Commission 2011, *Performance benchmarking of Australian business regulation: Planning, zoning and development assessments, Productivity Commission Research report, vol. 1*, Australian Government, Canberra.

Pusey, M. 1991, *Economic rationalism in Canberra*, Cambridge Press, New York.

Randolph, B. & Judd, B. 2000, 'Community renewal and large public housing estates', *Urban Policy and Research*, vol. 18, no. 1, pp. 91–104.

Randolph, B. & Judd, B. 2006, 'Qualitative methods and the evaluation of community renewal programs in Australia: Towards a national framework', *Urban Policy and Research*, vol. 24, no. 1, pp. 97–114.

Residential Development Council (RDC) 2007, Boulevard of broken dreams: The future of housing affordability in Australia, Residential Development Council, Property Council of Australia, Sydney.

Rhodes, R. 1991, 'Theory and methods in British public administration: The view from political science', *Political Studies*, vol. 39, no. 3, pp. 533–54.

Ruming, K., Gurran, N. & Randolph, B, 2011, 'Housing affordability and development contributions: New perspectives from industry and local government in New South Wales, Victoria and Queensland', *Urban Policy and Research*, vol. 29, no. 3, pp. 257–74.

SCRGSP (Steering Committee for the Review of Government Service Provision) 2006–2013, *Reports on government services 2006 to 2013*, Productivity Commission, Canberra.

SCRGSP (Steering Committee for the Review of Government Service Provision) 2014, *Report on Government Services 2014*, Volume G: Housing and Homelessness, Canberra, Commonwealth of Australia.

ShelterNSW February 2006, The supply and allocation social housing in New South Wales, Submission to the Public Bodies Review Committee, Legislative Assembly, Parliament of New South Wales, Sydney.

Treasury 2013, National Housing Supply Council, http://www.treasury.gov.au/ Policy-Topics/PeopleAndSociety/completed-programs-initiatives/NHSC, Accessed 24 July 2014.

von Hoffman, A. 2009, 'Housing and planning: A century of social reform and local power', *Journal of the American Planning Association*, vol. 75, no. 2, pp. 231–44.

Whitehead, C. 2007, 'Planning policies and affordable housing: England as a successful case study?', *Housing Studies*, vol. 22, no. 1, pp. 25–44.

Wiesel, I., Davison, G., Milligan, V., Phibbs, P., Judd, B. & Zanardo, M. 2012, Developing sustainable affordable housing: A project level analysis, Australian Housing and Urban Research Institute, UNSW–UWS Research Centre, Sydney.

Yates, J. 2002, 'The limits of choice in the private rental market', *Just Policy*, vol. 24, pp. 32–48.

8

Money and markets in Australia's healthcare system

Fran Collyer, Kirsten Harley and Stephanie Short

Since the 1980s, changes in government policy, including legislation to enable third-party insurance contracting, increased levels of state support for private health insurance, and public–private partnerships,[1] have encouraged corporate investment into the hospitals, medical centres, pathology laboratories and diagnostic facilities of the Australian healthcare system. Driven by the 'new public management' (NPM) reform agenda (English 2005, p. 93), and in conformity with the contradictory and crisis-driven nature of neoliberalism (Peck, Theodore & Brenner 2012, p. 25), the government's explicit agenda of privatisation and marketisation has profoundly altered the way the system is financed and organised. The sector, once dominated by public and not-for-profit, charity or religious institutions, with their own distinct

---

Collyer, F., Harley, K. & Short, S. 2015, 'Money and markets in Australia's healthcare system', in *Markets, rights and power in Australian social policy*, eds G. Meagher & S. Goodwin, Sydney University Press, Sydney.

---

1 Public–private partnerships refer to the involvement of private consortia with government to provide infrastructure and related services to the public. The origin of these in Australia, in their current form, can be traced to the election of conservative state governments in New South Wales (1989) and Victoria (1992) (English 2005, p. 92).

but complementary functions, has lost its universal character and been transformed into a highly protected market system. This new system has been very much a creation of government, intent on building private healthcare and health insurance markets, and its presence raises questions about the financial sustainability of a system which is largely uncapped, and about the extent to which healthcare, driven by market rather than medical considerations, can continue to deliver the high quality, accessible healthcare services once envisaged under the concept of Medibank.

This chapter begins with a brief overview of the Australian healthcare system and relevant policies. This leads on to an exploration of the history of private and public health insurance schemes, followed by the history of private and public healthcare services. These narratives reveal the extent to which the system has become corporatised and privatised, demonstrating the connections between government policy, the entry of corporate investment, the growth of for-profit organisations, and the changing balance between the private and public sectors. The chapter concludes by examining some of the implications of these changes for the healthcare budget, for the effective planning and delivery of services and for access to essential healthcare services for all Australians.

The Australian healthcare system

The Australian healthcare system is composed of both public and private facilities, and public and private sector workforces, and funded through a complex mix of Commonwealth and state government, corporate, religious, philanthropic and individual sources. Citizens have access to free medical care in public hospitals, and under the national, compulsory health insurance scheme, Medicare, are provided with free or subsidised access to doctors and various medical and health facilities – even though many of these are in the private sector and charge on a fee-for-service basis. The Pharmaceutical Benefits Scheme is also universal and government-funded, providing patients with pharmaceuticals from privately owned pharmacies at a significantly reduced cost where these are recommended by a doctor and on the list of essential medicines.

The Commonwealth government supplies the funds for both Medicare and the Pharmaceutical Benefits Scheme, thus providing the bulk of funds for medical services occurring outside hospitals. State and territory governments join with the Commonwealth to fund public hospitals and community care for aged and disabled persons, while the states and territories are the main providers for ambulance, public dental services (most dental services are provided in the private sector and are not subsidised), public health activities and community health services. Government-owned and operated community health centres are mostly found in locations that are not attractive to the private sector. They do not charge patients for services or access to facilities.

The healthcare system has long been dominated by its large public hospital sector, where most of the research and training is conducted and the specialities of medicine are found (Productivity Commission 2009). These public hospitals provide both in-patient and out-patient services at no charge to Australian citizens. However, the healthcare system also includes an array of small and large private hospitals and facilities (both religious not-for-profits, and corporate for-profits) that patients can access through private health insurance or personal payment. The non-government, religious and charitable sector provides a substantial level of residential aged care, but also a number of hospitals. These services are mostly financed by government.

The funding of healthcare in Australia

In the latter half of the 19th century, healthcare services in Australia developed from their colonial, military roots into a heterogeneous system funded from private, government, military and religious sources. During the first 60 years of the 20th century, several attempts were made by Commonwealth governments to introduce funding reform into this fragmented array of services. The first was in 1928 by Earle Page, a surgeon and Treasurer in the Country–Nationalist Coalition government led by Stanley Bruce (1923–28). Page's national insurance scheme for maternity, old age, sickness and invalidity, based on compulsory contributions from individuals and their employers, was thwarted by the friendly societies (voluntary health insurance associations), employers and doctors' groups. A second proposal came in 1938 from Treasurer

Richard Casey of the newly formed United Australia Party in the conservative government led by Joe Lyons (1932–39). This plan involved a public insurance scheme funded out of the wage system, and was also opposed by the medical profession, employers and even the Australian Labor Party, with the latter insisting on public provision and arguing contributions should not come from wages (Collyer 2012, p. 119).

In 1944, the Labor government created the *Pharmaceutical Benefits Act*, which aimed to provide essential medicines free of charge. Doctors, fearful of 'civil conscription' and the imposition of a 'socialist' health system styled on the British National Health Service, opposed this Act. The matter ended in the High Court and led to a referendum in 1946 to extend the Commonwealth's powers to legislate on healthcare services. These powers remained limited, for the constitutional amendment prohibited the government from requiring medical professionals 'to work in a nationalised health or dental service' (de Voe & Short 2003, p. 348). Given the continuing opposition of doctors (organised at this time by an Australian branch of the British Medical Association), and the newly formed conservative Liberal Party, the consequence for the next few years was the operation of a very limited – and patchy – national health program, with various subsidies offered to *some* hospitals in *some* states for the treatment of *some* public patients.

Further reform to the system occurred in 1953 under a Liberal–Country Party government, when Earle Page, this time as Minister for Health, proposed an alternative, voluntary, government-sponsored health insurance program in consultation with the medical profession. The 'Earle Page scheme', as it came to be known, offered public insurance administered by private, non-profit funds. These benefits were subsidised by the Commonwealth government and met part of the cost of medical expenses. Tax deductions were also provided by the Menzies Coalition government to assist with the cost of health insurance premiums (Stebbing & Spies-Butcher 2010, p. 591). Nevertheless, healthcare services during the 1950s and 1960s remained inaccessible to many individuals, for the scheme required patients to purchase private insurance before they could access government benefits. Indeed, the high cost of services led to an accumulation of bad debts which then drove up doctors' fees, and resulted in 17 percent of Australians without medical coverage. In 1968, the Committee of Inquiry into Health Insurance, established by the Gorton Coalition government (1968–71), confirmed criticisms of the scheme's failure to cover the entire population, the often large gap between fees charged and insurers' refunds, and the program's complexity and cost (Palmer & Short 2010, p. 61). The committee also pointed out that many of the insurance companies were not only delivering substandard benefits, but appropriating an unreasonably high proportion of the contributions (de Voe & Short 2003, p. 349).

Ideas for alternative healthcare schemes were fiercely debated during these years. In large part, this level of public discussion was made possible by the expansion of the middle class, itself stimulated by growth in the university sector where the new professions (such as social work) and new disciplines (such as health economics, public health and sociology) were beginning to make an impact in the Australian setting (Collyer 2012, pp. 124–25). In opposition in 1969, the Australian Labor Party sought to win over the public by promising to mend the inefficiencies of Australia's existing 78 private medical insurance funds and 109 private hospital insurance funds, with a proposal for a population-wide, compulsory health insurance program funded from a health tax. The scheme, eventually called Medibank, drew heavily on the work of economists Dick Scotton and John Deeble and was put forward as a more equitable and efficient alternative, with patients' costs proportional to incomes and multiple health funds replaced by one government-administered fund (Palmer & Short 2010, p. 62).

Medibank: the national health insurance scheme

After Labor was elected at the 1972 federal election, the Whitlam government set about implementing this health insurance program. Again, efforts to construct a national, publicly funded program were strongly opposed: this time by the Australian Medical Association (AMA),[2] private health funds and the opposition political parties. The legislation to introduce Medibank was twice rejected by the Senate but finally passed after a dissolution of both houses of parliament, a federal election in which health was again a major issue, and a joint sitting of both houses

---

2   Branches of the British Medical Association were formed in Australia in the 19th century, and these branches eventually merged to establish the AMA in 1962.

to resolve the continuing deadlock over this and other legislation (Scotton & Macdonald 1993).

Medibank commenced from mid-1975, beginning with the establishment of the Health Insurance Commission (HIC) on 1 July to administer this public medical insurance scheme. Unlike its proposed precursors, the scheme was initially funded entirely from Commonwealth revenue. Doctors were able to bill patients, or the HIC, and accept 85 percent of the scheduled fee as full payment. Later that year free medical care in public hospitals was made available under Medibank, with patients still able to choose to be treated privately, because private health insurance was also available to fund private patient costs in either public or private hospitals (Palmer & Short 2010, p. 63). Under Medibank, all Australians were for the first time provided with full access to hospital care, subsidised for their essential medicines, and able to access services (without cost, or with the assistance of a generous subsidy), when visiting a general practitioner (GP) or having diagnostic tests.

Immediately upon election in 1975, the Fraser Liberal–National Party government commenced the dismantling of Medibank, allowing individuals to opt out of the health tax by paying for private health insurance, and imposing a levy of two point five percent of taxable income for those covered only by the HIC. This was essentially a return to the voluntary Earle Page scheme of the 1950s, for changes in 1981 directed Commonwealth subsidies only to those who paid to join private health insurance funds (with contributions eligible for tax rebates), and it thus eliminated free hospital treatment (Gray 1996, p. 592). These were strong incentives to take out private health insurance coverage. It was a policy designed to reverse the decline in fund membership which had occurred since the introduction of Medibank (Palmer & Short 2010, p. 63).

The Hawke Labor government (1983–91) re-introduced a tax-funded public health insurance scheme on 1 February 1984. Like its predecessor Medibank, it was administered by the HIC but renamed Medicare Australia. In addition to general taxation revenue, the scheme was funded from a one percent levy on taxable income, with lower and upper limits.[3] Fees for each specified service were set out in the Medicare Benefits Schedule (MBS), and insurance companies were not allowed to offer 'gap' insurance to meet the difference between the scheduled fee and the actual fee charged by the doctor or hospital (Palmer & Short 2010, pp. 63–64). On this occasion, opposition to the introduction of Medicare from the medical profession was relatively muted. Nonetheless Medicare, like Medibank before it, led to a decline in the proportion of the population covered by private hospital insurance, from above 55 percent in the early 1980s, to 48 percent in 1985 and 30 percent in 1998 (Harley et al. 2011). This decline was not constructed as a 'policy problem' until after the Liberal–National Coalition government took office in 1996. Over the next 11 years, the Coalition continued to 'pay lip service' to Medicare while focusing its efforts on building a financially viable private health insurance sector.

The Coalition government re-built the private health insurance sector by introducing a series of measures to encourage the uptake of private health insurance, including both 'carrots and sticks' (Hall, de Abreu Lourenco & Viney 1999). The 'carrot' of the Private Health Insurance Incentives Scheme (PHIIS) subsidised the cost of premiums for those with low incomes, while the 'stick' was the Medicare Levy Surcharge: a one percent tax on high-income earners who did not purchase cover. The combination of government measures, but especially Lifetime Health Cover (Butler 2002), and the 'fear factor' about being uninsured (Deeble, in Gray 2004, p. 38), arrested and reversed the decline in insurance membership rates. These lifted from a low of 32 percent for hospital insurance and 33 percent ancillary coverage in March 2000, to 46 percent (hospital) and 41 percent (ancillary) in September 2000, and 45 percent (hospital) and 51 percent (ancillary) by June 2009 (Harley et al. 2011, p. 308). In 1999, the PHIIS was extended to a universal 30 percent private health insurance rebate (increased to 35 percent for individuals aged 65–69 years and 40 percent for those 70 years and older in 2005) (PHIAC 2009, p. 12; Kay 2007, p. 587).

Both the Liberal Coalition and Labor parties have shifted positions on the role of Medicare and private health insurance. In the run-up to the 1996 election, Liberal leader John Howard announced his new-found support for Medicare, a strategic move which assisted the Liberal Coalition to win government:

---

3   The Medicare levy has subsequently been increased to 1.5 percent and the upper limit (of $700) removed.

Medicare gives people a sense of security ... when Medicare was first introduced I was critical of it ... But over the years people have grown to support it ... And there's no law in politics that says that you can't over a period of time change your view about an issue (Howard 1996, p. 9).

It was a new policy narrative, offering support for the public insurance scheme but constructing the low rate of private health insurance membership as a 'policy problem' requiring an immediate solution (Elliot 2006, p. 133). Changes also occurred on the other side of politics. While in opposition, Labor had opposed the Coalition's private health insurance incentive schemes. However, in the lead-up to the 2007 federal election it committed to retaining the rebate (Biggs 2009, p. 4). Following their election, the Rudd and Gillard Labor governments adopted the language of 'balance' previously employed by the Coalition (Elliot 2006), calling for the rebate to be means-tested and proportionately reduced, and the Medicare Levy Surcharge increased for those on high incomes. A 2009 budget announcement proposed the scheme would be 're-balanced' so that the highest income earners (around one in 10 adults) would 'receive less "carrot" and more "stick" to be insured' (Roxon & Swan 2009). Under this proposal, the private health insurance rebate would no longer be available to the highest income tier, and reduced (by 20 and 10 percent respectively) for the two tiers below; conversely, the Medicare Levy Surcharge would be increased from one percent to 1.5 and 1.25 percent respectively for the top two tiers.[4] Legislation to this effect was fiercely opposed by the Coalition opposition and defeated in the Senate in 2009; however, the re-introduced Fairer Private Health Insurance Incentives Bill 2011 (and related bills) were passed in 2012. While this change removed or reduced the transfer of public financial support for the highest income earners to purchase private insurance, and reduced annual government expenditure by some

---

4   As a consequence of this legislation, citizens are eligible for a tax rebate depending on their level of income, whether they have dependents, and whether they are single. The threshold for payment varies each year, changing with the growth in Average Weekly Ordinary Time Earnings. Information about the three tiers of rebate can be found at Department of Human Services (n. d).

$746.3 million in 2012–13, the rebate scheme preserves substantial public funding of the private health insurance sector.

The private health insurance sector

The private health insurance sector is diverse, including small restricted membership organisations (generally associated with a particular employer or union), the large and influential Blue Cross funds (until recently HCF, HBA, HBF, Mutual Hospital and MBF), friendly societies, regional hospital funds and, since the 1980s, commercial for-profit funds and the national government fund, Medibank Private (the largest insurer). While legislation to privatise Medibank Private was passed in the final term of the Howard Coalition government, the sale was not implemented. The Rudd Labor government transformed this into a 'for-profit' entity with capacity to submit surpluses to Treasury (Shamsullah 2011, p. 27). In contrast, most of the Blue Cross funds were established and run by healthcare providers (doctors, hospitals and associated charities) with little contributor representation on their boards. They have thus traditionally been seen as working in the interests of providers, contributing to the cost control problems associated with voluntary insurance (Shamsullah 2011, p. 26).

The 1990s and 2000s have seen significant consolidation of the private health insurance sector, with 56 health benefits organisations (or insurers) operating in 1989, 44 in 2001 and 34 in 2011 (Industry Commission 1997, p. 97; PHIAC 2001, 2011). However, this consolidation or concentration has not meant a diminishing commercialisation of the sector. The overall *number* of for-profit organisations in the private health insurance sector has varied since they were allowed to operate in Australia after the introduction of Medicare (Shamsullah 2011, p. 27). Indeed, the number of for-profit insurers fluctuated between two and four during the 1990s (Industry Commission 1997), grew to six by 30 June 2001 (PHIAC 2001), increased to seven (of a total of 38 funds) by 2008, nine (of 37) in 2009 and 10 in 2010, dropping back to seven (of 34) in the next year with a number of mergers (PHIAC 2007, 2008, 2009, 2010, 2011). Nevertheless, there has been a significant growth in the *amount of business* conducted by this commercial segment of the insurance sector, for 'the bulk of the health insurance business is now conducted by funds classed as "for-profit"' (Shamsullah 2011, p. 29). These organisations include Medibank Private, the state-owned corporation with the largest market share (PHIAC 2011), followed closely by BUPA (British United Provident Association), which provides health insurance and healthcare service facilities in almost every country in the world (BUPA 2012). This new concentration of private enterprise in the health insurance sector is evident. At 30 June 2011, the seven for-profit insurers had 69 percent of market share, up from 42 percent in 2009 (PHIAC 2009, 2011), and from less than 13 percent in 1997 (Industry Commission 1997).

A protected industry

Private health insurance is an arena where we can see the direct coupling of government policy to strategic, corporate investment. This can be seen at the level of individual organisations as well as the industry as a whole. Medibank Private, the for-profit with the largest market share, for example, was created in 1976 and rapidly developed into the largest fund by 1982. As a new fund, it attracted a younger, lower-risk membership, but was advantaged from the start by its connection with the government fund, Medicare. Administered by the same government authority, the HIC, and able to share its shop front offices with Medicare, the private company's infrastructure costs were significantly reduced (Shamsullah 2011, p. 27). Complaints from its competitors led to the Howard government's attempt to privatise the organisation, and when this was unsuccessful, its eventual corporatisation. Medibank Private's initial market advantage has continued to assist its prosperity, perhaps because it is still regarded by many members of the public as a public entity. With regard to the private health insurance industry as a whole, Shamsullah (2011, p. 23) argues it has 'never been distinguished by profit-driven firms competing whole-heartedly in a dynamic, free market'. Indeed it has a unique position among industry sectors in Australia, protected from market competition and market downturns through government subsidies and a suite of legislation. The subsidy itself is large. Through the Private Health Insurance Tax Rebate, several billion dollars are shifted to the private health sector each year. In 2011–12, the subsidising of private health insurance amounted to $4.7

billion (AIHW 2013a, p. 38). The figures for 1999–2010 are presented in Table 8.1.

Table 8.1: Private health insurance subsidy, Australian Government 1999–2010

Year	Health insurance premium rebates ($ million)
1999–00	1,576
2000–1	2,031
2001–2	2,118
2002–3	2,250
2003–4	2,387
2004–5	2,645
2005–6	2,883
2006–7	3,073
2007–8	3,587
2008–9	3,643
2009–10	4,262

Source: Australian Institute of Health and Welfare (AIHW) 2011, p. 27. Table 3.5: Funding of health expenditure by the Australian Government, current prices, by type of expenditure.

Government legislation also protects this industry from market competition. Aiming to ensure insurance products were accessible to all (regardless of health status), the fair treatment of contributors and the sound management of the funds; 'competition between funds on price and product innovation and differentiation has been deliberately stifled' (Shamsullah 2011, p. 27). Government action has meant the industry's policies must comply with a comprehensive body of rules,[5] and its activities are intensively scrutinised by the Private Health Insurance Administration Council (Shamsullah 2011, p. 27). Restrictions include the inability to exclude high risk members, the provision of standard

---

5   The rules pertaining to the private health insurance industry can be found at Department of Health (2011).

statements of all policies, and price control. There is, consequently, little differentiation between the funds.

One of the implications of state support for the private health insurance sector is that it translates into support – and profit – for private providers of healthcare services. This is clearly seen in the increases in net profits for the largest health service providers that immediately followed the Howard government's promotion of private health insurance. These increases ranged from 34 percent for Healthscope to 142 percent for Ramsay in 2000–1, and were attributed in their annual reports to 'improving market conditions associated with increases in private health insurance coverage' (Hopkins 2001, pp. 232–33). Indeed, the private healthcare services sector, which includes the large for-profit companies Ramsay Health Care and Healthscope, as well as the private but not-for-profit Catholic Hospitals, benefit significantly from the state promotion and subsidisation of private health insurance. Over a 12-month period, the private hospital sector alone expanded its bed capacity by two percent to 28,351 and increased its income by nine percent to $10.7 billion (2010–11 figures, ABS 2012). Although the relationship between the private health insurance sector and the private provision of healthcare services is a complex one, these figures are indicative of the importance of private health insurance to the sustainability of the private healthcare sector. This is particularly important given that 37 percent of the funding for private hospitals is derived from the state, including 21 percent from the private health insurance rebate.[6] We turn now to consider healthcare services provision.

The provision of healthcare services

During the 1980s and 1990s, the healthcare services landscape in Australia began to radically alter as corporate players realised the potential

---

6   Private hospitals in Australia are funded from a variety of sources. In 2009–10, the breakdown of its sources of funding was: health insurance funds (45 percent), individuals (12 percent), other (six percent), and government (37 percent). This latter figure is a combination of Department of Veteran Affairs (nine percent), Australian government (three percent), rebates of health insurance premiums (21 percent), and state/territory governments (four percent) (AIHW 2012a, p. 4).

for expansion of private healthcare and began to systematically enter the market. This pattern, of significant government funding for health-care services followed by a heightening of corporate and investor in-terest, is not unique to Australia. It also occurred, for instance, in the United States, where the establishment of the public health insurance schemes in 1965, Medicare and Medicaid, supported and encouraged the growth of private hospitals (Collyer & White 2001, p. 4). Over the subsequent decade, the for-profit hospital sector in that country grew by 55 percent compared with only 28 percent for the non-profit sector (Sax 1990). Publicly funded insurance schemes guarantee *government* income for the medical profession, and given this would otherwise rep-resent the greatest expense to a hospital, provides a significant incentive for investors to enter the healthcare sector.

The rise of the corporate hospital

In Australia, the entry of corporate capital into the healthcare services sector would eventually – and profoundly – alter the provision of ser-vices as diverse as pathology laboratories and general practice. It was hospitals, however, that were the first to show the effects of marketisa-tion. The Australian hospital system has unique characteristics and a unique history. Unlike the European model with its basis in religious and private hospitals, the earliest hospitals in this country were military facilities, catering for convicts and military personnel (Daniel 1990, p. 71). The first non-military hospitals were state-owned facilities, created in 1848, seven years after the end of convict transportation and the for-mal handing over of the military hospitals to government for the use of civilians (Hicks 1981, p. 6). This event also followed the first *Hospi-tals Act 1847*, where although government took the major responsibility for the cost, hospitals were provided with the autonomy to receive do-nations and own land (Hicks 1981, p. 6). In contrast to England and Europe, religious and philanthropic hospitals only started to appear in Australia in the middle of the 19th century, as did the private hospitals (Daniel 1990, p. 71; Hicks 1981, pp. 6–7). Moreover, all hospital types were given some government funding, particularly the religious ones (Hicks 1981, p. 6; Sax 1984, p. 25), and historically this has remained the case, with all Australian hospitals relying heavily on government subsidies (Gray 1996, p. 589).

Until the mid-1970s, however, state funding was uncertain and irregular, varying enormously across jurisdictions, and subject to radical change with shifts in government, preventing hospital boards from effectively planning for expansion or renewal. While the Australian Labor Party has always supported the principle of public hospitals, private hospitals (with minimal subsidy) have been the preference of the conservative parties (Gray 1996, p. 590). Thus the renewed support for public hospitals introduced by the Australian Labor Party in the 1940s, ended in the 1950s (Gray 1996, p. 591). Only with the introduction of Medibank, which provided a regular and secure funding basis for hospitals for the first time (Collyer 2012, pp. 128–29; Whitlam 1968), were the large, publicly owned and publicly run institutions able to strengthen and become dominant features of the healthcare system.

From the mid-1980s, however, investors began purchasing the numerous, owner-operated, small private hospitals offering a limited range of services and interspersed throughout the sector. Some investors built new facilities, often luxurious, with an eye to attracting offshore clientele, and sometimes co-located with a large public hospital (Bloom 2000; Brown & Barnett 2004). There were also purchases of some larger, publicly owned institutions, and investors entered into commercial contracts with governments to manage and/or build these 'public' hospitals (Collyer 1997; Collyer & White 2001; Collyer, Wettenhall & McMaster 2003; Collyer, McMaster & Wettenhall 2001).

The result was a rapid concentration of hospital ownership in Australia, with a few large corporations purchasing, building, or otherwise owning 'chains' of sizeable hospitals (White & Collyer 1998, p. 492). This new hospital landscape emerged with an overall growth in the number of private hospitals from the early 1990s (from 430 in 1991–92 to 593 in 2010–11), and a 'modest contraction' in the number of public hospitals (758 in 1991–92, 752 in 2010–11) (an issue discussed in detail below). Table 8.2 shows the change in the relative number of private and public hospitals between 1991–92 and 2010–11, indicating the rapid growth of the private, free-standing, day hospital facilities over the same period.

A similar pattern of change in the hospital sector can be seen in the figures for hospital 'separations' (that is, episodes of care). Between 1995–96 and 2004–05 these increased for all hospitals by 35.7 percent. In the public sector the increase was 19.5 percent (acute hospitals),

Table 8.2: Hospital sector growth 1991–2011. For sources and notes, see appendix at the end of the chapter

Sector and type of hospital	1991–2	1996–7	2001–2	2006–7	2010–11
Public hospitals (acute and psychiatric)	758	729	746	758	752
Private hospitals (acute and psychiatric)	319	319	301	289	279
Private free-standing day hospital facilities	111*	153	246	268	314
Total private hospitals	430	472	547	557	593

but it was a much larger 73.8 percent in the private sector (including free-standing day facilities) (AIHW 2006, p. x). We can best examine these changes over time in terms of 'bed' numbers, a ready measure of 'throughput'. Table 8.3 indicates a remarkable growth in the number of private hospital beds available in the Australian healthcare system between 1991 and 2011. Bed numbers in the public sector have not increased to the same extent over the same period.

The 'modest contraction' or lack of growth in the public hospital sector needs further explanation, as it is of significance to the story of corporate growth and consolidation. Hospitals 'lost' to the public sector over the period were primarily psychiatric hospitals. Two were the result of administrative changes (with three hospitals in Tasmania becoming one 'reporting unit' in 2009–10), and others closed or sold in the process of de-institutionalisation. The number of acute hospitals in the public sector has remained fairly stable, in part due to the growth and preference for day surgery (where medically appropriate). Yet these hospital statistics do not reveal the number of 'public hospitals' now owned and/or managed by the private sector, where 'public' patients are admitted under contract to government. Such hospitals are classified as 'public' within the ABS and AIHW collections, and its patients identified only as public or private.[7] In other words, there is no separate

---

7   'A public hospital is defined as one that is operated by, or on behalf of, the government of the state or territory in which it is established. This includes hospitals which are owned by private or charitable groups but are authorised or

Table 8.3: Available hospital 'beds/chairs' 1991–2011

Sector and type of hospital	1991–92	1996–97	2001–2	2006–7	2010–11
Public hospital (acute and psychiatric) beds	57,053	56,836	51,461	55,904	57,772
Private free-standing day hospital beds	–	1,163	1,851	2,251	2,957
Other private hospital beds	–	22,966	25,556	24,427	25,394
Total private hospital beds	19,923	24,129	27,407	26,678	28,351

Source: Compiled from ABS (1995) for 1991–92 data and AIHW (2002, 2003, 2012b, 2013b) with AIHW Australian Hospital Statistics reports for other years also consulted.

category for these privately owned/managed 'public' hospitals, nor a category for 'publicly admitted patients' who represent a profit-making unit for the corporations concerned. Hence what appears to be a 'modest contraction' of the public hospital sector in fact obscures another area of growth in corporate activity – at the cost of state-owned facilities and state-provided care. Moreover, the financial costs of these activities to the state are not available for public scrutiny, as they are only documented in the commercial-in-confidence contracts these corporations have with state governments, and details are not provided even under freedom of information requests. This is a problem of privatisation and has been evident also in the United Kingdom, the United States (White & Collyer 1998, p. 503) and Canada (Whiteside 2013).

Integration and concentration in health services

These dramatic changes to the Australian hospital sector eventually began to have ramifications for other health services as the hospital corporations began to diversify through 'vertical integration': the purchasing of radiology and pathology testing laboratories, general practices (White & Collyer 1998; White 2000) and even pharmaceutical

---

contracted by the government to deliver public hospital services' (Productivity Commission 2009).

and research facilities (Collyer 2004). Since 2000 there has been an increasing consolidation of the medical market and a concentration of ownership, with ongoing corporatisation, consolidation and integration of pathology companies and diagnostic imaging, and both vertical and horizontal integration of companies and services. For instance, between January 2000 and June 2001, the corporate share of the private radiology market jumped from less than 10 percent to an estimated 46 percent, dominated by Medical Imaging Australasia (20 percent share), Sonic Health Care (12 percent), Mayne (10 percent) and I-Med (eight percent) (Quinlivan 2001); and by 2010 the top four public corporations' share of the private radiology market was above 60 percent (Jones 2010). In pathology, four companies had a 79 percent share of the private market by 2005 (Sonic 36 percent; Mayne 30 percent; Healthscope nine percent; Primary Health Care four percent). In 2009, following Primary Health Care's acquisition of Mayne's pathology interests, the remaining three accounted for 86 percent share, with the non-profit, St John of God, having an additional five percent share (NEHTA 2009).

Companies in both radiology and pathology benefit from the sizeable flow of Medicare funding (Quinlivan 2001). Diagnostic imaging services for example, which include ultrasound, magnetic resonance imaging (MRI) and computed tomography (CT scans), constitute six percent of all medical claims to Medicare, and expenditure on these services represents $2.15 billion or 14 percent of the Medicare budget (Medical Benefits Reviews Task Group 2012, p. 4). These technologies are distributed across both sectors (for example, 76 MRI machines are in private and 49 in public settings (see Medical Benefits Reviews Task Group 2012, p. 4), and public funding, via Medicare, is provided for both capital and recurrent costs on a fee-for-service basis for both public and private patients.

The arena of general practice demonstrates the complexity of privatisation in healthcare provision. When Medibank was devised in the early 1970s, no attempt was made to alter the fee-for-service nature of this sector. Most GPs operate their own, or work within a private practice, and the introduction of the Medibank system only altered their method of payment, not their status as private sector, self-employed workers. This status nevertheless shifted with the corporatisation of general practice. This began in the 1980s and 1990s with the luxuriously decorated high-traffic 'super clinics' established by the doctor and entrepreneur, Geoffrey Edelsten, quickly followed by various competitors including Viscount Holdings (Collyer & White 2001, p. 11). The rate of corporatisation has since settled into a more sustainable pattern, with three main companies involved in their ownership (down from seven in 2007). Two are listed on the Australian Securities Exchange (ASX), and are among the top 100 companies: Sonic Healthcare and Primary Health Care. Sonic leads in terms of market capitalisation ($5.3 billion), followed by Primary ($1.8 billion) (ASX 2012). A third large company, the Healthscope Group, though de-listed from the ASX in 2010 with its acquisition by transnationals (The Carlyle Group and TPG, both with headquarters in North America), also owns medical centres in Australia, alongside its pathology and hospital businesses.

In this industry sub-sector, medical centres represent a business opportunity. Medicare benefits paid by the federal government for general practice (across the industry sector) totalled $4.2 billion for the year ending June 2012 (Healthscope 2013, p. 47). There are approximately 9,380 medical centres and over 27,000 GPs in Australia, and 12 percent of the latter work for either Independent Practitioner Network Ltd (IPN) (Sonic's general practice company since 2008), Primary or Healthscope. The Healthscope Group owns and operates 46 medical centres in Australia (Healthscope 2013, p. 54). Primary Health Care, which acquired Mayne Nickless' health assets in 2008, operates 58 large-scale medical centres (Primary Health Care 2013) and IPN manages over 190 multi-disciplinary medical centres around Australia (IPN 2011; Sonic Healthcare 2011).

During the early 2000s, corporate medical centres appeared to be unprofitable ventures, with their commercial value primarily in the generation of referrals to pathology and diagnostic services owned by the same vertically integrated companies (Jones 2007). It was also thought that many GPs, while valuing the management and support services provided in corporate practice, were averse to restrictions to their clinical autonomy that might be entailed in making for-profit corporatisation profitable (Anderson et al. 2005). In this second decade of the millennium, the sub-industry has consolidated, with medical centres a staple of the larger, for-profit, healthcare sector.

The ownership of private hospitals, and the provision of hospital services, are other significant businesses in the corporate healthcare sector. In Australia there are currently 1,345 hospitals (including free-standing day hospital facilities), with public hospitals constituting, at most, 56 percent of these.[8] This has been reduced from its 1991 level of 65 percent, when there were 1,188 hospitals, and public hospitals were the dominant form. Within the corporate hospital sector, there are two leading hospital operators: Ramsay Health Care and the Healthscope Group. Both are large companies, with Ramsay Health Care listed on the ASX (with $4.8 billion in market capitalisation and revenues of $2.1 billion for the whole group), and the Healthscope Group, the second largest hospital operator, with revenues of $2.1 billion (Healthscope 2013, p. 14). Ramsay's Australian hospital portfolio includes a total of 66 hospitals and day facilities (Ramsay 2012a), including many 'public' hospitals – such as the Mildura Base Hospital in Victoria, the Joondalup Health Campus in Perth, and the Peel Health Campus in Western Australia – that it has built or operates as public–private partnerships with state governments. Healthscope has a portfolio of 44 private hospitals across Australia, and its hospital division generates its largest proportion of revenues. Six of its hospitals are co-located with large public teaching hospitals, three are operated on behalf of the Adelaide Community Healthcare Alliance, and a further 11 are leased (Healthscope 2013, p. 52).

The corporate hospital market in Australia is thriving. Although there has not been a growth in the *number* of for-profit companies owning and/or managing hospitals since the 1980s, these companies have nevertheless grown in size and extended their operations into all areas of healthcare, including laboratories and rehabilitation services. And while some companies are independent, owning only one hospital, others are 'group' or 'chain' operations. In 1986 there were 14 for-profit groups, owning an average of six hospitals each. By 2002, the 11 for-profit groups owned an average of 12 hospitals, with 104 between them (O'Loughlin 2002, p. 106). By 2013, over 120 of the 593 private hospitals are for-profit hospitals, including those owned by Ramsay (52 hospitals), Healthscope (44), Healthe Care (12) and Independent Private Hospitals (seven), as well as numerous independent hospital operators. The 'group' sector continues to grow. Indeed, the Manag-

---

8 The phrase 'at most', is used at this point to remind readers that the ABS and AIHW 'public' category for hospitals does not take into account the number of hospitals owned or managed by the private sector.

ing Director of Ramsay, Christopher Rex, suggested in a February 2012 ASX Announcement that 'given the emerging theme of public/private partnerships, the role of the private sector could grow even further' (Ramsay 2012b).

The politics of health service reform

Support for public, universal, compulsory health insurance has long been a feature of Australian Labor governments. Likewise, Labor has historically shown a greater preference for supporting the *public* hospital system and providing *public* healthcare services. Nevertheless, the reshaping of the healthcare services landscape through marketisation and corporatisation has been the product of the action of all major parties – albeit unequally – at both Commonwealth and state government levels. The Coalition's new-found support for Medicare from 1996 (alongside a strengthened advocacy for private health insurance), was only marginally pre-dated by another significant shift, this time legislative, introduced in 1993 by the Keating Labor Commonwealth government (1991–96). Charged with the responsibility for managing a highly complex private-public system that has never been able to effectively cap medical fees, the government's response to continually rising costs was to amend the *Health Insurance Act 1973* and the *National Health Act 1953*, to allow third parties to sign contracts with individual doctors or hospitals so that health services could be supplied for fixed fees.

This legislation enabled health insurance companies (or other bodies such as unions or employer groups) to offer direct contracts with hospitals (which could then sign up appropriate specialists) for services supplied to their members. It also allowed the insurance funds to offer 'gap' coverage to members, and limit this to members treated in the hospitals nominated by the funds. The legislation provided greater power to the insurance companies to negotiate with practitioners and hospitals, altering their previously passive role in price setting, shifting the risk to the hospitals themselves by changing the means by which the funds pay the hospitals from a bed day to per-episode basis, and in turn, encouraging investors to purchase several hospitals to improve their bargaining strength (O'Loughlin 2002, p. 113). The private hospitals and new hospital 'chains' also responded by strategically seeking opportunities for vertical integration, increasing the possibility of corporate control over the referral process. Such changes occurred relatively quickly, even though the contract system itself has not been, and remains, unpopular with doctors. The resistance to contracts is largely the result of its strong parallels with the American health system, where Health Maintenance Organisations combine insurance with the provision of services, and hence control access to services as well as determining the nature of services provided. Concern about the imposition of an American-style health system in Australia, with its restrictions on the autonomy of doctors, led to a sustained level of public outrage led by the AMA and the Doctors Reform Society (Collyer & White 2001, pp. 11–12). Under the Howard government, concessions were made to the professions to allow non-contractual agreements with funds, and to the providers, enabling hospitals to obtain the same benefits where no contracts were entered into (Shamsullah 2011, p. 29). Despite this reform, professional resistance continues and few contracts have been finalised.

The legislation also increased the capacity of state governments to introduce market principles into the healthcare services sector. State governments have traditionally played a key role in encouraging investment and managing hospitals and other services within their jurisdiction. Thus the flood of corporate investment into the sector during the 1980s and 1990s was welcomed and actively encouraged by various state governments (Collyer & White 2001). For example, the Liberal Greiner (1988–92) and Fahey (1992–95) governments in New South Wales (NSW) sold most of the state psychiatric hospitals and closed hundreds of public hospital beds. They promoted the construction of new private hospitals, and put out tenders for 24 hospital co-location opportunities on public hospital campuses (Bloom 2000, p. 236). Likewise the Liberal Kennett government in Victoria (in power 1992–99), was responsible for the closure of many public hospitals and the use of market mechanisms to 'reform' public services: including the introduction of a casemix system of funding hospitals and widespread competitive tendering (Collyer & White 2001, p. 5).

While the privatisation of healthcare services slowed with the subsequent election of Labor state governments in NSW (Carr/Iemma/Rees/Keneally, 1995–2011) and Victoria (Bracks/Brumby, 1999–2010), it did not stop. A particular focus has been hospitals built – and operated – through public–private partnerships, of which there were 12 in Australia by December 2006 (four each in NSW and Victoria, two in Western Australia and one each in Queensland and Tasmania) (English 2006). Data about the extent of hospital public–private partnerships in Australia is severely limited, but they continue to be created in most states of Australia, particularly, but not exclusively, where Liberal or Coalition governments are in power. The Bracks Labor government established Partnerships Victoria, which oversaw public–private partnerships for the construction of several hospitals including the Casey Community Hospital (opened 2004), Royal Women's Hospital (opened 2008), the new Royal Children's Hospital Project (2011) and the New Bendigo Hospital (Partnerships Victoria 2012). The election of a conservative Liberal Coalition government in Western Australia in 2008 (led by Colin Barnett) led to the renewal of a privatisation agenda and the significant contracting out of labour and services at a series of public hospitals, including the Albany, the Midland, the Royal Perth and the Fiona Stanley hospitals. In Queensland in 2012, under the Newman Coalition government, Exemplar Health won the tender to design, finance, construct and maintain (for 25 years) the Sunshine Coast University Hospital under a public–private partnership, and Ramsay Health Care given the right to build, operate and own a private hospital on the same site (Queensland Health 2012). In South Australia, under the Rann Labor government, a public–private partnership with a 35-year contract was used to build and finance the new Royal Adelaide Hospital (South Australia Health 2011); and the NSW Liberal government, despite the failure of its previous for-profit, public–private partnership (the Port Macquarie Base Hospital, see Collyer 1997), announced plans in 2013 for a public–private partnership for the new Frenchs Forest public hospital.

Some implications for the healthcare system

Over the past 100 years, the public–private balance of the Australian healthcare system has altered as successive governments, with distinct philosophical and ideological perspectives, have pursued diverse policy and financing strategies. In recent decades however, an entirely new system began to emerge with the adoption – by both major parties – of the NPM agenda and amidst the rhetoric and free-market ideologies of neoliberalism. Key principles of this reform program have included minimising the role of government in the provision of services, and funding institutions based on outcomes rather than inputs. Reforms have focused on 'the sale of public assets; the adoption of market models and competitive management and information reporting systems for a wide range of public sector organisations' (English 2005, p. 94). In the Australian case, these have been combined with an increasing preference for using social tax expenditures as a policy mechanism (such as the private health insurance rebate). These operate as fiscal welfare to the wealthier segments of society but at the same time allow governments to promote markets and support private firms (Stebbing & Spies-Butcher 2010, pp. 591–93; see also Meagher & Wilson and Stebbing, in this volume). Various policies of Australian governments, based on this agenda, have enabled the growth of *corporate* healthcare, bringing a qualitatively different approach to the financing of services and a reshaping of the system's structure and form. The new system is unlike its predecessor because the clear distinctions between the public and private sectors, which had developed by the middle of the 20th century, and the once dominant position of the public sector, have now given way to a more even spread of healthcare services across the public, for-profit and not-for-profit sectors, with increasing activity in the for-profit sector. Differences between the tasks performed by the public and private sectors are less apparent than they once were. In the past, private hospitals rarely offered a full range of services, but tended to specialise in a small number of surgical procedures, particularly elective surgeries (Productivity Commission 2009, p. 56). Moreover, few provided emergency department services, undertook research or clinical training for health and medical staff and students, or assumed the community functions of their public counterparts (Brown & Barnett 2004, p. 428). In contrast, the public hospitals had a full range of specialist units (such as domiciliary care, obstetrics and maternity, alcohol, drug and coronary care units) as well as undertaking the clinical research and training activities essential for sustaining the hospital sector, determining best practice, and setting its quality and standards.

Although the large metropolitan public hospitals continue to offer the full range of services, new funding mechanisms (such as casemix) have provided the financial incentive for the private sector to improve its services (O'Loughlin 2002, p. 113). Government has also encouraged the broadening of the operations of the private hospitals and broken down distinctions between the two sectors – particularly with regard to research and training activities – with programs such as the Expanded Specialist Training Program (Productivity Commission 2009, pp. 59–60). In addition, the private hospital sector has actively responded to pressures for diversification, with some now including emergency departments. Although this particular development is mostly restricted to the densely populated metropolitan areas, it is the result of several pressures, including the rising expectations of insured patients who prefer not to attend a public hospital in an emergency. It has been adopted by a small number of private hospitals as a means to source new patients for the hospital independently of the specialists; as a strategy to attract new specialists by offering them a more diverse casemix and complexity; and as a way of financing a medical staff presence 24 hours per day (Productivity Commission 2009, pp. 60–61). The distinction between the two sectors has been further blurred with the advent of the privatised public hospitals and the use of government contracts with the not-for-profit sector to operate public hospitals with a full range of facilities. The full extent of this latter development however, is obscured by the inclusion of these hospitals within the category of 'public' hospitals within all official statistical collections, including those of the Australian Bureau of Statistics and Australian Institute of Health and Welfare.

Another feature distinguishing the current healthcare system from previous iterations is its rapidly diminishing universality. The growth in private health insurance membership over the past decade has attracted larger numbers of patients into the private sector, leaving individuals without private insurance, and without the means to pay for private healthcare, in the public system (Moorin & Holman 2006, pp. 248–49). With elective surgery increasingly being moved into the private hospitals (Griffith 2006, p. 42), and the higher remuneration of surgeons operating in private hospitals (Duckett 2005, p. 88), a two-tier system has developed, whereby the least wealthy – and those most in medical need of services – are denied access to timely surgery. While the increase in private hospital usage is often seen as a positive outcome for the healthcare budget, and phrased in terms of 'taking the load off the public sector'; this is a controversial change. The total amount contributed to the health bill by the private health insurance sector has continued to fall (Kay 2007, p. 587), the relative levels of funding to the public sector have dropped and the amount contributed by individual patients has risen. Yet at the same time, the government's subsidy of the industry has increased (Griffith 2006, p. 22). Hence the subsidy is rapidly becoming a 'significant and rising fiscal burden for the Commonwealth Government' (Peter Dawkins in Griffith 2006, p. 39). Clearly, the movement of patients into the private sector has not reduced the healthcare costs to either government or the individual patient, nor assisted the public hospitals. The planning of these 'reforms' was based not on evidence but on assumptions about the greater efficiency of the private sector, for there is little evidence of any savings to the healthcare budget from the private health insurance subsidies (Duckett & Jackson 2000; McAuley 2005; Richardson & Segal 2004), or from public–private partnership schemes in the healthcare sector (Acerete, Stafford & Stapleton 2012; English 2005). Such schemes are ostensibly introduced to reduce public expenditures:

[y]et greater profit making for private partners and contractors does not necessarily translate into lower costs for taxpayers, especially when hospital infrastructure is privately financed. P3s [public–private partnerships] are often used by government to avoid upfront capital expenses and as a way of shifting costs and risks away from the public sector – however higher interest rates, hidden fees, inadequate or misleading risk transfer, and higher private partner overhead costs all add up, producing more expensive infrastructure and services over the long run (Whiteside 2013).

The increasing government support of the private healthcare sector also removes resources from the public system. In a small market such as Australia, where almost all surgeons operate in both the public and the private sectors, increases in the level of private sector work (particularly where it is for private patients and elective surgery) diminishes the profession's capacity to attend to those in the public sector (Duckett 2005, p. 88). And it is the public sector which cares for a much larger proportion of patients with relatively low socioeconomic status and more complex medical needs (Productivity Commission 2009, p. 29, 55). Moreover, instead of reducing public waiting lists, growth in the use of the private sector may have the opposite effect because the higher remuneration of private hospitals provides surgeons with a 'perverse incentive to maintain high waiting times in the public sector to encourage prospective patients to seek private care' (Duckett 2005, p. 88; also Pratt 2005).

The new healthcare system is fundamentally different in yet another way. Although the two sectors may be becoming more alike with regard to their functions, their historically divergent operational motives, incentives and responsibilities have been brought into tension. Under the NPM agenda, and triggered by the signing of the 1995 National Competition Policy (NCP) – which bound state and federal governments to the 'competitive norms and rules' of the private sector (English 2005, p. 95) – corporate medical facilities and the expansion of for-profit insurance firms were ushered into the Australian marketplace. Under the NCP, a 'competitive neutrality between the private and public sectors became enshrined in law' (English 2005, p. 95). In other words, governments are compelled to ignore the diverse operational motives of the two sectors.

This largely explains the lack of parliamentary debate about the extent to which health funding is ending up in the private sector. Where previous Commonwealth and state health budgets were primarily spent on the provision of public services and the building of its infrastructure, an increasing proportion of those budgets is now channelled into corporate profits and other private surpluses. In 1990, for instance, private hospitals received five percent of their total recurrent funds from the Commonwealth. By 1999, it was providing 23 percent of their funds (O'Loughlin 2002, p. 11). By 2009–10, this has risen to 33 percent (AIHW 2012a, p. 4). With rising numbers of patients treated within the for-profit hospital sector, and growth in the number of public hospitals now under for-profit, private ownership and/or management, government expenditures are rising. Indeed, corporations such as Ramsay Health Care expect health expenditure, as a proportion of GDP, to increase to 14.5 percent by 2050 (Rex 2013).

Despite this change to healthcare financing, corporate healthcare has not been constituted as a policy 'problem' in need of a 'solution'. Yet the contrasting operational agendas of the two sectors lies at the heart of this issue. Privately owned/managed hospitals have an incentive to increase 'throughput' as they operate under a fee-for-service funding model, and for-profit hospitals have a duty to maximise returns to shareholders/owners. In the not-for-profit sector, the revenue-generation motive is less obvious, but there is nevertheless an aim to avoid losses (Productivity Commission 2009, p. 47).[9] In the public sector, a 'core function may be to assemble infrastructure, workforce and knowledge around the care of patients to improve their health' (Productivity Commission 2009, p. 82), and the cost efficiency of its services is only one of many concerns. Introducing marketisation into the healthcare sector does not simply mean bringing in more private firms, but also increasing the overall demand for services. This occurs because private health insurance incentives raise expectations about the increased capacity of the private system, and thus in themselves increase demand for services (Pratt 2005). It is also because there are greater incentives in the private sector to clinically or surgically intervene and provide services to patients. And there is evidence of 'over-servicing' in the private sector. For example, patients admitted to private hospitals are significantly more likely to receive intensive treatments, requiring more specialists to be transferred out of the public sector (Richardson & Segal 2004, p. 40).

The new healthcare system then, is no longer government-driven but market-shaped. Planning decisions are increasingly informed by market considerations rather than medical need. Private facilities are placed geographically to maximise revenue for corporate investors, even where this will compete with local public services and duplicate resources, leaving other regions undersupplied. This situation is currently occurring across Australia, because even while private hospital beds are increasingly available in capital cities, they are being reduced in regional areas where profitability is lower (Productivity Commission 2009, p. 65). Governments are unable to control the planning of appropriate hospital facilities, because the legal framework within which

9   It should also be noted that organisations in the not-for-profit sector may have their own agendas. While often considered to offer an alternative to the profit-motive of the corporate hospitals, the institutional mission of the not-for-profits can also shape the services they provide. For instance, the code of ethics of Catholic Health Australia, Australia's largest not-for-profit group (Productivity Commission 2009), precludes direct provision or referrals for abortion, some fertility treatments, vasectomy and other forms of sterilisation and birth control, including for women who have been raped (Catholic Health Australia 2001).

claims are heard is based on the needs and property rights of entrepreneurs, not the user rights of patients or the service responsibilities of government (Duckett 1989). Given that all medical services and hospitals in Australia rely heavily on public funding, this situation wastes scarce resources and produces no net gain in services for the community (White & Collyer 1998, p. 502). Equally, marketisation means standards of accountability and transparency are weakened, with less information provided about where the health budget is spent. This is particularly apparent when funding is subject to the 'commercial confidentiality' clauses of the public–private contracts, but also where important government data collections have been discontinued (including class-based disease categories and mortality rates) or simply not updated, obscuring the role and impact of radical changes in the healthcare system.

Conclusion

This chapter has provided a description and analysis of how the Australian healthcare system has developed since European settlement, and its radical transformation over the past three decades. The focus has been two areas within the healthcare system: the national insurance scheme of Medicare and its private health insurance counterpart, and the private and public hospital sectors. These areas are closely linked in the private sector, given that the health funds are a major source of a private hospital's revenue, and hospital services constitute most of a fund's expenditures. Our analysis has concentrated on the private sector, particularly the role of the large, for-profit corporations rather than the small independent private entities, religious institutions and not-for-profit insurance schemes. This is because there has been relatively little discussion or analysis of *corporate* healthcare in the Australian setting, even though it has been the most significant development since the introduction of Medibank.

Corporate healthcare has, as we have seen, brought a new complexity to an already complex healthcare system. Prior to their entry, the mixed system contained private, primarily not-for-profit religious providers of healthcare services and not-for-profit insurance services. With the growth in corporate healthcare and for-profit insurance companies, new administrative and regulatory processes have become essential. For instance, in the hospital sector, the introduction of public–private partnerships and contracts to care for public patients has forced governments to create new regulatory and monitoring mechanisms to ensure comparable quality across all services, and new programs and policies to ensure sufficient medical and specialist training positions. Corporate, for-profit healthcare has also transformed the landscape of the services sector, creating new scarcities within the public system, new demands on the healthcare budget, new obstacles to the efficient planning of services, and new constraints on the provision of information and the maintenance of previously high standards of transparency and accountability. In this new healthcare system, market actors and market principles have a much larger role than ever before.

Acknowledgments

Thanks to Karen Willis and Marika Franklin for helpful suggestions and assistance towards this chapter and to the editors for their insightful and careful feedback on earlier drafts. The authors, together with Karen Willis, are recipients of Australian Research Council (ARC) Discovery Project funding for the project, 'How Australians navigate the health care maze: The differential capacity to choose', 2013–15.

Appendix

Sources and notes to Table 8.2.

- Compiled from ABS (1995) and AIHW (1999) for 1991–92 data and AIHW (2002, 2003 [updated version of table 2.1], 2012b, 2013b) with AIHW Australian Hospital Statistics reports for other years also consulted. It should be noted that each hospital is a reporting unit rather than necessarily one separate building, and there has been some variance in administrative definitions over the period above. * Figures for these facilities in 1991–92 are not available, hence 1993–94 figures are supplied as an indicator of growth in this sub-sector.

References

Acerete B., Stafford, A. & Stapleton, P. 2012, 'New development: New global health care PPP developments – a critique of the success story', *Public Money and Management*, vol. 32, no. 4, pp. 311–14.

ABS (Australian Bureau of Statistics) 1995, *Hospitals, Australia, 1991–92*, Cat. no. 4391. 0, ABS, Canberra.

ABS 2012, *Private hospitals, Australia, 2010–11*, Cat. no. 4390. 0, ABS, Canberra.

AIHW (Australian Institute of Health and Welfare) 1999, *Australian hospital statistics, 1997–98*, Health Services Series, Cat. no. HSE 6, AIHW, Canberra.

AIHW 2002, *Australian hospital statistics, 2000–01*, Health Services Series no. 19, Cat. no. HSE 20, AIHW, Canberra.

AIHW 2003, *Australian hospital statistics, 2001–02*, Health Services Series no. 20, Cat. no. HSE 25, AIHW, Canberra [updated version of Table 2. 1 available at: http://www.aihw.gov.au/WorkArea/DownloadAsset.aspx?id=6442473475]

AIHW 2006, *Australian hospital statistics 2004–05, Cat. no. HSE 107*, AIHW, Canberra.

AIHW 2011, *Health expenditure Australia 2009–10*, Health and Welfare Expenditure Series no. 46, Cat. no. HWE 55, AIHW, Canberra.

AIHW 2012a, *Australia's hospitals 2010–11 at a glance*, Health Services Series No. 44, Cat. no. HSE 118, AIHW, Canberra.

AIHW 2012b, *Australian hospital statistics 2010–11*, Health Services Series no. 43, Cat. no. HSE 117, AIHW, Canberra.

AIHW 2013a, *Health expenditure Australia 2011–12*, Health and Welfare Expenditure Series No. 50, Cat. no. HSE 118, AIHW, Canberra.

AIHW 2013b, *Australian hospital statistics 2010–11*, Health Services Series no. 50, Cat. no. HSE 134, AIHW, Canberra.

Anderson, R., Haywood, P., Usherwood, T., Haas, M. & Hall, J. 2005, 'Alternatives to for-profit corporatisation: The view from general practice', *Australian Journal of Primary Health*, vol. 11, no. 2, pp. 78–86.

ASX (Australian Securities Exchange) 2012, Health care & biotechnology sector profile, June. http://www.asx.com.au/research/pdf/health_care_sector_factsheet.pdf

Biggs, A. 2009, 'Fairer private health insurance incentives bill 2009', *Bills Digest*, no. 152, 2008–09, Parliamentary Library, Canberra. http://www.aph.gov.au/Parliamentary_Business/Bills_Legislation/bd/bd1112a/12bd020

Bloom, A. 2000, 'Hospital co-locations: Private sector participation in the hospital sector in Australia', in *Health Reform in Australia and New Zealand*, ed. A. L. Bloom, Oxford University Press, Melbourne, pp. 235–250.

Brown, L. & Barnett, J. R. 2004, 'Is the corporate transformation of hospitals creating a new hybrid health care space? A case study of the impact of co-location of public and private hospitals in Australia', *Social Science & Medicine*, vol. 58, no. 2, pp. 427–444.

BUPA 2012, The global BUPA family. http://www.bupa.com.au/about-us/about-bupa/bupa-group

Butler, J. R. G. 2002, 'Policy change and private health insurance: Did the cheapest policy do the trick?', *Australian Health Review*, vol. 25, no. 6, pp. 33–41.

Catholic Health Australia 2001, Catholic Health Australia, Red Hill, ACT. http://www.cha.org.au/code-of-ethical-standards.html

Collyer, F. M. 1997, 'The Port Macquarie base hospital: Privatisation and the public purse', *Just Policy*, vol. 10, pp. 27–39.

Collyer, F. M. 2004, 'The corporatisation and commercialisation of complementary and alternative medicine', in *The mainstreaming of complementary and alternative medicine in social context: An international perspective*, eds P. Tovey, G. Easthope & J. Adams, Routledge, New York, pp. 81–99.

Collyer, F. M. 2012, *Mapping the sociology of health and medicine: America, Britain and Australia compared*, Palgrave Macmillan, Basingstoke.

Collyer, F. M., McMaster, J. & Wettenhall, R. W. 2001, *Public enterprise divestment: Australian case studies*, University of South Pacific Press, Fiji.

Collyer, F. M., Wettenhall, R. W. & McMaster, J. 2003, 'The privatisation of public enterprises: Australian research findings', *Just Policy*, no. 31, December, pp. 14–23.

Collyer, F. M. & White, K. N. 2001, Corporate control of healthcare in Australia, Discussion Paper No. 42, Australia Institute, Canberra.

Daniel, A. 1990, *Medicine and the state*, Allen & Unwin, Sydney.

de Voe, J. E. & Short, S. D. 2003, 'A shift in the historical trajectory of medical dominance: The case of Medibank and the Australian Doctors' Lobby', *Social Science and Medicine*, vol. 57, no. 2, pp. 343–53.

Department of Health 2011, Private health insurance – Legislation. http://www.health.gov.au/internet/main/publishing. nsf/Content/health-privatehealth-consumers-legislat.htm

Department of Human Services n.d., Rebate amounts. http://www.humanservices.gov.au/customer/enablers/medicare/australian-government-rebate-on-private-health-insurance/rebate-amounts

Duckett, S. 1989, 'Regulating the construction of hospitals or vice versa', *Community Health Studies*, vol. 13, no. 4, pp. 431–40.

Duckett, S. 2005, 'Private care and public waiting', *Australian Health Review*, vol. 29, no. 1, pp. 87–93.

Duckett, S. & Jackson, T. J. 2000, 'The new health insurance rebate: An inefficient way of assisting public hospitals', *Medical Journal of Australia*, vol. 172, no. 9, pp. 439–42.

Elliot, A. 2006, ' "The best friend Medicare ever had?" Policy narratives and changes in Coalition health policy', *Health Sociology Review*, vol. 15, no. 2, pp. 132–43.

English, L. M. 2005, 'Using public-private partnerships to achieve value for money in the delivery of healthcare in Australia', *International Journal of Public Policy*, vol. 1, no. 1–2, pp. 91–121.

English, L. M. 2006, 'Public private partnerships in Australia: An overview of their nature, purpose, incidence and oversight', *UNSW Law Journal*, vol. 29, no. 3, pp. 250–62.

Gray, G. 1996, 'Reform and reaction in Australian health policy', *Journal of Health Politics, Policy and Law*, vol. 21, no. 3, pp. 587–615.

Gray, G. 2004, *The politics of Medicare: Who gets what, when and how*, University of New South Wales Press, Sydney.

Griffith, G. 2006, *Commonwealth-state responsibilities for health: 'Big bang' or incremental reform*, NSW Parliamentary Library Research Service Briefing Paper 17/06.

Hall, J., de Abreu Lourenco, R. & Viney, R. 1999, 'Carrots and sticks – the fall and fall of private health insurance', *Health Economics*, vol. 8, no. 8, pp. 653–60.

Harley, K., Willis, K., Gabe, J., Short, S., Collyer, F. M., Natalier, K. & Calnan, M. 2011, 'Constructing health consumers: Private health insurance discourses in Australia and the United Kingdom', *Health Sociology Review*, vol. 20, no. 3, pp. 306–20.

Healthscope 2013, Prospectus – Healthscope subordinated notes II, Prospectus for the offer of Healthscope Subordinated Notes II to be listed on ASX.

Hicks, R. 1981, *Rum regulation and riches*, RT Kelly P/L, Sydney.

Hopkins, S. 2001, 'The rise of private health insurance in Australia: Early effects on insurance and hospital markets'. *Economic and Labour Relations Review*, vol. 12, no. 2, pp. 225–38.

Howard, J. W. 1996, Transcript of the First Great Debate with Ray Martin and Paul Keating, Channel Nine, 11 February.

Industry Commission 1997, *Private health insurance*, Report no. 57, Commonwealth of Australia, Canberra.

IPN (Independent Practitioner Network) 2011, About IPN. http://www.ipn.com.au/ index.php?option=com_content&view=article&id=20&Itemid=3

Jones, J. 2007, 'Integration and diversification in healthcare: Financial performance and implications for Medicare', *Health Sociology Review*, vol. 16, no. 1, pp. 27–42.

Jones, J. 2010, Organisational diversification and financial performance in health care: A longitudinal study of public Australian companies, PhD thesis, Faculty of Social Sciences, Flinders University of South Australia.

Kay, A. 2007, 'Tense layering and synthetic policy paradigms: The politics of health insurance in Australia', *Australian Journal of Political Science*, vol. 42, no. 4, pp. 579–91.

McAuley, I. 2005, 'Private health insurance: Still muddling through', *Agenda*, vol. 12, no. 2, pp. 159–71.

Medical Benefits Reviews Task Group Diagnostic Imaging Review Team 2012, *Review of funding for diagnostic imaging services: Final report*, Department of Health and Ageing, Commonwealth of Australia.

Moorin, R. & Holman, C. 2006, 'The influence of federal health care policy reforms on the use of private health insurance in disadvantaged groups', *Australian Health Review*, vol. 30, no. 2, pp. 241–51.

NEHTA (National e-Health Transition Authority) 2009, Environment scan: The pathology industry, NEHTA, Sydney. http://www.nehta.gov.au/component/docman/doc_details/762-e-pathology-environment-scan-of-the-pathology-industry-v10-f

O'Loughlin, M. A. 2002, 'Conflicting interests in private hospital care', *Australian Health Review*, vol. 25, no. 5, pp. 106–17.

Palmer, G.R. & Short, S.D. 2010, *Health care and public policy: An Australian analysis*, 4th edn, Palgrave Macmillan, South Yarra.

Partnerships Victoria 2012, Public Private Partnerships, Projects. Department of Treasury and Finance, Victorian Government. http://www.partnerships.vic.gov.au/CA25708500035EB6/WebProjects?OpenView

Peck, J., Theodore, N., & Brenner, N. 2012, 'Neoliberalism, interrupted', in *Neoliberalism: Beyond the free market*, eds D. Cahill, L. Edwards & F. Stilwell, pp. 15–30. Edward Elgar, Cheltenham, UK.

PHIAC (Private Health Insurance Administration Council) 2001, *Operations of the private health insurers annual report 2000–01*, PHIAC, Canberra. http://phiac.gov.au/wp-content/uploads/2012/08/82pa2001.pdf

PHIAC 2007, *Operations of the private health insurers annual report 2006–07*, PHIAC, Canberra. http://phiac.gov.au/wp-content/uploads/2012/08/264152007.pdf

PHIAC 2008, *Operations of the private health insurers annual report 2007–08*, PHIAC, Canberra. http://phiac.gov.au/wp-content/uploads/2012/08/26415.pdf

PHIAC 2009, *Operations of the private health insurers annual report 2008–09*, PHIAC, Canberra. http://phiac.gov.au/wp-content/uploads/2012/08/264-152009.pdf

PHIAC 2010, *Operations of the private health insurers annual report 2009–10*, PHIAC, Canberra. http://phiac.gov.au/wp-content/uploads/2012/08/110201%20264-15%20Annual%20Report.pdf

PHIAC 2011, *Operations of the private health insurers annual report 2010–11*, PHIAC, Canberra. http://phiac.gov.au/wp-content/uploads/2012/08/ Annual-Report-on-Operations-2010-11-web-version.pdf

Pratt, A. 2005, '*Public versus private? An overview of the debate on private health insurance and pressure on public hospitals*', Research Note, Parliamentary Library, Parliament of Australia, Canberra.

Primary Health Care 2013, Results for announcement to the market, Primary Health Care Limited, Appendix 4D – Half year report, for the half year ended 31 December 2012, Notes provided to the ASX. http://www.afr.com/rw/ Wires/Stories/2013-02-06/ASXAnnouncements/PRY_01379998.pdf

Productivity Commission 2009, *Public and private hospitals: Research report*, Productivity Commission, Canberra.

Queensland Health 2012, The project. http://www.health. qld.gov.au/scuhospital/ the_project-procurement. asp

Quinlivan, B. 2001, 'The uncanny x-ray men', *Business Review Weekly*, 22 June.

Ramsay 2012a, Ramsay Health Care Limited Annual Report, Ramsay, Sydney. http://www.ramsayhealth.com.au/Investor-Centre/docs/AR2012.pdf.

Ramsay 2012b, ASX Announcement, Ramsay Health Care reports 14. 0% rise in first-half core net profit & upgrades FY12 guidance, 23 February. http://www.ramsayhealth.com/Investor-Centre/docs/ Market_Briefings_23022012a.pdf

Rex, C. 2013, Emerging themes in the Australian and global health systems, presented at the Annual Stockbrokers Conference, 31 May. http://www.ramsayhealth.com/Investor-Centre/docs/ Market_Briefings_31052013.pdf

Richardson, J. & Segal, L. 2004, 'Private health insurance and the pharmaceutical benefits scheme: How effective has recent government policy been?' *Australian Health Review* , vol. 28, no. 1, pp. 34–47.

Roxon, N. & Swan, W. 2009, Rebalancing support for private health insurance, Media release, 12 May. http://www.health.gov.au/internet/budget/publishing. nsf/Content/budget2009-hmedia13.htm

Sax, S. 1984, *A strife of interests: politics and policies in Australian health services*, George Allen & Unwin, Sydney.

Sax, S. 1990, *Healthcare choices and the public purse*, Allen & Unwin, Sydney.

Scotton, R. B. & Macdonald, C. R. 1993, *The making of Medibank*, Australian Studies in Health Service Administration No. 76. University of New South Wales.

Shamsullah, A. 2011, 'Australia's private health insurance industry: Structure, competition, regulation and role in a less than 'ideal world" ', *Australian Health Review*, vol. 35, no. 1, pp. 23–31.

Sonic Healthcare 2011, Our history. http://www.sonichealthcare.com/about-us/
our-history.aspx

South Australia Health 2011, Public private partnership and the new Royal
Adelaide Hospital. http://www.sahealth.sa.gov.au/wps/wcm/connect/
Public+Content/SA+Health+Internet/Health+reform/
The+new+Royal+Adelaide+Hospital/
Public+Private+Partnership+and+the+new+Royal+Adelaide+Hospital

Stebbing, A. & Spies-Butcher, B. 2010, 'Universal welfare by "other means"? Social
tax expenditures and the Australian dual welfare state', *Journal of Social
Policy*, vol. 39, no. 4, pp. 585–606.

White, K. N. 2000, 'The state, the market, and general practice in Australia',
International Journal of Health Services, vol. 30, no. 2, pp. 285–302.

White, K. N. & Collyer, F. M. 1998, 'Healthcare markets in Australia: Ownership of
the private hospital sector', *International Journal of Health Services*, vol. 28,
no. 3, pp. 487–510.

Whiteside, H. 2013, 'Public-private partnerships: Re-conceptualising the "public
interest" ', Canadian Political Science Association 2013 Annual Conference,
4–6 June, University of Victoria, Victoria.

Whitlam, G. 1968, 'The alternative health program', *Australian Journal of Social
Issues*, vol. 3, no. 4, pp. 33–50.

9
Marketisation of immigrant skills assessment in Australia

Anna Boucher

Over the 1990s and 2000s, private actors have played an increasing role in the selection and integration of new migrants. An individual applying as a skilled immigrant to Australia must have his or her skills accredited before lodgment of an application with the Department of Immigration and Border Protection (DIBP)[1]. This assessment forms a vital part of the immigration process for a wide range of visa categories. Historically, such assessments were undertaken by immigration officials. Since 1999, the preliminary step of skills assessment of immigrant applicants has been carried out by 35 different assessing authorities independent of the department. Some of these authorities are private

---

Boucher, A. 2015, 'Marketisation of immigrant skills assessment in Australia', in *Markets, rights and power in Australian social policy*, eds G. Meagher & S. Goodwin, Sydney University Press, Sydney.

---

1 The name of the department has changed several times in recent decades. From 2007–2013, it was called the Department of Immigration and Citizenship; following the election of the Coalition government in 2013, the name was changed to Immigration and Border Protection (DIBP 2014a). In this chapter, department names at the time of writing are given, unless the responsible department at the time of a reported past event or inquiry was different, and in the case of institutional authorship.

professional bodies, others are commercial arms of government agencies. While this trend towards marketisation has been considered in light of privatised detention centres for asylum seekers (Crock & Berg 2011, pp. 132–33; Crock, Saul & Dastyari 2006), privatisation and marketisation of the bulk of immigration selection for skilled immigration in Australia have not been analysed extensively. Yet, given the centrality of immigration to Australia's sovereign identity, and the importance of skilled immigration within immigration and labour market policy more broadly, such an assessment is warranted. This chapter outlines marketisation in the assessment of immigrant skills since 1999 and evaluates the realisation of key public policy goals in light of this development.

The effects of marketisation of skills assessment upon skilled immigration assessment are evaluated using five public policy indicators: i) the *timeliness* of skills assessments; ii) the *accuracy* of decision-making; iii) the *cost shifting* that has occurred; iv) the *transparency* of the skills assessment process and opportunities for review; and v) the *fairness* of the assessment system, across different assessing agencies, both public and private. These indicators have been selected based on their prevalent usage in public policy analysis of privatisation and marketisation processes. Marketisation is often justified on the basis that expertise in pricing and business can lead to better and faster delivery of goods and services (Aman 2009, p. 269; Leunig 2010, p. 160; Quiggin 2010, p. 186; Webster & Harding 2000, p. 10), although whether this is actually the case may depend upon whether there is real competition at play (Kelman 2009, p. 156). The specialisation that comes with marketisation can also be seen to increase the accuracy of decision-making (Aman 2009, p. 269). More critically, marketisation has been seen to reduce the transparency and fairness of policy processes, insofar that certain forms of public law review are reduced, or hidden from sight (Freeman 1999; Freeman & Minow 2009, pp. 4–5; Kelman 2009, p. 178; Ramia & Carney 2000; Sapotichne & Smith 2011, p. 89). Aside from the theoretical basis for the selection of these indicators, the empirical research undertaken for this chapter demonstrates their practical importance to stakeholders engaged in the skilled immigration field, including immigrant applicants and their representatives.

Given the dearth of current academic research on how these theoretical concerns play out in the area of immigrant skills assessment, a range of original research was undertaken for this chapter, coupled with desk analysis of existing policy documents. First, I undertook a survey of migrant agents registered with the Migration Institute of Australia in 2012 to ascertain their perceptions of skilled migration assessment in the present day and across time. Second, I drew upon elite interviews conducted in 2009 with senior immigration officials engaged in the 1999 policy reforms (Boucher 2011). Third, I analysed the report of a Joint Standing Committee on Migration review of migrant skills accreditation and assessment – *Negotiating the maze* (JSC 2006) – and the government response to that inquiry (JSC 2011). Submissions to this review were also examined. Finally, I considered several legal cases and relevant rules pertinent to this area of regulation. This chapter states the law and application fees as stated in public documents in January 2012.

The public policy context of skills assessments for immigration purposes

Skilled immigration plays an important role in Australia's immigration program and economy more broadly, as structural ageing and skill gaps in the domestic workforce, particularly in the mineral and resource sectors, create labour market pressures. Skilled immigration selection comprises 65 percent of Australia's permanent immigration program and a significant component of Australia's temporary immigration (DIAC 2011a, p. 3).[2] The size of the immigration program is also significant. In the year 2010 to 2011, 113,725 immigrants entered Australia under the permanent skilled category and 90,120 under the temporary skilled category (DIAC 2012a, p. 6, 49). Over the 1990s and 2000s, Australia's skilled immigration system has grown in scale and become more complex in its design through a proliferation of visa classes and associated rules and provisions (Crock & Berg 2011, Ch 9). Within this complex and increasingly vital area of labour market activity, analysis of skills assessments is of broad public policy salience.

---

2   Together, permanent skilled and temporary skilled entrants comprise around 33 percent of net overseas migration and this is projected to rise to 40 percent by 2014–15 (DIAC 2011b, p. 10). Net overseas migration comprises all immigration flows minus all emigration flows.

A successful skills assessment is required prior to lodgment of an application for points-tested general skilled immigration. As such, skills assessment is a separate, independent but also necessarily preliminary step prior to the application for a skilled immigration visa. Skills assessments are required by many classes of skilled visa applicants.[3] Skills assessments fulfill a number of important policy functions, predominately to ensure that 'the overall objectives of the skilled program are met in terms of economic benefit to Australia' (MIA 2005, p. 8). This is because, at least in principle, a skills assessment should guarantee that the applicant has the necessary skills upon arrival in Australia. Second, skills assessments provide consumer protection and a gatekeeping function, including in the 'high risk' medical, allied health and aviation occupations (MIA 2005, p. 8). Australia has undertaken some form of skills assessment since at least the late 1960s. These assessments have classically fallen into a white collar/blue collar demarcation. In 1969, the Committee on Overseas Professional Qualifications was established within the Department of Immigration (Iredale 1997, pp. 101–4). This committee originally took the form of an information body for prospective migrants but later adopted an assessment function.[4] In 1989, the National Office of Overseas Skill Recognition (NOOSR) within the Department of Employment, Education and Training, as it was then known, replaced the committee. NOOSR staff, located in Canberra, undertook the paper assessments of professional occupations. NOOSR also published a variety of papers on occupational recognition, which were used as guidelines by assessors

---

3 Applications by recent international student graduates for ongoing residency require a skills assessment, as do applications under some temporary migration visas and for some categories of the Employer Nomination Scheme, by which an employer nominates a migrant for entry to work permanently in Australia (Policy Advice Manual 3; Migration Regulations 1994, Schedule 1, Item 1136(3)(ba)(ii); Item 1229(3)(aa-ab); Schedule 2, 487. 214; 487.223; 856.213(b). There are several important exceptions to the requirement to undertake a skills assessment. Applicants who apply under a Temporary Business (Long Stay) (Subclass 457) visa sponsored by an employer (457 visa) and who do not work in a trade are not required to undertake such an assessment. Further, no skills assessment is required for migrants sponsored under a Regional Sponsored Migration Scheme.
4 Cully and Skladzien (2001, p. 24) note that, prior to 1969, those in white collar jobs were required to 'fend for themselves in the market, or rely on ... bilateral arrangements'.

to identify the 'usual occupation' of skilled immigrant applicants. The assessment of trades was dealt with through the *Tradesmen's Rights Regulation Act 1946* (Cwlth), which was administered through various Central Trade Committees and Local Trade Committees. By convention, these committees were comprised of members from relevant employer and trade union associations who were responsible for creating 'standards, policies and recognition criteria' for trades as well as considering 'applications for migration assessments' (DEWRSB 1998, pp. 5–6) with immigration officials located overseas (Crock 1998, pp. 103–4; Cully & Skladzien 2001, p. 86; Iredale 1997, p. 104). Following a legislative inquiry in 1998, the *Tradesmen's Rights Regulation Act 1946* (Cwlth) was repealed through the Tradesman's Rights Regulation Repeal Bill 1999. By the late 1990s, about 60 percent of assessments were undertaken by immigration officers and the remainder by NOOSR, Trades Recognition Australia (TRA) and a very small number of external bodies (DIMA 1999a, p. 78).

Throughout the 1980s and 1990s, government officials raised concerns over the difficulties for immigration officers in undertaking skills assessments (CAAIP 1988, pp. 53–54; cited in House of Representatives Standing Committee on Community Affairs 1996, p. 55). However, it was not until the election of the Howard Coalition government in 1996 that decisive policy reform was initiated in this area. Marketisation and privatisation of previously governmental functions occurred across a number of policy areas at the time (ARC 1998; Aulich 2011; Ramia & Carney 2001) and within a number of aspects of the immigration portfolio (DIMA 1999b, p. 31, cited in Crock & Berg 2011, p. 129). This marketisation was justified on the basis that it would 'improve service delivery by government' and 'ensure that resources [were] used efficiently'. The marketisation of skills assessment in particular was undertaken as part of the review of general skilled immigration, which overhauled not only the process of skills assessment, but also the points test for skilled immigration more broadly (DIMA 1999a, p. 76).

A number of arguments were provided by government in favour of marketisation of skills assessment. First, external skills assessment was expected to improve the timeliness of skills assessment by separating out skills assessment from visa processing (DIMA 1999c). Second, outsourced skills assessments may be more accurate in their appraisal of skill than those undertaken by immigration officials. This spoke to the difficulty for immigration officials in identifying the 'usual occupation' of the applicant, as well as the lack of expertise on the part of immigration officials in particular skill areas (DIMA 1999a, p. 76, 78). As Mark Cully and Tom Skladzien (2001, p. 32) argued of the pre-1999 system: 'This system was regarded as costly (to government) and prone to error as assessments for many occupations were done by those without any knowledge of, or training in, the relevant field'. The claim, as put by Cully and Skladzien (2001, p. 32), is that the new system improved the accuracy of skill assessments undertaken by departmental officers: 'The new system reduces the risk of error by accrediting a competent assessing authority for each occupation on the Skills Occupation List'.

A senior immigration official questioned the accuracy of skill assessments undertaken by his department in more colourful terms:

> I saw a case years ago of a gentleman … and this is creative, called himself a 'forecourt engineer'. Would you hazard a guess as to what a 'forecourt engineer' does? Petrol pump attendant. You know what I mean, how do you describe yourself? And immigration officers, that's not our game. We are there to process, we are there to apply the law and the regulations on lots of things, and this is part of our business, but not really the core part of our business, because we are not a skills assessing body. (Interview with official of the Department of Immigration and Citizenship, Canberra, 24 September 2009)

A final and related argument was that marketisation would reduce cost to the state, in the sense that an activity once included within visa assessment is now outsourced and paid for by the migrant applicant separately as part of the visa application process. As outlined in more detail below, this may, however, depend upon whether the skills assessment is undertaken by a government body, or a private authority. Government bodies must operate on a cost recovery basis, requiring a fee-for-service (DIIRSTE 2013, p. 6), which does not appear to be the case for private assessing authorities. An official from the Department of Immigration summarised the benefits of marketisation as follows: 'It was beneficial to the migrant, beneficial for the labour market. And it removed a decision-making role for immigration officers, which really they weren't in a position to do' (Boucher 2011).[5]

Following marketisation in 1999, NOOSR was delegated a narrower, oversight function in the skills assessment process. Its role was redefined as a clearinghouse for information and advice on overseas qualifications including determining the equivalent Australian standard of overseas qualifications (Cully & Skladzien 2001, p. 27). In 2014, NOOSR's name was changed to the Qualifications Recognition Policy Unit, within the Department of Education and Training (DET n.d.). TRA retained oversight over most (but not all) of the trade occupations and has been overseen since 2011 by the Department of Industry and Science. The Vocational Education Training and Assessment (VETASSESS) provider established in 1997 is the commercial arm of the Melbourne-based Kangan Batman TAFE (VETASSESS 2013). VETASSESS is responsible for the assessment of the bulk of professional occupations and some trades (JSC 2006, p. 50), and is a government business enterprise. While government documentation reveals that VETASSESS is 'contracted by DIMA [the Department of Immigration and Multicultural Affairs]' (JSC 2006, p. 50), the exact nature of the contractual relationship is not clear from this documentation, and an attempt by the author to interview the head of VETASSESS to clarify the relationship was refused. A range of private professional associations undertake the remainder of skill assessments. These assessing bodies are the same organisations responsible for domestic accreditation of skills of Australian graduates, such as the various Legal Practitioner Admissions Boards, the Architects Accreditation Council of Australia, or Engineers Australia (DIBP 2014). As such, in many cases, the bodies responsible for assessing the skills of potential immigrants, are also those who regulate professions. The power to declare a body as an assessing authority lies with the Minister for Education or Employment (Migration Regulations 1994, r2.26B [1–1A]).

Skills assessment had been marketised to assessing agencies for six years when in 2005, the Joint Standing Committee on Migration of the Federal Parliament held a parliamentary inquiry into, among other things, migrant skills recognition. Entitled *Negotiating the maze: Review of arrangements for overseas skills recognition, upgrading and licensing* (JSC 2006), henceforth *Negotiating the maze*, the inquiry in-

---

5 Interview with senior official of the Department of Immigration and Citizenship, Canberra, 30 October 2009.

vestigated the complex systems of skills assessment and the structural barriers to skills recognition for new Australians upon settlement (JSC 2006, pp. ix–x). The inquiry followed a series of federal, state and academic inquiries into skills assessment and migrant skill recognition held over the preceding two decades, which had highlighted the need for ongoing attention to these issues (JSC 2006, p. xxx). Specifically, following *To make a contribution: Review of skilled labour migration programs*, a separate inquiry into general skilled immigration in 2005, the then Minister for Immigration and Multicultural Affairs, Senator Amanda Vanstone, sought the agreement of the Joint Standing Committee on Migration to review skills recognition (JSC 2006, p. xxxi). Five years later the Gillard Labor government responded to the *Negotiating the maze* inquiry and accepted some but not all of the recommendations (JSC 2011). Details of the inquiry and subsequent government responses are canvassed below. First, I set out the details of the survey I undertook with members of the Migration Institute of Australia.

Empirical approach: A survey of members of the Migration Institute of Australia

One important source for the analysis in this section of this chapter is an original survey administered electronically via SurveyMonkey in January 2012 to all Migration Institute of Australia (MIA) members working in the field of skilled immigration. The MIA assisted in administering the survey to ensure the anonymity of its members. There were 249 responses to the survey, which represents an estimated 15 percent response rate of eligible MIA members. Respondents to the survey work with both public and private assessing bodies and some of the respondents have been employed in the field prior to 1999. Migration agents were selected as a source of expertise on the issue of skills assessment for a number of reasons. First, migration agents are responsible for submitting the majority of skilled migration applications. On most recent estimates, migration agents lodge between 24 and 100 percent of relevant skilled immigration visas, depending on the particular visa subclass (DIAC 2012b). As a group, migration agents therefore possess considerable knowledge in the area of skills assessment. Second, given this expertise, migrant agents are more likely to understand the

Table 9.1: Assessing bodies most used by migrant agents

Assessing body	Most used	Second most used
Trade Recognition Australia (TRA)	49.6%	20.0%
Vocational Education and Training Assessment Services (VETASSESS)	56.3%	32.1%
Australian Computer Society (ACS)	33.6%	14.9%
Engineers Australia	24.2%	11.2%

Note: These percentages do not add up to 100 as respondents in some cases selected more than one organisation for the most used. The Department of Immigration does not provide a table of the distribution of skills assessments across all assessing bodies.

complexities of the skilled immigration system than their clients, who have only undergone their own, singular immigration application experience. Third, recruitment of migrant agents was assisted through the MIA, the peak representative body for migration agents.

Respondents were asked both closed and open questions about their involvement and experience of skill assessments, across a number of assessing bodies (public and private) and about their views on the efficiency, cost, accuracy, review rights and fairness of skill assessment. Depending upon their length of engagement in the field, agents were also asked to compare skill assessments before and after 1999. Although there are limitations in surveying agents about their views on assessment that occurred over 10 years ago, this was the best available method to compare policy indicators across time.

Table 9.1 shows the assessing agencies identified by respondents as the most used and the second most used. As the table makes clear, the majority of respondents identified TRA and VETASSESS as the most used assessing bodies, while the private Australian Computer Society (ACS) and Engineers Australia (EA) were the third and fourth most used assessing authorities. Nonetheless, given that respondents identified over 32 of the 35 organisations responsible for skill assessment across the survey, a variety of public and private authorities were represented in the responses and accordingly, in the analysis in this chapter. Unfortunately, these response details from the survey cannot be compared against agency details of the number of assessments undertaken each year, as assessing agencies do not all make this information publicly available on their websites.

Analysis

Drawing upon this survey data and the desk analysis of major government inquiries into skills assessment, the remainder of this chapter assesses marketisation of skills assessment against a number of key public policy indicators: timeliness, accuracy, cost-shifting, accountability and transparency, and, finally, the fairness of skill assessments. The rationale for each of these indictors is set out in each section below.

Timeliness

Perhaps one of the most prominent arguments in favour of marketisation and privatisation of government services is that it improves timeliness. Such improvements may arise from the specialisation that can occur within the private sector, as a result of particular expertise in pricing and business (Aman 2009, p. 269) and in terms of better, faster work practices (Webster & Harding 2000, p. 10, cited in Chalmers & Davis 2001, p. 75) and service delivery (Leunig 2010). As noted above, arguments around improved service delivery were presented in favour of the marketisation of skills assessment in 1999 (DIMA 1999c). In fact, marketisation became the status quo in the migration setting more broadly 'unless there were clear reasons for not doing so' (DIMA 2000, p. 22, cited in Crock & Berg 2011, p. 131).

Insofar that the skills assessment process in Australia is perceived as more streamlined than in other immigrant selecting countries, the marketisation of skills assessment may also have made Australia a more attractive destination country for skilled immigrants (Cully & Skladzien 2001, p. 11). Given that a successful skills assessment is the necessary first step for a successful application for skilled migration, it is clear that any delay in skills assessments will also delay final processing times. This can be particularly problematic when an applicant is relying upon points under the skilled immigration points test for age. These points diminish if the processing times are extended, as the applicant ages. This may appear to be a minor issue, yet given the high pass mark for the points test for Skilled-Independent visas, processing times can actually be decisive in whether an application for skilled immigration is successful or not. A delay in processing can also see an applicant lose their temporary provisional visa status in some instances.

It is clear that the processing period for skill assessments is a key measure of timeliness that holds ramifications not only for the administration of the immigration program at large, but also for individual applicants. Reduction in processing times was seen as one key advantage of marketisation by departmental officials (Interview by author with senior official of the Department of Immigration and Citizenship, Canberra, 30 October 2009). Yet, concern over processing times have persisted since and had already been raised in submissions to a Joint Standing Committee Inquiry into skills accreditation for new migrants, the *Negotiating the maze* inquiry in 2005–6 (see ILAA 2005, p. 6, pp. 113–14). The survey of migration agents undertaken for this chapter reveals large differences in perceived processing times across assessing bodies, and concerns around timeliness with some assessing agencies. Given sensitivity around this issue, it is unsurprising that assessment bodies do not advertise this information on their websites.

As such, we must rely upon survey results, which provide an initial indication of processing times. Respondents were asked about the time taken on average for application processing, by the authority with which the respondent had the most dealings. The survey offered the time periods show in Table 9.2. As this table makes clear, the reported average processing times for skills assessment as reported in the survey are between three and six months.

Concerns over processing times were raised by 40 percent of respondents in a general open field question.[6] Further, concerns were raised over processing times for both private and public assessing bodies. Qualitative responses to this open question indicated that processing times change quite dramatically depending upon the current pressures on the immigration system as a whole and due to changes in

---

6 This open field question asked 'Are there any further comments you would like to make about the skills assessment process that have not been covered in the survey?' and gave respondents the opportunity to provide qualitative feedback on their experience with skills assessment.

Table 9.2: Average time for skills assessments by assessing bodies

Length of time	Response (percent)	Response (count)
Less than one month	8.5%	21
One to two months	38.9%	96
Three to six months	48.6%	120
In excess of six months	4.0%	10
	100%	247

N = 247

selection rules, such as a new requirement introduced in 2011 that skill authorities assess work experience as well as professional qualifications for general skilled immigration. Those migration agents who had been active since before 1999 were asked to reflect on differences in skills assessment since marketisation. Those respondents were more likely to find that there had been a slowing of assessment times since 1999 (25 percent) than a speeding up of times over the same period (nine percent). However, over the last decade, the entire system of skilled immigration has become much more complex, meaning that changes in processing times before and after 1999 should not simply be attributed to the marketisation process. More subtly, marketisation may have affected the speed at various stages of the application process, as one respondent to the survey pointed out:

> In our opinion, the outsourcing process has led to improved post-lodgment processing times for skilled immigration applicants, but has caused significant delays and difficulties in skilled immigration applicants' pre-lodgment procedures. For instance, applicants cannot lodge a subclass 885 [Skilled-Independent] visa application until they have obtained a positive skills assessment result from skills assessment authority prior to application. This very often causes significant delays in pre-lodgment as some skills assessment authorities take up to three to four months to process an application. However, once the positive skills assessment result is available, it could be

submitted to DIBP to speed up the post-lodgment processing time-frame.

Accuracy

One of the strongest arguments in favour of marketisation of skills assessment was that it would increase the reliability and accuracy of this activity. When asked about their views on the effects of marketisation upon the accuracy of assessments, 43 percent of respondents who have worked in the field since before 1999 said that they believed that the process had increased accuracy. Eighteen percent said it led to less accurate skills assessments. Thirty-nine percent believed that it had no effect on the accuracy of skills assessments. The qualitative comments suggested that concerns over accuracy arise for both public and private assessing bodies, but particularly for VETASSESS, a government business enterprise that, as noted, is responsible for a large percentage of skill assessments. The survey revealed fewer concerns over accuracy with the smaller, professional assessing bodies. This suggests that at least with regard to the accuracy of assessments, the specialisation that occurs through marketisation may have led to better outcomes in skills assessment for some occupational groupings.

Cost shifting

The marketisation of skills assessment has led to a deflection of the cost of assessment from the Department of Immigration to the individual applicant. Prior to 1999, the cost of assessment was built into the overall cost of visa applications, as the Department of Immigration had oversight over this entire process. Since 1999, the two-step system means that the applicant must pay both for the skills assessment and separately for the visa application. Marketisation amounts to a form of cost deflection and is consistent with federal government cost recovery policy in place in 2002. As a recent policy document summarises, the 'underpinning principle' of cost recovery 'is that entities should set charges to recover all the costs of products or services where it is efficient and effective to do so, where the beneficiaries are a narrow and identifiable group' (DIIRSTE 2013, p. 6). In light of this policy, a recent draft review of TRA's pricing for skills assessment recommends increased fees across most visa classes (DIIRSTE 2013, p. 12).

Visa charges have also increased significantly across the immigration field since the late 1990s (Crock & Berg 2011, p. 155). One respondent in the survey commented of these changes: 'It seems to me that the assessment of migrants has become big business. Considering the costs involved in migrating and settling, I believe the assessments charges are at the most extreme'. The suggestion here is that assessing authorities are charging large and perhaps incommensurate fees for skills assessment, relative to the time it takes to undertake such assessment. Particular concerns were raised by respondents to the survey about the implications of these high costs for applicants from developing countries, with the suggestion from one respondent that individuals from these countries 'simply cannot afford to pay for a formal skills assessment'. This resonates with findings in the *Negotiating the maze* inquiry that there is significant variation across assessing bodies in fee charges and that 'a number of participants to the inquiry commented on the costs of overseas skills recognition' (JSC 2006, p. 114).

Analysis of top assessing agencies indicates skills assessment fees vary dramatically across the top 10 assessing bodies, from as low as $200 for some forms of skills assessment with the ACS to up to $737 with VETASSESS. The 'Job Ready Program', which allows recent international student graduates to gain domestic employment experience and a skills assessment as a combined package, can be as high as $2000 (TRA 2011a, p. 8). The range in initial fees for the top 10 assessing bodies identified in the survey are set out in Table 9.3.

Table 9.3 shows that there is considerable variation in fees, even within VETASSESS, where initial fees range from $330 to $737, depending upon the occupations. The table only presents initial fees to allow for comparability, although in fact, when the full range of fees is included, costs increase significantly. Some of the smaller associations, which are not represented in the top 10 skills assessing bodies reported in Table 9.3, have even higher fees. For instance, the Australian Dental Council requires all applicants who have not completed dentistry qualifications in Australia, Ireland, the United Kingdom or Canada, to undertake two clinical examinations prior to skills assessment. The first preliminary examination costs $1,100 and the second $6,615 (ADC 2012). As the Immigration Lawyers' Association of Australasia (ILAA

Table 9.3: Cost of initial assessment of top 10 assessing bodies. For sources and notes, see appendix at the end of the chapter

Assessing body	Cost of initial assessment
1. VETASSESS	$330–$737
2. TRA	$300
3. ACS	$200–$550
4. Engineers Australia	$605
5. Certified Practising Accountants of Australia	$475
6. Institute of Charted Accountants in Australia	$400–$550
7. Australian Nursing and Midwifery Council	$346–$450
8. Institute of Public Accountants	$400–$600
9. Australian Institute of Management	$475
10. Australian Institute of Welfare and Community Workers	$500

2005, p. 6) pointed out in its submission to the *Negotiating the maze* inquiry, high fees charged by some assessing authorities may constitute protectionist obstacles to the inflow of skilled immigrant labour into Australia, rather than representing a genuine fee for services. One respondent to the survey suggested that if the system was truly competitive (with several assessing agencies competing for skill assessments in the same area) that fees would not be so high. Yet, as private assessment agencies are often also professional peak bodies, there is frequently only one assessing agency for a relevant skill assessment, rendering any competition non-existent.[7] This raises some concerns over professional closure by some professional bodies. Yet, without further research, this possibility cannot be comprehensively assessed.

---

7   An important exception is accounting, where the Certified Practising Accountants of Australia (CPA Australia), the Institute of Charted Accountants in Australia (ICAA) and the Institute of Public Accountants (IPA) all may assess applications.

Accountability and transparency

Accountability and transparency, central goals of public regulation, are often seen as being under threat following privatisation and marketisation of previously public functions. In essence, this critique relates to the restricted capacity for public accountability mechanisms, secured through the democratic logic of public power, to translate into the private sphere of regulation (Freeman 1999, p. 6). The central question is whether similar – or equivalent – accountability mechanisms can be established between private actors and citizens as between public bodies and citizens. In a related but separate fashion, critics of privatisation and marketisation ask whether the opportunity for public engagement in decision-making is reduced or narrowed through these processes (Aman 2009, p. 277). The central issue here is the extent of transparency in decisions when private rather than public bodies undertake these processes. The concern is that by taking decision-making outside of the realm of public power, and therefore legislative and executive politics, there may be a depoliticisation of the relevant policy issues, in turn contributing to a lack of transparency in assessment of that process (Aman 2009).

Prior to 1999, the Immigration Review Tribunal could review the facts considered in making skill assessments (*Mak v IRT* [1994] 48 FCR 314; see also Crock 1998, pp. 104–5). Since 1999, cases of this nature cannot be brought before public law tribunals, for reasons outlined below. Any legal concerns can only be pursued on the basis of contractual breaches. Before assessing the details of the legal decision that limited public law review of skills assessments, it is important to outline the implications for applicants of this change for the cost of review, the scope of grounds for review and for available remedies. The capacity to seek review on the basis of particular public law grounds (such as error of law, improper exercise of power or taking into account irrelevant considerations) is denied under a contractual case, which focuses on breach of the contractual agreement and monetary remedies. Further, it is more expensive to bring a private contractual case than to bring a public tribunal matter to the Migration Review Tribunal (as it is now known).

The restriction upon public law review of skills assessments is a product of a court case conducted shortly after the 1999 changes. In

Silveira v Australian Institute of Management [2001] FCA 803, Justice Emmett of the Federal Court of Australia held that a decision by an assessing authority was not a 'decision under an enactment', thereby rendering it ineligible for administrative law review (*Administrative Decisions [Judicial Review] Act 1977* [Cwlth], s3[a]). Justice Emmett did not distinguish between public and private assessing bodies (paragraphs 40–41). Instead his decision turned on the fact that the skills assessment was viewed as a mere 'step along the way in a course of reasoning', rather than either the final determination or a 'condition precedent to a reviewable decision'. If Ms Silveira were to have recourse against the decision of the institute, this lay in contract rather than administrative law (paragraph 47). The case was unsuccessful on appeal (*Silveira v Australian Institute of Management [2001] FCA 1358*).

The notion that a skills assessment is not a necessary first step for a decision regarding skilled immigration is highly artificial. Without a skills assessment, an immigration applicant is unable to lodge an application for many immigration visas. Despite these shortcomings with the *Silveira* reasoning, the case stands. Since the *Silveira* decision, no cases have tested the proposition that given their different legal structures to private assessing bodies, decisions by TRA or VETASSESS could be a 'decision under an enactment' and therefore subject to public law review. Yet, there are reasons to believe that the *Silveira* decision might now be challenged both on this and several other bases. A recent High Court of Australia case, *M61/201E v Commonwealth; Plaintiff M69 of 2010 v Commonwealth* (2010) 85 ALJR 133 (*Wizard* hereafter), found that the decision by an external refugee review body, which employs case assessors from the private company, Wizard People Pty Ltd, was reviewable. This decision did not adjudge directly on the issue of the general reviewability under administrative law of decisions made by private companies contracted by the Department of Immigration. Yet, it would appear to leave the door open in this regard (see Crock & Ghezelbash 2011, pp. 106–7). This decision challenges the *Silveria* decision in two respects. First, it suggests that the immigration decisions of private assessing bodies contracted by the Minister for Immigration might be reviewable. Second, *Wizard* indicates that, although the exact review process of the independent reviewers is not provided for in the Migration Act or regulations, it is still a form of delegated governmental power and therefore might be considered a 'decision under an enactment' for the purposes of the *Administrative Decisions (Judicial Review) Act 1977* (Cwlth), s3.

Nonetheless, in light of the current restriction against administrative review, the capacity for internal review within assessing bodies must also be considered. Review of original decisions is available, although at least in the current survey, was not reported as utilised by the majority of migrant applicants. Fifty-two percent of respondents to the survey indicated that they do not seek review either because the outcome for the client was positive, or because clients did not instruct review. Qualitative responses to the survey indicate that migration agents have a number of reasons for not seeking internal review on behalf of their clients. These include the cost and timing of reviews; a perceived lack of transparency in the review process; the inability to lodge new evidence as part of a review; a belief that it is easier to lodge a new application rather than to seek review of the original decision; delays in reimbursement for the cost of a successful review; and the general concern that a review process was not fully independent of the original decision-maker. For instance, many respondents to the survey complained that internal review failed to take relevant factors into consideration. Yet, taking relevant considerations into account is a well-established basis for review under administrative review (*Administrative Decisions [Judicial Review] Act 1977* [Cwlth], s5[2][b]). The majority of agents reported that their clients paid between $200 and $400 for a review, although in all cases where the review was successful, the full cost of the review was eventually recouped. Only a very small number of respondents (eight out of 247) reported using political means of review, by appealing either to the Department of Employment and Workplace Relations, the Department of Immigration, or the Minister for Immigration and none used the Commonwealth Ombudsman. Interestingly, as TRA is a public body, applicants may bring complaints from TRA to the Commonwealth Ombudsman. No respondent in the survey had used the Ombudsman for review process. Nor is skills assessment for immigration purposes mentioned in the latest Commonwealth Ombudsman annual report (2012), although it has been referred to in previous reports (2009) and several high-profile matters in this area have been referred to the Ombudsman previously (Skelton 2012).

Migration agents who appealed decisions on behalf of their clients expressed different levels of satisfaction with different assessing bodies and their internal review procedures. Respondents were asked in open-ended questions to reflect on their views of the review process. Of the 46 open responses to this question, only two expressed satisfaction. Many saw the review process as too lengthy and costly, lacking in transparency, failing to provide clear reasons for rejection, inconsistent across applicants or inefficient. There have been complaints about a lack of an open review procedure at TRA (ILAA 2005; MIA 2005, pp. 21–22). The Immigration Lawyers' Association of Australasia argued that TRA and the ACS were not always clear about the reasons for their decisions. VETASSESS, on the other hand, was viewed by the Immigration Lawyers' Association of Australasia as quite good in this regard (ILAA 2005, p. 23). It is clear that there is considerable variation across assessing bodies in terms of the cost, speed and reasons given for the determination of internal reviews. On this basis, some respondents to the survey argued that all assessing bodies should be subject to administrative review. One respondent argued:

There must be more administrative law accountability of the process performed by the skills assessing authorities. They are performing a segment of the government's administrative process, and therefore should be accountable to the same standards of procedural fairness, and natural justice. There should be an independent appeal tribunal for skills assessment outcomes.

Accountability also plays out at a larger level with regard to the central issue of oversight of assessing bodies. The lack of clear monitoring of the field of assessment bodies was raised as a key concern within the *Negotiating the maze* inquiry. According to the inquiry, there was an absence of statutory clarity over whether the Department of Immigration or the Department of Education, Science and Training (now the Department of Industry and Science) was responsible for oversight of assessing agencies and that 'the general "washing of hands" of the problem [was] a concern' (JSC 2006, p. 94). While DIS is clearly responsible for approving a body as an assessing authority under the Migration Regulations 1994, regulation 2.26B, the responsibility for ongoing monitoring of these authorities is unclear (JSC 2006, pp. 97–99). Some but not all of the inquiry's other recommendations regarding monitoring and oversight appear to have been implemented. For instance, the inquiry recommended that the immigration department ensure that its Australian Skills Recognition Information website 'provide an overview of the various organisations involved in administering, monitoring and delivering overseas skill recognition services' (JSC 2006, p. xix). This has been undertaken (JSC 2011, p. 8). In contrast, the review also recommended that the DEST undertake a review of fees charged by assessing bodies to 'ensure these fees are reasonable and have been determined on a not-for-profit basis' (JSC 2006, p. xxii). However, it is unclear whether such monitoring is being pursued and the basis upon which private assessing authorities determine fee structures remains opaque.

Fairness

This chapter has identified some concerns over consistency in treatment of migrant applicants, within and across assessing bodies. This goes to the central issue of fairness, which can be viewed as a key public policy goal (Freeman 1999, p. 13). It could be argued that fairness is a difficult policy goal to achieve in the immigration field, which by nature is concerned with discriminating between applicants (Dauvergne 2009). However, while immigration is clearly about selection, it is important that there is consistency in the way that applicants are treated in the *process* of such selection. In 1996, the House of Representatives Standing Committee on Community Affairs (1996, p. 58, cited in Iredale 1997, p. 107) identified concerns over migrant applicants having to deal with two agencies (NOOSR and TRA) in the process of skilled immigration applications. This 'silo' effect is now even greater. The diversification of assessing bodies post-1999, and the proliferation of visa categories that has accompanied an increasingly complex immigration program, raises concerns over a related diversification in the quality of service provided to applicants.

In its submission to the *Negotiating the maze* inquiry, the Immigration Lawyers' Association of Australasia (ILAA 2005, p. 6) raised concerns about the diversity of approaches and the resultant inequality across assessing bodies. Although not directly questioned about their perceptions of fairness in the skills assessment process, respondents to the open-ended question in the survey also expressed concern about inconsistent decisions, sometimes even within the same assessing bodies. Issues with inconsistency can also play out in more subtle ways, for instance in different interpretations of English language qualifications and requirements by different assessing bodies.[8] Such concerns arise both with regards to public and privately run assessing bodies. Given that TRA is responsible for a large proportion of assessments, it is unsurprising that more complaints are raised about TRA than other agencies in this regard.

Fairness can also be considered in terms of whether migrant applicants are treated equally by assessing authorities, depending upon their existing qualifications. MIA agents were asked whether they experienced differences in processing times for different occupations processed by the same agency. Twenty-one percent of respondents said that they had and 60 percent said that there was no major difference across occupations, while for another 19 percent, the question was irrelevant as they only dealt with one occupational group. Looking at the qualitative responses, some migrant agents reported that certain occupations, such as accountancy, were being processed faster than others, while others noted that it had less to do with the particular occupation and more to do with the vagaries of the individual assessing officer.

For other respondents, the country of origin of existing applicant qualifications were central, with those from non-English-speaking and non-Western countries at a distinct disadvantage in terms of processing, given a perceived mismatch among assessors between applicant qualifications and Australian qualifications. As such, the nature of the client, as well as the assessing authority, may affect processing times. The extent of this problem could be further examined by surveying individual immigrants about their experience of skills assessment. Such an assessment of the role of country of origin may be necessary in order to reduce any discriminatory bias in immigration policy – a central tenet of immigration selection since the end to race-based selection in 1973 (DIAC 2009). Marketisation of the skills assessment field has led, as noted, to an array of public and private assessment bodies. It is im-

---

8 This concern was raised by a number of migration agents at an event on skills assessment attended by the author: Skills Assessment Forum, Migration Institute of Australia, 11 October 2011.

portant to ensure that these bodies provide equal adherence to these central principles of the immigration program, despite not being under the direct remit of the Department of Immigration.

Conclusion

The immigration regulation field in Australia has changed dramatically since 1999. The immigration system has become more complex, there are far higher rates of skilled and temporary migration and there is a greater emphasis on skill of new entrants within the immigration program as a whole than 10 years ago. In light of these developments and the marketisation of skills assessment in 1999, examination of the skills assessment process is essential. It is clear that the marketisation documented in this chapter differs in important ways from other policy areas considered in this book. For while responsibility for skills assessment has moved away from the DIBP, and while there has been a diversification of public and private providers, much of the assessment function is still undertaken by public, or semi-public entities. Nonetheless, as documented in this chapter, the diversification in assessing authorities raises some important policy issues.

This chapter has not considered the relationship between pre-migration assessment and skills accreditation after arrival in Australia. In fact, the marketisation of skills assessment was partially justified on the basis that the organisations undertaking skills assessment for migratory purposes are also often the registration bodies for professional accreditation. Accordingly, one argument in favour of the 1999 changes was that it would improve new migrant labour market outcomes by ensuring that skills assessments and professional accreditation would be coupled in the one stage (see Cully & Skladzien 2001, p. 7). Although not the focus of this chapter, it is important to acknowledge that evidence to the contrary has also emerged. The *Negotiating the maze* report (2006, pp. 109–13, pp. 160–65) and recent research by Lesleyanne Hawthorne (2011) identify ongoing obstacles to accreditation faced by newly arrived migrants in Australia, even for those who had undertaken skills assessments as part of the migration process. A comprehensive analysis of the enduring disjuncture between pre- and post-migration skills assessment and recognition is a separate topic, which touches only in part upon marketisation issues, and is also related to the federal system of trade recognition, and a raft of other governance concerns. The survey of migration agents presented in this chapter, coupled with secondary desk analysis, suggests that marketisation has been mixed in its achievement of key policy goals. Marketisation appears to have deflected the cost of skills assessment from the Department of Immigration onto individual migrant applicants and their sponsors. Review rights have also been truncated, in that administrative review opportunities have been removed and internal reviews offer fewer remedies. The multitude of agencies now responsible for assessment, with differing costs, procedures and processing times, raises concerns about consistency across immigration applicants as well as concerns over oversight and monitoring of the entire industry. Despite these apparently negative outcomes, there is also evidence, particularly with regard to specialised assessing agencies, that the accuracy of skills assessments has increased and in some cases, that assessment times have been reduced.

Acknowledgments

Thanks to the Migration Institute of Australia, particularly Dr Pamela O'Neill, for assistance in administering the survey to MIA members. Thanks to all migration agents and other members of the MIA, as well as several government officers, who responded to the survey and in some cases, provided detailed email comments about their experience in skills assessments (Mick Keegan, Helen Duncan, Mark Glazbrook, Kevin Lane, Vanesse Loo, Angela De Marco and Mark Cully). Thanks to Ariadne Vromen, Peter Chen, Mary Crock, the Public Policy Research Cluster at the University of Sydney and the editors for feedback on earlier versions of this chapter and assistance with survey design. This chapter refers to several interviews conducted with senior officials of the Department of Immigration and Citizenship in 2009 as part of doctoral research undertaken at the London School of Economics and Political Science (LSE) in 2006–10. Ethics approval to conduct the survey was granted by the Human Ethics Committee of the University of Sydney. Ethics approval to conduct the interviews was granted by the Research Office of the LSE.

Appendix

Sources and notes to Table 9.3.

- ACS (2012); ANMC (2012); ACWA (2012, 3); AIM (2012); CPA (2012); EA (2012); ICCA (2012); IPA (2012) VETASSESS (2012); TRA (2011b, 5).
- Fees vary within associations depending upon the particular skills assessment sought, whether a standard or fast-tracked application processing period is requested, and sometimes, the relevant visa category. This table reflects the general range of fees. These fees are based on those reported at the time of publication, but are subject to indexed increases.

Legislation and case law

Administrative Decisions (Judicial Review) Act 1977 (Cwlth)
M61/201E v Commonwealth; Plaintiff M69 of 2010 v Commonwealth (2010) 85 ALJR 133
Mak v IRT (1994) 48 FCR 314
Migration Act 1958 (Cwlth)
Migration Regulations 1994 (Cwlth)
Silveira v Australian Institute of Management [2001] FCA 803
Silveira v Australian Institute of Management [2001] FCA 1358

References

ACS (Australian Computer Society) 2012, Costs and charges. https://www.acs.org.au/index.cfm?action=show&conID=costcharge
ACWA (Australian Community Workers Association) 2012, Information relevant to application form 1182 for welfare workers. http://www.acwa.org.au/sites/ www.acwa.org.au/files/Form%201182%20Information%20Pack.pdf
ADC (Australian Dental Council) 2012, Schedule of fees. http://www.adc.org.au/ fees.pdf
AEI (Australian Education International) 2013, *Assessment of overseas qualifications: Our assessments*, Canberra, Australian Education International.

AIM (Australian Institute of Migration) 2012, *Migration fees*.
http://www.aim.com.au/migration/fees.html

Aman, A. C. 2009, 'Privatisation and democracy: Resources in administrative law', in *Government by contract: Outsourcing and American democracy*, ed. A. C. Aman Jr, Harvard University Press, Cambridge, Massachusetts and London, England, pp. 261–88.

ANMC (Australian Nursing and Midwifery Council) 2012, Application form, general registration, graduated or trained overseas, nursing and midwifery. http://www.nursingmidwiferyboard.gov.au/ Search.aspx?q=skills%20assessment%20fee

ARC (Administrative Review Council) 1998, *Report to the Attorney-General: The contracting out of government services*, Administrative Review Council, Canberra.

Aulich, C. 2011, 'It's not ownership that matters: It's publicness', *Policy Studies*, vol. 32, no. 2, pp. 199–213.

Boucher, A. 2011, Venue-setting and diversity-seeking: Gender and immigration selection policy in Australia and Canada, PhD in Political Science, Department of Government, London School of Economics.

Chalmers, J. & Davis, G 2001, 'Rediscovering implementation: Public sector contracting and human services', *Australian Journal of Administrative Law*, vol. 60, no. 2, pp. 74–85.

CAAIP (Committee to Advise on Australia's Immigration Policies) 1988, *Immigration, a commitment to Australia: The report of the committee to advise on Australia's immigration policies*, Australian Government Publishing Service, Canberra.

CPA (Certified Practising Accountants of Australia) 2012, Migration assessment. http://www.cpaaustralia.com.au/cps/rde/xchg/cpa-site/hs. xsl/ become-how-migration.html

Commonwealth Ombudsman 2012, *Annual report: Investigations, reports and submissions*, Commonwealth Ombudsman, Canberra.

Commonwealth Ombudsman 2009, *Commonwealth Ombudsman annual report 2008–2009*, Commonwealth Ombudsman, Canberra.

Crock, M. 1998, *Immigration and refugee law in Australia*, Federation Press, Sydney.

Crock, M., Saul, B. & Dastyari, A. 2006, *A future seekers II: Refugees and irregular migration in Australia*, Federation Press, Sydney.

Crock, M. & Berg, L. 2011, *Immigration, refugees and forced migration: Law, policy and practice in Australia*, Federation Press, Leichhardt, Sydney.

Crock, M. & Ghezelbash, D. 2011, 'Due process and rule of law as human rights: The High Court and the "offshore" processing of asylum seekers', *Australian Journal of Administrative Law*, vol. 18, pp. 101–14.

Cully, M. & Skladzien, T. 2001, *Assessment of overseas qualifications and skills: A comparative analysis*, South Australian Department of Education, Training and Employment/ National Institute of Labour Studies, Flinders University of South Australia, Adelaide.

Dauvergne, C. 2009, 'Globalising fragmentation – New pressures on the women caught in the migration law – Citizenship law dichotomy', in *Migration and mobilities: Citizenship, borders and gender*, ed. C. Dauvergne, New York University Press, New York/London, pp. 333–55.

DET (Department of Education and Training), n.d. Our role. https://internationaleducation.gov.au/Services-And-Resources/ourrole/Pages/Our-role.aspx

DEWRSB (Department of Employment, Workplace Relations and Small Business) 1998, *Report of the legislative review of the Tradesmen's Rights Regulation Act 1946*, Department of Employment, Workplace Relations and Small Business, Canberra.

DIAC (Department of Immigration and Citizenship) 2009, *Fact sheet 1 – Immigration: The background part one*, Department of Immigration and Citizenship, Canberra.

DIAC 2011a, *2010–11 Migration program report: Program year to 30 June 2011*, Department of Immigration and Citizenship, Canberra.

DIAC 2011b, *The outlook for net overseas migration*, Department of Immigration and Citizenship, Canberra.

DIAC 2012a, *Populations flows: Immigration aspects, 2010–2011*, Department of Immigration and Citizenship, Canberra.

DIAC 2012b, *Percentage of visas lodged by migration agents, January–March 2012*, Department of Immigration and Citizenship, Canberra. http://www.immi.gov.au/media/statistics/pdf/migration-agent-stats-jan-mar-2012.pdf

DIBP (Department of Immigration and Border Protection) 2014a, What's in a name? http://www.immi.gov.au/about/anniversary/whats-in-a-name.htm

DIBP 2014b, Contact details for assessing authorities. http://www.immi.gov.au/Work/Pages/skilled-occupations-lists/assessingauthorities.aspx

DIIRSTE (Department of Innovation, Industry, Science and Research and Tertiary Education) 2013, *Draft cost recovery impact statement: Charges under the Trades Recognition Australia's program*, Department of Industry, Innovation Science, Research and Tertiary Education, Canberra.

DIMA (Department of Immigration and Multicultural Affairs) 1999a, *Review of the independent and skilled-Australian linked categories*, Department of Immigration and Multicultural Affairs, Canberra.

DIMA 1999b, *Portfolio budget statement 1990–2000*, Department of Immigration and Multicultural Affairs, Canberra.

DIMA 1999c, *About the department: DIMA annual report 1999–2000, management and accountability, contracting legal services and litigation*, Department of Immigration and Multicultural Affairs, Canberra.

DIMA 2000, *Portfolio budget statement 2000–2001*, Department of Immigration and Multicultural Affairs, Canberra.

EA (Engineers Australia), 2012 Migration Skills Assessment. http://www.engineersaustralia.org.au/about-us/migration-skills-assessment

Freeman, J. 1999, 'Private parties, public functions and the new administrative law', in *Recrafting the rule of law: The limits of legal order*, eds J. Freeman, Hart Publishing, Toronto, pp. 331–70.

Freeman, J. & Minow, M. 2009, 'Introduction: Reframing the outsourcing debates', in *Government by contract: Outsourcing and American democracy*, ed. J. Freeman & M. Minow, Harvard University Press, Cambridge, Massachusetts and London, England, 1–6.

Hawthorne, L. 2011, Australian–Canada roundtable on foreign qualification recognition: Complete backgrounder, paper presentation, Melbourne, 13–15 April.

House of Representatives Standing Committee on Community Affairs 1996, *A fair go for all: Report on migrant access and equity*, Australian Government Printing Service, Canberra.

ICCA (Institute of Charted Accountants Australia) 2012, Fees and processing times. http://www.charteredaccountants.com.au/The-Institute/Migration-assessment/Fees-and-processing-times.aspx

ILAA (International Lawyers Association of Australasia) 2005, Submission to the joint committee on migration: Inquiry into skills recognition, upgrading and licensing. Immigration Lawyers Association of Australia.

IPA (Institute of Public Accountants) 2012, Qualifications assessment for migration. http://www.publicaccountants.org.au/media/220306/assessmentmigrationform_web3.pdf

Iredale, R. R. 1997, *Skills transfer: International migration and accreditation issues*, University of Wollongong Press, Wollongong.

JSC (Joint Standing Committee on Migration) 2006, *Negotiating the maze: Review of arrangements for overseas skills recognition, upgrading and licensing*, Joint Standing Committee on Migration, Canberra.

JSC 2011, *Negotiating the maze: Review of arrangements for overseas skills recognition, upgrading and licensing: Government response*, Parliamentary Joint Standing Committee on Migration, Canberra.

Kelman, S. J. 2009, 'Achieving contracting goals and recognising public law concerns: A contracting management perspective', in *Government by contract:*

Outsourcing and American democracy, eds J. Freeman & M. Minow, Harvard University Press, Cambridge, Massachusetts and London, England, pp. 53–191.

Leunig, T. 2010, 'Post–World War II British Railways: The unintended consequences of insufficient government intervention', in *Paradoxes of modernisation: Unintended consequences of public policy reform*, eds H. Margetts, P. 6 & C. Hood, Oxford University Press, Oxford, 155–84.

MIA (Migration Institute of Australia) 2005, A review of qualification assessment for skilled people applying to migration to Australia: Submission to the Joint Standing Committee on Migration of the Parliament of the Commonwealth of Australia, Migration Institute of Australia, Sydney.

Quiggin, J. 2010, *Zombie economics: How dead ideas still walk among us*, Princeton University Press, New Jersey.

Ramia, G. & Carney, T. 2001, 'Contractualism, managerialism and welfare: The Australian experience with a marketised employment services network', *Policy & Politics*, vol. 29, no. 1, pp. 59–83.

Sapotichne, J. & Smith, J. M. 2011, 'Venue shopping and the politics of urban development: Lessons from Chicago and Seattle', *Urban Affairs Review*, vol. 48, pp. 86–110.

Skelton, R. 2012, 'Blunder a threat to foreign job visas', *Sydney Morning Herald*, July 28.

TRA (Trades Recognition Australia) 2011a, *Job ready program: Participant guidelines, September 2011*, Department of Education, Employment and Workplace Relations, Canberra. http://www.deewr.gov.au/Skills/Programs/SkillsAssess/TRA/residenceVisa/JobReady/Documents/JobReadyProgramGuidelines.pdf

TRA (Trades Recognition Australia) 2011b, *TRA migration skills assessment, applicant guidelines*, 20 June 2011, Department of Education, Employment and Workplace Relations, Canberra. http://www.deewr.gov.au/Skills/Programs/SkillsAssess/TRA/residenceVisa/Skilled/Documents/MigrationSkillsGuidelines.pdf

VETASSESS (Vocational Education Training and Assessment Services) 2012, Fees and payment. http://www.vetassess.com.au/migrate_to_australia/qa2_fees_payment.cfm

VETASSESS (Vocational Education Training and Assessment Services) 2013, Our organisation and history. http://www.vetassess.com.au

Webster, E. & Harding. G. 2000, Contracting public employment services: The Australian experience, Melbourne Institute Working Paper Series No. 3, University of Melbourne, Melbourne.

10

Markets in education: 'School choice' and family capital

Helen Proctor and Claire Aitchison

From about the mid-1980s both state and federal governments in Australia effected a series of market-oriented reforms in education. In the late 1990s, Simon Marginson (1997a, 1997b) produced the first monograph accounts of this development, one of which was called, *Markets in education* (1997b), in which he proposed that by the end of the 20th century:

> The dominant paradigm was no longer that of education as a common public service. It had become an education market, steered from the background by government, in which students and parents were consumers, teachers and academics were producers, and educational administrators had become managers and entrepreneurs. (1997b, p. 5; see also Welch 1996)

More recently, Raewyn Connell (2013) described a 'neoliberal cascade' of interventions in education by successive state and federal governments since the 1980s, urged on by both major political parties and various business organisations, and informed by 'market logic'.

Proctor, H. & Aitchison, C. 2015, 'Markets in education: "School choice" and family capital', in *Markets, rights and power in Australian social policy*, eds G. Meagher & S. Goodwin, Sydney University Press, Sydney.

Since the late 1990s terms like 'markets', 'marketisation' and 'neoliberalism' have come to be near universal in the sociology of Australian education to describe a set of public policy interventions that have ostensibly sought to apply the energy, flexibility and efficiency of capitalist private enterprise to the provision of teaching and learning in mass institutions, including schools – the focus of this chapter. Such educational reforms are widespread internationally (Apple 2004; Davies & Bansel 2007; Musset 2012) and there has been considerable 'policy borrowing' (Lingard 2010), with key influences for Australia coming from the United Kingdom, New Zealand and the United States (Forsey, Davies & Walford 2008; Marginson 1997b). Internationally, the term 'quasi-markets' has been coined to emphasise that, in practice, schooling markets are multiple, complex and imperfect, typically experiencing high levels of government regulation, with competition located across multiple and unequal sites (Whitty 1997). It is certainly the case in Australia that governments still play more than just a regulatory or 'steering' role in schooling. For example, the majority of school premises in Australia are still publicly owned and the majority of school students attend public schools. Despite the introduction of degrees of decentralised school management since the 1990s, and an increase in casual employment, the majority of public school teachers are still permanent employees with traditional sick leave benefits, standardised wages and so on. Nor has any Australian government or major interest group seriously suggested that public schools should be privatised, as has happened with some other kinds of public services and infrastructure (see Meagher & Wilson, this volume).

Nevertheless, there has indeed been substantial market-oriented change in the provision, operation and experience of schooling over the past quarter century, most notably in the allocation of students to schools. Some consider Australia to be a world leader in the market reform of schooling, specifically in the related encouragement of school 'autonomy' and school 'choice' (Jensen, Weidmann & Farmer 2013; Musset 2012). Before we turn to our discussion of families and school choice, we briefly address some of the main features of contemporary Australian school markets that have been encouraged, supported or driven by public policy: the private/public divide in school provision; the introduction of new measures of school accountability and public school 'autonomy'; and the public funding of non-government schools.

Australian schooling has historically been characterised by the strength of its non-government sector and, even during the 1960s and 1970s, 'the high point of the development of centrally controlled and bureaucratically managed public education' (Campbell & Sherington 2006, p. 90), the reach of government schooling was less than universal. In 1975, just over three-quarters of all Australian secondary school students attended government high schools (Campbell, Proctor & Sherington 2009, p. 58). In the 21st century, Australia has one of the largest non-government sector enrolments in the OECD, especially in secondary schools (Musset 2012). In 2012, less than 60 percent of secondary school students were in government schools, with just over 22 percent in Catholic schools and just under 18 percent in other non-government schools (Campbell & Proctor 2014, p. 261). (Nearly 69 percent of primary school students were enrolled in public schools.)

In Australian common usage the word 'public' describes schools that are owned and managed by the state departments of education and 'private' describes schools that are run by non-government bodies such as churches or corporations. Non-government schools outside the Catholic systems (including some Catholic schools) usually describe themselves as 'independent' schools. The terms, 'private' and 'independent' are misleading in that the majority of such schools in Australia are heavily publicly subsidised, as we explain below, and all are subject to detailed public regulation, and because the terminology has the effect of eliding the diversity that exists within both 'public' and 'private' school sectors. Broadly speaking, however, the non-government school sector comprises a small group of elite high-fee schools, the less expensive Catholic systemic schools and a growing number of low or moderate fee 'independent' schools which were mainly founded during the last quarter of the 20th century. The majority of non-government school students attend Catholic schools but the strongest growth has been in the relatively new low to moderate fee schools. In the early 1960s more than 80 percent of non-government school pupils were enrolled in Catholic schools (Ryan & Watson 2004) but in 2012 the figure was about 60 percent (Campbell & Proctor 2014, p. 261). Most non-government schools have a Christian religious affiliation of one kind or another, though there is a small and rapidly growing Islamic sector (McNeilage 2013) and small numbers of 'non-denominational' schools, Jewish schools and 'alternative' schools such as Steiner schools.

The historical shift away from public schooling has occurred disproportionately among the children of higher income or 'middle-class' households (Campbell 2005; Preston 2013). The government school sector is less representative than it was in the 1970s and 1980s, enrolling disproportionately large numbers of children from low-income families (and of children with disabilities) (Campbell 2005; Gonski 2011; Musset 2012; Nous Group 2011; Preston 2013;). Although there are some exceptions, as we show in this chapter, in the main it has become possible to think of 'private' schools as schools of 'choice' and public schools as schools of 'compulsion'.

The relative extent of the influence of public policy in the shift to non-government schooling is debatable (see, for example, Ryan & Watson 2004) but there is no doubt that the promotion of choice and competition by successive state and federal governments has contributed to the change – in addition to fostering competition *within* all schooling sectors (on shifts within the public school sector, see Vickers 2004). Since the mid-1980s NSW state government activity has included the de-zoning of enrolments for public schools and the creation of new specialist and academically selective high schools (Campbell & Sherington 2006; Sherington & Hughes 2012). Public school devolution or 'autonomy' programs have been undertaken by a number of state governments beginning with Victoria under the Liberal Party Premier, Jeffrey Kennett, in the 1990s. School autonomy programs ostensibly encourage the reorientation of public schools away from their centralised bureaucratic system ties and towards a more engaged and responsive relationship with their local clientele. Federally, the establishment of the 'MySchool' website in 2010 – which records and compares school test results – provides systematic comparisons among schools to inform the choice-making of parents and encourage competition between schools.

As we have said, all non-government schools in Australia are eligible for degrees of state and federal government funding, with federal governments being the principal source of public subsidy. The history of government funding to non-government schools – or 'State Aid' – has been long and politically controversial, but since the early 1970s the principle of reliable recurrent public subsidy to non-government schools has been accepted by all the main political parties (Ryan & Watson 2004; Wilkinson et al. 2007) except, within the past decade or so, the Greens. Most non-government schools are heavily subsidised: in

2010 some 72 percent of independent schools received more than 50 percent of their net recurrent income from governments and the average Catholic systemic school more than 75 percent (Gonski 2011, p. 15).

Markets and choice

This chapter examines the practice of 'school choice', which we argue has been fundamental to the development and operation of market-oriented schooling in Australia – and internationally. Rather than simply enrolling their child in the nearest government (or Catholic) school, as might have been the case in the 1970s, parents in 21st-century Australia have increasingly been positioned as active consumers who may or must choose a school for their child from a number of options, especially at the secondary school level. The public vigilance of parents acting as individuals, yet coordinated by the market mechanism, is meant to be a key driver of quality control. Under-performing schools, it is argued, will be forced to make improvements in order to attract parents. Well-managed schools will be validated in the marketplace. According to Bob Lingard (2010, p. 132), 'a basic assumption [of the Rudd government's public accountability agenda, including the MySchool website, was] that competition between schools and parental pressures will push up standards and strengthen accountabilities'. In theory, parents (as consumers) make rational, objective, self-interested choices between competing providers (schools) who offer goods (education) in a competitive environment. Thus children are positioned as human capital, and education is the commodity which families purchase as an investment in their child's (and the whole family's) future wellbeing (Strober 2003). Parents' wealth and knowhow has always been important, even decisive, in the educational fortunes of children (see, for example, Connell et al. 1982), but under current policy arrangements parental agency is explicitly validated and encouraged.

The standard critique of school choice is that choice operates to prioritise the demands of those students whose parents are savvy and well resourced (Ball 2003; Brown 1990; Windle 2009) and that children, as well as schools, can become commodified, with some children having more exchange value than others (Kenway & Bullen 2001). We further argue that the neoliberal marketised frame has reconfigured both schools and families as new, different kinds of entrepreneurial citizens acutely aware of their own and each other's role in the marketplace – and that a particular kind of entrepreneurial parent has been produced and affirmed by the encouragement of markets in education (see also Connell 2008). This chapter is concerned with how families, as consumers, are shaped by, and respond to marketised schooling. Within this frame, financial capacity is more important than ever before – indeed the success of these reforms depend on a strong middle class. Nevertheless, we argue that school choice is predicated on more than the capacity to pay. School markets are complex and unique environments of competing interests, tensions and roles, potentially requiring specialised expertise and strategy to negotiate. Success in a market context may require families to operationalise a range of skills and capacities including social and cultural capitals (Bourdieu 1984, 1986). We argue that marketised schooling impels parents to be 'alert' and 'strategic' (Ball 2003) and to behave as 'unequivocally middle-class' (Davies & Bansel 2007) in pursuit of the 'right' school for their child.

The chapter draws on two of the earliest studies in the small but growing field of school choice in Australia: an Australian Research Council–funded study focusing on the decision-making processes of middle-class parents (Campbell et al. 2009) and a doctoral study of mothers' secondary school choice-making (Aitchison 2006). Both studies interviewed parents in Sydney, Australia, with Craig Campbell and colleagues (2009) interviewing 63 parents or couples who had recently enrolled their child in the first year of high school, and Claire Aitchison (2006) conducting return interviews with 20 mothers over a 14-month period as they engaged in secondary school decision-making. Aitchison was particularly interested in the labour of mothers as key agents in familial decision-making. Among other things, she found that the mothers she interviewed followed recognised patterns of consumer behaviour, namely information gathering, evaluating options to make a shortlist of preferences, investigating procedures for maximising access to those schools, and then taking appropriate actions to secure choices (Aitchison 2010). Campbell, Proctor and Sherington were principally concerned with historical questions of middle-class formation and the retreat from common schooling.

Choice and capital

In this section we turn to four vignettes – two from each of our collections of data – that illustrate how some families activate different
capitals in the school market. The first and fourth come from Aitchison's study, the second and third are from interviews conducted by
Helen Proctor. The first of these stories highlights how the realities of a
restricted school market can force families to make choices against their
wishes, even forcing them to draw on limited finances and place themselves in unfamiliar contexts which are at odds with family traditions
and practices. The second is an example of conflict between parents
over whose traditions and values will be prioritised in their child's education and the third illustrates the complexities of finding a compatible
school for a child who is not necessarily considered a valuable commodity in the educational marketplace. The fourth of these vignettes
was chosen because it is an uncommon example of a family that chose
not to participate in the school market according to the expectations
associated with capacity to pay.

Following Pierre Bourdieu (1986), we understand capital to include
various kinds of resources available to a person operating within a
social system where certain things are valued more than others, and
where these can be exchanged for benefit. One form of capital, economic capital, is usually understood as cash or financial assets. According to Bourdieu, other forms of capital share similarities with economic
capital in that they can be accumulated, passed down through the
family and 'cashed in' when necessary. In our studies we found that
economic capital was significant, but not the only kind of capital that
families called upon in the process of school choice. In some situations
cultural capital, that is, intellectual, cultural or educational resources,
was a powerful force framing how parents regarded schools and navi-
gated school choices. For others, social capital or the social networks of
informants or influence, impacted on decision-making and even school
choice outcomes. It seemed that this increasingly marketised system
encouraged a more sustained and active engagement in school choice
whereby parents accessed a 'portfolio' of capitals as required in pursuit
of their interests.

May: School choice in a restricted market with limited finances

Few of the families in either of our studies reported that financial considerations were insignificant to their consideration of schools. Parents were acutely aware of the impact of money on a child's education; to buy into a school and to sustain learning. Money could be used to support a child's academic development, thus facilitating their desirability to a school, and success in a school. Financial security could also provide parallel educational support, irrespective of the child's school. As this first vignette illustrates, even though this family was not particularly financially secure, when faced with very restricted school choices, the family as a whole was forced to consider undertaking the significant financial burden of enrolling a child in a fee-paying school.

May and her husband had one child at a neighbouring boys' high school, but when she came to consider schools for her daughter, she was unhappy with the government schools. May's children had struggled academically, and they were not in a position to consider academically selective schooling. They were out of area for the nearest government girls' school, and the family believed the local comprehensive high school had a poor reputation. In addition it had a very high male to female pupil ratio, which May considered an additional disadvantage given her daughter's personality. When it became apparent that they were not likely to be accepted into the girl's school, they decided to 'pull out all stops' and try to enrol their daughter in the local systemic Catholic girls' school.

Acting on the belief that this was their only option, the family was faced with a significant and unplanned financial impost. They felt that they had to choose a school other than the available local government school, but not having the right social and financial capital restricted their set of options. In concrete terms, even the relatively modest fee-charging Catholic school meant this family would have to make significant sacrifices. May would have to take on more work, they would have to forgo family holidays and they would most likely have to eat into their savings.

There were a number of other non-economic challenges, too. Firstly, May had to work hard to 'talk her daughter around' to the idea of the Catholic school. Like many other children of her generation growing up on a farm in rural Australia, May had gone to boarding school – in her case, Anglican. However neither she nor her family was religious:

> I'm not religious … I see myself as being an Anglican if anything. My husband is a Catholic. I don't believe in it, so I said 'If you want to take them to church you can', and I knew he wouldn't, so it was a safe offer!

May had no experience of Catholicism and the thought of a Catholic education was unfamiliar and discomforting: 'I'd rather they spent time on arithmetic and writing … I'd rather have somewhere which had the same mindset as ourselves, you know, their kids and us in the same mindset'. None of their friends were planning to attend Catholic schools.

Further, the first child felt an acute sense of injustice and complained of inequity saying that he, and the whole family 'would have to pay for this!' May agreed, commenting that the non-government option 'means the whole family just can't do any of the other things it wants to do, and I just don't agree with that either'. There were mixed emotions all around, as the family realigned their thinking towards the non-government sector. There were to be financial costs draining the family's economic capital, but the family was also entering into an unfamiliar social/cultural space, and without friends joining them, they were unable to draw on relevant social capital to smooth the transition.

Megan: An unhappy child and parents at odds

At the time of her interview, Megan was co-parenting with her ex-partner with whom she was on polite but not warm terms. Megan and her former partner had divergent views about education, arising from their rather different family histories of schooling. Her daughter's father comes from a well-to-do family who supported their children through prestigious single-sex high-fee schools. His parents were very proud that they had provided him that start in life, according to Megan. It was an important part of who they were and they were at ease in that milieu.

In Bourdieuian terms, Megan's former partner had significant social, cultural and economic capital to facilitate his daughter's path through high-fee private schooling. From the time of her enrolment in a prestigious kindergarten, her father had apparently mapped out a trajectory that would include a professional university degree. He was happy to pay the school fees and in Megan's telling he saw this as a crucial part of his parenting contribution, especially as the non-custodial parent. Megan's history of schooling was quite different. She grew up in a country town where she attended the local public high school, which was the only secondary school in town. She described herself as having a much more relaxed and progressive attitude to schooling. She preferred her daughter not to feel pressured by thoughts of the far future but rather to feel free 'to explore different pathways' through education. Despite finding her ex-partner's plans too prescriptive, Megan described herself as initially happy enough to go along with them until there was a crisis which, among other things, exposed the differences between their world views.

Their daughter was apparently badly bullied at the private school and Megan reported that she was unable to gain a satisfactory response from the school. Megan reported feeling uncomfortable: that she was different from many of the other mothers – 'less wealthy, less polished' and 'less leisured'. Nor did she feel that she was treated by the school as someone with an entitlement to speak. In other words, she lacked the 'right' social and cultural capital. Moreover she felt that the bullying was more than just the antics of a few children; rather she saw it as deriving from by the school's elitism, wealth and exclusivity. While a number of other parents in our studies admired what they saw as the discipline and smooth operation of elite schools, Megan argued that her daughter's school was too focused on its market position at the expense of the children's individuality. She identified an undue emphasis on appearances and a damaging lack of tolerance for anything spontaneous, messy or disorganised.

For several years Megan struggled with this situation and investigated other schools. She wanted to move her daughter to the local comprehensive public school because she felt it would be a better social and cultural fit but she was blocked by the child's father. The NSW public education system provided a compromise for this family in the form of an academically selective public high school, for which their daughter was clever enough to qualify. Megan eventually moved her daughter with the tepid support of her former partner, who was apparently mollified by the idea that the school was selective. The new school was quite a contrast to the old. Megan spoke affectionately about the scruffiness of the students, the rundown buildings and even the noticeable swearing. There were quite different kinds of social and cultural capital operating there. Megan found the new school more suited to her tomboy daughter and more 'real'. She felt more comfortable as a parent and became involved in the school community. But according to Megan it took her ex-partner some weeks to confess the school change to his parents. For this family, the new school symbolised a significant change. Where their daughter's former school had symbolised her father's social, economic and cultural capital investment, Megan's social and cultural capital were now dominant.

Olivia: Using knowhow and networks to place an 'unmarketable' child

At the time of Olivia's interview she was worried about whether, having spent two years doing intensive research in order to choose the right public high school for her son, she should continue to try to work with the chosen school or cut her losses and move him. Rather than choosing from a number of options, Olivia had found it difficult to actually find a school to suit a child with 'special needs', a child for whom it takes 'a bit of extra effort' to keep up with his classmates. Olivia explained that she and her son are not 'marketable' or 'valid' for the schools for two reasons: first because of her son's special needs and second because of their family's lack of money. Finding a school had been hard work and emotionally upsetting because there seemed to be no really good options. It had just been a question, Olivia said, of 'the best of a bad bunch ... picking the best out of what we had, compromising'. Had they been able to afford it they may have tried a local Christian school, which they had heard has resources for special needs children.

At the time of the interview Olivia had chosen a school for her son which was working to build its enrolment numbers. Under a charismatic principal the school, which formerly had apparently had a long-standing reputation for being 'rough', was now gentrifying to attract a different enrolment profile from its demographically mixed local community. This had included insisting on a detailed uniform code. The pressure to keep up had been stressful: 'they're very, very careful about making sure that the kids all wear uniform every day, and that sort of stuff, but they're not careful about how they treat the kids'. Olivia and her husband had had trouble paying for the Year 7 camp, the text books (which used to be free for all public school children), and the regulation black leather shoes that have to be replaced every few months as their child grows. The school might be publicly successful, argued Olivia, 'they want to be known as a good school', but she felt that she and her son were the casualties of that success.

Despite these problems, Olivia was by no means powerless. She had excellent research skills and came from an old Sydney family with a three-generation deep knowledge of the public education system. She was confident and articulate and has good networks. In other words she was well positioned to activate cultural capital – her knowhow – and her social capital – her networks.

When asked how she found out about schools, Olivia said:

> Talking to other parents ... I read the local paper every day and you read about what's going on at schools ... you chat to other parents at playgroup, or where your kids go to school. And often parents are very willing to say 'oh don't send him to so-and-so. This is the experience we've had there'. And particularly growing up in the area, I know a lot of people ... And you do talk about it as a general topic. A lot of parents I know, we talk about schools a lot, and how disappointed we are, or how pleased we are. We swap information very quickly, and it becomes like wildfire after a while. Everyone knows.

Olivia had also worked with the school to ensure her son had a teachers' aide, had sought action over bullying and had organised counselling for her son from outside the school. At home she worked to encourage him and build his 'self-esteem'. She was able to call on considerable stores of cultural capital to confidently and competently oversee homework and to compensate for classroom deficiencies. Later she used her social capital to facilitate a move to a new school. Olivia discovered that a school she had previously dismissed had acquired a new, well-regarded principal. She made the decision to move her son and by the end of Year 7 he was 'progressing in leaps and bounds' at the new school.

Clover: Unlimited familial capital does not guarantee consumer behaviour

The vast majority of families in our research took advantage of their economic, social and cultural capital to participate in the schooling market to purchase the 'best' school available to them. The family described in our final vignette made a deliberate decision to seek out a comprehensive government school for their son, even though both parents had been educated outside the government school sector. They made an assessment that their social, cultural and financial capital could be better employed in supporting the child at an 'ordinary' school, rather than invested in seeking out the 'best' school.

Clover and her partner were both lawyers and were among the highest income earners in our studies and, further, Clover intended to take on more work when their only child went to high school. Clover herself was educated in Sydney's rapidly expanding postwar suburbs in a 'Catholic working class school' until the final year it was available, whereupon she transferred to the local single-sex government high school to complete her schooling. Typical of that kind of Catholic schooling at the time, classes were overcrowded, facilities substandard, and the teaching force often under-trained. Of her schooling Clover said: 'In my day ... there was never a discussion about where to go for high school, there was never a choice'. By comparison, Clover's partner attended 'the best Church of England grammar school' in Queensland. He did not particularly enjoy this experience, claiming that the best teaching was reserved for the brightest students.

Clover stated that both she and her partner support public education and therefore she narrowed her choice making to neighbouring government schools only. In addition she was opposed to academically selective schooling for both ideological and educational reasons. The local co-educational high school had an academically selective stream, and they preferred the comprehensive co-educational school in the next suburb. Despite their own childhood experiences of different school systems, these parents both sought a local government school for their son.

Clover and her partner recognised that their views on schooling differ from many of their peers. They were financially well-off and their social circle included others in similar circumstances, the majority of whom would have chosen private schooling for their children. And yet

Clover observed: 'We have friends that have really achieved and they didn't go to fancy schools ... but we are in no doubt ... that going to the right school does give an advantage – we are not naïve'.

For this family, decisions about school were predominately ideological rather than economic, or religious. Unlike those motivated by religious beliefs, for example, these parents were supporters of public, comprehensive schooling – albeit a view held from a position of advantage. The family was stable economically, but also, their academically able child would be supported by parents and a wider community of well-educated professionals in a culturally rich home where learning was valued and supported.

Of all the people in Aitchison's study, Clover and her partner had the greatest economic, social and cultural capital. Unlike other participants, there was no talk of opportunity cost in discussions about secondary schooling. Their social circles included successful professional people schooled in both the public and private sectors. They were confident their child would succeed on his own merits rather than through the networks afforded by a private education. They were, however, in no doubt about the security of their cultural and economic capital, nor of how that enabled them to take chances that others experienced as too risky. They were confident that their economic, social and cultural capital provided a safety net; that they had the knowhow and resources to identify and remedy any problems should they arise. Their son could be more easily moved or supported if things started to go wrong, than if he was from a less advantaged family. In reflecting on their decision to send their child to a non-selective government school, Clover said:

> We felt confident. He is a healthy, intelligent child and we come from a position of privilege and so we're lucky ... we always felt confident that he'd make his own way in the world; wherever he went to school, he'd be successful. We're lucky he [her son] has similar views, we feel very strongly about public education. If he had not wanted the same thing, I don't know, but probably we wouldn't have let him go to a private school. We have some friends who have changed to private schooling against their own ideology.

Conclusion

This chapter has outlined historical changes in the organisation of school education in Australia, with a particular focus on contemporary neoliberal formulations that impact on the ways Australian families relate to their schools. Key to this relationship is the market-oriented framing of education, facilitated by policies and practices of state and federal governments of all political persuasions, around the concept of 'choice'. Vast numbers of families are engaging in school choice and the overall trend away from the government sector to private schooling is significant and profound. Moreover, a generation of market-informed mobility has undoubtedly contributed to the social segmentation of Australian schools. On average, Australian schools have a narrower socioeconomic mix than schools in other OECD nations (Nous Group 2011), and a narrower socioeconomic mix than was the case a generation ago (Preston 2013).

Drawing from two major studies of how middle-class families negotiate this new school marketplace has enabled us to illustrate here how these policy changes played out for these families. As we have shown, parents use various strategies, sometimes over extended timeframes, to investigate and position their children and the family to maximise chances of being accepted into preferred schools. This operation of choice turns on familial capital in all its forms. As we illustrated, economic capital constrains or liberates choosers, but family decision-making is more complex and nuanced as family structures, beliefs, individual histories and needs vary, thereby constricting or informing the options parents pursue. Sometimes school choice processes and outcomes fit well with both parents' own inherited familial capitals. At other times, views, values and aspirations are contested between family members, sometimes causing long-term anxieties and disharmony. We saw, too, where some families were forced to choose schooling that did not match their social or cultural heritage and – where this combined with limited economic capital – the resultant strains and pressures. For parents of children with special needs, school choice options are even more constrained and the capacity to call on social and cultural capital sometimes became as important, if not more important, than economic capital.

For many of the families in our studies, school choice was a significant, even defining moment in the family biography. Unlike previous
generations where children mostly attended schools in their local or
Catholic communities, the parents in our studies were very aware of a
right to choose. However, some did so with reservations about the impact of this new way for their local communities and for the schools
themselves. Many found the process of school choice to be labour intensive, and emotionally and intellectually challenging. And for some,
the outcome was tinged with dissatisfaction as they recognised and experienced the limitations of choice in practice.

By engaging in school markets, schools and families were themselves changed – each feeling the pressure to conform to the expectations of a market which favours and normalises traditional notions
of the family and of schools. Megan and Olivia, for example, each experienced problems with schools that seemed overly preoccupied with
market image. May's experience forced her to consider options well
outside of her comfort zone and financial capacity to pay. By contrast,
despite having ample capital to facilitate a wide set of school choices,
Clover's family were motivated by an ideological perspective to choose
the local government school.

The simplistic rhetoric of the market that consumer choice is rational, self-interested and individuated (Apple 2001) was challenged by
our studies. Parents were driven to maximise benefits to their families, but their actions were rarely simple or straightforward. Our studies
showed that school choice was complex and multifaceted, involving an
interplay of subjective, emotional and intergenerational influences connecting networks of informants, and sometimes including collaborative
behaviours by families and communities. It showed that successful engagement in school choice was uneven, and regularly favoured particular kinds of children and families, and educational forms. Parents in
our studies had different preferences and capacities in regard to school
choice and these were impacted by the particular material conditions
within which they operated.

Finally, recent work by Joel Windle and Rodrigo Rocco Fossa
(2012) provides an important caution that the kinds of activities we
document in this chapter (and elsewhere) – while very powerful as discourse – are still not universal as practice. Interviewing parents from a
cluster of 'disadvantaged' suburbs in Melbourne, Windle found:

Most families were not engaged in school choice in the ways that the Rudd government hoped when it urged families to 'vote with their feet' and abandon bad schools for good ones. Families that spoke a language other than English in the home, had lower socio-economic status, and had children with lower academic performance levels were even less likely than others to consider more than one option. Families expressed strong attachment to local community, and to schools where they had pre-existing family connections.

While many of the families in our larger studies did express attachments to local community and historical family connections, by and large this was not enough for them. Individual self-interested decisions are at the heart of neoliberal market philosophy and most of the families we heard from acted to advance their own interests. In so doing, they interpreted their own situations and worked strategically to activate the kinds of capitals that were available to them. The market-oriented schooling system compelled them to examine and assess their resources (capitals) and to adjust their behaviours to maximise their chances of achieving a desired outcome. An examination of this process revealed how some families (and their children) are privileged over others. It is evident that some families have more choice than others, and that it is more than a simple question of money.

References

Aitchison, C. 2006, Mothers and school choice: Effects on the home front, PhD Thesis, University of Technology, Sydney.

Aitchison, C. 2010, 'Good mothers go school shopping', in *The good mother: Contemporary motherhoods in Australia*, eds S. Goodwin & K. Huppatz, Sydney University Press, Sydney, pp. 88–110.

Apple, M. 2001, 'Gender meets neo-liberalism', *Discourse: Studies in the Cultural Politics of Education*, vol. 22, no. 1, pp. 115–118.

Apple, M. 2004, 'Creating difference: Neo-liberalism, neo-conservatism and the politics of educational reform', *Educational Policy*, vol. 18 no. 1, pp. 12–44.

Ball, S. J. 2003, *Class strategies and the education marketplace: The middle classes and social advantage*, Routledge-Falmer, London.

Bourdieu, P. 1984, *Distinction: A social critique of the judgement of taste*, trans. R. Nice, Routledge and Kegan Paul, London.

Bourdieu, P. 1986, 'The forms of capital', in *Handbook of theory and research for the sociology of education*, ed. J. G. Richardson, Greenwood Press, New York.

Brown, P. 1990, 'The "third wave": Education and the ideology of parentocracy', *British Journal of Sociology of Education*, vol. 11, no. 1, pp. 65–85.

Campbell, C. 2005, 'Changing school loyalties and the middle class: A reflection on the developing fate of state comprehensive high schooling', *Australian Educational Researcher*, vol. 32, no. 1, pp. 3–24.

Campbell, C. & Proctor, H. 2014, *A history of Australian schooling*, Allen & Unwin, Sydney.

Campbell, C., Proctor, H. & Sherington, G. 2009, *School choice: How parents negotiate the new school market in Australia*, Allen & Unwin, Sydney.

Campbell, C. & Sherington, G. 2006, *The comprehensive public high school: Historical perspectives*, Palgrave Macmillan, New York.

Connell, R. 2008, 'The neo-liberal parent and schools', in *Breaking the iron cage: Resistance to the schooling of global capitalism*, ed. G. Martell, Canadian Center for Policy Alternatives, Ottawa, pp. 175–93.

Connell, R. 2013, 'The neoliberal cascade and education: An essay on the market agenda and its consequences', *Critical Studies in Education*, vol. 54, no. 2, pp. 99–112.

Connell, R. W., Ashenden, D., Kessler, S. & Dowsett, G., 1982, *Making the difference: Schools, families and social division*, Allen & Unwin, Sydney.

Davies, B. & Bansel, P. 2007, 'Neoliberalism and education', *International Journal of Qualitative Studies in Education*, vol. 20, no. 3, pp. 247–59.

Forsey, M., Davies, S. & Walford, G. 2008, 'The globalisation of school choice? An introduction to key issues and concerns', in *The globalisation of school choice?* eds M. Forsey, S. Davies & G. Walford, Symposium Books, Oxford, pp. 9–25.

Gonski, D. (Chair) 2011, *Review of funding for schooling: Final report*, Australian Government, Canberra.

Jensen, B., Weidmann, B. & Farmer, J. 2013, *The myth of markets in school education*, Grattan Institute, Melbourne.

Kenway, J. & Bullen, E. 2001, *Consuming children: Education – entertainment – advertising*, Open University Press, Buckingham.

Lingard, B. 2010, 'Policy borrowing, policy learning: Testing times in Australian schooling', *Critical Studies in Education*, vol. 51, no. 2, pp. 129–47.

Marginson, S. 1997a, *Educating Australia*, Cambridge University Press, Cambridge.

Marginson, S. 1997b, *Markets in education*, Allen & Unwin, Sydney.

McNeilage, A. 2013, 'Islamic student numbers soar', *Sun Herald*, 4 August, p. 5.

Musset, P. 2012, School choice and equity: Current policies in OECD countries and a literature review, OECD Education Working Papers, No. 66, OECD Publishing.

Nous Group 2011, Schooling challenges and opportunities, Melbourne Graduate School of Education, Melbourne.

Preston, B. 2013, The social make-up of schools: Family income, Indigenous status, family type, religion and broadband access of students in government, Catholic and other nongovernment schools, Barbara Preston Research, Canberra.

Ryan, C. & Watson, L. 2004, The drift to private schools in Australia: Understanding its features, Centre for Economic Policy Research, Australian National University, Canberra.

Sherington, G. & Hughes, J. P. 2012, 'Education', in *From Carr to Keneally: NSW Labor in office 1995–2011*, eds R. Smith & D. Clune, Allen & Unwin, Sydney, pp. 138–49.

Strober, M. H. 2003, 'The application of mainstream economics constructs to education: A feminist analysis', in *Ten years beyond economic man*, eds M. Ferber & J. Nelson, University of Chicago Press, Chicago, pp. 261–91.

Vickers, M. 2004, 'Markets and mobilities: Dilemmas facing the comprehensive neighbourhood high school', *Melbourne Studies in Education*, vol. 45, no. 2, pp. 1–22.

Welch, A. 1996, *Australian education: Reform or crisis?* Allen & Unwin, Sydney.

Whitty, G., 1997, 'Creating quasi-markets in education: A review of recent research on parental choice and school autonomy in three countries', *Review of Research in Education*, vol. 22, pp. 3–47.

Wilkinson, I., Caldwell, B., Selleck, R., Harris, J. & Dettman, P. 2007, *A history of state aid to non-government schools in Australia*, Department of Education, Science and Training, Commonwealth of Australia, Canberra.

Windle, J. 2009, 'The limits of school choice: Some implications for accountability of selective practices and positional competition in Australian education', *Critical Studies in Education*, vol. 50, no. 3, pp. 231–46.

Windle, J. & Rocco Fossa, R. 2012, Democratisation through school choice? Rhetoric and reality in the Australian 'Education Revolution', paper presented to the International Sociological Association, 2nd Forum of Sociology, Social Justice, and Democratisation, Buenos Aires, 1–4 August.

11

Conditional income transfers and choice in social services: Just more conditions and more markets?

Terry Carney

Privatisation is not the only force re-sculpting the rights, power and dignity of recipients of welfare in Australia. As predicted by Peter Dwyer's idea of the 'conditional welfare state' for social security (Dwyer 1998, 2004, 2008), Australian social security *payments* are becoming more conditional, restricting individual choice (Carney 2011), whereas welfare services are expanding consumer choice (Needham 2011) along with greater reliance on market forces in service delivery. Drawing on the examples of the increasing conditionalisation of social security and the 'personalisation' of aged care in Australia, this chapter illustrates this convergence towards a middle ground between respect for individual choice and state paternalism and a rebalancing of the tension between the state and markets.

Social policy writers have long observed that conditions on income support payments can run from negligible, such as Britain's early history of having, 'but generally not applying', a work test on the unemployed (Wikeley 1989, p. 296), to very burdensome, as under contemporary 'activation' policies in many countries (Handler 2009, pp. 81–87). Changes in the degree and intensity of such conditions can

Carney, T. 2015, 'Conditional income transfers and choice in social services: Just more conditions and more markets?', in *Markets, rights and power in Australian social policy*, eds G. Meagher & S. Goodwin, Sydney University Press, Sydney.

be studied for their 'disciplinary' and 'surveillance' effects (Henman & Adler 2001, 2003) or in terms of the political economy of welfare.[1] Recent changes to the *form* of social security illustrate a move away from reliance on the cash/electronic funds transfers toward 'in-kind' transfer schemes. Examples include longstanding 'food stamps' in the United States (Tschoepe & Hindera 2001) and other recent voucher schemes, such as the French experiment with low value vouchers (Dallongeville et al. 2010) and Australia's Forrest Report proposal for a more universal 'healthy welfare' card (Forrest 2014); utilisation of representative payee, or 'nominee', provisions enabling third parties to control and spend welfare payments for people with reduced decision-making capacity (*Social Security [Administration] Act* 1999 'S[A]A, 1999', ss 44, 123A–123S; see also Creyke 1991; Komlos-Hrobsky 1989); and hybrid forms (Katz 2010), such as Australia's 'welfare quarantining', which limits what a proportion of a social security payment may be used to purchase, or the method of payment, through the issue of a debit card rather than cash (Billings 2011; Bielefeld 2014). All of these can be evaluated in terms of the impacts on recipient choice, dignity, human rights and impacts on vulnerable populations (Billings 2011; Coven 2001; Ries et al. 2004).

More recently, social policy writers have turned their attention to questions of how welfare services are arranged and provided. Services such as job-matching, or residential care of the aged, for example, were initially configured as state-funded, state-delivered (job-matching) or state-auspiced (aged care), and 'state-standardised' services. These packages of services offered few real choices, either for unemployed people (originally managed by a branch of government called the Commonwealth Employment Service), or for frail older people requiring

---

1 As Joel Handler (2009, p. 84) observes of the differences between US workfare and EU activation or active labour market programs: 'Activation and ALMP [Active Labour Market Programs] are considered different from workfare. The Europeans maintain that the idea behind ALMPs is that actively seeking work is about rights and opportunities as opposed to the US-style workfare model that is focused on duties and sanctions ... ALMPs embrace a wide range of measures from voluntary training, human capital development, employment and wage subsidies, and job creation to compulsory work programs. There are combinations of carrots and sticks. In contrast, US workfare lacks rewards/carrots and focuses on job first and sanctions/sticks'.

residential care. More recently, such policies have been criticised for neglecting values of human choice and agency, for their alleged inefficiency and inflexibility, and for failing to recognise the diversity and pluralism of modern society. New approaches to service delivery, involving contracting out of state services for-profit companies or not-for-profit agencies, and private arrangements, through measures such as the individual budget and individual choice and engagement of services, have come to the fore (see Meagher & Goodwin, this volume). The various forms taken by such 'new public management' (NPM) arrangements for delivery of welfare services in turn raise important issues regarding distributional equity, transparency and public accountability, and outcomes for vulnerable populations.

This chapter steps slightly sideways from these debates to explore an apparent 'convergence' towards new forms of social security and social welfare provision whereby, to put it simply, income support is growing 'sticky tentacles' that reduce individual lifestyle choices while state services programs are being 'hollowed out' to make greater space for consumer choice, under the rather elusive banner of 'personalised services' (Needham 2011). The chapter opens by briefly mapping the conceptual landscape being examined, focusing on the key concepts 'conditional welfare' and 'welfare service choice'. Drawing on (minimally updated) examples exant at the time the chapter was first written in 2012, it then presents some Australian examples of a new paradigm taking the place of the traditional welfare state characterised by unconditional cash social security transfers and standardised state-run programs of social services. This 'new paradigm' is illustrated through a discussion of the increasing conditionalisation of Australian social security and the increasing 'personalisation' of residential aged care. It is tentatively argued in the final section that both trends can be attributed to a recalibration of the welfare state. This recalibration centres on the age-old tension between the state and the market and the search for the elusive middle ground.

What is meant by conditional welfare and social service 'choice'?

Conditional income support

In the real world, all income support is conditional to some extent. Even the as yet utopian idea of a guaranteed minimum income ('negative income tax') would be conditional on citizenship for qualification. Classical European social insurance schemes have long tied entitlement durations to the numbers of years of contributions, and may also now impose conditions of 'activation' for people of workforce age/capacity. Likewise in the case of taxpayer-funded social assistance schemes operating either as a safety net or as the primary social security system (as in Australia), job search and residence requirements have long placed 'conditions' on receipt of payments. The origins of such conditions for the able-bodied run deep into history, including the British Poor Laws (Garraty 1978).

The intensification of conditions attached to workforce age payments across the developed world has been part of a conversion of social security from a so-called passive 'right' into an 'active' reciprocal bargain between recipients and the state, often now packaged under 'welfare-to-work' welfare reforms (Handler 2009; Larkin 2011). As Martin Powell (2000, p. 47) explained of the once quite fashionable Third Way policies of Tony Blair's Britain, '[i]n short, the third way of citizenship moves from "dutiless rights" towards "conditional welfare" '. While the convergence of welfare-to-work policies across countries should not be overstated (Handler 2009, p. 88), there does appear to be a trend toward increased targeting of income support to people of working age and increased sanctions for non-compliance with new conditions.

What is distinctive in Australia and other countries is the *selective* imposition of additional conditions on certain groups of social security recipients, such as the United Kingdom requiring participation in treatment on the part of addicts (Harris 2010) or, in common with many countries, extension of conditionality to disability payments (Patrick 2011) and, more recently, payments to sole parents. Australia's trajectory started with active policing of a work test on workforce age payments, before intensifying with adoption of 'work-fare' (such as 'work for the dole' programs), or requirements to vaccinate children or take action to collect child support as a condition of certain family payments. This has culminated most recently in measures restricting the way half or more of the amount of a welfare payment for an Indigenous client is spent, 'quarantining' part of the money for food and essentials (Billings 2010), an approach later extended to cover behaviours such as child neglect or school truancy in selected regions (Hutchinson, Dickson & Chappell 2011).[2] Although not pursued, in December 2008 a government white paper on homelessness (*The road home*) had also flagged compulsory rent deductions for public tenants (Gilbert 2009, p. 13), in part based on British Third Way thinking about supported housing (Carr 2005). As was the case with supervisory 'new paternalist-inspired' welfare reforms in the United States (Mead 1997), such extended conditionality aims to change *values* or inculcate certain *behavioural* standards in specific groups of 'welfare dependent' people.

Markets and 'choice' in welfare services

Choice and efficiency are the benefits claimed from application of markets to welfare, but welfare markets take many different forms and often combine with *other* organisational configurations. As Ingo Bode (2009, pp. 164–65) reminds us in *On the road to welfare markets*, organisational partnerships for the administration of social services are not new: non-government agencies and non-profit organisations, local government, unions and employers, advocacy and pressure groups, professional organisations, and many others have long had a hand in shaping and delivering social services around different parts of the world (Bode 2009, p. 168). Co-payments for accessing a public good like health or aged care, for instance, spread costs between the public purse and private pockets, as well as curbing 'unnecessary' utilisation

---

2   School Enrolment and Attendance Measures trials were located at Mornington Island and Doomadgee in north-west Queensland, and the suburb of Logan in Brisbane. According to Terry Hutchinson and colleagues (2011, p. 107), at February 2011 there were 82 suspensions of payment (79 for failure of children to attend school, three for failure to enrol). From July 2012 quarantining expanded to five regions (Logan and Rockhampton in Queensland, Bankstown in Sydney, Greater Shepparton in Victoria and Playford in South Australia), and 'financial vulnerability' joined child neglect as a basis for quarantining of between 50 and 70 percent of each payment (Billings 2011).

through a compression of choice. Examples of this include patient co-payments for medical consultations or drug prescriptions (Carney & Ramia 2009; Sweeny 2009).

Bode's focus is government pursuit of '*some* purposeful social policy objectives ... by means of distinctive regulations', through what he terms '*managed welfare markets*' (Bode 2009, p. 165 [emphasis in original]). Often called 'quasi-markets', these involve government contracting with private providers for provisions of services, also referred to as the purchaser–provider model (Wanna, Butcher & Freyens 2010, Ch 5). The radical transformation of the state job placement service, the Commonwealth Employment Service, into the dispersed network of privately contracted employment services providers known as the Job Network (now Jobs Services Australia) has been told extensively elsewhere (Carney 2005; Carney & Ramia 2002a; Considine 2001; Considine, Lewis & O'Sullivan 2011) including most recently its implications for non-state (civil society) providers (Wright, Marston & McDonald 2011). In a more heavily regulated form, the Australian residential aged care arrangements discussed later in the chapter also already incorporate a purchaser–provider model.

Public subsidies rewarding private action, such as tax incentives for buying additional private superannuation coverage, for their part serve to *shape* individual choices within private markets (see Adam Stebbing's contribution to this volume), though Bode argues that neither co-payment nor subsidy models create a *welfare market* properly so-called. Rather, for the purposes of the present chapter, Bode's concept of a *subsidised welfare market* is most pertinent. For Bode, these are characterised by more interventionist controls and conditions; and what he terms *direct payments*, including vouchers, enabling consumers to choose and control the purchase of services such as for disability, personal care or other human services (Bode 2009, p. 166). As explained later, this maps conceptually to Australia's aged care (and disability) reforms of interest in this chapter.

In sum, the emergence of managed and subsidised welfare markets have constituted a hollowing out of former state 'template-delivered' social services, ostensibly in the interests of greater consumer choice and government efficiency. This has occurred in conjunction with a trend towards greater conditionality of income support. This brief sketch of the territory being considered is perhaps better understood in light of two recent Australian case studies.

Case studies of Australian conditionality in social security and welfare services

Conditional social security through 'quarantining'

Historically, all Australian social security, other than compulsory superannuation, has taken the form of tax-funded social assistance. With its history of a 'workers welfare state' constructed around a highly selective and means-tested program covering all major life contingencies (Carney 2002, 2006), Australia's social security system until very recently relied entirely on unrestricted cash transfers, combined with concession cards[3] qualifying holders for various 'fringe' benefits, such as lower utility charges or transport fares.

However, in 2007, selected groups such as Indigenous communities and neglectful parents were singled out by the former conservative Howard government (1996–2011) for an authoritarian form of involuntary management of their welfare payments, as part of a suite of health, education and other measures presented as being designed to tackle coordination of school attendance or policies to regulate alcohol and drug abuse and child protection (Goodwin 2011).[4] While distantly supported by the government's McClure *Report on welfare reform* (2000), which favoured 'bundling' income with other needed supports, the

---

3   Such as the pensioner concession card or the seniors and (lower income) healthcare cards: *Social Security Act 1991* (Cwlth), Chapter 2A, Part 2A. 1. These cards qualify holders for certain advantages such as lower caps on charges for pharmaceutical prescriptions, and state and territory governments which for convenience choose to direct transport, utility and other concessions to the aged or low-income groups to card holders.
4   These reforms have their origins in the Aurukun 'community justice agreements' and the wider knitting of education, health, housing and income support (Hatami 2006, p. 27), and the 'mutual responsibility agreements' (McCausland & Levy 2006) developed for 100 or so Indigenous health, housing and other programs when the Aboriginal and Torres Strait Islander Commission (ATSIC) was abolished in 2004 (Anderson 2006).

whole package of measures was highly paternalistic and redolent of 'social control' measures. So far as income support was concerned, a new 'income management' regime was legislated, covering three different groups of people (Sutton 2008): (i) *all* citizens living in declared (Indigenous) geographic *areas* (essentially confined to the Northern Territory); (ii) *individual* Australians anywhere in Australia selected for income management due to concerns about child protection, school enrolment or truancy; and (iii) those Indigenous citizens living in Queensland, individually selected for income management after a hearing by the Family Relations Commission, a new state body with membership from Indigenous communities (S(A)A, 1999: s123TA). In the Northern Territory alone, as at June 2008, there were 'over 13,300 individuals' subject to the scheme; covering '53 communities within prescribed areas and in 46 town camps located in major centres' (Australian Government 2008).

The legislation provides for half or more of payments to be received in the form of a 'voucher' akin to a food stamp (in practice 50 to 70 percent of the payment) and the remainder in cash, with the restricted 'basics card' portion confined to paying for 'priority needs' as defined (such as food, clothing, housing etcetera), and unable to be spent on 'excluded items' (such as alcohol, gambling, tobacco and pornography). The scheme was expanded late in the term of the Gillard Labor government to include non-Indigenous citizens and by including additional behavioural conduct (such as child protection or addictions), and indicators of individual vulnerability (teenage mothers[5] and jobless families[6]), piloted in regions with a high population incidence of such

---

5   When the youngest child reaches six months of age, a Centrelink information interview explains 'what they will be required to do ... once their youngest child turns one, including the services and assistance that they can access'. This includes 'developing a participation plan'. Plans focus on reaching Year 12 or equivalent and 'getting good early health and education outcomes for their children'. Parents need to agree to comply with the plan. They are supported by a range of extra services in these locations.

6   Trial participants were obliged to satisfy certain requirements. Failure to attend appointments/workshops without a reasonable excuse, including to discuss an Employment Pathway Plan, or failure to sign a plan, led to suspension of payments until attendance at a rescheduled appointment/workshop releases payment (with full back pay). Under ongoing versions of these sanctions, advice of a reasonable

indicators. While the sanctions of loss of payments for some of these new groups are less punitive (for example, for teenage mothers) than for other workforce age payments for which recipients are subject to participation plans (Employment Pathway Plans) and/or quarantining, intensive case management contacts are still required for all, leaving such people vulnerable to loss of income for failure to co-operate with more active engagement.[7]

These measures can be viewed in a positive light as designed to tackle the more entrenched pockets of disadvantage, in accordance with contemporary thinking about how to shape a social inclusion agenda. However, from a more critical standpoint they remain problematic on both human rights (discrimination in the provision of welfare) and efficacy grounds (Billings 2010), despite being broadened beyond the Indigenous community (Billings 2011). Choice rights of some recipients are still being compromised in the interests of ill-defined broader welfare objectives, and clients' power and dignity are diminished.

The predicate here is that lack of employment or other conditions of welfare dependency for individuals or their families (such as a focus on child neglect or addictions) not only can be attributed to *individual* rather than external structural factors (problematic in itself), but also that the individual retains sufficient *agency* or choice over behaviour for it to be ethical to utilise loss of benefit payments or other sanctions to alter that behaviour. Behaviours such as gambling or addiction (both included on the list of prohibited expenditures) are just two of those which fail this test (Macdonald et al. 2001). Both are well recognised

---

excuse avoids suspension, but failure to attend rescheduled appointments/ workshops may again trigger suspension. Plans may include activities that focus on the health, wellbeing and education of the child and the education of the parent, as an alternative to looking for work, but will not include compulsory requirements to place children into childcare or to look for or accept work. Where activities are voluntarily included in the plan, and cannot subsequently be met, the plan must be renegotiated. Parents in the teenage parent trial failing to comply with activities in their plan could have their income support suspended until they provide evidence of participation, but jobless family trial participants were exempt from this.

7   Centrelink states that neither 'sanctions' nor 'debts' are incurred for failure of jobless families to comply with activities of their Employment Pathway Plan, 'but other sanctions such as more frequent interviews with Centrelink and suspension of income support will apply'.

as having medical or learned components necessitating often lengthy treatment programs, and thus are not responsive to simplistic moral notions of 'deciding' not to gamble or drink. That is not to say that major benefits might not accrue to the *dependants* of the person (for whom money otherwise devoted to the grog will be available for food and necessities), but however worthy as an objective, this does not validate the assumption for quarantining the income support of the *individual* recipient.

A different narrative unfolds in the next case study, analysing expansion of choice in welfare services for the aged requiring residential care.

Easing conditional social services for the aged in Australia

Australia's model of residential care is a mixed model, reliant on for-profit or not-for-profit providers, funded through a combination of means-tested elements along with universal characteristics, akin to schemes found in Austria and France (Productivity Commission 2011a, vol. 2, p. 22, Appendix D).

Residential aged care is a small sub-set of Australian aged care services, accounting for approximately 220,000 people at any one time, with around 60,000 each year accessing respite care (see detailed elaboration in Productivity Commission 2011b, p. 11, pp. 15–16). More than nine in 10 (92 percent) of older Australians live in private residences (with family or alone). Approximately 2.3 million people provide some informal care of the aged, a proportion of whom qualify for income support, a carer allowance or carer payment.[8]

---

8 Carer payment, paid at effectively the pension rate ($776.70 per fortnight single from September 2014), requires a high minimum objective rating score under an objective rating instrument regarding the needs of the person cared for (under the Adult Disability Assessment Tool, 'ADAT'), care in a private home, and 'constant care' (broadly interpreted as care equivalent to a full time job): s 198; *Re Del Vecchio and Secretary DFaCSIA* [2007] AATA 1145, and *Re Confidential and Secretary DFHCSIA* [2010] AATA 551. Carer allowance, paid at a low rate ($121.70 per fortnight in September 2014) also available only on the basis of a minimum ADAT score, must be provided daily in a private home, and also must be for at least 20 hours a week where the person cared for lives elsewhere in another private

Government involvement in Australian residential aged care arrangements began with capital funding of non-government providers in the mid-1950s, followed by payment of 'nursing home benefits' in 1963. Market failure as 'for-profit' providers replaced not-for-profit (often religious) providers from the 1970s (Carney 1997; Carney & Hanks 1986, pp. 204–21) led to united political action to regulate the quantity, price and quality of residential care (Courtney, Minichiello & Waite 1997; Productivity Commission 2011b, Appendix E). To correct for concerns such as over-institutionalisation of the aged population, inequitable access, or poor standards of care, operators have been required to be approved[9] and obtain an allocation of places approved for each geographic region, based on demographic indicators of expected need. Entry into residential care has depended on obtaining a favourable recommendation from multi-disciplinary 'aged care assessment teams' (ACAT), based on medical need and capacity for community care (Productivity Commission 2011b, p. E15; Carney 2013a),[10] though limited places meant approval did not guarantee entry (Productivity Commission 2011a, vol. 1, pp. 104–11), and quality control through sanctioning of unsatisfactory providers proved to be a rather crude and ineffective quality assurance device (Ellis & Howe 2010).

The Productivity Commission's inquiry report, *Caring for older Australians* (2011a) recommended a radical restructure of these regulatory (and associated subsidy) arrangements in order to promote values of individual 'choice' and generally create a more diversified market for aged care services, mirroring similar trends discerned in provision of disability services (Fisher et al. 2010). The commission pointed out that

---

home: *Social Security Act 1991* (Cwlth) ss 954(1), 954A; *Re Walsh and Secretary DFaCS* [2002] AATA 881.
9   Approval requires demonstrated compliance with 'aged care principles' and other conditions under Part 2.1 of the *Aged Care Act 1997* (Cwlth), along with the 'certification' process set out in Part 2.6, and quality accreditation standards in Part 4.1.
10   The national target ratio of aged care per 1,000 people aged over 70 be achieved by June 2011 was set at 113, made up of 88 residential (evenly split between high and low care) and 25 community-based predominantly low care places (AIHW 2010, p. 15), and in June 2009 it stood at 110, though actual provision in Western Australia, Queensland and the ACT was lower (AIHW 2010, p. 16).

the system struggled to meet demand for residential care, or diversify to cater to the needs of residents' expectations of being able to purchase 'extras' in order to better tailor care to their individual aspirations (Productivity Commission 2011a, vol. 1, pp. 101–38). An overall perceived lack of variety of service offerings underpinned its recommended shift to a more flexible, more market-sensitive, model of delivery.

The Productivity Commission's proposed package of reforms (Productivity Commission 2011a, vol. 1, pp. xxiv–xcii) have since been partially adopted by government (Australian Government 2012), including abolition of the former distinction between high and low care residential places, access to entry bonds and higher co-payment contributions for all residents who can afford to pay and an ability for facilities to charge for 'extras' (de Boer 2012). Accountability and regulatory agencies proposed by the commission were fully established: an Aged Care Financing Authority (to set a price, which may or may not reflect the cost of providing the service), an Aged Care Quality Agency and an Aged Care Reform Implementation Council.

Of these, the personalisation of care to realise greater choice is the issue of greatest interest for present purposes.

Personalisation of support

The idea of 'personalisation of support' through a more consumer-directed, person-centred residential aged care system offering greater choice (Productivity Commission 2011a, vol. 1, pp. 111–13), was adopted in a very modest way by the Australian government.

The proposal for a single 'gateway agency' into all services, assessing client needs (and to some extent preferences) regarding an overall 'package' of subsidised services, was adopted, though its scope was initially unclear (de Boer 2012). However, the idea of making a 'choice' between competing service packages offered by approved providers, (Productivity Commission 2011a, vol. 2, pp. 166–74) is only to be trialled (de Boer 2012). This was welcome recognition that choice can be very problematic, especially for groups such as the frail aged, with empirical studies showing that even Australia's present system proves very difficult to comprehend both for aged people and their families, arguably overtaxing their capacity to make wise choices (Wilson, Setterlund & Tilse 2003). Even so, as public resourcing models switch

from program-based funding to individualised cash funding allocations which can be spent as service *users* sees fit (for an Australian
review: Fisher et al. 2010, pp. 7–13), the complexity of the choices demanded of aged care recipients can only increase, along with workforce
pressures on providers (Baxter, Wilberforce & Glendinning 2011).

Since many users of residential aged care are frail or very elderly,
family or other carers will increasingly be in short supply, placing added
demands on the pool of potential substitute decision-makers appointed
under (now disfavoured) durable powers of attorney or public
guardianship. This will also challenge the viability of the 'supported
decision-making' approaches so strongly favoured under the *Convention on the Rights of Persons with Disabilities* (Carney 2012) and the
blueprint provided by the Australian Law Reform Commission (2014)
and the equivalent but largely untested brokerage/substitute decision-
making in other fields such as disability services (Tilse et al. 2003; Tilse
et al. 2005). By risking not being able to deliver the informal support
promised, this set of reforms arguably taxes the ability of civil society or
government systems to deliver equity and security to match the theoretical expansion of 'choice' rights (Carney 2013b). Personal budgets, then,
are potentially empowering of individuals and their rights if soundly
implemented and well resourced but, if poorly implemented, also risk
short-changing citizens by detracting from the right to quality welfare services, leaving vulnerable consumers open to exploitation such
as 'elder abuse' at worst or disregard of their wishes and values at best
(Carney & Beaupert 2013).

In assessing the advantages of personalised support, account must
also be taken of *other* counter forces pushing to re-homogenise what
markets offer. In an analysis of National Health Service (NHS) hospitals
in the United Kingdom, Patrick Brown and Mike Calnan (2010, p. 16)
argue that a pervasive 'culture of targets and audits' has accompanied
the widespread contracting out of services to third-party providers, under the neoliberal philosophy of NPM. Among other casualties, clinical
trust and professionalism are undermined, while institutions experience 'risk colonisation', leading to bland or lowest common denominator provision of services (Brown & Calnan 2010, p. 15). Illustrative
examples in residential aged care can include food hygiene standards
precluding serving of soft-boiled eggs, or excessive incursions on the

rights of aged residents to form sexual relationships (especially those with mild dementia).

Explaining and theorising the trend towards conditional welfare

Various theoretical explanations might be suggested as drivers of this convergence of choice and paternalism, a social policy trend which can be read equivocally either as 'beneficial' (in the sense of building individual capacity and resilience) or conversely as rights-restricting and disempowering, as discussed in this chapter. However, none of the theories briefly outlined below are entirely convincing, leaving this writer to suggest that pragmatic political trends may be more important in explaining Australian trends.

New governance?

A range of social policy commentators suggest we have shifted to a new form of governance whereby various levels and types of public and private decision-makers form flat structures of mutually interdependent networks, yielding consensual positions which achieve governance through 'soft law' rather than Weberian command-and-control methods (see, for example, Héritier & Rhodes 2011; Lindsay & McQuaid 2009; Van Berkel 2010). One theoretical explanation of the trends reviewed in this chapter, then, is that they reflect these changing fashions of *governance*. Paul Smyth (2008, p. 55), for instance, argues that we are witnessing a new era of closer partnership between the various 'pillars' of social policy. Whereas the former welfare state era policies either promoted 'citizen-based social development' or adopted market-based models which 'sought to restrict welfare to the deserving few', he contends that 'a new set of goals is forming around social investment in an inclusive society in which all people have the opportunities to realise their capabilities', entailing such a new form of collaborative or 'networked' governance (see also Damgaard & Torfing 2010; Hemerijck 2009, p. 89; Wanna et al. 2010, pp. 289–95).

Certainly, the Australian convergence of the state-imposed control of social security alongside expanded client-choice-autonomy settings for social services can be partially explained by the rise of network governance, given its focus on consensual or lowest common denominator elements, though some contest this as just another expression of neoliberalism (Davies 2009). But it is a partial explanation at best, as there are many other forces at work in the 'recalibration' of the welfare settlement, including: globalisation, demographic ageing, changed family and work patterns, and so forth. Indeed, trends towards reconfiguring the former welfare *state* to 'create and develop welfare *markets*, that is social welfare provision operated by market actors' (Bode 2009, p. 162 [emphasis in original]), were noted over a decade ago as characteristic of 'third way' policies (Lazar & Stoyko 1998, p. 22), as under quasi-markets like Australia's Job Network.

Neoliberalism

Neoliberal confidence in markets is frequently advanced as a basis for welfare reform (Beeson & Firth 1998; Carney & Ramia 2010; McClusky 2003). Although there are a range of arguments against 'leaving social provision to markets' – including the view of the then Australian Treasury Secretary Ken Henry, who pithily observed (2009, p. 10) 'leaving fairness solely to the market to determine should be unacceptable to a civilised society' – in its emphasis on individual choice and market mechanisms, the Productivity Commission was undoubtedly strongly influenced by neoliberal sentiments in framing its residential aged care reform proposals.

While it is somewhat ironic that history suggests that adverse social equity outcomes resulted from the mistakes of under- and mis-regulation of publicly financed Australian aged care at its very inception in the 1960s and 1970s (Carney & Hanks 1986, pp. 206–12), it is also true that neoliberalism is by no means the only reason for the rising popularity of personalised welfare support. As Andrew Power, Janet Lord and Allison deFranco explain in their detailed comparative study of 'personalisation' and empowerment reforms of disability services in the United States, Canada, England, Northern Ireland, Sweden, France and the Irish Republic, there are also strong philosophical, human rights and theoretical justifications for the shift, including the influence of ideas of active citizenship, the 'developmental welfare state' and obligations under international treaties such as the *Convention on the Rights of Persons with Disabilities* (Power, Lord & deFranco 2013, p. 8). Again, this theory offers an incomplete explanation at best.

Remaking and restricting citizens?

The expansion and intensification 'conditional' social security brings also offers itself to several interpretations in addition to those canvassed already. Analyses suggestive of Foucaldian extended (and almost invisible) social control through technological 'soft' surveillance and moulding of the lives of citizens clearly have some purchase in explaining the trends in social security (Henman 2004; Henman & Adler 2001, 2003), as also does the idea of construction of the 'docile' citizen (Hartman 2005). However, so far as conditional welfare is concerned, much of its intellectual underpinnings can actually be traced to writing in the vein of Lawrence Mead (Carney & Ramia 2002b; Mead 1997) and to the somewhat simpler social policy idea that people cannot be re-empowered as autonomous human agents without *supervision* and direction to remake their values and attitudes in ways more congenial to society and the domains of work (Green 2002; Macgregor 1999).

As has been shown in this chapter, the Australian experiment with welfare quarantining does fit this narrative of use of state power to remake individual values, in that it openly and directly targets socially dysfunctional behaviours such as excessive drinking, school absenteeism, child neglect and consumption of pornography (Billings 2010; Bielefeld 2014). Likewise, the requirements imposed on addicts in the United States and United Kingdom are another example of the 'responsibilisation' agenda (Harris 2010). As John Chamberlain (2013, p. 100) writes in a review of the extensive literature by authors such as Nikolas Rose on the notion of the 'enterprise self' and neoliberal governmentality, its agenda of 'dual advocacy of the self-regulating free individual and the free market' has assumed a 'near-hegemonic position'. This self-actualised or 'enterprised self' is shaped and governed by a series of 'rationalities' such as those of individual activation (citizens as 'entrepreneurs of the self'), competition, self-reliance and accountability for actions and consumerist framing (Chamberlain 2013, pp. 98–100). Or as Nikolas Rose and Peter Miller (2010) write specifically on welfare, it can be portrayed as an exercise in the construction of citizens capable of exercising 'regulated freedom'. But once again, the material canvassed in this chapter also resonates with a more pragmatic and less theoretical explanation.

Conclusion: No single or clear overarching narrative?

Convincing overarching narratives are hard to find for this convergence around the hybrid forms of 'managed-markets' exemplified by conditional welfare and the greater personalisation of social care services like residential aged care.

At a purely descriptive level it is evident that two different images of choice are in play. In conditional welfare the fungibility of cash payments and the alleged lack of sufficient conditions or obligations is constructed as failing to re-shape poor behavioural characteristics (such as lack of a work ethic or irresponsible spending or addictions); here paternalist corrective intervention is the virtue to be pursued. With the personalisation of welfare services, choice itself is constructed as a virtue which is being unreasonably compressed by rigid bureaucratic state service delivery systems or excessively detailed controls; here paternalism is the vice to be tackled. As each sector moves from polar extremes of comparatively untrammeled choice (as-of-right cash transfers for social security) and paternalism (one-size-fits-all state-run services), towards a rebalancing of choice and paternalism, it might be argued that this degree of convergence is just a welcome pragmatic embrace of more nuanced and sophisticated policies.

On the other hand, as this chapter has shown, the theoretical justifications for the restriction of choice (quarantining) or its expansion (personalised support) proved to be rather thin. Such recalibrations thus risk falling victim to excessively zealous and sweeping adoptions of new configurations without a sufficient evidence-based foundation or subsequent critical evaluation of the impact of the policy change. For example, currently popular narratives like 'personalisation' of welfare conceal old dilemmas. Catherine Needham (2011, pp. 62–63) raises one of the more pertinent to this chapter when she asks:

[H]ow do you make sense of your relationship to the state when you are placed in control of a personal budget, and exhorted to strive for self actualisation, while at the same time being subject to strictures to enter the labour market on whatever basic terms it is possible to get a job?

Networked governance is another popular contemporary concept to come into question for blurring important policy debates, including from commentators such as Jonathan Davies (2009).

To take a contemporary policy example, it is therefore cautioned that Australia should not rush too quickly into legislation replacing substitute decision-making with 'supported decision-making' schemes. Such reforms need to be well grounded in an evidence base and rigorous evaluation of the quite distinctive (and limited) contributions able to be made by law, formal policy or other normative civil society and family processes. Otherwise, such reforms may fail to provide the intended complementary assistance in the realisation of the objective of 'personalisation of choice' in services for vulnerable populations such as people with a disability (Carney & Beaupert 2013). Identical conclusions have been reached from a meta-review of international studies (Kohn, Blumenthal & Campbell 2013). Similar warnings about the lack of specificity of proposals have been levelled at 'social inclusion' programs, which Davies (2005, p. 23) earlier rather tartly characterised as:

[A] contract, in which the individual pledges to take responsibility across the full spectrum of social life – from maintaining employability to maintaining a healthy life style. The state is re-shaped to bear part of the risk that such responsible individuals face, but in ways that minimise dependency and the social wage. The wealthy appear to be largely exempt from any additional obligations.

Again, these debates have salience for Australia (Carney 2007).

One of the broader goals tapped by ideas of personalisation, networked governance and social inclusion is greater responsiveness of welfare systems to the variety of individual needs and capacities of consumers and to the diversity of values and interests of modern society. However, consistent with the aim of cultivation of 'responsibilisation' of the individual, there are elements in all of these of a somewhat woolly assumption of localised, deliberative democratic engagement in crafting individual or collective policies within outer bounds set by the state; a form of 'guided self-regulation'. Of course, such policy configurations *can* bring important benefits despite these concerns; it all depends on close examination of the detail of particular schemes, as demonstrated by Power, Lord and deFranco's international review of personalisation programs (Power, Lord & deFranco 2013). But the *public policy* problem is that this detail – as illustrated by NPM and neoliberal governance reforms – tends to be hidden *further away* from public scrutiny and accountability than was the case under predecessor policy settings (Diller 2000; Gilman 2001).

The way forward cannot confidently be mapped fully at this stage. Certainly, the trend towards market provision and conditional welfare calls for creative thinking on how to reinstate respect for values of accountability and transparency (Mashaw 2006; Mulgan 2006). However, as Tara Melish (2010, pp. 56–60, 69ff) implies, this must surely also be accompanied by rethinking the degree of 'convergence' that is appropriate. While there *is* undoubtedly an intensifying trend under the Abbott government both to make income support more conditional and to inject greater choice in those service provision programs for which it continues to accept responsibility for funding after any devolution to the states and territories, the jury remains out on whether and to what degree this is desirable. While both can be rationalised as being a product of a common influence – such as in striving to realise the 'ensuring' state or Bode's 'subsidised welfare market' – history may yet show that the trend towards convergence between choice and paternalism was a mere temporary coincidence in the workings of Australia's democratic polity. As this chapter reveals, both possibilities seemingly remain open.

Legislation and cases

Aged Care Act 1997 (Cwlth)
Social Security Act 1991
Social Security (Administration) Act 1999
Re Confidential and Secretary DFHCSIA [2010] AATA 551.
Re Del Vecchio and Secretary DFaCSIA [2007] AATA 1145
Re Walsh and Secretary DFaCS [2002] AATA 881

References

AIHW (Australian Institute of Health and Welfare) 2010, *Residential aged care in Australia 2008–2009*, Australian Institute of Health and Welfare, Canberra. http://www.aihw.gov.au/publications/index.cfm/title/11628

Anderson, I. 2006, 'Mutual obligation, shared responsibility agreements and Indigenous health strategy', *Australia and New Zealand Health Policy*, vol. 3, no. 10, pp. 1–10.

Australian Government 2008, Report of the NTER Review Board, NTER Review Board, Canberra. http://www.nterreview.gov.au/docs/report_nter_review/default.htm

Australian Government 2012, *Living longer. Living better. Aged care reform package*, Australian Government, Canberra.

Australian Law Reform Commission 2014, *Equality, capacity and disability in Commonwealth laws: Final report*, Australian Law Reform Commission, Sydney.

Baxter, K., Wilberforce, M. & Glendinning, C. 2011, 'Personal budgets and the workforce implications for social care providers: Expectations and early experience', *Social Policy and Society*, vol. 10, no. 1, pp. 55–65.

Beeson, M. & Firth, A. 1998, 'Neoliberalism as a political rationality: Australian public policy since the 1980s', *Journal of Sociology*, vol. 34, no. 3, pp. 215–31.

Bielefeld, S. 2014, 'Compulsory income management and indigenous peoples – Exploring counter narratives amidst colonial constructions of "vulnerability"', *Sydney Law Review*, vol. 36, no. 4, pp. 695–726.

Billings, P. 2010, 'Social welfare experiments in Australia: More trials for Aboriginal families?', *Journal of Social Security Law*, vol. 17, no. 3, pp. 164–97.

Billings, P. 2011, 'Income management in Australia: Protecting the vulnerable and promoting human capital through welfare conditionality', *Journal of Social Security Law*, vol. 18, no. 4, pp. 167–91.

Bode, I. 2009, 'On the road to welfare markets: Institutional, organisational and cultural dynamics of a new welfare state settlement', in *The welfare state in post-industrial society: A global perspective*, eds J. Powell & J. Hendricks, Springer, Dordrecht, pp. 161–77.

Brown, P. & Calnan, M. 2010, 'The risks of managing uncertainty: The limitations of governance and choice, and the potential for trust', *Social Policy and Society*, vol. 9, no. 1, pp. 13–24.

Carney, T. 1997, 'Ageing and the law: Perspectives and prospects', in *Aging and social policy in Australia*, eds A. Borowski, S. Encel & E. Ozanne, Cambridge University Press, Melbourne, pp. 249–75.

Carney, T. 2002, 'Australia: Workers' welfare state or responsive pragmatism?', *Zeitschrift fur austlandisches und internationales Arbeits- und Sozialrecht*, vol. 16, no. 4, pp. 360–90.

Carney, T. 2005, 'Lessons from Australia's fully privatised labour exchange reform (job network): From "rights" to "management"?', *Zeitschrift fur austlandisches und internationales Arbeits- und Sozialrecht*, vol. 19, no. 1, pp. 77–105.

Carney, T. 2006, *Social security law and policy*, Federation Press, Sydney.

Carney, T. 2007, 'Reforming social security: Improving incentives and capabilities', *Griffith Law Review*, vol. 16, no. 1, pp. 1–26.

Carney, T. 2011, 'Social security law: What does the politics of "conditional welfare" mean for review and client representation?', *Australian Journal of Social Issues*, vol. 46, no. 3, pp. 233–52.

Carney, T. 2012, 'Guardianship, "social citizenship" and theorising substitute-decisionmaking law', in *Beyond elder law: New directions in law and ageing*, eds I. Doron & A. Soden, Springer, Dordrecht, pp. 1–17.

Carney, T. 2013a, 'Where now Australia's welfare state?', *Diritto Pubblico Comparato ed Europeo*, no. IV, pp. 1353–70.

Carney, T. 2013b, 'Participation & service access rights for people with intellectual disability: A role for law?', *Journal of Intellectual & Developmental Disability*, vol. 38, no. 1, pp. 59–69.

Carney, T. & Beaupert, F. 2013, 'Public and private bricolage: Challenges balancing law, services and civil society in advancing CRPD supported decision-making', *University of New South Wales Law Journal*, vol. 36, no. 1, pp. 175–201.

Carney, T. & Hanks, P. 1986, *Australian social security law, policy and administration*, Oxford University Press, Melbourne.

Carney, T. & Ramia, G. 2002a, *From rights to management: Contract, new public management and employment services*, Kluwer Law International, Dordrecht.

Carney, T. & Ramia, G. 2002b, 'Mutuality, Mead & McClure: More big 'Ms' for the unemployed?', *Australian Journal of Social Issues*, vol. 37, no. 3, pp. 277–300.

Carney, T. & Ramia, G. 2009, Emerging patterns of social protection in Australia, paper presented to XIX World Congress on Labour and Social Security Law, International Society for Labour and Social Security Law [Country Report on Theme lll, 'Emerging Patterns of Social Protection in Light of Structural Change'], Sydney, 1–4 September. http://www.labourlawsydney.com/downloads/NationalReports/AUSTRALIA%20Carney-RamiaISLSSLNovember2008C.pdf

Carney, T. & Ramia, G. 2010, 'Welfare support and "sanctions for non compliance" in a recessionary world labour market: Post-neoliberalism or not?', *International Journal of Social Security and Workers Compensation*, vol. 2, no. 1, pp. 29–40.

Carr, H. 2005, ' "Someone to watch over me": Making supported housing work', *Social & Legal Studies*, vol. 14, no. 3, pp. 387–408.

Chamberlain, J. M. 2013, *The sociology of medical regulation: An introduction*, Springer, Dordrecht.

Considine, M. 2001, *Enterprising states: The public management of welfare-to-work*, Cambridge University Press, Cambridge.

Considine, M., Lewis, J. & O'Sullivan, S. 2011, 'Quasi-markets and service delivery flexibility following a decade of employment assistance reform in Australia', *Journal of Social Policy*, vol. 40, no. 4, pp. 811–33.

Courtney, M., Minichiello, V. & Waite, H. 1997, 'Aged care in Australia: A critical review of the reforms', *Journal of Aging Studies*, vol. 11, no. 3, pp. 229–50.

Coven, M. B. 2001, 'The freedom to spend: The case for cash-based public assistance', *Minnesota Law Review*, vol. 86, no. 4, pp. 847–911.

Creyke, R. 1991, 'Whose pension is it? Substitute payees for mentally incompetent pensioners', *University of Tasmania Law Review*, vol. 10, no. 2, pp. 102–28.

Dallongeville, J., Dauchet, L., de Mouzon, O., Réquillart, V. & Soler, L. -G. 2010, Are fruit and vegetable stamp policies cost effective?, Toulouse, Institut d'Économie Industrielle (IDEI), University of Toulouse, School of Economics.

Damgaard, B. & Torfing, J. 2010, 'Network governance of active employment policy: The Danish experience', *Journal of European Social Policy*, vol. 20, no. 3, pp. 248–62.

Davies, J. S. 2005, 'The social exclusion debate: Strategies, controversies and dilemmas', *Policy Studies*, vol. 26, no. 1, pp. 3–27.

Davies, J. S. 2009, 'The limits of joined up government: Towards a political analysis', *Public Administration*, vol. 87, no. 1, pp. 80–96.

de Boer, R. 2012, Changes to community care. FlagPost Information and research from Australia's Parliamentary Library, Canberra. http://tiny.cc/x03yrx

Diller, M. 2000, 'The revolution in welfare administration: Rules, discretion and entrepreneurial government', *New York University Law Review*, vol. 75, no. 5, pp. 1121–220.

Dwyer, P. 1998, 'Conditional citizens? Welfare rights and responsibilities in the late 1990s', *Critical Social Policy*, vol. 18, no. 4, pp. 493–517.

Dwyer, P. 2004, 'Creeping conditionality in the UK: From welfare rights to conditional entitlements?', *Canadian Journal of Sociology*, vol. 29, no. 2, pp. 265–87.

Dwyer, P. 2008, 'The conditional welfare state', in *Modernising the welfare state: The Blair legacy*, ed. M. A. Powell, Policy Press, Bristol, pp. 199–218.

Ellis, J. M. & Howe, A. 2010, 'The role of sanctions in Australia's residential aged care quality assurance system', *International Journal for Quality in Health Care*, vol. 22, no. 6, pp. 452–60.

Fisher, K. R., Gleeson, R., Edwards, R., Purcal, C., Sitek, T., Dinning, B., Laragy, C., D'aegher, L. & Thompson, D. 2010, *Effectiveness of individual funding approaches for disability support*, Department of Families, Housing, Community Services and Indigenous Affairs, Canberra.

Forrest, A. (Chair) 2014, *Creating Parity – The Forrest Review*, Commonwealth of Australia, Canberra.

Garraty, J. 1978, *Unemployment in history*, Harper and Row, New York.

Gilbert, T. 2009, 'A place to call home? Challenges facing people who are homeless in Australia's 21st century rental market', *Parity*, vol. 22, no. 3, pp. 12–13.

Gilman, M. 2001, 'Legal accountability in an era of privatized welfare', *California Law Review*, vol. 89, no. 3, pp. 569–642.

Goodwin, S. 2011, 'Analysing policy as discourse: Methodological advances in policy analysis', in *Methodological choice and design*, eds L. Markauskaite, P. Freebody & J. Irwin, Springer, pp. 167–80.

Green, K. 2002, 'Welfare reform in Australia and the United States: Tracing the emergence and critiques of the new paternalism and mutual obligation', *The Drawing Board: An Australian Review of Public Affairs*, vol. 3, no. 1, pp. 15–32. http://www.australianreview.net/journal/v3/n1/green.html

Handler, J. F. 2009, 'Welfare, workfare, and citizenship in the developed world', *Annual Review of Law and Social Science*, vol. 5, pp. 71–90.

Harris, N. 2010, 'Conditional rights, benefit reform, and drug users: Reducing dependency?', *Journal of Law and Society*, vol. 37, no. 2, pp. 233–63.

Hartman, Y. 2005, 'In bed with the enemy: Some ideas on the connections between neoliberalism and the welfare state', *Current Sociology*, vol. 53, no. 1, pp. 57–73.

Hatami, N. 2006, 'Aboriginal authority brings justice and welfare reform: Introducing community justice agreements', *Public Administration Today*, vol. 6, Jan/Mar, pp. 26–28.

Hemerijck, A. 2009, 'In search of a new welfare state in Europe: An international perspective', in *The welfare state in post-industrial society: A global perspective*, eds J. Powell & J. Hendricks, Springer, Dordrecht, pp. 71–98.

Henman, P. 2004, 'Targeted!: Population segmentation, electronic surveillance and governing the unemployed in Australia', *International Sociology*, vol. 19, no. 2, pp. 173–91.

Henman, P. & Adler, M. 2001, 'Information technology and transformations in social security policy and administration: A review', *International Social Security Review*, vol. 54, no. 4, pp. 23–47.

Henman, P. & Adler, M. 2003, 'Information technology and the governance of social security', *Critical Social Policy*, vol. 23, no. 2, pp. 139–64.

Henry, K. 2009, 'How much inequity should we allow?', *Impact*, Summer, pp. 10–14.

Héritier, A. & Rhodes, M. (eds) 2011, *New modes of governance in Europe: Governing in the shadow of hierarchy*, Basingstoke, Palgrave Macmillan.

Hutchinson, T., Dickson, E. & Chappell, D. 2011, 'Juvenile justice and truancy legislation', *Alternative Law Journal*, vol. 36, no. 2, pp. 104–9.

Katz, M. B. 2010, 'The American welfare state and social contract in hard times', *Journal of Policy History*, vol. 22, no. 4, pp. 508–29.

Kohn, N. A., Blumenthal, J. A. & Campbell, A. T. 2012/2013, 'Supported decision-making: A viable alternative to guardianship?', *Penn State Law Review*, vol. 117, no. 4, pp. 1111–57.

Komlos-Hrobsky, P. 1989, 'Representative payee issues in the social security and supplementary security income programs', *Clearinghouse Review*, vol. 23, no. 4, pp. 412–17.

Larkin, P. 2011, 'The legislative arrival and future of workfare: The Welfare Reform Act 2009', *Journal of Social Security Law*, vol. 18, no. 1, pp. 11–32.

Lazar, H. & Stoyko, P. 1998, 'The future of the welfare state', *International Social Security Review*, vol. 51, no. 3, pp. 3–36.

Lindsay, C. & McQuaid, R. W. 2009, 'New governance and the case of activation policies: Comparing experiences in Denmark and the Netherlands', *Social Policy & Administration*, vol. 43, no. 5, pp. 445–63.

Macdonald, S., Bois, C., Brands, B., Dempsey, D., Erickson, P., Marsh, D., Meredith, S., Shain, M., Skinner, W. & Chiu, A. 2001, 'Drug testing and mandatory treatment for welfare recipients', *The International Journal of Drug Policy*, vol. 12, no. 3, pp. 249–57.

Macgregor, S. 1999, 'Welfare, neoliberalism and new paternalism: Three ways for social policy in late capitalist society', *Capital and Class*, vol. 67, Spring, pp. 91–119.

McCausland, R. & Levy, M. 2006, 'Indigenous policy and mutual obligation: Shared or shifting responsibility agreements?', *Australian Journal of Social Issues*, vol. 41, no. 3, pp. 277–94.

McClure, P. 2000, Final report: Participation support for a more equitable society, Reference Group on Welfare Reform, Canberra.

McClusky, M. 2003, 'Efficiency and social citizenship: Challenging the neoliberal attack on the welfare state', *Indiana Law Journal*, vol. 78, no. 2, pp. 783–876.

Mashaw, J. 2006, 'Accountability and institutional design: Some thoughts on the grammar of governance', in *Public accountability: Designs, dilemmas and experiences*, ed. M. Dowdle, Cambridge University Press, New York, pp. 115–56.

Mead, L. (ed.) 1997, *The new paternalism: Supervisory approaches to poverty*, Brookings Institution Press, Washington DC.

Melish, T. J. 2010, 'Maximum feasible participation of the poor: New governance, new accountability, and a twenty-first century war on the sources of poverty', *Yale Human Rights and Development Law Journal*, vol. 13, pp. 1–133.

Mulgan, R. 2006, 'Government accountability for outsourced services', *Australian Journal of Public Administration*, vol. 65, no. 2, pp. 48–58.

Needham, C. 2011, 'Personalization: From story line to practice', *Social Policy & Administration*, vol. 45, no. 1, pp. 54–68.

Patrick, R. 2011, 'Disabling or enabling: The extension of work-related conditionality to disabled people', *Social Policy and Society*, vol. 10, no. 3, pp. 309–20.

Powell, M. A. 2000, 'New labour and the third way in the British welfare state: A new and distinctive approach?', *Critical Social Policy*, vol. 20, no. 1, pp. 39–60.

Power, A., Lord, J. & deFranco, A. 2013, *Active citizenship and disability: Implementing the personalisation of support*, Cambridge University Press, Cambridge.

Productivity Commission 2011a, *Caring for older Australians*, Productivity Commission, Melbourne. http://www.pc.gov.au/projects/inquiry/aged-care/report

Productivity Commission 2011b, *Caring for older Australians: Draft report*, Productivity Commission, Melbourne. http://www.pc.gov.au/projects/inquiry/aged-care

Ries, R., Dyck, D., Short, R., Srebnik, D., Fisher, A. & Comtois, K. 2004, 'Outcomes of managing disability benefits among patients with substance dependence and severe mental illness', *Psychiatric Services*, vol. 55, no. 4, pp. 445–47.

Rose, N. & Miller, P. 2010, 'Political power beyond the state: Problematics of government', *The British Journal of Sociology*, vol. 61, no. s1, pp. 271–303.

Smyth, P. 2008, 'Collaborative governance: The community sector and collaborative network governance', in *Collaborative governance: A new era of public policy in Australia?*, eds J. O'Flynn & J. Wanna, ANU E Press, Canberra, pp. 51–57.

Sutton, J. 2008, 'Emergency welfare reforms: A mirror to the past?', *Alternative Law Journal*, vol. 33, no. 1, pp. 27–30.

Sweeny, K. 2009, 'The impact of copayments and safety nets on PBS expenditure', *Australian Health Review*, vol. 33, no. 2, pp. 215–30.

Tilse, C., Setterlund, D., Wilson, J. & Rosenman, L. 2005, 'Minding the money: A growing responsibility for informal carers', *Ageing & Society*, vol. 25, no. 2, pp. 215–27.

Tilse, C., Wilson, J., Setterlund, D. & Robinson, G. 2003, Families, asset management and care giving: Developing issues in policy, research and practice, paper presented to 8th Australian Institute of Family Studies Conference, Melbourne, 12–14 February.

Tschoepe, G. J. & Hindera, J. J. 2001, 'Explaining state AFDC and food stamp caseloads: Has welfare reform discouraged food stamp participation?', *The Social Science Journal*, vol. 38, no. 3, pp. 435–43.

Van Berkel, R. 2010, 'The provision of income protection and activation services for the unemployed in 'active' welfare states: An international comparison', *Journal of Social Policy*, vol. 39, no. 1, pp. 17–34.

Wanna, J., Butcher, J. & Freyens, B. 2010, *Policy in action: The challenge of service delivery*, UNSW Press, Kensington.

Wikeley, N. 1989, 'Unemployment benefit, the state, and the labour market', *Journal of Law and Society*, vol. 16, no. 3, pp. 291–309.

Wilson, J., Setterlund, D. & Tilse, C. 2003, ' "I know I signed something": Older people, families and social workers' understanding of the legal aspects of entry to residential care', *Australian Social Work*, vol. 56, no. 2, pp. 155–65.

Wright, S., Marston, G. & McDonald, C. 2011, 'The role of non-profit organizations in the mixed economy of welfare-to-work in the UK and Australia', *Social Policy and Administration*, vol. 45, no. 3, pp. 299–318.

About the contributors

Claire Aitchison works in the Office of the Pro-Vice Chancellor, Research, at the University of Western Sydney in researcher education, supporting the writing of academics, supervisors and students. Her research interests include these fields and the marketisation of education.

Anna Boucher is a lecturer in the Department of Government and International Relations at the University of Sydney and a founding member of the Migration Studies Unit at the London School of Economics and Political Science. Her research focuses on comparative immigration policy, gender, ethnicity and the welfare state.

Dick Bryan is professor of political economy at the University of Sydney. He researches the new social foundations of money, including the ways in which financial calculation is intruding into, and increasingly ordering, daily life.

Terry Carney is emeritus professor of law at the University of Sydney. He is a fellow of the Australian Academy of Law, a past president (2005–7) of the International Academy of Law and Mental Health, and has chaired the National Advisory Council on Social Welfare and the Board of the Institute of Family Studies, along with various state enquiries on adult guardianship and health law. A part-time member of the Social Security Appeals Tribunal, his research and publications concentrate on social security and health law issues.

Fran Collyer is a sociologist at the University of Sydney, National Convenor of the Health Section of *The Australian Sociological Association*, a member of the Health Governance Network and former editor of the *Health Sociology Review*. She publishes in the fields of the sociology of knowledge, the history of sociology, disciplines and institutions, and the sociology of health.

Leanne Cutcher is an associate professor in the Discipline of Work and Organisational Studies at the University of Sydney's Business School. Her research explores issues of gender, race, space and age in a range of organisational settings and has been published in leading journals, including: *Organization Studies, Journal of Management Studies, Gender Work and Organisation* and *Work, Employment and Society*.

Bob Davidson is a private consultant who is undertaking a PhD at the Social Policy Research Centre at the University of New South Wales. He has had extensive experience in the government, community and corporate sectors, in a range of social, economic, and environmental areas. His current research interests focus on the economics of human services and the impact of marketisation on service providers.

Susan Goodwin is an associate professor in policy studies in the Faculty of Education and Social Work at the University of Sydney. Her research focuses on gender, social policy analysis and contemporary forms of governance, including governing through 'community'.

Lucy Groenhart joined Swinburne University, Melbourne in 2013 as the Australian Housing and Urban Research Institute Postdoctoral Fellow. Her research interests are housing and urban policy.

Nicole Gurran is a professor within the University of Sydney's Faculty of Architecture, Design and Planning. Her research interests focus on urban policy, planning and housing.

Kirsten Harley is a lecturer in behavioural and social sciences in the Faculty of Health Sciences and an honorary associate in the Department of Sociology and Social Policy at the University of Sydney. She publishes in areas of health sociology, the history of sociology and theory use and, with Nick Osbaldiston, co-edits *Nexus*, the newsletter of The Australian Sociological Association.

Johann Loibl works as a Business Improvement Consultant in the eCommerce industry. Prior to this he spent several years working in project and process management in the agricultural sector. He has a Master of International Business from the University of Sydney.

Gabrielle Meagher is professor of social policy in the Faculty of Education and Social Work at the University of Sydney. She is co-convenor of the Nordic Research Network on Marketisation in Eldercare and of the Australian Paid Care Research Network, and editor of the *Australian Review of Public Affairs*. Her research interests include care work and marketisation in social services.

Angela Mitropoulos is a researcher in the School of Social and Political Sciences at the University of Sydney. She is the author of *Contract and contagion: From biopolitics to oikonomia* (2012), and her current book project is titled *Infrastructures of uncommon forms*.

Ruth Phillips is an associate professor in the Social Work and Policy Studies Program in the Faculty of Education and Social Work at the University of Sydney. Her core research interests include social policy, global social policy, the third sector and the application of feminism in these areas.

Helen Proctor is a senior lecturer at the University of Sydney. Her research focuses on the complex relationships between schools and families. Her most recent book, jointly authored with Craig Campbell, is *A history of Australian schooling* (2014).

Stephanie D. Short is professor and head of the Discipline of Behavioural and Social Sciences at the University of Sydney in the Faculty of Health Sciences. She has written extensively on the sociology of healthcare and is convenor of HealthGov, an international network of regulators, professionals and researchers.

Adam Stebbing is a lecturer in the Department of Sociology at Macquarie University and a fellow at the Centre for Policy Development. He is broadly interested in the interactions between social policy and social inequality, particularly hidden forms of middle-class welfare delivered through the tax system.

Shaun Wilson is a senior lecturer in the Department of Sociology at Macquarie University. His interests lie in political and economic sociology, social survey research, social democracy and the electorate, and social policy. In collaboration with others, he has recently written on the sociology of the emotions in the economy, on Australia's unemployment and disability support policies, and comparative welfare politics in Australia and New Zealand. He has also recently written on the fiscal and political dilemmas involved in Australia's low-tax version of social democracy.

Index